Marooned
in
Moscow

Marguerite Harrison

Edited and Annotated by
William Benton Whisenhunt

Russian Life
BOOKS

ISBN 978-1-880100-64-6

Library of Congress Control Number: 2011927745.

Russian Information Services, Inc.
PO Box 567
Montpelier, VT 05601-0567
www.russianlife.com
orders@russianlife.com
phone 802-223-4955

For Michele,
an extraordinary woman

Contents

INTRODUCTION: *Pluck and Luck: The Story of Marguerite E. Harrison* 7

FOREWORD 25

CHAPTER I: *Warsaw to No Man's Land* 27

CHAPTER II: *A Red Army Billet* 34

CHAPTER III: *Work and Play in the Red Army* 42

CHAPTER IV: *A Trip in a Box Car* 50

CHAPTER V: *An Unwelcome Guest* 58

CHAPTER VI: *News Gathering in Moscow* 65

CHAPTER VII: *The Gods and Their Machine* 79

CHAPTER VIII: *The Woman's Part* 90

CHAPTER IX: *Soviet Weddings* 98

CHAPTER X: *Bourgeois* 105

CHAPTER XI: *Under Suspicion* 117

CHAPTER XII: *Bureaus and Bureaucrats* 127

CHAPTER XIII: *Icons and Anti-Christ* 138

CHAPTER XIV: *Radical Anti-Reds* 147

CHAPTER XV: *Sukharevka* 157

CHAPTER XVI: *Moscow Foyers and Salons* 165

CHAPTER XVII: *A Provincial Junket* 177

CHAPTER XVIII: *Pageants and Plots* 186

CHAPTER XIX: *A Modern Babel* 193

CHAPTER XX: *Al Fresco Adventures* 205

CHAPTER XXI: *The Shadow of the Cheka* 212

CHAPTER XXII: *The Trap is Sprung* 227

CHAPTER XXIII: *Odinochka* 234

CHAPTER XXIV: *Close Quarters* 239

CHAPTER XXV: *Prison Holidays* 250

CHAPTER XXVI: *The Mills of the Gods* 257

CHAPTER XXVII: *An Attic Cell* 267

CHAPTER XXVIII: *Wherein a Jailbird Turns Jailer* 275

CHAPTER XXIX: *Prison De Luxe* 285

CHAPTER XXX: *Release Number 2961* 292

AFTERWORD 299

APPENDIXES

  The Russian Socialist Federal Soviet Republic 307

  New Documents from Russian and U.S. Archives 313

INDEX 320

ACKNOWLEDGEMENTS 325

ABOUT THE AUTHOR AND EDITOR 327

Marguerite Harrison

INTRODUCTION
Pluck and Luck: The Story of Marguerite E. Harrison

"Marguerite Harrison is both plucky and lucky." Thus did the *New York Times* characterize Harrison's Russian adventure in a 1921 book review of *Marooned in Moscow: The Story of An American Woman Imprisoned in Russia*. The reviewer explained that Harrison's "pluck is proved by what she endured: her luck consists of being alive."[1] In fact, Marguerite Harrison's book did not receive much fanfare when it was published in late 1921, but in the few publications where it was reviewed, the comments were usually full of amazement. Most were astonished at her daring and bravery, but all were stunned by her treatment in Russian prisons. One reviewer claimed that "the best book by a woman on Soviet Russia since Clare Sheridan's *Mayfair to Moscow* is Marguerite Harrison's *Marooned in Moscow*."[2]

In fact, in the early 1920s, there were several books published by foreign visitors to Soviet Russia, including John Reed, Louise Bryant, Emma Goldman, and others.[3] The stories of their authors, especially Reed, Bryant and Goldman, are well-documented and provide a fascinating tale of the turmoil that gripped Russia in the days, weeks, months, and years after the Bolshevik Revolution of 1917. Yet Harrison's book seemed to fall out of public view rather quickly. And her book, first published in late 1921, has never been republished in its entirety, until now.

....

1. William Lyon Phelps, "A Composite Picture of Russia," *New York Times* (January 8, 1922), p. 47.
2. "An American Woman's Adventure in Soviet Russia," *Current Opinion* LXXII, no. 5, (May 1922), p. 641.
3. Clare Sheridan, *Mayfair to Moscow: Clare Sheridan's Diary* (New York: Boni and Liveright, 1921); John Reed, *Ten Days That Shook the World* (New York: Boni and Liveright, 1919); Louise Bryant, *Six Months in Red Russia* (New York: George H. Doran, 1918); and Emma Goldman, *My Disillusionment in Russia* (New York: Doubleday, Page, and Co., 1923).

Why is this so? There are several reasons. First, Harrison was not an anarchist firebrand like Goldman, nor did she meet a tragic end like Reed, so her personal story was comparatively less compelling. Second, she was, by most accounts, a rather impartial observer of the events she witnessed and even those in which she participated. So, neither partisans for nor against the Bolsheviks could claim her as an ally or spokesperson. (According to the *New York Times* reviewer: "She writes without bias.... I have not seen any book on contemporary Russia more interesting and valuable than this, and none that inspires more credence.") Third, despite her many adventures in Russia and around the world in the 1920s, she did not seek celebrity but lived in relative normalcy until her death in the 1960s. Lastly, her writing style and non-partisanship understated the drama of the events she experienced and witnessed. One reviewer noted that the book's "style is simple and vivid, and it tells a story that makes an instant appeal." Yet just a few lines later the same reviewer stated, somewhat contradictorily, that "she tells what she saw in so matter-of-fact a fashion as to blind the reader to the really amazing nature of her whole adventure."[4] A reviewer from the *Washington Herald* agreed that Harrison's account was impartial and concluded that "since Mrs. Harrison left Russia, correspondents of every complexion have been permitted to enter, but the Russia they describe is not the Russia Mrs. Harrison saw, and her account is needed as a picture of a period which has been both misrepresented and misunderstood."[5]

Marooned in Moscow provides a fascinating first-hand account by an unlikely American journalist and spy in early Bolshevik Russia. Harrison begins her work by recalling her attempt to enter Russia in the fall of 1919, less than two years after the Bolshevik seizure of power. ("Recall" is a key word here. By Harrison's account, she was not allowed to leave Russia with a single scrap of notes, and so the whole book, in all its remarkable detail, was composed from memory.) Harrison entered a Russia racked by the devastation of World War I. A war of this magnitude had not been fought in Europe since the days of Napoleon, a century before. Yet when it began, all of the major powers greeted the war enthusiastically, with parades, volunteerism, and fanfare. Most believed the war would be short, and that it would allow them to reclaim or establish their national prestige and settle old scores with neighbors. Russia was no exception. In 1913, Russia had celebrated the three hundredth anniversary of the Romanov dynasty with unrivaled displays of imperial pomp, which Tsar

....
4. "An American Woman's Adventure in Soviet Russia," p. 641.
5. "Narrative of a Soviet Rule Impartial and Penetrating," *Washington Herald* (January 22, 1922), p. 4.

Nicholas II surely hoped would erase memories of Russia's embarrassing defeat by the Japanese in 1905 (a failure that, coupled with a general strike in 1905, nearly brought the regime down). Indeed, on the eve of the Great War, despite the turmoil of rising radicalism and intensified police action in many major Russian cities, the tsarist regime seemed secure.[6]

The First World War proved disastrous for Russia. It did not have the industrial capacity to compete with Germany, leading to battlefront shortages of supplies, food, and weapons. Yet Nicholas continued to send troops to the front, as if he were using soldiers as ammunition. For years, radical groups had criticized the imperial regime. And, as losses mounted, moderate members of the government also began to raise concerns about the course of the war and Nicholas' leadership abilities. The tsar tried to boost morale among the troops by leading them personally at the front. There was a temporary improvement, but turmoil continued both at the front and at home.[7]

Food and fuel shortages, rising protests, and army mutinies made Petrograd, the capital, chaotic. Nicholas II's absence raised concerns about who was running the country. That his wife, Empress Alexandra, was of German birth raised suspicions of disloyalty. In addition, faith healer Grigory Rasputin – brought to court to tend to the royal couple's hemophilic son Alexei – was widely viewed as a mysterious monk wielding more power than he should (leading to his murder in 1916 by a noble cabal). By February 1917, protests in the streets of Petrograd called for bread, for soldiers to mutiny, and for Nicholas II to abdicate. Despite warnings from Alexandra not to, Nicholas decided to return from the front. But before he could reach Petrograd, he was forced to abdicate, ending the 304-year Romanov reign.[8]

In the months that followed, Russia plunged further into chaos. The Provisional Government, under the leadership of Alexander Kerensky, was weak and ineffectual, yet it promised to stay in the war and honor Russia's alliances with France and Britain. Despite the fact that this promise, along with the scheduling of elections later in 1917, helped bring the United States into the war, it doomed Russia's fragile democracy. Internal dissent over the war reached a fever pitch in the summer of 1917, leading to a failed military coup. Teetering on the brink of collapse, Kerensky sought support from an unlikely source:

6. Richard Wortman, *Scenarios of Power: Myth and Ceremony in Russian Monarchy,* Volume 2 (Princeton: Princeton University Press, 2000), pp. 439-80 and Orlando Figes, *A People's Tragedy: A History of the Russian Revolution* (New York: Viking, 1996), pp. 157-80.
7. Figes, *A People's Tragedy,* pp. 253-70.
8. Ibid., pp. 307-50.

radical groups, including the Bolsheviks. This weakness opened the door to a Bolshevik takeover. In the final days of October 1917, the Bolsheviks seized power by force, though in considerably less dramatic fashion than later depicted in Soviet films like Sergei Eisenstein's *October*.[9]

MARGUERITE E. (BAKER) HARRISON was born October 23, 1878, to a prominent and wealthy Baltimore family. Her father, Bernard Baker, made his fortune in trans-Atlantic shipping. This took young Marguerite across the Atlantic several times in her youth, her exposure to European life enhancing her natural ability for languages – a facility that was to prove vital in her later adventures. In her autobiography, published in the 1930s, Marguerite recalled that she had had a rather contented childhood. Yet her frequent travels to Europe left her with few friends in Europe or America, and she did not attend school regularly while abroad; she generally had tutors and governesses. When Marguerite was twelve, her mother became seriously ill, and Marguerite was sent to live with her grandparents at the family estate – Elton Park in Catonsville, Maryland, where she also attended St. Timothy's School as a day student. Her education there combined college preparatory courses with the domestic sciences. She warmly recalled two teachers – the sisters Polly and Sally Carter – who influenced her views on literature, history, Germany and the world.[10]

Marguerite had a real fondness for her father and her grandparents, yet she never had a very close relationship with her mother or younger sister. In fact, her strained relationship with her mother played a role in her early marriage. After finishing at St. Timothy's, Marguerite enrolled in Radcliffe College. There, far from home, she fell in love with Thomas Harrison, her landlady's son, whose family was of a lower social and financial standing. The couple became engaged without telling Marguerite's parents. But Marguerite's mother found out and packed her off to Italy after just one semester of college, hoping that the separation would kill the relationship. It didn't. Marguerite and Thomas were married when she returned to the United States, and the couple settled in Baltimore. At about the same time, Bernard Baker's shipping business fell on hard times, but this did not lessen his family's social standing.

In 1902, Marguerite and Thomas had their only child, Tommy. While they lived a rather ordinary and more modest life than she had known as a child,

---

9. Ibid., pp. 406-52.
10. Marguerite E. Harrison, *There's Always Tomorrow: The Story of a Checkered Life* (New York: Farrar & Rinehart, 1935), pp. 18-25.

Marguerite described her married life as blissful. She dedicated most of her time to charity work, including the founding of the Children's Hospital of Baltimore in 1905. The bliss ended in 1915, however, when Marguerite's husband died suddenly of a brain tumor. What is more, Marguerite found out that her husband had accumulated significant debts of which she knew nothing. She resolved to go to work to support herself and her son, and to pay off her husband's debts.[11] She continued to work in the Flower House Studio (her interior design shop which predated her husband's death) until 1916, yet knew it would not generate enough income to live on. She also took in boarders. By 1916, she had also been appointed to the State Board of Motion Picture Censors. Personal connections proved crucial. Her deceased husband's stepfather was Dr. Joseph S. Ames, President of Johns Hopkins University, and her sister had married Albert Ritchie, a prominent Maryland politician who would become the state's 49th governor. Through these connections Harrison was hired as a society reporter at the *Baltimore Sun* newspaper, despite the fact that she could not type and only had one semester of college. Interestingly, her typing deficiency proved to be a larger problem than her lack of formal higher education.

Marguerite knew the Baltimore society scene, so this position was a natural fit. Yet with the First World War well underway and American neutrality being tested by 1916, Harrison began to take a more direct interest in what was happening in Europe. Her extensive experience on the continent and her facility in French and German began to make her think she could contribute to the war effort more directly. After American intervention in April 1917, her sense of duty increased, but it was not until the spring and summer of 1918 that she discussed the idea seriously with friends and family. Then, on September 15, 1918, she applied to the Military Intelligence Division (MID) to serve as a spy in Germany. In her application, she described herself as having "absolute command of French and German, am very fluent and have a good accent in Italian and speak a little Spanish. Without any trouble I could pass as a French woman and after a little practice as German-Swiss."[12] Through her political connections and with the cooperation of the publishers of the *Baltimore Sun*, she went to Germany as a spy under journalistic cover, leaving Tommy with relatives in England. By the time she reached Germany, however, an armistice had been signed. She nonetheless stayed in Germany until the middle of 1919,

11. Ibid., pp. 50-75; Catherine Mary Griggs, "Beyond Boundaries: The Adventurous Life of Marguerite Harrison," (Ph.D. dissertation, George Washington University, 1996), pp. 1-60.
12. "Information Blank," File PF-39205, RG 165 (War Department General Staff), Military Intelligence Division, Box 607, National Archives. See page 318.

collecting information on post-war Germany. While there, she began to be intrigued by events in Russia and within a few months of her return from Germany, in the summer of 1919, she was on her way to Russia, again as an MID spy with journalistic cover, this time working for the Associated Press and the *Baltimore Sun*.[13]

The Russian assignment proved to be a far different, far more difficult mission than her foray into Germany. While she spoke German fluently, she knew no Russian; she had had official permission to enter Germany as a journalist, yet, the Bolsheviks were only letting in a few journalists, and only fellow-travelers. As described vividly in Chapter 1, she had to find her own way into Russia. And this time she left Tommy not in England with relatives, but at a boarding school in Switzerland. When the trip that was to last two months turned into two years, it understandably put a strain on their relationship.

So why did Harrison do this? What made a thirty-nine year old widow and single mother of a young boy become a spy? While Harrison wrote extensively about her life and her adventures in Russia, Asia, and the Middle East, she never made clear her motivation for undertaking espionage and foreign journalism at this stage of her life. It could be that after the sudden death of her husband (and her mother, who also died in 1915), she felt the need to escape life as she knew it. Yet three years span these events, so this seems an unsatisfactory explanation. It could be Marguerite simply had a strong sense of patriotic duty, and felt that her skills could be useful abroad. This seems likely, as is the simple explanation that she was just a very curious person with an insatiable and fearless wanderlust.

ONCE THE Bolsheviks had seized power, they controlled a very fragile state. With problems too numerous to count, Vladimir Lenin focused on consolidating political power. Two key tools for this were the creation of the Cheka (an acronym for All-Russian Extraordinary Commission for Combating Counter-Revolution, Profiteering and Sabotage) and withdrawal from the First World War. The Cheka was created in late 1917 and the ruthless ascetic Felix Dzerzhinsky was placed at its head. Its purpose was to seek out and destroy the Bolshevik regime's multitudinous opponents, and it had become a truly powerful force by the time of Harrison's stay in Russia. Meanwhile, by March 1918, with the Treaty of Brest-Litovsk, Bolshevik Russia had negotiated a

---

13. Harrison, *There's Always Tomorrow*, pp. 50-96; Griggs, "Beyond Boundaries," pp. 78-100; Elizabeth Fagg Olds, *Women of the Four Winds: The Adventures of Four of America's First Women Explorers* (New York: Mariner Books, 1999), pp. 155-180.

separate peace with Germany. But the move angered Russia's allies – France, England and the U.S. – and led those countries to intervene in Russia's Civil War, which broke out in 1918 and would last until 1923 (though serious fighting ended by 1920).

As if all this were not enough, in early 1919 the young Bolshevik regime was at war with Poland (making Harrison's trek through "No Man's Land" into Russia all the more remarkable). In the late eighteenth century, Poland had been partitioned three times. Its neighbors – Austria, Prussia and Russia – had benefited territorially, and in the late nineteenth century, parts of eastern Poland were fully incorporated into the Russian Empire. In the aftermath of World War I, as the Germans retreated from Western Russia, Poland was reconstituted as an independent nation, but the boundaries between Poland and Russia were not defined in the Treaty of Versailles. Fighting lasted until October 1920 and a peace treaty was signed in Riga in March of 1921.[14]

THE READER WILL immediately recognize that Harrison's work covers an extraordinary number of topics, especially in the first two-thirds of the book, before her imprisonment. After she completed her taxing journey into Russia, she spent eight months in relative freedom, soaking up every aspect of Russian life.

Harrison's harrowing journey into Russia revealed much about her character and dedication to her assignment. On her way into Russia, she encountered numerous problems. She did not have proper documentation to move through the contested "no-man's land" between Polish and Russian forces. Poles and Russians alike warned her of negative consequences if she dared continue her journey any farther. She, with the aid of her translator, Dr. Anna Karlin, pushed forward regardless. They traveled by sleigh, motorcycle, lorry, train and, more often than not, on foot. She met mostly friendly soldiers and peasants along the way. All were stunned by the fact that she had gotten so far, with so little, into a zone that was very unsafe for fighting men, much less traveling women.

Harrison describes in great detail the many people who helped her and the lives they led in this dangerous territory. She found the Russians to have less discipline and formality than the Poles. Yet, when she was waiting for transportation to Moscow, she did have a good time with the Red Army soldiers who were her hosts. Their inclusion of her into their social life seemed to bring her comfort as she continued into the unknown. Some peasants she met along

14. Figes, *A People's Tragedy,* p. 700-702.

the way asked her to make contact with relatives who had gone to America and posed questions about American politics, yet others seemed totally isolated. She speculated that she "was the first person who had come to them from the outside world. Most of them had never seen a Western European, much less an American woman, before." (38)

Once in Moscow, Harrison's eight months of freedom were filled with extraordinary experiences. She pursued her role as a journalist with gusto and spent much of her time interviewing a wide range of subjects. The list of prominent Bolsheviks with whom she had at least a passing conversation is impressive. While her encounter with Trotsky was unplanned, most of the others were by arrangement. She interviewed some, like Karl Radek and Leonid Krasin, only once. There were others, like Georgy Chicherin, with whom she had repeated conversations, given that he handled the censoring of foreign press at the Foreign Office. Harrison noted that her most interesting interview, ironically, was with Cheka head, Felix Dzerzhinsky. While she did not have a formal interview with Lenin, she did hear him speak once and was quite impressed. Other foreign journalists had informed her that formal interviews took a long time to arrange and they were often rather stilted. Harrison never even mentions the name Joseph Stalin, except in her appendix listing members of the leadership. It is clear, at least from Harrison's experience, that he was not a key public face of the Party at that time.

Harrison also met and attended lectures given by notable female Bolsheviks, like Alexandra Kollontai and Angelica Balabanova.[15] Kollontai shared ideas on how children ought to be raised and how the Bolshevik leadership were not taking women's issues seriously enough. Harrison had far more contact with Balabanova. She attended two of the Russian feminist's speeches on March 8, International Women's Day. The first speech, while electric, was disappointing to both Balabanova and Harrison. Balabanova was trying to encourage unskilled working women to assert their rights. Yet, the questions at the end of the speech tended to focus on such mundane, albeit essential, concerns as where to get bread and shoes. Balabanova's second speech at the Prokorov Factory was far more engaging. The skilled workers were more politicized and responded to Balabanova's call for equality. While Harrison appeared to disagree with some of Kollontai's views on children and the state, she seemed to be very impressed

---

15. Alexandra Kollontai (1872-1952) was the Commissar for Social Welfare. She founded the Zhenodtel ("Women's Department") in 1919. Angelica Balabanova (1878-1965) was Secretary of the Comintern, but broke with the Bolsheviks in 1922.

with Balabanova's main points. In sympathy to the plight of Russian women, Harrison concluded that

> When you work from six to eight hours a day, spend three or four standing in line outside of one of the cooperatives waiting for food and clothing issued on cards, or dragging a hand sled loaded with wood for several versts, cook your own meals, feeding four mouths where there is enough for two, you have little time for anything else. (94)

For each of the prominent Bolsheviks she covers, Harrison gives a remarkably accurate biography of each, given that the book was purportedly composed from memory after ten months in prison. Her contacts were far from limited to Bolsheviks, however.

Harrison met foreigners from all over the world, as many were housed where she was, in the main foreign visitors' guesthouse, on Maly Kharitonevsky lane. She traveled within Moscow and beyond its bounds with delegations of sympathetic foreign journalists and politicians from the United States, Germany, India, Great Britain and other countries. Among prominent Americans, she got to know Emma Goldman, Alexander Berkman, and Louise Bryant. She even helped nurse Berkman back to health, leaving her to wonder "what my conventional American friends would think if they could see me sitting by the hour in Berkman's bedroom administering medicines and changing water bottles." (150) And she was one of the last people, aside from Louise Bryant, to see John Reed alive.

By the summer of 1920, Harrison's connections expanded to include between eight and ten American prisoners being held by the Bolsheviks. She traded in illegal markets, collected money from other foreigners, used her own money and sold her own possessions to prepare packages for these prisoners. She aided Xenophon Kalamantiano (a spy in his own right), Royal R. Keeley (an economic advisor) and "Corporal Francis Mosher" (who was actually a Captain Merian C. Cooper, of the Kosciusko Squadron). She put herself in great danger to help these captured Americans. While Cooper would escape in early 1921, the other two were released when Harrison was, in July of 1921. Harrison and Cooper met again in Berlin in 1921, following her release. Then, four years later, they traveled together across Persia and Central Asia to make what is known as the first film documentary, *Grass*, in 1925. Cooper later went on to greater fame, as the director of *King Kong*.

Of course, Harrison also encountered plenty of ordinary Russians, many of whom were peasants, and some of whom were facing starvation on a daily basis, due to the Soviet government's inadequate rationing system. Other Russians, however, benefited from their status in the system and seemed to have enough to get by. Still others were caught between two worlds. One of these was General Alexei Brusilov, formerly a general in the Imperial Army, but still well-regarded. His status under the new Bolshevik regime seemed ambiguous, yet Harrison got to know him and his wife rather well. One of the most extraordinary sections of Harrison's work is her open and matter-of-fact descriptions of attending Cheka trials of pre-revolutionary figures who were now considered to be enemies of the state, including Leo Tolstoy's daughter.

Harrison also met Patriarch Tikhon, head of the Russian Orthodox Church, and offers interesting impressions of him (Tikhon was arrested in the mid-1920s and died mysteriously). Her observations of church matters more generally revealed that, while marriages were officially state sanctioned ceremonies, in the summer of 1920 a significant number of them were still being held in churches. Such ambiguity also ruled the lives of dispossessed nuns living at Novodevichy Convent. Much of the famous convent was being used to house working people, while the nuns maintained their vows, but received very poor rations and were banned from doing any work.

In the relatively short time that Harrison was free in Moscow, she also attended poetry readings, ballets, operas, and many other cultural events. She records encounters with Vladimir Mayakovsky, Alexander Scriabin, and Fyodor Chaliapin. Her theatre attendance revealed that the Soviets were performing not only Russian plays, but also some by British and American authors. She also attended some smaller theatres, children theatres and circuses (where she encountered the famous clown duo, Bim Bom). In one of the children's theatres she noted that they performed Rudyard Kipling's *Jungle Book* under the title *Mowgli*. The motion picture theatres, however, Harrison found to be uninspiring. They simply replayed old films and did not seem to add much to the cultural life. Harrison recorded her belief that all Muscovites, whether educated or not, benefited from all of the cultural activities in the capital city, but that the "peasants were usually mystified, and often frankly bored at efforts made to cultivate them." (176)

Harrison's opinion of peasants was actually not so categorical, and was shaped partially by her journey from Poland to Moscow, but also by a trip down the Volga with a British Labor Delegation. She was the only foreigner on that trip who spoke any Russian, and she circulated rather freely among peasants in several provincial villages. She always applauded the hospitality and friendliness of the Russian people (especially when they discovered she could speak some Russian). Yet, she seems amazed that the peasants she met did not fully grasp the reality of the new government. They resented the requisitions of livestock and supplies by the government and many believed that there would be another revolution to displace the Bolsheviks.

Back in Moscow at the end of July 1920, the city was enlivened by the Second World Congress of the Comintern (Third International). This congress assembled delegates from many socialist parties from all over the world. Harrison witnessed a sight in Red Square that would become ever so common during Soviet times. The buildings were draped in banners and placards, balloons floated revolutionary images overhead as speakers rallied the crowds and soldiers paraded past St. Basil's Cathedral. While the pageant was brilliant and evoked a sense of celebration, Lenin's mission at this congress was to clearly define what was a Communist party as opposed to merely a socialist party – in other words, who could be counted on and who could not.

As a testament to her straight-forward style, Harrison recounts with great calmness the events of her arrest on October 20, 1920. When she heard the knock at the door, she said she thought "It's all up," and did not even rise to open the door, but simply called for the Cheka officials to "Come in." (227) She recalled that the Cheka soldiers were young and apprehensive. She tried to relieve them by stating "I suppose you have come to arrest me." (228) After she was given the arrest order (on page 232) and had been searched, she left for prison for ten months, without fanfare or drama.

HARRISON'S OWN prison experience occupies the last third of her book. Her depiction of life in a Soviet prison stands by itself and may have been the first detailed description of life in a Soviet prison published in English. It shows a penitentiary world that, while awful, is considerably less horrific than the hellish Gulag system that was just beginning to be constructed. Her ability to survive under very difficult conditions with little contact with the outside world is a testament to her "pluck." Her release from prison in late July 1921 also is a testament to her "luck."

In the spring 1921, the Harding Administration had replaced that of Woodrow Wilson, and the American Relief Administration (ARA), headed by Herbert Hoover, began negotiating with the Bolsheviks to negotiate the terms of American relief in a Russia racked by famine. Despite grave suspicions of the ARA, Lenin recognized that Russia was in dire straits. On August 20, 1921, an agreement was signed whereby Lenin allowed the ARA into Russia in exchange for the release of all American prisoners, including Harrison and about a dozen others.[16]

Public and political pressure, in part, also helped gain Harrison and the others their release. Major newspapers like the *Baltimore Sun* and the *New York Times* ran occasional stories in their pages about Harrison's plight, but also about some of the other prisoners like Keeley. Most of these stories depicted the Americans as being in the wrong place at the wrong time. For Keeley, this seemed to be the case. However, Harrison and Kalamantiano were spies, and their circumstances were different despite the favorable coverage from the American press. Political pressure also played a part. Harrison's personal contacts, Dr. Joseph S. Ames, now president of Johns Hopkins University, and Maryland Governor Albert Ritchie worked with the publishers of the *Baltimore Sun*, MID and Maryland Senator Joseph I. France to broker the ARA deal.[17]

EVEN BEFORE she was released, on July 29, 1921, a controversy erupted concerning Harrison's role in Russia. Some people suspected that she had become a double agent while in Moscow. As a condition of her release from her first arrest in April 1920, Harrison agreed to pass information on foreigners in Moscow to the Cheka. Harrison claimed that she only passed bogus information and worked hard to distance herself from the foreign community, in order to protect them from being guilty by association. However, a British agent, Mrs. Stan Harding, believed that Harrison was a double agent who had informed on her, resulting in her being imprisoned. After Harding was released in 1920, she began to publish articles about Harrison's duplicity that angered many of Harrison's supporters at home and in Russia, like Louise Bryant. Harrison knew nothing of the controversy until after her release, but Harding kept pursuing the issue.

Harrison and Harding had known each other in Berlin, but there is no evidence that Harrison betrayed her or any others during her time in Russia. Harding's demands were loud and gaining attention, though. She demanded

---

16. Bertrand M. Patenaude, *The Big Show in Bololand: The American Relief Expedition to Soviet Russia in the Famine of 1921* (Stanford: Stanford University Press, 2002), pp. 36-45; Griggs, "Beyond Boundaries," pp. 235-42; and Harrison, *There's Always Tomorrow*, pp. 410-442. At its peak, the ARA employed 300 Americans, more than 120,000 Russians, and fed 10.5 million people daily.
17. Griggs, "Beyond Boundaries," pp. 235-42; Olds, *Women of the Four Winds*, pp. 180-85.

reparations from the Soviet government for her imprisonment, but she also demanded reparations from the American government for Harrison's alleged role. After much haggling, the Soviet government paid her £3,000 (the modern equivalent would be about $500,000), primarily to preserve a new trade deal with Britain. Some in the British government believed that Harding was mentally unstable. She continued for year to make wild allegations and even contrived charges against Harrison. Harrison, for the most part, ignored it all, maintained her innocence, allowed those in the MID and at the *Baltimore Sun* to defend her, and went on with the rest of her life. Even though Harding had had some initial support for her charges, that faded by the end of the 1920s, because her claims seemed more about publicity and her moment of fame than it did any real claims against Harrison.[18]

Once Harrison was released, she made her way back to the United States with her son Tommy. She spent the fall of 1921 writing *Marooned in Moscow*, and it was published by the end of that year. Yet her desire for adventure had not been sated. She no longer worked for the MID, but she did write for several magazines and newspapers. In June 1922, less than a year after her release, she set off for Asia alone to write articles about rising nationalism in the region. She spent several months in Japan before moving on to Sakhalin Island, China and Mongolia. Her Asian trip was not well planned. She was fascinated by Asian culture, yet what she really wanted was to return to Russia. She ended up in Urga (Ulan Bator), along the way riding in wagons, small paddleboats and cars. She slept in the open air, on mats, and even in a brothel. The trip was anything but luxurious.[19]

Harrison crossed into Siberia's Far Eastern Republic from Mongolia with a visa she had acquired while in China. The Far Eastern Republic was a semi-autonomous region of the Soviet Union, and just days before Harrison set out from Urga to Chita, on November 15, 1922, the Soviets claimed their sovereignty over the republic. Two days after she arrived in Chita, on November 21, Harrison was arrested by the GPU (successor to the Cheka).[20] Her harrowing trip to Moscow along the Trans-Siberian Railway took more than a week. The compartment had vermin, few blankets and little food. Once in Moscow, she was returned to the Lubyanka prison where she had spent time during her first adventure into Russia. She also shortly learned that her former interrogator,

18. Griggs, "Beyond Boundaries," pp. 225-38.
19. Olds, *Women of the Four Winds*, pp. 180-94.
20. GPU stands for Gosudarstvennoye Politicheskoye Upravleniye (State Political Directorate).

Solomon G. Mogilevsky, had been tracking her in Asia and had ordered her arrest.

Some controversy exists about what came next. It is known that Harrison spent the next ten weeks in prison. Her son, Tommy, claimed much later that his mother was asked to be a Soviet spy in Moscow, in order to inform on Russians. Some scholars, like Catherine Mary Griggs, doubt this, contending that her earlier adventure was now so exposed that it would have been difficult to create a plausible cover. However, others believed that Harrison and Mogilevsky might have been romantically involved. Harrison, in her writing, confirmed neither account. However, she did write with a certain guarded fondness for her former jailer. Whatever the truth was, it will probably never be known. What is certain is that Harrison was even more perplexed by this prison stay. She feared falling into the prison system and being lost. While she had advocates in the United States pushing for her release through the ARA, she did not know this. She was released in March 1923, visibly weakened, yet hardly discouraged from an adventurous life.[21]

Harrison and Tommy lived in New York after her return. She published her second book, *Unfinished Tales from a Russian Prison,* in 1923 – an expansion on prison stories from her first stay in Russia. She also lectured and began writing her third book, *Red Bear or Yellow Dragon.* Within a year after her return from Russia, she again grew restless. Reacquainted with Merian C. Cooper, who had become interested in filmmaking, the two, along with Ernest B. Shoedsack, a cameraman from Iowa who had served in World War I, decided to produce a film about an isolated tribe. Their original idea was to visit the Kurds in eastern Turkey, but some of Harrison's friends encouraged her to travel further into Persia, to film the nomadic Bakhtiari. But their funds were limited (mostly raised by Harrison), so they settled for filming the Kurds. Once they reached Turkey, however, they decided nonetheless to push further into Persia. They endured many hardships of travel, permits, and even illness (Cooper); but they pressed on. Along the way, Harrison studied Turkish and Persian, wrote for the *New York Times* and others, and finished her book, *Red Bear or Yellow Dragon.*

Fearing the Bakhtiari would move before they could reach them, Harrison and her colleagues rushed to reach Persia in the spring of 1924. Harrison's linguistic ability surprised many and was instrumental in the trio's success, as they battled heat, cold, wind, dust, sand, flies, snow, cheating guides, and the danger of running out of supplies, money and film. The filming was hot

----
21. Griggs, "Beyond Boundaries," pp. 289-301.

and intense, but the three American adventurers, and especially Harrison, had impressed the leader, Haidar Khan. This goodwill allowed them, over a span of nearly 50 days, to capture many hours of the tribe's activities on film. About a month into the migration, Harrison contracted malaria and had a high fever. She took large doses of quinine and recovered. By the end of the extraordinary migration, Harrison and Shoedsack were ready to leave the Bakhtiari people, whom they found to be crude, treacherous and without culture. Cooper, however, had developed a real affection for them.[22]

The film, *Grass*, premiered in the spring of 1925 in New York. Most viewers and critics did not know how to receive the documentary – an unknown genre at the time. In her autobiography, published about a decade later, Harrison noted that the film was not what she had wanted it to be. In her view, Cooper and Shoedsack had sensationalized the film through some of their scene selections and subtitles. She wanted a more authentic and natural approach. The film ran for several months in New York, made very little money, but proved to be a watershed work in the documentary film world.

During and between her several adventures, Harrison had grown tired of the sexist questions and persistent rumors about her personal life. There were constant whispers that this attractive widow was having affairs across the world. This is part of what led Harrison, in early 1925, along with three other women explorers, Blair Niles, Gertrude Mathews Selby, and Gertrude Emerson, to found the Society of Woman Geographers in Washington, DC, to promote the work and achievements of women as explorers.

In 1926, Harrison married an English actor, Arthur M. Blake. The marriage seemed to bring an end to her adventurous life. Harrison noted later that "during my wander years I never met any man for whose sake I would have given up even a small part of my personal freedom."[23]

Harrison and Blake lived much of the next twenty years in Hollywood, in order that he could pursue his acting career, until his death in 1949. During that span Harrison published *Asia Reborn* (1928) and her autobiography, *There's Always Tomorrow* (1935).

After Blake's death, at the age of seventy-one, Harrison moved back to Baltimore to be closer to her son Tommy and his family. However, by her later seventies her wanderlust returned, and she traveled to South America, Australia,

22. Harrison, *There's Always Tomorrow*, pp. 569-610. See also Bahman Maghsoudlou, *Grass: Untold Stories*, (Costa Mesa, CA: Mazda Publishers, 2009).
23. Quoted in Olds, *Women of the Four Winds*, p. 229.

and Africa. In her early eighties, she even returned to Berlin and claimed to have crossed to the eastern side employing her German and Russian again without incident. She was a healthy chain-smoker until the very end of her life. She died after a series of strokes on July 16, 1967. She was 88.[24]

Harrison unquestionably broke the then prevalent gender barriers in the United States, though it must be admitted that her privileged origins provided her with more opportunities than most women of her time. Once Harrison entered the public eye, she was never content to return to a traditional life. Yet she was at odds with American feminism. She did not accept the limitations placed on her by gender, but she felt that feminists, in their drive for equality, were emphasizing those very differences. Harrison felt that equality was essential but that it could and should be achieved without emphasizing those qualities that made the genders different.

Harrison was also a creature of her own background. She was an elite who rarely expounded on the life of privilege she enjoyed. Yet, she held views often associated with her class and certainly of her era. One striking feature the reader will find in this work is her constant reference to Jews. Many of the original Bolsheviks were Jews and there was a widely held notion at the time that the Bolshevik Revolution was a Jewish conspiracy. Harrison does not seem to endorse that conspiracy theory, but it is clear in her writing that she is constantly aware of who were Jews and who were not. Several key passages from her text illustrate her awareness, if not racist views, toward Jews. She notes when describing Leonid Krasin, Commissar of Ways and Communications, that he "is a man of education and refinement, and there is nothing about him to suggest the Jew, although it has been said that he is of Jewish ancestry." (69) Of Radek, she says he is "typically Jewish in appearance." (70) Of Zinoviev, she said "a rugged, unprepossessing looking individual of a distinctly Jewish type, with an extremely forceful, dominating personality." (201) And of Trotsky speaking, she wrote, "There was something almost exultant in his expression as his eyes swept the enormous crowd in front of him, and it seemed to me that subconsciously it was mingled with a certain amount of racial pride. I could almost imagine him saying, 'For the first time since the days of the Maccabees, I, a Jew, am the head of a great army.'" (82) While such comments are deplorable in our day, bigotry like this was pervasive in the U.S. and Europe in the pre-WWII era (and certainly not limited to anti-Semitism), and Harrison is thus a fair representative of her times. Though most of Harrison's such comments are

....

24. Ibid, pp. 220-30.

not positive, they are not hostile, a conclusion supported by her fair assessment in Chapter XIV of the difficult situation of Jews in Bolshevik Russia. (151-2)

In sum, human shortcomings notwithstanding, Harrison was a remarkably astute and thorough observer. She gained an amazing level of access, interviewing nearly every important political and social leader in Bolshevik Russia, save Lenin and Stalin. She is also an invaluable guide to life in early Soviet Russia. Indeed, she met everyone from John Reed to General Brusilov, from Patriarch Tikhon to the Anarchist Emma Goldman, and offers profiles that are richly textured and full of information and events not elsewhere available. Finally, as stated above, her reporting on prison life may well have been the first detailed account by a foreigner in the Soviet period.

A note about spelling and editing of this volume. The original edition of this book included transcriptural and factual errors that are understandable, given the haste with which the book was published and the extreme shortage of Russian experts in the United States in the 1920s. In point of fact, such errors were rather few, given the limitations Harrison and her editors faced. Our general practice was to edit with a light hand, preferring to not interfere with Harrison's voice or language, unless some small edit was required to make something understandable to a modern reader, yet in most all instances this was achieved through footnoting. Most edits in fact consisted of the correction of misspellings and Russian transliterations, plus the occasional placement of commas, in those cases where their absence particularly infuriated our modern sensibilities.

INTERESTINGLY, HARRISON'S adventures in Russia and elsewhere left her without a place in the world. She often noted that she never felt comfortable back in the United States when she returned from her trips to Russia, Asia and Persia. While she was curious about many parts of the world, Russia consistently held a special place in her heart. In her autobiography, she recalled her feelings as she was expelled from Russia in 1923 after her second imprisonment. She noted that

Although I was eager to get back to America and above all to see my boy again, I lingered on until the *permis de sejour* had nearly expired. I hated to leave Moscow! Eugenia and several other friends saw me off by the Diplomatic Express for Riga and I crossed the Latvian frontier fifteen minutes before the expiration of my five-day permit. There was something final about my departure this time. I felt that I would never see my beloved Russia again.[25]

Strangely, Harrison felt a profound affection for a country that had imprisoned her twice, totalling nearly a year of her life. In the pages that follow, that affection certainly shines through. But, more than that, this fascinating tale in Harrison's own words offers an extraordinary image of an extraordinary time in Russia, by an extraordinary woman.

William Benton Whisenhunt

---

25. Harrison, *There's Always Tomorrow*, p. 561.

FOREWORD

*I*n the early part of February, 1920, I crossed into Russia through the Polish Front, as correspondent of the *Baltimore Sun* and the Associated Press, intending to remain for six weeks. I stayed for eighteen months, ten of which were spent in prison. This was due to the manner in which I entered the country, and my actions while there, which I shall describe fully in the following pages, telling what happened to me as well as what I heard and saw in Russia. My treatment while in prison was no different from that accorded any other prisoners, native or foreign, and I can honestly say that I have come through it all with absolutely no personal bitterness and with what I believe to be a purely impartial view of conditions in the Soviet Republic.

My account of my experiences is written entirely from memory, as I was permitted to take no notes out of the country when I was released on July 28, upon the acceptance by the Soviet government of the terms of the American Relief Association for famine relief in Russia, which was made conditional on the release of all American prisoners.

Marguerite E. Harrison

CHAPTER I
Warsaw to No Man's Land

To get into any country by the back door, after having been refused permission to come in by the front way, does not sound like a simple thing to do, yet, as a matter of fact, I accomplished the feat without any great difficulty in February, 1920, when I entered Soviet Russia from Poland while a state of war existed between the two nations.[1] My method was simplicity itself-I passed through the Polish lines into No Man's Land, and gave myself up to the first Red Army patrol. By this means I succeeded two weeks later in reaching Moscow, where I stayed for eighteen months, during which I was arrested twice by the Cheka,[2] living for six months under surveillance and for nearly ten in prison.

Under the circumstances I consider that I fared rather well. If, as an American citizen, I had tried to get into Germany through the front lines from France after diplomatic relations had been broken off between the United States and that country, I doubt if I would have been as lucky with either the French or the Boches,[3] for I would have run a pretty good chance of being taken for a spy by both sides.

---

1. As the Russian Civil War (1918-1920) was nearing its end, the newly-recreated Polish state launched an attack on Ukraine in early 1920, in what is known as the Russo-Polish War (1920-1921). By early 1921, the Treaty of Riga ended the war through a compromise on border territories between Poland and the new Soviet Union.
2. In December 1917, the Cheka was created. The acronym stood for the Extraordinary Commission and then later the All-Russian Extraordinary Commission for Combating Counter-Revolution, Profiteering, and Corruption. The new Bolshevik government used this organization as a political police to eliminate counter-revolutionary activities. Its first head was Felix Dzerzhinsky.
3. A disparaging French term for a German. Related to the word *caboche* (cabbage), usually translated as blockhead.

My decision to get into Russia by the underground route was reached only after I had tried and failed to get in by legitimate means. I had been in Germany as the correspondent of the *Baltimore Sun* during the six months of readjustment and revolution immediately following the Armistice, and there, through persons identified with the Socialist movement, I had heard many things, which made me realize that we, in Western countries, knew little or nothing of what was actually happening in Soviet Russia. I wanted to see something at close range of the great social experiment of the Bolsheviks. Consequently, on my return to America in the early autumn of 1919, I applied at the Martens Bureau[4] in New York for permission to enter Russia for the *Baltimore Sun,* of which I was a staff correspondent, the *New York Evening Post,* which had given me credentials as occasional traveling correspondent, and Underwood & Underwood,[5] for whom I had agreed to take pictures in Europe. I was told flatly that this would be impossible. The Soviet government at that time was not encouraging the entrance of bourgeois press correspondents. It was felt that the privileges accorded correspondents in Russia had been so often abused by deliberate misstatements intended to further anti-Bolshevik propaganda that, with few exceptions, the Foreign Office was refusing permission to the representatives of non-Socialist papers. I was even warned that it would be extremely unwise for me to attempt to get into the country.

In spite of this fact, I started for Europe in October determined to try my luck. In London I had a conversation, confirmed later in writing, with Mr. Collins, European manager of the Associated Press, who had agreed to accept my services as Moscow correspondent, should I succeed in entering Russia. The refusal of the Martens Bureau closed the only legitimate routes through Estonia, Finland and the Soviet courier service via Murmansk. It also barred me from applying to the only other agency which could have given me permission – Litvinov's bureau at Copenhagen.[6]

---

4. This organization was established in New York during the Russian Civil War by Ludwig Martens. It served as an unofficial embassy for the Soviet government, because the United States refused to extend official diplomatic recognition to the new Soviet government after October 1917. In 1921, Martens was deported after several U.S. Senate and U.S. Department of Labor investigations revealed illegal activity. The U.S. officially recognized the USSR in 1933.

5. Underwood and Underwood was a company that was a pioneer in photographic images (including for journalism). It got its start in Kansas in the 1880s, but by this time had offices in Baltimore and New York.

6. Maxim Litvinov (1876-1951) was a long-time Bolshevik who held many positions within the party before and after the revolution. During the Russian Civil War he served as a roaming ambassador for the new Soviet government, mainly based in London and Copenhagen.

There remained another possibility — entrance through one of the countries with which Soviet Russia was then at war: Latvia, Lithuania or Poland. I chose the last named route, not because it was the easiest, but because it promised the most interesting experiences, and laid my plans accordingly. I wish to emphasize these facts because they had an important bearing on what happened to me later. I was deliberately taking a desperate risk, and I had no one but myself to blame for the consequences.

I arrived in Warsaw in December with no very definite plans except that somehow or other I was determined to get to Russia. At that time I spoke very little Russian, so the first thing that was absolutely essential was an interpreter. It was necessary to find someone who would be acceptable to the Bolsheviks and at the same time did not have too bad a standing with the Polish authorities. For some time I failed to find anyone meeting these requirements. Then by chance I met Doctor Anna Karlin. She was a Russian who had emigrated to the United States some ten years previously, had taken out American citizenship papers, and lived for some time in Chicago, where she was identified with Socialist activities. At the beginning of the revolution she had gone to Russia via Siberia and had worked for a year as a Red Army physician, being assigned to duty in Galicia.[7] When the Poles occupied this territory in the Autumn of 1919, she was made a prisoner, but, as she claimed American citizenship, she was allowed to go unmolested to Warsaw. For some months she tried to obtain an American passport, but without success. I found her out of work, unable to return to the United States and practically destitute. She still retained her Red Army papers, and I felt that, once in Russia, she would be able to take care of herself. I suggested that she should accompany me to Russia as an interpreter. She agreed, and we left together for Minsk, then occupied by Polish troops in command of General Jelikovski.

My first difficulties were encountered when I applied for a permit for her to leave Warsaw. As a Jewess, and as a person who had formerly been in the service of the Red Army, the Polish authorities were naturally inclined to be suspicious of her, and it took me some time to obtain the necessary papers. On my arrival in Minsk I called on General Jelikovski, explained to him that I was anxious to get into Soviet Russia, and asked for a safe conduct through the Polish lines on that sector of the Berezina front.[8] I was met with a point-blank refusal. In the

---

7. Galicia is a region in eastern Poland often disputed between the Poles and the Russians.
8. Berezina was a key front along the Berezina River in the Russo-Polish War. Notably, Napoleon suffered heavy losses here in 1812-1813 during his retreat from Moscow.

first place, the general told me, he would not be responsible for my personal safety. If I crossed the front in that manner I would certainly be shot as a spy by the Bolsheviks. In addition, I would naturally learn much about the disposition of the Polish troops, and either unwittingly, or under pressure, I might give valuable information to the Reds. As for taking with me a Jewish woman, who had been with the Red Army and afterwards lived in Warsaw, that was utterly preposterous!

After several interviews, I realized that General Jelikovsky knew his own mind and that it was impossible to do anything with him. Meanwhile, I had made many acquaintances in Minsk among the Jews who were bitterly antagonistic to the Polish occupation on account of the unjust persecutions to which they were subjected. While not Communists by conviction, most of them secretly sympathized with the Bolsheviks on account of the attitude of the Poles. As Minsk was formerly a Russian province, nearly all of them had ties connecting them with Soviet Russia. There was a flourishing trade in contraband between the Jews in Minsk and their co-religionists in Russia, and a well organized underground railroad of communication between the Russian and Polish branches of various Jewish benevolent organizations such as the "Oze"[9] and the "Jakopo."[10] Most of these people crossed the lines through the Berezina sector, because it was the least guarded of all the fronts and also because it was used for the repatriation of Germans, and for exchange of hostages between the Poles and Russians. For this purpose a sort of tacit armistice had been established. On all other sectors of the front, while there was no actual fighting, there were frequent skirmishes and to cross between the lines was much more difficult. I had determined that if I was unsuccessful in getting a safe conduct from the military authorities I would throw in my luck with the Jewish contrabanders, but if I had been caught this would have blocked all my future chances of getting into Russia through Poland.

---

9. OZE is an acronym for the *Obshchestvo Zdravookhraneniya Yevreyev* (Society for the Protection of the Health of Jews). It was established in 1912 in St. Petersburg by a group of Jewish professionals (doctors, lawyers, etc.) who wanted to promote proper sanitary and medical practices.

10. Jakopo, also known as Ekopo, was a Jewish philanthropic organization in Petrograd during World War I. The acronym stands for *Yevreysky komitet pomoshchy zhertvam voiny* (Jewish Committee for Aid to War Victims).

I had heard that General Szeptycki,[11] who was in command of the Vilna[12] sector, was a much more approachable person. I therefore determined to go to Vilna and try to get a permit from him. So, leaving Dr. Karlin at Minsk, I started for Vilna. At that time, travel in eastern Poland was anything but luxurious. I made the trip from Minsk to Vilna in a fourth-class car, packed with Polish soldiers and a large convoy of Bolshevik prisoners. The trip, which in normal times is a matter of three hours or so, took us just twenty-two hours, owing to the sabotage of the railroad employees, all of whom were White Russians[13] and bitterly antagonistic to the Polish occupation. At Moledechno,[14] midway between Minsk and Vilna, the engine crew struck and we were held up for four or five hours while the Polish officers in command of the train tried in vain to secure another crew. Finally they collected a purse of two thousand marks and presented it to the strikers, upon which they condescended to take us to Vilna.

Some days after my arrival I had an interview with General Szeptycki, and told him what I had in mind. At first he emphatically refused, but I finally succeeded in persuading him to give me a safe conduct through the Polish lines. Armed with this, I returned to Minsk determined to give the slip to General Jelikovsky and cross through his sector. The best route was from Minsk through Smolovichi to Borisov.[15] There I had Jewish friends who were in constant communication with persons across the border and they would be able to give me letters of introduction, which would help me considerably in Russia. I calculated that, once on the front, a permit from General Szeptycki, who was well known and much loved throughout the entire army, would be sufficient to induce the officer in command of the front line troops to pass me through unless he received orders from Minsk to the contrary. So, as a military permit was necessary to travel on the train to Borisov we left Minsk early one morning in a sleigh furnished us by Jewish contrabanders. We covered the one hundred and twenty versts[16] to Borisov in a day, arriving late at night by a circuitous route, so that we would not be challenged by Polish sentries.

....

11. General Stanislav Szeptitzki (Szeptycki) (1867-1950) served in World War I on the side of Austria-Hungary before he joined the Northeast Front, near Minsk, in the Russo-Polish War against the Bolsheviks. He later opposed Polish leader Joseph Pilsudski for which he was removed from active service.
12. Vilna is the name of the current city of Vilnius, Lithuania.
13. This is another name for Belarusans (Byelorussians).
14. Moledechno is a town near Minsk that shifted between Polish and Soviet control during the Russo-Polish War. In 1921, the Treaty of Riga made it a part of Poland. After World War II, it became a part of Belarus.
15. Smolovichi and Borisov are two towns near Minsk.
16. A verst is an old Russian unit of measurement that equals 3,500 feet or 1.07 kilometers.

The next morning I interviewed the commanding officer, showed my permit from General Szeptycki, carefully concealing the fact that I had come from Minsk and it was arranged that I should be conducted through the front lines on the following day.

Having accomplished this much, my only anxiety, as far as the Poles were concerned, was that I might be searched for letters before leaving the country. On the way to Poland I had received several letters of introduction for Moscow from Paul Birukov,[17] a Russian, friend and biographer of Tolstoy, whom I had met in Geneva. One was to M. Bonch-Bruevich[18] who was associated with Lunacharsky, Commissioner of Education; another to Krupskaya, wife of Lenin.[19] Besides, I had a letter from a well-known Polish Communist, and a number of personal letters from Jewish people in Poland to their relatives in Russia. The latter, for all I knew, might be a disadvantage to me with the Bolsheviks as well, for in most cases I had no idea of the politics of the people who had given them to me. I even had three thousand Kerensky rubles[20] from a Doctor Szabad of Vilna, for his wife, who was living in Petrograd,[21] and letters from members of Jewish benevolent associations to fellow members in Orscha, Vitebsk, Smolensk and Moscow. Much to my relief, the subject was never brought up, and as a matter of fact I was not searched until my arrival in Moscow.

We left Borisov for the front in a sleigh early on the morning of February 8th, with a Polish soldier who acted as our escort during an exciting drive of seven versts, along a rough highway rutted by heavy motor lorries, through a winding track in a dense forest where we often had to stop and bridge the trenches with spruce boughs to permit the passage of our sleigh. We finally arrived at a dugout built of logs, camouflaged with evergreens, where I found an officer who had

....

17. Paul Birukov (1860-1931) was a biographer of Leo Tolstoy who later, in 1930, signed the "Manifesto Against Conscription and the Military System," with such notable figures as Jane Addams, Thomas Mann, John Dewey, Sigmund Freud, Albert Einstein and others.

18. Vladimir D. Bonch-Bruevich (1873-1955) was a long-time revolutionary who first met Lenin in 1893. He worked in many positions in the Bolshevik party before the revolution and after including the executive secretary of the Sovnarkom.

19. Anatoly Lunacharsky (1875-1933) was a long-time Bolshevik who held many positions within the party both before and after the revolution. His most notable position was Commissar of Public Enlightenment, which, after 1917, put him in charge of education. Nadezhda Krupskaya (1869-1939) was Vladimir Lenin's wife and a formidable Bolshevik in her own right.

20. Kerensky rubles were a new currency issued during the Provisional Government era (February-October 1917) and were named for this government's primary leader, Alexander Kerensky (1881-1970). Harrison notes later in this work that the exchange rate was 2500 rubles for 1 U.S. dollar.

21. St. Petersburg was renamed Petrograd during the World War I, as Tsar Nicholas felt St. Petersburg sounded too German. The city was renamed Leningrad after Vladimir Lenin's death in 1924, and became St. Petersburg again in 1991.

been notified of our coming from staff headquarters at Borisov. He was none too cordial and evidently did not relish his task of conducting me to No Man's Land. We had coffee together and all the while he entertained me with accounts of Bolshevik atrocities, predicting that I would probably be shot within twenty-four hours and suggesting that perhaps I should like to change my mind and go back to Borisov. Finding me adamant, he started out leading the way through a network of barbed wire entanglements with my carryall slung over his shoulder. I followed with my suitcase and knapsack, and the little doctor, who was very fat and short of breath, brought up the rear.

Finally we emerged from the woods and I found myself on the edge of No Man's Land, a wide, open expanse of snow covered fields dotted here and there with peasant villages. Apparently it was absolutely uninhabited. There were no signs of life, not even an occasional peasant or a village. Dogdead silence brooded over everything. I knew that somewhere, just beyond, were detachments of the Red Army, but there was no evidence of their proximity. Some distance away was a small settlement of about six houses and the officer informed me that there we would be able to find a sleigh to take us to the nearest village. We covered the distance in a few minutes and knocked at the door of one of the houses, a rough board structure with a thatched roof. A bearded peasant with a sheepskin coat and Astrakhan cap[22] appeared at the door. He eyed my escort in a rather unfriendly manner and was decidedly disgruntled when ordered to bring out his sleigh and take us to the nearest village, where, I was told, I would probably meet the Red Army patrol in a few hours. Presently he brought up a moth-eaten horse and a broken-down sleigh into which we piled our bags, following him on foot to the village, which we reached after a half-hour tramp. We stopped in front of a schoolhouse, the only decent building in the place, where we were received by the teacher, a very pretty Russian girl who spoke Polish well, and seemed to be on excellent terms with my officer. They had a long conversation during which she evidently gave him a certain amount of important information for which he paid several pounds of chocolate and a package of tea. Then he said good-bye to me, wishing me luck, and Doctor Karlin and I were left to await the arrival of the Red Army patrol.

---

22. An astrakhan cap is a traditional Russian fur hat that has many variations across the Middle East and Central Asia.

CHAPTER II
A Red Army Billet[1]

$\mathcal{T}$he room in which we were sitting served as the teacher's living and bedroom. It was large and cheerful, with geraniums in the windows, a comfortable drugget[2] on the floor, and a big porcelain stove in the corner that made us forget the intense cold outside—in fact several degrees below zero. In a few minutes, with true Russian hospitality, the teacher brought in a bubbling samovar,[3] some small oaten cakes with bacon fat instead of butter, and invited us to have a cup of real tea, which she had probably received on a previous visit from our officer. It was all very different from what I had imagined. I had thought that I would find No Man's Land a desolate waste, but here was no sign of war and destruction—even comparative comfort. To tell the truth, I never had the feeling that I was in the zone of military operations, either on the Polish or Russian front lines.

To anyone who was at all familiar with the Western Front in the Great War, the Berezina front was like going back to the days of, say, Napoleon. The Poles had an irregular line of entrenchments and barbed wire entanglements, seven versts east of the Berezina, a few batteries of light artillery and machine guns. Their supplies were brought to within a few versts of the advanced posts by a small number of decrepit motor lorries, which had much difficulty in ploughing their way through the heavy snow. Then they were loaded on sleighs or carried in packs to the front line trenches. There were no narrow gauge lines, no funny little dummy engines, no strings of supply trains passing one another. Everything was primitive and simple to a degree; there was none of the paraphernalia of

....
1. A billet is a term for a soldier's living quarters.
2. A *drugget* is a coarse woolen rug with a pattern on one side.
3. A samovar is a traditional Russian metal container for heating water, usually for tea.

modern war. The soldiers were poorly armed, poorly equipped, and lived in the rudest shelters imaginable.

The Bolsheviks did not even pretend to have a line of entrenchments. Between them and the Poles was a wide stretch of open territory, perhaps five versts across in the narrowest portion. Behind this debatable ground were the scattered villages, in which the Red Army detachments were billeted. On that sector of the Russian front I never saw a trench or a dugout. The entire army was like a flying squadron, ready to advance or retreat at a moment's notice. Of course the Russian climate makes a winter campaign practically impossible, and the Bolsheviks were quite safe as they were. Besides, both sides at that time confidently expected peace in the spring, and were simply maintaining an attitude of watchful waiting.

So far I had seen no evidence of the presence of the Red Army, but in about an hour the door opened and three men in rough khaki colored coats, high boots and Astrakhan caps came in. Each wore on his cap a five-pointed star, and one had pinned to his coat the Communist insignia, a star surrounded by a silver wreath. He was a splendid looking fellow, of the peasant type, with clear blue eyes and a wholesome, ruddy skin, very young and very much impressed with the importance of his office, for he was a political commissar. I explained to him in my very best Russian, that I had come from America to learn the truth about the Soviet Government, and that I wished to go on to Moscow.

"That is very good of you," he said simply, with the friendliest smile imaginable, "but I have no authority to let you go farther. I must telephone to the company commander in Lochnitsa, the next village. Meanwhile we will do all we can to make you comfortable here."

While we were waiting for a reply, the teacher invited me to have a look at the schoolroom across the hall. School was over for the day, and I found a meeting of the village Soviet[4] going on. There were women as well as men gathered around the chairman, who was reading a decree from Moscow ordering the mobilization of all men of the classes of 1883, 1884 and 1885 to cut and haul wood for the railroads and the army. This was followed by the announcement that all villagers who had not a sufficient supply of wood to last through the winter would be allotted a certain amount, and a list of names of those in need of wood was read. Instantly several hands were raised.

---

4. A soviet is a local council that dates back to 1905, but lasted through the Russian Revolution of 1917 as a form of local government. Many of them, especially in urban areas, were quite radical.

"My neighbor, Dmitri Pavlovich, is not on the list," said one man. "He has not enough wood to last a month." Dmitri's name was promptly written down, as was that of a woman who claimed that she had been overlooked, and various other matters affecting the commune were taken up one by one. Few of the members could read or write, and yet they were governing themselves in an orderly and efficient manner.

"We are doing our best," said the young commissar,[5] who had come back with the news that I was to be sent to the company command fifteen versts away, "but we are greatly handicapped because of the lack of cooperation of the intelligent classes. We want them to work with us."

Our trip was made in two requisitioned sleighs, Doctor Karlin and I occupying the first, the second containing our baggage and two soldiers. The way led down the broad highroad that runs from Minsk to Moscow, which I had already traveled on the Polish side. It was built by Catherine the Great;[6] to this day it is bordered in many places by double rows of birch trees planted in her time, and the peasants still call it the "Ekaterina Chaussee." Our driver was a typical *muzhik*,[7] big, blond, gentle and childlike, with a certain underlying shrewdness. He was extremely talkative and the fact that I was a foreigner gave him an added degree of confidence. Indeed he was childishly eager to explain his perplexities and get my advice. "We are a dark people, Barina,"[8] he said; "we know little beyond our own villages. It was bad for us under our father, the Tsar, that much we know. Now we have a new government. Will it be better for us, do you think?"

I told him it would be hard for me, as a foreigner, to judge, and asked him how the people of his village had been treated by the Red Army.

According to his accounts, on the whole, they had fared much better since the revolution. A commissar had taken charge, and had made a list of foodstuffs and livestock available. Each peasant had been allowed enough for his needs, and the surplus had been requisitioned for the army. There had been no robbery and no lawlessness. On certain days he was compelled to report for work with his horse and sleigh, but otherwise he was left free to attend to his own affairs. In his village, he told me, there was enough food, with the exception of salt, but salt was extremely expensive, and almost unobtainable. Parties constantly crossed the Polish lines to smuggle in supplies, but they were frequently arrested and

....

5. A commissar is an early Bolshevik term for a government official.
6. Catherine the Great was the Empress of Russia from 1762 to 1796.
7. *Muzhik* is a term used to refer to a Russian peasant before the Bolshevik Revolution of 1917.
8. *Barina* is Russian for "baroness" and is a generalized term of respect from the pre-revolutionary era.

shot by the Poles. As for the soldiers of the Red Army, they had as a rule been very good to the peasants, often sharing their supplies with them, or giving salt in return for eggs, milk and bacon.

Other peasants with whom I talked in the districts through which we passed, which are among the poorest agricultural regions in Russia, told the same story, with variations. In some villages there was no surplus and often a shortage of food supply, and there requisitions had been made very sparingly. There was some dissatisfaction over the failure of the government to provide food, but no antagonism to the administration as such.

Among the few richer *muzhiks* who owned good-sized tracts of land, there was a strong sentiment against nationalization, but as a matter of fact the government had decided the previous year to leave the question of nationalization in abeyance. Actually, under the Soviet Government there is less communism in the matter of land holdings than there was under the Tsar. Under the old system, much land was owned in common by the villages and parceled out among the peasants. At present, the peasants are in possession of their farms. Many of them are dubious about this free gift from the government, and officials are often approached by the peasants with offers to pay for their newly acquired interests. The peasants may be dissatisfied with taxes or requisitions, they may complain of the lack of the government to supply them with seeds, farm implements and manufactured goods, but they will never rise *en masse* against any government which leaves them in possession of the land.

Meanwhile they are actually rich as far as money goes, and nearly every peasant has his hoard of "Nikolai" rubles[9] tucked in his boots or hidden under the family feather bed on the stove. At present, however, his money does him no good. Many of the village cooperatives are closed or are operating on a restricted basis, on account of lack of supplies.

We arrived after dark in a driving snowstorm and stopped in front of an *izba*[10] that served as company headquarters. It had two rooms. In the first a family of *muzhiks* was living. An enormous earthenware stove, on top of which the grandmother and children had already gone to bed, was the most prominent article of furniture in the room. The father and several grown up sons were sitting on a long wooden bench, smoking pipes, filled with a vile weed called "*makhorka*,"[11] the peasant substitute for tobacco. In front of the fire, the

9. Nikolai rubles was a currency issued under the last emperor of Russia, Tsar Nicholas II (1894-1917).
10. An *izba* is a traditional Russian peasant home usually resembling a log cabin.
11. *Mahorka* is an inexpensive Russian tobacco.

mother was spinning flax on a spinning wheel that looked as if it might have been made in the seventeenth century. The other room served as living and sleeping quarters for the commandant and his political commissar.

The latter was at first inclined to be somewhat suspicious and put me through a rigid cross-examination, but as he showed no intention of having me shot on the spot, I began to feel slightly encouraged, especially as I knew something of army psychology. These Red Army men on the Berezina were very much like our own troops on the Western front—they were lonely and homesick; they had news and mail only intermittently. Life was very dull between the intervals of hostilities and they were thirsty for news and amusement. I was the first person who had come to them from the outside world. Most of them had never seen a Western European, much less an American woman, before. It was curiosity and boredom, coupled, perhaps, with a certain admiration of my audacity, that carried me through the Red Army from this small village on the edge of No Man's Land to Division Headquarters at Vitebsk.

Having successfully passed through the ordeal of cross-examination, we were received with simple unaffected friendliness, and deluged with questions with regard to happenings in the outside world. Why did the Entente[12] wish to prevent Russia from settling her own affairs in her own way? What was the attitude of the American people with regard to their Russian comrades? Who would be the next American president? When would the blockade be lifted? When would Russia have peace?

While I was endeavoring to answer in my limited Russian, with the help of my interpreter, supper was brought in. There were no plates, and we shared a community dish of delicious country bacon with black bread, butter and hot tea with milk. After supper the commander himself took us to our billet in an "*izba*" across the way. It was quite a luxurious one, boasting three rooms. Ours was the best in the house, the principal articles of furniture being a wooden bed with big down pillows and an American sewing machine. The entire family assembled to greet us, and from that moment we were never left alone. They had never seen an American woman before and their curiosity was flattering if a bit overwhelming. Every piece of baggage was inspected and I undressed and went to bed before a breathlessly interested audience. The women of the family gathered in my room to watch the process, and the men, I felt sure, peeped

----

12. The Entente was the alliance system that opposed the Central Powers in World War I. Russia was part of the Entente before the Bolshevik Revolution, along with France and Great Britain. The French, British, Americans, and Czechs intervened in the Russian Civil War by sending troops to guard munitions, undermine the Bolsheviks, and support the Whites in this conflict.

through the cracks in the wooden partition. In the morning my sponge bath in a small tin basin was a source of untold entertainment. We had a breakfast of pancakes and tea, after which the commander appeared. It was ten o'clock and he had just gotten up. Nobody in Russia ever wants to go to bed or get up in the morning, and reveille is unknown in the Red Army. Soldiers and officers get up when they please.

He invited me to go out and inspect the schools and the hospital. "School!" I said. "Is it possible that you have a school here?" for we were only fifteen versts from No Man's Land.

"Yes, indeed," he answered, "and we have more pupils than before the Revolution."

I found that there had formerly been one primary school in Lochnitsa, with sixty-five pupils. At that time, four hundred pupils were registered in the primary schools and the *gymnasium* or secondary school. The entire equipment for the gymnasium had been gotten together very hurriedly. There were three classrooms, in each of which I found about thirty pupils hard at work. The benches had been knocked together from boards, with log supports. Similar benches, a little higher, served as desks. The blackboards were homemade and the pupils were doing their exercises on sheets of wrapping paper, cut to the required size, with pencils that had been divided into three to make them go around.

The schoolmaster was teaching a class in geometry when I came in. He had only two textbooks. He was an elderly man who had formerly taught in one of the *gymnasia*. All his life he had had theories about education which he had never been allowed to put into practice, and here he was in this out of the way place, within range of the Polish guns, carrying out his life's ambition with next to nothing in the way of equipment. He had planned for his pupils an up-to-date course, corresponding to that in our high schools, including modern languages, bookkeeping, scientific and agricultural courses. He was very much interested in the American public school system and asked me when I thought they would be able to get some pedagogical books from the United States. His attitude towards the Soviet Government was purely nonpolitical, but I think it was rather favorable than otherwise.

In the primary schools there was the same lack of technical equipment. I talked to one of the teachers who was the daughter of a *pomeshchik*,[13] one of

. . . .

13. *Pomeshchik* is a term that dates to the 14th century. The term originated with the practice of land grants (*pomestye*) given as a condition for lifetime military service. During the 18th century the *pomestye* were

the former landlords in the neighborhood. She was frankly uninterested in her work and resentful at being obliged to teach French and German to the children of her father's *muzhiks*. Nothing good could come of it, she said, and I could easily see that here was the sabotage of which I had already heard.

From the schools we went to the hospital. It was a well arranged building, with light, airy wards, each containing twenty beds, a dispensary and an operating room, but it was absolutely empty. There was not a piece of linen, a yard of surgical dressings, a pound of soap or disinfectant, nor an ounce of medicine. The physician in charge told me that it was impossible to receive patients.

"All I can do is to handle a few surgical cases in the dispensary," he said, "and yet the number of new cases of typhus averages twenty a week."

Before we finished our tour of inspection, a regular blizzard was raging, and it was bitterly cold, so we decided to remain in Lochnitsa for another night. I had just started to give the commander an English lesson, after explaining the delightful mysteries of my folding typewriter, when he was called to the telephone. He came back with a rueful expression.

"I have bad news for you," he said.

"Here's where we go back over the border," I thought, but it proved that he had orders to send us on at once to regimental headquarters at Nacha,[14] twenty-five versts away; so we bundled up and set off in two sleighs down the long, broad Chaussee. Our hosts flatly refused to accept money for our meals and lodgings, the old mother only begging me to take a letter to her son in New York. She had lost the address, but she was quite sure that I would be able to find him, and I hadn't the heart to undeceive her.

We reported at regimental headquarters, where the political commissar offered us his own billet, a warm, comfortable room in a clean little "*izba*," where we had supper with him and the commander of the regiment. They were an interesting pair. The commander, Shevilov, was an actor by profession, and an artist to his fingertips, and the commissar, Shevchenko, who was an ardent Communist, had been an upholsterer. The latter told me much about the activities of the Communist party in the army.

"Every officer shares authority with a political commissar, who is invariably a Communist," he said. "We are placed in the army to guard against purely military authority. All complaints, all matters of regimental discipline, and

---

transformed into real private holdings, the landowners were released from the requirement of service, and the gentry became a privileged estate with virtually unlimited power over their resident serfs. The term continued to be used, especially derogatorily after the 1917 revolution, to refer to landowners.

14. Nacha is a town in western Russia.

all questions affecting relations between the army and the civilian population must be referred to us, although with regard to technical matters the officer has full liberty of action. It is required of an officer simply that he must be an expert in his line, and that he shall attend to his business. Under this system it is possible for us to make use of former army officers, irrespective of their political convictions, because their activities are controlled. There are, in addition, Communists among the enlisted men in every regiment, and we choose some of our best men for that job, because we realize the importance of propaganda."

The commander was plainly not interested in politics, and our talk drifted to music, the theater, books and finally to Russian songs. One after another he sang lovely folk melodies, boat songs from the Volga, harvest songs from the Ukraine, songs of forgotten heroes. Soon a crowd of soldiers gathered at the door and we all joined in the chorus. Then followed revolutionary songs, such as the splendid funeral march of the Communists, the famous "Varshavyanka" and the "Dubinushka,"[15] perhaps the finest of all Russian folk songs, for it is the heart cry of the Russian people. For generations the untranslatable chorus was sung by factory workers toiling twelve hours a day, by the slaves of the *pomeshchiki* and by the political prisoners in the Siberian mines, who were kept from dropping at their tasks by the steady rhythm. The hours slipped by and it was five o'clock in the morning before we wished each other "*Spokoynoy nochi,*"[16] a peaceful night.

We were left to sleep undisturbed until nearly noon, when the commissar knocked at our door. He had communicated with brigade headquarters at Krupki, some twenty-five *versts* away, and had received instructions to send us on as soon as possible. From there, he told us, we would get direct rail communications with Moscow. So far we had traveled entirely by sleigh, as the railroad had been torn up in anticipation of the Polish offensive. At Krupki we would be behind the front lines and would find much more comfortable accommodations.

....

15. The *Varshavyanka* (The Warsawian) and the *Dubinushka* (the Little Club) were extremely popular work songs that were sung widely among laborers and soldiers.
16. *Spokoynoy nochi* means "Good night" in Russian.

CHAPTER III
Work and Play in the Red Army

𝒦rupki, as brigade headquarters, was quite an important town, with a correspondingly important staff. The commanding officer was away at the time of our arrival, and we were received by the political commissar, a Pole named Sinkiewicz. I had much more difficulty in getting by the first examination with him than with the other commissars, for he was both inquisitive and suspicious, besides being exceedingly intelligent, and a devoted Communist. Finally, however, he decided to let us stay at Krupki, I rather think in order that he might observe us himself. He gave up his own room to me, and left nothing undone to make us comfortable. We stayed for nearly a week, and I grew to know him very well. Before the war he had been a joiner, and he had had only a rudimentary education, but he had natural ability, real enthusiasm, and unlimited capacity for work. No detail was too small to receive his attention. He worked from nine or ten of one morning till three or four of the next, and the soldiers, while not fond of him, for he was a rather unapproachable person, respected him greatly. Outwardly, in his command there was very little of what we would call discipline; the soldiers never stood at attention or saluted; there were apparently no fixed hours for anything, but when he gave an order it was instantly obeyed.

With him I visited many of the enlisted men's billets. They were comfortably housed, and there was none of the overcrowding which I had noticed in the Polish army. The men's equipment was excellent, though not uniform. Each man had two suits of underwear, a uniform consisting of a flannel blouse or an army tunic somewhat on the American pattern, loose, baggy trousers, stout leather boots or shoes and felt boots for extreme weather, called *valenki*,[1] an Astrakhan cap, a greatcoat or a sheepskin jacket. Their rifles were in good order, but not of the latest pattern, and mostly remade. There was no army kitchen, each man receiving his rations in bulk, and preparing them in his own billet.

The officers had a mess in the schoolhouse across the way from my own billet, and I was invited to share their meals. They received the same rations as the men, but employed a woman to cook for them, and pooled their supplies. I prepared my breakfast in my room, but had dinner and supper with them. The former meal consisted of a meat soup, meat cutlets, with potatoes or *kasha*, the Russian national dish (a cereal, usually whole wheat, buckwheat or millet), tea, with occasionally marmalade. Supper was soup, *kasha*, tea, and sometimes bacon.

There were few officers at headquarters, most of them being stationed in adjoining towns, but they often came into Krupki for orders and I met many of them. Most of them were former imperial army officers, soldiers by profession, who had no political ideas, and cared little for whom they fought as long as they got their pay; others may have been working against the Soviet Government, hoping for a chance to put something over, but on the surface everything worked smoothly, and the political commissar's word was law. The only place where I noticed sabotage or friction was in the Red Cross, which is in charge of the Red Army Sanitary Service, and there also I began to observe evidences of discontent among the Jews, which is far more prevalent in Soviet Russia than people on the outside believe. Many of the physicians and a large proportion of the personnel were Jews, few of them were Communists, nearly all of the men had entered the sanitary service to escape active duty, and there was plenty of sabotage. The Synagogue had been converted into an emergency field hospital, the church being spared, which caused a great deal of feeling among the Jewish population. This was almost invariably the case in small towns unprovided with sufficient hospital facilities, and with no large buildings except the church and synagogue. It was quite natural that the latter should have been chosen as it was always lighter and dryer than the church, but the Jews did not appreciate this fact and were in many cases very bitter against the army authorities.

The head physician at Krupki was a most entertaining person, who played the harmonica like a virtuoso, and regaled me with roast goose and baked apples in his billet, but he was very slipshod in his methods and profoundly indifferent.

---

1. *Valenki* are traditional Russian felt boots.

The hospital, while well equipped with medicines and supplies, was very dirty, and ran itself without any system whatever.

The peasants at Krupki I found exactly like the others I had met—they were very well pleased at owning their land, dumbly submissive to the requisition system, which they evaded whenever they could, totally apolitical, and only vaguely conscious of the great changes that had come to Russia. They had always been in the fighting zone since the beginning of the war, military rule prevailed then, and it was still in force. Their food ration had been getting steadily shorter, supplies of manufactured goods less and less, but then that was war. They had the land, their children were getting a better education, that was the Revolution.

On the whole, they were rather pleased than otherwise with the change. It was easy to see that if they were left in possession of their fields, and received a scant supply of salt and manufactured articles, they would care very little about the form of government in far-away Moscow or even in the provincial capital of Vitebsk. The members of the village Soviet were simple, hardworking men for the most part; a few of them, however, were Communist propaganda workers who took the lead, and the others let them run things.

The Jewish population, composed entirely of former small tradespeople, was, on the other hand, bitterly discontented. Their stores had been closed, they were compelled to do work for the army in order to draw their rations; speculation was punished with arrest or imprisonment. Many of them were very poor, far worse off indeed than the peasants. In the small towns in the war zone there are not multifarious commissariats[2] in which the Jews can find comfortable jobs; they do not care for hard physical work and many of them existed on secreted supplies or devious and dangerous contraband trade with Poland.

While in Krupki I had an opportunity of seeing one of the Red Army schools for illiterates. These schools are splendidly organized. There is a school for every two hundred and fifty men throughout the entire Red Army. Attendance is compulsory and by an intensive system of teaching, illiterates are taught to read the newspapers and to write a fairly legible hand in six weeks. In the class I saw there were about fifteen pupils, mostly sturdy young boys of the peasant class from nineteen to twenty-four. They sat around a big table, at the head of which stood the teacher. He distributed a number of cardboard letters among the pupils, then formed with the letters which he had retained a word of one syllable. After all had taken a good look at it, he swept the letters into a pile in the center of the table and then a race started among the pupils to form the

---

2. A commissariat is a division of the government under the Bolsheviks in early Soviet Russia.

word from memory, the man who made it first and correctly winning the game. They were as keen about it as children, a score was kept and there was hot rivalry among them to see who would come out ahead at the end of the lesson.

It was very interesting to note that while teaching the soldiers the alphabet, the teacher also inculcated the first principles of Communism. Words employing all vowels and consonants were most cleverly brought into the lesson, each chosen with a view to propaganda. A more advanced class was using a primer for adult illiterates, which had been published by the department of education. The first sentence was: "*Muy ne rabuy—muy radi.*" "We are not slaves—we are glad." Then follows (this time I will only give the English translation): "We are all equal—our masters are sorry." "We used to work for our masters, now we work for ourselves." "We elect our Soviets." "The Soviets are the tocsin of the people." "Our army is an army of workers and peasants," and so on. When words of three syllables were reached, there were a number of short expositions of the principles of Soviet government, the relation between town and city workers and finally a brief sketch of the growth of the Communist movement from the foundation of the First International.[3] The first "piece" was a speech of Trotsky.[4]

Reading of dates and numbers was taught by such historical landmarks as the birth of La Salle and Karl Marx, the Decembrist revolution, the assassinations of Alexander the Second and Stolypin, the March and October Revolutions and the meetings of the International.[5]

....

3. The formal name of the First International was the International Workingman's Association. It was founded in London, in 1864, in order to unite workers in class struggle. Later, radicals viewed this organization as the beginning of class struggle in Europe.

4. Leon Trotsky (Lev Bronstein, 1879-1940) was a key revolutionary figure in Russia. He was once a member of the Menshevik Party, but just before the Bolshevik Revolution of 1917 he joined Vladimir Lenin's movement to oust the Provisional Government. During the Russian Civil War, he led the Red Army to victory against the Whites.

5. Rene-Robert Cavelier, Sieur de La Salle, (1643-1687) was a French explorer who traveled through the Great Lakes region in the United States and claimed the Mississippi River region for France. Karl Marx (1818-1883) was a German philosopher whose ideas were a key inspiration for the Bolshevik Revolution in Russia. The Decembrist Revolt (1825) was an unsuccessful revolt of mainly Russian veterans of the Napoleonic Wars against the new emperor, Nicholas I, and in favor of republicanism. Alexander II (1818-1881) was the emperor of Russia between 1855 and 1881. He instituted massive reforms in Russia including the freeing of the serfs, but he was still assassinated by radicals in 1881. Peter Stolypin (1862-1911) served as Prime Minister of Russia from 1906 to 1911. He was assassinated in Kiev by radicals because of his repressive policies. The two revolutions in Russia in 1917 took place in February and October by the Russian (Julian) calendar. The Western (Gregorian) calendar was thirteen days ahead, so these two revolutions actually took place in March and November. Harrison was mixing the two calendars.

The educational system in the army is so well organized that I believe that every man who serves six months or more in the Red Army will go home with at least a rudimentary education.

Social amusements as well are not lacking in the Red Army. One night while I was at Krupki, I was invited to a ball in the brigade recreation center, a short distance outside of the town. This was a house that formerly belonged to one of the large landowners in the neighborhood. On the first floor were recreation and lounge rooms for the soldiers, well supplied with newspapers and propaganda literature. Upstairs, a large room had been converted into a combination theater and ballroom. All the stage settings had been designed and made by the soldiers themselves. The curtain was made of strips of muslin, which Russian soldiers are in the habit of wrapping around their feet instead of stockings under their high boots or *valenki*.

The ball was preceded by three one-act plays, in which the women's parts were taken by girls from the village. The first two plays were the production of local Red Army talent. One was a sort of condensed version of *Ten Nights in a Barroom*,[6] the other frankly militaristic propaganda about a boy who redeems a worthless past by valiant service in the Red Army. The third, much to my amusement, was a conventional society farce with all the earmarks of class, and it was played and applauded with more zest than either of the others.

After the performance, chairs were pushed back and the dance began, the music being furnished by a regimental band, which alternated Russian national dances with American ragtime. We had *A Hot Time in the Old Town, On the Mississippi*, Sousa's marches, including the *Stars and Stripes Forever*,[7] and I danced the two-step for the first time in ten years. The Russian dances were far more intricate and proved a great tax on my adaptability, but I managed to get through without any serious mistakes.

Officers and enlisted men mingled indiscriminately, for when not on duty no distinction of rank is officially recognized. The uniforms are supposed to be all the same, the only difference being that the officer wears on his left arm the Red stars and bars, the insignia of rank. But I found that practice in this rule was not always strictly observed; the officers' uniforms were usually of better quality

---

6. A book by American author Timothy Shay Arthur published in 1854 and depicting the evils of alcohol.

7. *A Hot Time in the Old Town* is an American ragtime song composed by Theodore August Metz in 1896. John Philip Sousa (1854-1932) was an American composer of patriotic marches including *Stars and Stripes Forever*.

than those of the men. Some of them sported British uniforms or tunics and Sam Browne belts,[8] from army stores captured in Siberia or Archangel.

The word "officer" is never used in the Red Army, being replaced by the word "Commander"; thus a company commander is addressed "Comrade Company Commander," a general "Comrade Division Commander." The organization of the army is similar to the organization of other armies, beginning with the *rota*, or company, and going to the division, which consists of a minimum of ten thousand men. Several divisions form an "army," which is a slightly larger unit than an American division. There were forty thousand men in the Seventeenth Army, whose guest I was, and which had its headquarters at Smolensk.

In the middle of the party dancing stopped and we played a game called "Post Office." Pencils and paper were distributed, each guest was given a small slip of paper on which was written a number. These we pinned on our chests, and then proceeded to write letters to the people we wanted to meet, addressing them by number, and signing our own numbers. The letters were dropped in a mailbag and distributed by a soldier postman. If Citizeness 27 received a letter from Citizen 17 she was supposed to ask him to dance.

I had a number of letters, some of them very touching in their naive joy at seeing someone who brought news from the outside world. Others welcomed me simply and heartily to Soviet Russia, and some were very amusing. One man wrote in English, "You danced very well." I promptly asked him to try it with me and then inquired where he had learned English. He told me that he had been a sailor on the Russian American Steamship Company's[9] boats which ran between New York and Libau.[10] The first question he asked me about the United States was "Is Coney Island still running?"

In the intervals between dancing we often adjourned to the buffet, where tea was dispensed from a big brass samovar, and sausage and cheese sandwiches served. The girls at the party were all from the town or daughters of the peasants in the neighborhood. For the most part they were well dressed and looked rosy and happy. I talked to several girls as well as parents in Krupki and other towns in the army zone, and I never heard of an instance of women being outraged by Red Army men. The relation between the men and the girls was one of

---

8. Sam Browne belts were belts that went over the right shoulder on British military uniforms. The name comes from Captain Sam Browne, who served in India in the mid-nineteenth century.
9. A pre-revolutionary steamship line between the United States and the Russian Empire, better-known as the Russian-American Line.
10. A port city in Latvia on the Baltic Sea.

comradeship and absolute equality. There were many army weddings, both civil and religious.

A few days later I was invited to amateur theatricals followed by a dance at Bober, another army post a short distance from Krupki. My interpreter and I drove over in a sleigh, after an ineffectual attempt to take me in a motorcycle. There were very few motorcycles or lorries in the army, and messages and supplies were usually carried by sleigh, but in our battalion there was one decrepit English motorcycle. The young officer who operated it was as proud of it as of a child, and in spite of the heavy snow assured me that he could take me the thirty-five *versts* to Bober and back. I was ready on time, and watched him while he tinkered with the machine for an hour. Finally he announced that it was working all right. I got in and we started off at the rate of about sixty miles an hour, but suddenly something went wrong, we slackened speed, puffed and snorted, turned around three times and finally tried to climb up the steps of the village school. Then we made another start, bumped into a telegraph pole, and skidded off into a snowdrift. I got out and pushed from behind while the driver tried to get every possible ounce of power out of his wheezy engine. Suddenly he started unexpectedly. I gave a flying leap and landed on all fours in the sidecar, but we decided that while the going was good it would be better to go back to Krupki and take a sleigh to Bober.

At Bober I had dinner with an army physician and his wife. Officially they were not married, for it is forbidden for a man and wife to serve in the same unit in the Red Army, but she acted as his secretary, and what is more, the entire family, consisting of three children, a cow, a pet goat and six bantam chickens, accompanied them from one army post to another. It was an instance of "pull," which is not confined, as I discovered, to capitalistic countries. Indeed, there is no place where it is more flourishing at the present time than in Russia. They were both very intelligent; he, while not at all in sympathy with the existing regime, was devoted to his work. The evacuation hospital under his care was at that time mainly devoted to typhus and pneumonia cases, as there was practically an armistice on that sector of the front, and the men wounded some weeks previously had all been sent to the rear. He told me that some of the most necessary medicines were lacking, but that they obtained many drugs through contraband trade with the Poles. Actually, the Red Army was being supplied with a considerable quantity of drugs and surgical supplies by its enemies, Polish officers sometimes engaging in the underground traffic. At Orsha, a few days later, I saw a large room filled with American Red Cross supplies that had been bought from officers in the Polish Army.

The play at Bober was a classical comedy, very well acted and staged with considerable ingenuity, for everything had been made by the soldiers themselves. There was one boy of nineteen, a real artist, who played exquisitely on the violin, giving a number of Russian dances and folk songs as well as one of Wieniawski's Caprices,[11] which he interpreted in a masterly manner. Afterwards I was invited to supper at the Aviators' Club. The aviators were all old Imperial army officers; most of them spoke French or German, and we had a very jolly time. From their manners and conversation they might have been still in their old environment. Their squadron possessed, they told me, only five old French planes of the 1917 model, petrol was scarce and the winter storms did not permit them to do much flying. Altogether, they said, the air force of the Red Army was insignificant and could only be counted on for a small amount of scout work.

....

11. Henryk Wieniawski (1835-1880) was a Polish composer and violinist who wrote "L'Ecole Moderne: 10 Etudes-Caprices," which was taught to many young violinists at the turn of the twentieth century in Russia and elsewhere.

CHAPTER IV
A Trip in a Box Car

We had a funny time getting away from Krupki. It was an extremely good illustration of the Russians' quality of never being exact about anything, and their utter lack of a system. Our train was to leave at twelve o'clock by the new daylight saving schedule that went into force on the day fixed for our departure, but the army failed to move up its clocks to correspond with the railroads, and we arrived just an hour late. Incidentally, the Bolsheviks go in rather extensively for daylight saving. The difference between summer and wintertime is two and a half hours.[1] The next day we were on time, but the commander of the battalion had ordered places reserved for us in the post-office car. The official in charge of the car refused to admit us without authorization from the Commissariat of Posts and Telegraphs, and while he and the Red Army men who accompanied us to the station were disputing, the train moved off. As it was the only train that day, we were obliged to spend another twenty-four hours in Krupki.

Near the station I inspected a German repatriation echelon, loaded with civilians and prisoners of war, who were being repatriated through Poland. It was an up-to-date sanitary train, complete in every particular, with hospital, kitchen and refrigerator cars, steam heated and lighted by electricity. I also saw on a siding an ugly looking armored train, rather amateurishly constructed from converted flat cars, the guns being camouflaged with logs to make it appear like a lumber train.

....

1. Daylight Savings Time was first instituted in Russia in 1917 under the Provisional Government, but the Bolsheviks alternated between using it and abandoning it early in their reign. The confusion in this section for Harrison probably stemmed from the fact that the entire country was not uniform its use of this system.

We left Krupki in a boxcar with the members of a forestry commission and two Soviet officials who had been purchasing sole leather intended for the Polish army, from Polish officers on the Berezina front. There were ten of us in all, eight men, my interpreter and myself. The six foresters were the first civilian employees of the Soviet Government with whom I had been thrown in contact. They were not in the least interested in politics, and the only member of the party who was thoroughly discontented with the present regime was a Jew. The paymaster was an old man whom they called *babushka*, grandfather.[2] He sat up in a corner day and night on his money chest, smoked *makhorka* and never said a word, but the others were very talkative, and I got to know them well on the trip to headquarters at Vitebsk, which took three days and two nights, including a stop of some hours at Orshcha.

Our housekeeping arrangements were, to say the least, primitive. At both ends of the car were wide board shelves covered with clean hay, on which we slept, five on a side. In the center was a small sheet metal stove, around which was a bench roughly knocked together out of unplaned boards. We did all our cooking on this stove. The toilet arrangements consisted of a tin bucket and a dipper. In the morning when I washed my face and hands I followed the example of the others, leaning out of the door of the car, and cupping my hands while one of the "comrades" poured in water, with which I splashed my face. We made tea and pancakes on the stove, and heated cans of excellent meats which, with tea, black bread and sugar, were the army traveling rations. My companion and I were provided with these at Krupki. After supper in the evening we sat around the stove, told stories and the soldiers sang Russian songs for us by the hour to the accompaniment of a *balalaika*[3] with one string missing.

At Orshcha I was met at the station by the chairman of the local Ispolkom[4] (executive committee), to whom I had sent a telegram, as I had a letter for him from his mother, an old Jewish lady who lived in Borisov. He took us to his home, where he gave us a wonderful dinner: "*shchi*," a Russian vegetable soup, roast goose with potatoes and onions, Jewish style, pancakes, with sour cream, tea and cakes and apples for dessert. All the while, he kept telling me about the terrible food shortage in the towns. With him I visited one of the "People's Universities," where they had very good technical courses, and classes for adult

---

2. Harrison is confusing the term *babushka* for *dedushka*. *Babushka* means grandmother and *dedushka* means grandfather.

3. A *balalaika* is a traditional Russian instrument with three strings and a triangular body.

4. This is an abbreviation of *Ispolnitelny komitet* that means "executive committee." It was a common Bolshevik practice to abbreviate the names of their new government structures.

illiterates, and the hospital, which lacked the most necessary medicines and supplies. Everything available in that line had been requisitioned by the army and the civilian population was suffering greatly in consequence.

While waiting for our boxcar, or *tyeplushka*,[5] to be attached to the next train which was shortly due, I was invited to have a look at the "Agit Punkt," the army recreation and propaganda center, of which there is one in every large town through which troops pass. It was a large, airy room, formerly the first-class waiting room. As soon as I entered it I was struck with its resemblance to something I had seen before, then it occurred to me that it was as nearly as possible like an American "Y" center. There was the same arrangement of tables spread with periodicals and magazines, the same type of decorations on the walls, red flags and banners and portraits of Lenin replacing the stars and stripes and pictures of President Wilson, an American graphophone, a moving picture machine, and a platform with a piano and arrangements for impromptu theatricals.

I soon found out why. The director was an old American "Y" man—a Russian by birth, it was true, but he had worked with the American Y.M.C.A.[6] in Siberia and Russia for three years, drifting into the Red Army to carry on the same work after the departure of the American workers. He had been with them long enough to become thoroughly imbued with American ideas and was genuinely homesick for his old environment.

We arrived in Vitebsk early in the morning, and the doctor and I accompanied by an army dentist who had traveled with us from Orsha, went to report at Division Headquarters. We had all this time been traveling from place to place on army safe conducts, which carried us as far as Vitebsk, and it was necessary, we were told, for us to get permission from the general headquarters of the Seventeenth Army at Smolensk to take us through to Moscow. Division headquarters were in a large, ramshackle building which had formerly been used as a hotel, all the rooms being occupied by staff offices. The political commissar, a pleasant but rather ignorant man, who struck me as being much too young and inexperienced for his job, interviewed us, asking comparatively few questions, and promised to telegraph immediately for a permit for us to proceed to Moscow.

---

5. *Tyeplushka* – the name means literally a heated vehicle.
6. The American Young Men's Christian Association set up operations in Russia around the turn of the twentieth century in several Russian cities providing varying services. They would remain in the Soviet Union until 1940. See Matthew Lee Miller, *American Philanthropy Among Russians: The Work of the YMCA, 1900-1940* (Ph.D. dissertation, University of Minnesota, 2006).

He told us that his wife had been anxious for some time to go to Moscow, but had been unable to obtain permission as she had no business there which would entitle her to a *kommandirovka*, as official traveling orders are called in Russia, and that sending her as our escort would be an excellent pretext for getting her there.

While we were waiting, we were shown over headquarters, inspecting the commissary department, where we found a very efficient looking officer examining samples of flour for army use. He was well qualified for his job, for he had been a baker before the Revolution. The topographical section was well equipped with maps, and the communications seemed to be in excellent working order, judging from the number of telegraph and telephone instruments in operation. The commanding general was an austere looking man, evidently a former Imperial officer, for he clicked his heels together and made a stiff little bow when we were presented to him. He had perfect manners, but seemed rather diffident and uncommunicative. My judgment was that he was decidedly uncomfortable in his present position, and was watched rather closely, for the political commissar never left us for a minute and did most of the talking. The permit for us to go to Moscow arrived within an hour, and we were told that the train would leave at seven in the evening. Meanwhile, perhaps we would like to see the town. We said that we would very much, and set out in a sleigh, with a pleasant young commissar as our escort.

The first place we visited was the military hospital, which was clean and very well run, situated on a high hill, where are grouped most of the churches, former government buildings and the houses of the bourgeoisie. The buildings were substantial structures of stone or concrete, painted pink or white, some of them beautiful examples of the Russian Empire style dating from the early days of the nineteenth century. The streets in this part of the town were broad and fairly clean, with trees, public squares and picturesque glimpses of the frozen Dnieper winding around the foot of the hill, where were located the railroad station and the dirty, forlorn buildings of the lower town. These consisted mostly of small Jewish shops, nearly all of which were closed, though "free trade" was still nominally in force in Vitebsk. In the shops that were still open, the shelves were nearly bare of general merchandise, but the food stores exhibited geese and chickens, some meat, white bread, cakes and a few withered apples. Here and there a cafe was open. In one of these we had imitation coffee flavored with saccharin and watered milk, and some insipid little cakes, the former three hundred rubles a glass, the latter five hundred rubles apiece. The place was literally infested with beggars and apparently no effort was made to control them. They were mostly Jews, for Vitebsk was on the edge of what was known as the Jewish Pale,[7] the extreme Eastern limit of the zone wherein Jews were permitted to live in the old days, and it was a lively trading center between Central Russia and Poland.

The Revolution had put all these small traders out of business, there were neither factories nor a multiplicity of Soviet offices to absorb the workers, and those who were not conscripted for the Red Army or employed in one of the government departments were living in direst poverty. The official bread ration for those not classed as heavy workers was one-half a pound of black bread a day, and a little soup and *kasha*, which they obtained at the Soviet dining rooms. The fare in the children's dining rooms was better than that for adults, but they had no fats and no milk. Salt was almost impossible to get and the people were desperate for lack of it. We had dinner in the dining room for the employees of the general staff. It consisted of cabbage soup and *kasha*, and the employees had to bring their own bread.

Typhus was epidemic in the town, there were practically no disinfectants, soap or medicines, and the hospitals were not able to accommodate even a small percentage of the victims. In the afternoon, when we were left to wander about by ourselves, we visited a civilian hospital with a capacity of one hundred beds, which contained two hundred and forty patients, all ill with typhus. They were lying on straw pallets on the floors in the wards and in the hallways. On many of the beds the linen had not been changed for over a month; some of the patients were lying in bed quite naked, or covered with filthy rags.

In spite of the frightful appearance of everything, the doctor told us that the death rate among the patients was not over ten percent, as they were mostly peasants. Typhus has been endemic so long in Russia that the lower classes are semi-immunized and the death rate is always in inverse ratio to the intelligence of the population. Among persons of the upper class, it is twenty per cent and it is highest among the medical personnel, who are usually in poor condition to resist attacks from epidemics, owing to the fact that they are all overworked and

---

7. This was also known as the Pale of Settlement. It was an area on the western side of the Russian Empire where Jews were allowed to live. It originated in the 1790s under Catherine the Great and was enforced with varying intensity in the nineteenth century. Vitebsk in fact had a very sizable Jewish quarter, and was birthplace of the painter Marc Chagall, who was later made the Vitebsk region's Commissar for Arts, creating a People's Art College in the town, among other things. He left Vitebsk for Moscow in 1920, and left the USSR altogether two years later.

undernourished. The death rate among doctors in Russia during the past three years has been nearly forty percent.

Two of the most interesting places we visited in Vitebsk were the Army Political School and the Vitebsk branch of the Commissariat of Nationalities.[8] The former was for Red Army officers, men and political commissars. It was in a large building formerly used as a *gymnasium* or high school by the Russian government. Daily classes were held in history, political economy, the history of the Socialist movement, Marxism, the principles of the Communist Dictatorship; Communist propaganda workers were trained for field service in the army and among the peasant population. There were also classes in journalism for those who wished to acquire the art of writing the propaganda leaflets and brochures with which Russia is deluged at the present time, and art classes for designers of Bolshevik posters. We saw a rehearsal by the dramatic club of a Revolutionary play that was to be given at the main theater in a few weeks.

The Commissariat of Nationalities was divided into four sections: Russian, White Russian, Polish and Jewish. I found that the Soviet Government was placing no bar in the way of nationalistic feeling or aspirations. Each nationality was permitted to issue its own bulletins, and its own books and pamphlets, whenever the limited supply of paper and printers' ink permitted their publication, and the schools were conducted in all four languages. There was even a Polish school, where the little Poles, however, were taught to become good Communists. The churches were in the same position, and Catholic, Uniate[9] and Orthodox churches flourished side by side with the synagogues. There had been no very great effort to introduce a strictly Communistic system; free trade was permitted because the Soviet stores were obviously unable to give the people merchandise; many people had been left in undisturbed possession of their own homes, because there was no demand for lodgings, many of the population having emigrated further east, owing to the proximity of Vitebsk to the war zone. The general impression I got was of great squalor and misery caused by the war and the blockade, of general confusion and impermanence, with no evidence of either the benefits or disadvantages caused by Soviet rule.

....

8. This commissariat was headed at this time by Joseph Stalin (1879-1953) who would later be made General Secretary of the Communist Party of the Soviet Union, holding the post from 1928-1953. It was during his work in this commissariat that he began to build the political base that helped him acquire absolute power in the late 1920s.

9. Uniates are Eastern Orthodox Christians who are in communion with the Roman Catholic Church, but retain their own rituals, languages, and customs.

We left Vitebsk that evening, traveling in the army staff car with the commissar's lady, who proved a very good-natured but stupid companion, and a soldier who was detailed to carry our luggage and wait on us generally. As far as Orsha we occupied an ordinary second-class compartment, but there we changed to a staff sleeping car, which was to take us the thirty-six-hour journey to Moscow. At Orsha, where we arrived in the middle of the night, and had to wait for six hours, we found several regiments on the move. The station was literally one mass of filthy humanity. Every inch of floor space was covered with sleeping soldiers with indescribably dirty bedding rolls, bags and knapsacks. They slept overlapping, and the air was foul beyond description. Fortunately I found my "Y" man, who had not yet gone to bed, and he let us into the recreation room, which had been locked up for the night, where we slept on benches until it was time for our train to leave.

Our quarters in the staff car were close, to say the least, but we were lucky, it seemed, to have those. A compartment for two was reserved for the four of us, and there, with the exception of a few venturesome visits to the toilet, we spent the next thirty-six hours. I occupied the lower berth, the doctor and the commissar's wife the upper berth, and the soldier slept on the floor. It was stiflingly hot, and the window was hermetically sealed. Standing in the corridor was impossible, because it was already filled with a solid mass of soldiers, who insisted in defiance of discipline on occupying it. They made it almost impossible for us to open the door and our escort had to fight his way out to get hot water to make our tea from the samovar machines that are in operation at each station.

The rest of the train, which was entirely composed of boxcars, was packed, people even sitting on the roofs and bumpers, and there were fights at every station between persons trying to get on and off. The country through which we passed was mostly flat and uninteresting, though it had a certain historical interest for me as the region through which Napoleon passed in his Russian campaign. I had followed pretty much the same general route as the Imperial Eagles,[10] all the way from Borisov, where there was a column to commemorate his crossing of the Berezina, and a small house just outside the town, where tradition has it that he spent the night.

---

10. A figure of an eagle carried on the end of a staff by Napoleon's army as they invaded Russia in 1812.

We arrived at the Alexandrovsky Station,[11] Moscow, early in the morning of the second day. There the army's responsibility for us ended, and, as I had no credentials to stay in Moscow, I asked the doctor to telephone to the Foreign Office to announce our arrival. She was told rather shortly that a representative of the Western Section would be sent to meet us and that we were not to leave the station until his arrival. Meanwhile I tried to spell out the news in *Pravda*,[12] which I had purchased at the newsstand, for a limited number of papers were on public sale in Moscow at that time, and I wondered what was coming next. So far so good, but the Foreign Office at least was utterly unaware of the fact that I had already spent two weeks in Soviet Russia. Whether my presence was known or not to the secret police of the Extraordinary Commission,[13] they certainly had done nothing so far to stop me.

---

11. Originally known as Smolensky Station, this, Moscow's sixth train station when it was built in 1870, was soon renamed Belorussky, then Alexandrovsky in 1912, to Belorussky-Baltiysky in 1922, and simply Belorussky again in 1936.
12. *Pravda* (Truth) was the official newspaper of the Communist Party of the Soviet Union. It was founded in Vienna in 1908, by Leon Trotsky, and became the official organ of the Party in 1910, but did not publish between 1912 and 1917. It was shuttered by Boris Yeltsin in 1991.
13. This is a reference to the Cheka. See note 2, page 27.

CHAPTER V
An Unwelcome Guest

*I*n about half an hour I saw a small, thin, dark, nervous-looking man with a pronounced stoop that made him appear almost like a hunchback enter the waiting room, glancing about as if he were looking for someone. "That is the man from the Foreign Office," I thought. In two seconds he had singled me out, and made straight for the corner where I was sitting. "Good morning," he said curtly in excellent English. "I'm Rosenberg, head of the Western Section of the Foreign Office. Will you be good enough to tell me how you got to Moscow?" I explained while he stood holding his dispatch case, nervously biting his lower lip, a characteristic gesture. When I had finished he looked at me severely. "Do you know that you have done a perfectly illegal and very dangerous thing in coming to Moscow without permission?" he demanded.

I replied that I had traveled openly with safe conducts from the Red Army, and that if it had chosen it could have stopped me and sent me back at any time. "That is true," he returned, "and for that reason we will give you a hearing. You are not entirely to blame, and those who were responsible for your entering the country will be held to account, but I warn you that you have rendered yourself liable to immediate deportation if not something worse" – this with a searching look that gave me a decidedly uncomfortable feeling – "come this way, please," and so saying he led the way to a small room which belonged to one of the station officials. Once there he carefully closed the door.

"Now hand over your passport and all your papers," he said. I obeyed, pulling out letters of introduction, credentials, letters to private persons and the notes I had made while with the Red Army.

"Is that all?" he asked. I assured him that it was.

"And who is this woman?" he inquired, turning to the little doctor, who had stood all the while, very red in the face, not daring to say a word. She handed over her papers, which he glanced at and tucked in his dispatch case.

Then he explained to me that the present policy of the Foreign Office was to admit but a small number of correspondents from bourgeois papers, and then only after their credentials had been carefully passed on by Chicherin;[1] that he had already refused admission to representatives of the Associated Press and the *Evening Post*, and that my presence would be a source of considerable embarrassment to the Foreign Office. I presented my side of the case as well as I knew how, and the upshot of it all was that he agreed to put the matter before Chicherin, and to permit me to remain in Moscow for the night, pending his decision. He retained the papers, but the rest of our luggage was packed into a waiting limousine, in which we were whirled away to the government guest house, where I was to be virtually under house arrest until the Foreign Office had decided what was to be done with me.

My first glimpse of Moscow did not produce the impression of utter desolation that most travelers experience on their arrival in Russia at the present time. It was probably because I had become accustomed by degrees to ruin and disrepair through long sojourn in war-ridden countries. I had been in Germany and Belgium immediately after the Armistice;[2] in the previous December I had passed through Vienna, which was almost as badly off as Moscow; then I had spent over two months in Minsk and Vilna, which had been despoiled in turn by Germans and Bolsheviks, and finally turned over to the none too tender mercies of the Polish occupation. Boarded shops, deserted streets, houses with the paint peeling off their moldy facades, snow blocked pavements, long lines of patient citizens waiting outside government shops for rations were no new sight to me.

The people I saw on the street, every other one of whom was dragging a little sled laden with wood, bundles or provisions, were for the most part better dressed and seemed better nourished than the people I had seen in Minsk or Vienna. Outside of the station and in the public squares there were plenty of sleighs, with their picturesque *izvozchiks*, or Russian cabbies, in long coats of

---

1. Georgy V. Chicherin (1872-1936) served as Commissar of Foreign Affairs from 1918 to 1930. He had once been a Menshevik, but in 1917 his anti-war stance brought him in line with the Bolsheviks. The Mensheviks were a revolutionary party in Russia that emerged from the split of the Russian Social Democratic Labor Party in 1903. The Bolsheviks were the other major faction.

2. The Armistice was November 11, 1918, when the warring sides in World War I ceased hostilities and began negotiating a peace settlement.

black, green, or blue cloth, belted with metal-studded girdles or barbaric colored sashes. Occasionally, well-dressed men and women dashed by in luxurious sleighs with tinkling bells and fur robes. The only sinister impression I received was from the flocks of ravens that hovered over the city, sat in the bare branches of the trees in the parks and on the eaves of all the buildings. They are as thick in Moscow during the winter as the pigeons around St. Paul's in London or in the Piazza of St. Mark in Venice, and almost as tame.

All the public buildings were decorated with red flags and banners, for it was the second anniversary of the founding of the Red Army, and Moscow was in festival attire. Many of them displayed huge canvases showing brawny workers holding aloft the banner of the proletariat against a background of smoking factories and workmen's homes. At every corner were propaganda placards urging support of the working army, for an early peace with Poland was anticipated, peace with Estonia had recently been signed, and the government was conducting a great campaign in support of Trotsky's plan for the re-mobilization of the Red Army in a vast scheme of reconstruction.

Here and there were posters against the Entente, showing the capitalists of the world sitting on their money bags and lording it over the workers, Lloyd George[3] handing out toy battleships and cannon to Yudenich and Denikin,[4] caricatures of the "Big Four" at Versailles, and various other cartoons of that character. Most of them were crudely but vigorously drawn, startling as to color and design, but remarkably direct in their conveyance of a concrete idea.

We passed swiftly down the Tverskaya, Moscow's former shopping thoroughfare, into the Kuznetsky Most, where were formerly the great jewelers, and the most exclusive shops, up the Myasnitskaya,[5] where I noticed the closed offices of the Westinghouse Company and the Singer Sewing Machine,[6] and into a small side street, the Mali Kharitonevsky, where we stopped before number ten, the government guest house which was to be my home, though I did not realize it at the time, with a few interludes, for eight months.

....

3. David Lloyd George (1863-1945) served as British Prime Minister from 1916-1922.

4. Nikolai N. Yudenich (1862-1933) was a general for Russia in World War I. He also was a military leader for the White forces in the Russian Civil War (1918-1920). Anton I. Denikin (1872-1947) was a general for Russia during World War I. He also served as a military leader for the White forces in the Russian Civil War (1918-1920).

5. These are prominent streets in Moscow known for expensive shopping areas, artistic residences, and offices of major companies.

6. The Singer Sewing Machine Company opened a factory outside Moscow, in Serpukhov, in 1900, and an office in St. Petersburg in 1904. Russia was the largest foreign market for Singer at that time. The "American sewing machine" which Harrison mentions in Chapter 2 was certainly a Singer. The company's factories and property were nationalized after the Revolution.

It had been the private residence of a German named Roerich, who was one of Moscow's richest merchants.[7] Though it had suffered severely in the anti-German riots of 1915, when it was attacked by a mob, and had been further despoiled during the early days of disorder following the October Revolution, it was still comfortably, even luxuriously, furnished. We were taken into a beautiful oak-paneled dining room, where our baggage was courteously searched by an employee of the Foreign Office. I was allowed to retain my typewriter, and nothing was taken but my Kodak and films. After this formality we were shown to a large room with a brass bed with box springs which looked good to me after my Red Army experiences, comfortable arm chairs, an electric bed lamp, and an enormous sofa which was to serve as the bed for the doctor.

Soon dinner was announced, and in the dining room I met the other foreign guests, Michael Farbman, then correspondent of the *Chicago Daily News*, a Norwegian businessman named Jonas Lied, and a Korean, Pak, who was the official delegate to Russia of the Korean Socialist party. There were also several Russians, among whom was a man called Siryazhnikov, who had lived for some time in the United States and organized the first Russian cooperatives on the Pacific Coast. The remaining guests were several Russians employed in the Foreign Office and a potentate from Bukhara[8] who ate all his meals, prepared by a native attendant, in his room. He had many visitors, but rarely appeared himself, except to flit to and fro from his bath wearing a gorgeous smoking jacket, a round embroidered cap and stealthy velvet slippers.

Dinner, which was typical of the meals served in other guest houses and hotels for government employees, was as follows: A thin meat soup, thickened with cereal or noodles made of rye flour, mashed potatoes or *kasha*, tea, black bread and sugar. It was served at two o'clock. Supper, at nine o'clock, consisted of Soviet macaroni, *kasha* or mashed potatoes, black bread and tea. Breakfast, between nine and ten, was tea or Soviet coffee, black bread and margarine or butter, and two teaspoons of sugar. This was substantially my diet for my entire stay, except when I purchased eggs, milk, fruit or other luxuries in the markets, or when I was invited to private homes or patronized illegal restaurants.

Once or twice a week our dinner menu was varied by the addition of boiled salt pork, horse or mutton, either as a separate dish, or, more often, incorporated sparingly in the mashed potatoes. Occasionally we had a small tin of canned fish

---

7. The home was built in 1909 for A.V. Roerich; today the building houses Moscow's Hall of Marriage No. 1.
8. Bukhara is a city in Uzbekistan populated mainly by Turkic-speaking Uzbeks. The Bukhara People's Soviet Republic existed from 1920-1925, encompassing what had previously been the Emirate of Bukhara. After 1925, the borders were redrawn and the territory essentially became the Uzbek SSR.

or a piece of cheese for supper, and about once in two weeks we had stewed fruit in season. In winter it was Russian cranberries, thickened with potato flour and flavored with saccharin. When sugar was scarce we had two bonbons with our tea instead of sugar. This was far better than the average ration of the ordinary citizen in Moscow at that time. We also received as part of our ration twenty-five cigarettes every other day.

Despite the uncertainty as to my fate, I spent the first evening very agreeably, and enjoyed a fine rest in the comfortable bed. When I asked if I might take a bath in the beautiful tiled bathroom, I was told that there was hot water every Wednesday, and that I would have to wait until then if I wanted it hot. The scramble for the bath on Wednesdays was very amusing. No one made any engagements for that afternoon if possible, as hot water was on tap only from twelve noon till eight in the evening, and it was necessary to hang around and watch for your turn.

I was fully prepared to do my own chamber work the next morning, as I had imagined that in Soviet Russia there were no servants, but I discovered that we had four.

The heavy work was done by prisoners who were sentenced to compulsory labor for speculation or violation of other decrees of the Soviet Government. They came in squads periodically with armed guards, and washed floors and windows. The house servants were apparently not subject to the rules regulating the employment of labor, for they worked from eight in the morning till eleven or twelve at night, and scarcely ever had any time off. Occasionally they were given tickets to the theater. They received a small stipend, their clothes, and the regular workers' *payok* or rations, supplemented by tips and presents of food from the foreign guests. The laundress slaved from early morning till late evening doing all the house wash as well as the personal laundry of the guests, who varied in number from ten to fourteen.

Once during the summer the Foreign Office attempted to cut off their *payok* on the ground that as many of the guests frequently stayed out for meals, what was left over from our table would be sufficient for them, but they struck, and kept their rations, which they sent home to their families.

This state of affairs struck me as rather inconsistent, but I later found that the servant class, like many other bourgeois institutions, had by no means disappeared in Russia. Many of my Russian friends kept at least one maid, and I knew of several commissars who did the same.

Once I received a visit from a girl who had been employed at the Savoy Hotel, also a government guest house, where I spent several weeks. She was a Lett,[9] and was anxious to secure a position as cook to the Russian mission, then leaving for Riga with a retinue of servants to negotiate peace with Poland. She asked me to recommend her to Ioffe,[10] chief of the mission, who often visited the Kharitonevsky, and gave as a reference Mme. Steklov, wife of the editor of the *Izvestia*,[11] with whom she had lived for over a year, and she told me that they employed three servants. The Trotskys also keep several servants, and I often saw the Trotsky children in a private victoria[12] with a very correct looking coachman driving through the streets of Moscow.

Of course all this is in direct contradiction to Marxist theories, but the Communists in practice are not averse to accepting the services of that portion of the proletariat which has not yet become class conscious, and is perfectly content to remain as "hired help." In justice to Soviet principles it must be said, however, that the authorities recognize the fact that brain workers must have time free for work in their special field, and that they do not object to the employment of labor to do the manual tasks for those engaged in more important activities.

Eventually, in an ideal Communist state, the Communists say, there will be no need for labor of this class. All meals will be served in the public dining rooms, all washing done in the community laundries, children will be all cared for in Soviet homes and nurseries, apartments heated from a central plant, and cleaned by government workers. But at present it is impossible to organize things on this basis. Domestic service is a relic of capitalism which will disappear in due time, but meanwhile it is not worthwhile to regulate it, as it is only a temporary phase.

Shortly after breakfast, Rosenberg appeared with a car, and took me to the Foreign Office, where I was told that Chicherin had determined to allow me to remain in Moscow for two weeks. I sent a radio to the Associated Press

---

9. A term for a Latvian.

10. Adolf A. Ioffe (1883-1927) was a revolutionary from an early age who befriended Leon Trotsky in 1908. He supported Trotsky in his negotiation of the Treaty of Brest-Litovsk in 1918. He would also negotiate with the Baltic states and Germany before serving as ambassador in China. In ill health and in protest to Trotsky's expulsion from the party, he committed suicide.

11. *Izvestia* was founded in 1917 as a workers' newspaper which was more aligned with the Mensheviks and Socialist Revolutionaries. After the revolution, it became the official newspaper of the Soviet Government, while *Pravda* was the official newspaper of the Communist Party. Yuri M. Steklov (1875-1941) was the editor of *Izvestia* at this time.

12. An elegant nineteenth-century French carriage still in use in Russia in the twentieth century.

Maly Kharitonevsky 10 today.

announcing my arrival, arranged for an interview with Chicherin for the next day, and settled down to life in my new quarters, which were most comfortable. We had a billiard room, and there was a big garden behind the house, to which access was had from a terrace opening out of the dining room. The table linen was of the best quality, and we used real silver forks and knives for some time, until some of the cutlery was stolen, which resulted in the substitution of plated ware. Our bed linen was changed every two weeks, and all our laundry was done in the house. At first we paid nothing at all for this service, but afterwards the Foreign Office instituted a tariff of seven hundred and fifty rubles a day, explaining rather naively as the reason that Soviet emissaries in other countries were invariably charged for their accommodations.

CHAPTER VI
News Gathering in Moscow

On the morning after my arrival, having been provided with the necessary documents of identity, I started to take a walk through the town, and happened to see a most picturesque ceremony, the funeral of the Commissar of Posts and Telegraphs.[1] It took place from the building of the Moscow Soviet, a beautiful early nineteenth century structure facing what is now known as the Soviet square, which is adorned with a new monument commemorating the Revolution. He was to be buried in the Red Square, at the base of the Kremlin, with the victims of the October Revolution. Long before the time appointed for the funeral, the employees of the various departments of the commissariat began to assemble in the square, each section carrying its own banner draped in black. There must have been several thousand of them. All along the route of the cortege, Red Armists, as the Red Army soldiers are called in Russia, were stationed at intervals, and cavalrymen with khaki coats and the bright pink trousers of the old imperial cavalry dashed up and down giving orders, and holding back the crowds which began to gather early from all directions. Then delegations from workmen's clubs and trades unions commenced to arrive carrying banners and standards; among them I even noticed an Anarchists' Club[2] with a huge black flag, curiously somber and menacing in the blur of red.

1. Vadim Podbelsky (1887-1920). Born in Yakutia and a member of the Party since 1905, he lived in France from 1906 until the 1917 revolution.
2. The Moscow Anarchists' Club served as a radical opposition to the Bolshevik regime. American exiles Emma Goldman and Alexander Berkman were associated with this club. Harrison describes Goldman and Berkman in detail later in the book.

An old white hearse, harnessed with six white horses, and attended by six professional pallbearers in white frock coats and gloves and antiquated white silk beaver hats, was waiting to receive the coffin, but when it emerged from the building, carried on the shoulders of ten sturdy Red Armists, covered with a red flag like a huge blood spot, I could not help thinking how out of place and incongruous it would look on the pretentious bier that had probably carried many an Imperial functionary to his last resting place.

The commissar's comrades evidently thought so too, for they never even glanced in the direction of the waiting hearse with its plumes and outriders, but turned slowly down the street, followed by the huge silent cortege with bared heads. In front of the coffin marched a Red Army band, playing the glorious funeral march of the Nihilists,[3] which has been adopted by the Communists as their own. At intervals other bands took up the hymn, one by one, as they filed into line.

In the Red Square, a guard of honor was assembled around the open grave, and the Commissar was laid to rest with his dead comrades without benefit of clergy, according to Karl Marx, with Kamenev,[4] the president of the Moscow Soviet, and other speakers paying warm tributes to his singleness of purpose and devotion to the cause of Communism. The grave was filled, the bare earth covered with a mass of green wreaths and Red streamers, and the simple ceremony was over. A little more than half a year later, another funeral took place in the Red Square, but I was not there to see it, being at that time in prison. It was that of John Reed,[5] the leader of the American Communist party.

My interview with Chicherin took place on the evening of my second day in Moscow. The appointment was at twelve o'clock, for Chicherin only works at night, and it was nearly two before I was finally shown into his room, where he sat in front of a huge table buried under an avalanche of documents and papers. I had expected to see a tall, self-confident, rather masterful looking person, but instead I saw a thin, delicate looking man of about forty-eight, with

---

3. Nihilism was a movement that began in Russia in the 1860s. With a belief in nothing (nihil) they formed anti-government revolutionary cells in Russia. The term nihilist was made famous by Russian novelist Ivan Turgenev in *Fathers and Sons* in 1862. Nihilists were behind the assassination of Alexander II in 1881.

4. Lev Borisovich (Rosenfeld) Kamenev (1883-1936) was a key Bolshevik politician and head of the Politburo from 1923-4. For a brief time he was considered a possible successor to Lenin. In 1936, he was executed after being convicted in the first of Stalin's show trials.

5. John Reed (1887-1920) was an American journalist who was sympathetic to the Bolshevik Revolution. He wrote *Ten Days That Shook the World* in 1919. He died of typhus in the Soviet Union in 1920. See page 223.

sandy hair, decidedly thin around the temples, and a small, pointed blond beard and mustache. Around his neck was a woolen muffler that almost concealed his chin. During the entire winter and well into the spring, I never saw him without it. His pale greenish-blue eyes had the strained expression that comes from overwork, and as he talked to me he kept interlacing his long sensitive fingers, that, without a further glance at his physiognomy, proclaimed him as what he essentially is, a man of culture and a gentleman. There seem to be so many misapprehensions about many of the People's Commissars that I will repeat here what should be known to all intelligent persons, that Chicherin, like many leading Communists, is a man of very good family, and a real Russian. He is related by marriage to several old Polish families, among them that of Count Czapski,[6] who was at one time secretary to Mr. Hugh Gibson,[7] our minister to Poland. His cousin, Countess Plater, whom I met in Vilna, was in the habit of referring to him as "That devil, my cousin Chicherin," but there was nothing diabolical about his appearance as he sat at his desk facing me, though he at once gave me the impression of being an exceedingly subtle personality. He spoke English almost as well as an Englishman.

After asking me how I had managed to fool the Foreign Office by coming uninvited into Russia and telling me that, in spite of my illegal status, he had decided to permit me to take up my work as correspondent in Moscow, we proceeded to talk about other things. While inflexible in his devotion to Communism, I believe that Chicherin has always been in favor of a more liberal policy with regard to the foreign affairs than many of his colleagues, but things often get beyond his control, and he is not always listened to. Several times while I was in Moscow he was severely censured by the more intransigent Communists, and his report on his foreign policy to the Moscow Soviet last year was carried by an insignificant minority. At the same time, he is the only man in Russia today who has the experience and knowledge to handle the affairs of the Foreign Office. His notes are often masterpieces in their way, and he has a genius for showing up the weak side of European diplomatists. I consider that when it came to the matter of the retort courteous in the correspondence between Lord Curzon[8] and Chicherin, that Chicherin usually got the better of his British opponent. He is less inclined than some of his fellow commissars to

6. Andrew O. Czapski (1900-1976) was a young Polish military officer who worked with Herbert Hoover after World War I for the repatriation of prisoners.
7. Hugh S. Gibson (1883-1954) was the first American Plenipotentiary to Poland from 1919 to 1924.
8. George N. Curzon (1859-1925) served as viceroy of India from 1895 to 1905 and Foreign Secretary of Great Britain from 1919 to 1924.

have a supreme disregard for truth in his statements, though he often sanctions
the publication of utterly misleading reports in the Soviet bulletins.

For example, last year, when it was reported in the Soviet wireless that the
cathedral of St. Vladimir and the water works at Kiev had been blown up by the
retreating Poles, he never contradicted it, though it was later proved to be false. I
also tried to get through him confirmation of the published report that officers
of the American Red Cross with the Polish Army had refused to attend the Red
Army wounded, but failed. However, after all, this is not Chicherin's business.
He does actually censor and supervise material sent out to the foreign press, but
this is officially the responsibility of the government news agency, the Rosta,[9] of
which I shall have more to say later on.

My conversation with Chicherin was chiefly confined to the prospects
of peace with Poland, for which he confidently hoped at that time, and for
which I believe he was sincerely working. That his efforts were blocked was
due principally to the attitude of the Poles themselves, backed by France and
England, and in part to other causes originating in Russia. He regarded the
attitude of America as frankly inconsistent, declaring that President Wilson had
been the first to advocate the principle of self-determination and the first to
depart from it. Russia, he said, was the only country that had consistently lived
by this doctrine. He was prepared to make important concessions to Poland
in return for peace, which he regarded as vital at the moment, and stated that
he wished to see the country free to devote itself to the problems of economic
reconstruction. Besides Chicherin, the men who have the most flexible and
farseeing minds among those who are directing the affairs of the Soviet Republic
are Lenin, Krasin, and Karl Radek.[10]

Shortly after my talk with Chicherin I had an interview with Krasin, who
was then Commissar of Ways and Communications, but who expected soon
to leave on his London mission. He made an exceedingly frank and interesting
statement on the desperate state of Russian railroads, expressed hope for a
trade agreement with England and America, and outlined the policy of the
government towards concessions. There would be no difficulty, he said, for
Russia, in doing business with foreign nations, once a standard of value had
been fixed as the basis of payment or exchange. Instead of transacting business

9. Rossiyskoye telegrafnoye agentstvo, literally the Russian Telegraph Agency, was the Soviet news agency
from 1918-1935.
10. Leonid B. Krasin (1870-1926) served as Commissar of Foreign Trade from 1920 to 1924. Karl Radek
(1885-1939) served as the Secretary of the Comintern in 1920. He fell victim to Stalin's purge of the
"Rightists" in 1927 and was killed in a labor camp.

with a number of small capitalists, foreign interests would be dealing with one great capitalist, the Soviet Republic. While he did not believe there were enough raw materials on hand to begin trade to any great extent with outside countries, he was of the opinion that if Russia were given peace, the possibility of economic and industrial development, and be allowed to purchase locomotives, for which he claimed there was sufficient gold on hand, she would soon be able to furnish raw materials, though he considered that even under the most favorable circumstances it would be many years before Russia could produce any manufactured articles for export.

He spoke excellent German, which was natural, for he spent many years in Germany, and for some time was general agent of the Siemens Electric Company of Berlin, which, with the General Electric Company, formerly furnished practically all electrical supplies and machinery used in Russia. He is a man of education and refinement, and there is nothing about him to suggest the Jew, although it has been said that he is of Jewish ancestry.

A few days later I saw Karl Radek, who is the "Peck's Bad Boy" of the Soviet Government,[11] always making indiscreet utterances, always getting into trouble and wriggling out again with his clever tongue, but with such wit and talent as a publicist and propagandist that the Soviet Government cannot do without him. He is a Polish Jew, and was active in the Sparticist revolts[12] in Germany in 1919, and only adopted Russia after his release from prison in Berlin in the summer of that year.

We chatted for a while about German affairs, and then he began with the most amazing frankness to discuss the Polish question, declaring that Poland wanted the war, but even if she did not, she would be indirectly provoked to it by Russia, for whom it was absolutely essential to have contact with Germany. This could only be done by the conquest of Poland, not so much by arms as by propaganda, and he was firmly convinced that an invasion would be followed by a revolution in Poland. If the German Communist revolution did not come off, he believed that a profitable deal could be made with the German Junkers[13] to join with Russia against the Entente. For the future, he envisaged a possible

---

11. Peck's Bad Boy: the fictional star of newspaper stories and books created by George W. Peck in the late 1800s. In the stories, Hennery (or Henry) Peck was a mischievous prankster who delighted in creating mayhem. The stories were a huge hit, and the name Peck's Bad Boy became a popular term for any incorrigible rule-breaker.

12. The Sparticist Revolt was a workers' revolt in Germany between June 5 and June 12, 1919.

13. German Junkers were the landed nobility in Prussia. They were still very powerful after German Unification in 1871.

Georgy Chicherin

Karl Radek

alliance of Germany and Russia into which perhaps the United States would be drawn as a protection against the "yellow menace" of Japan. He also had a vision of the development of South America into a great power, which, backed by England, would rob America of her foreign trade and the domination of the Western Hemisphere.

It was a most entertaining interview. I wrote it, and, as required, I gave one copy to the press censorship of the Foreign Office for revision, and sent the other to Radek for correction. Needless to say I never received either back again. When I called Radek up by telephone, he told me that he had OK'd my copy and returned it to the Foreign Office, but it got mysteriously lost, and the interview was never put on the wireless.

Meanwhile, I had taken up my routine as Moscow correspondent of the Associated Press, my work centering in the Western Section of the Foreign Office under Rosenberg, who was in charge of all press correspondents. Rosenberg was generally unpopular with correspondents. In the first place, he was physically unprepossessing, typically Jewish in appearance, with vile manners, and a frank contempt for bourgeois ideals, which he was at no pains to conceal. He had no conception of newspaper ethics, and regarded newspaper work as simply an arm of propaganda. Objective statements or constructive criticism did not appeal to him.

Once, I summarized the main facts in a very interesting article on the situation of Russian railroads, which had appeared in *Economic Life*, emphasizing certain data which seemed to me important, and drawing my own conclusions, in my radio telegram. At the same time another story was written by an American newspaper man then in Moscow, based on the same facts, but drawing conclusions more favorable to the Soviet Government. I turned in my dispatch, the other correspondent did the same. Rosenberg read them both, then he turned to me and said, "Mrs. Harrison, your article is perfectly correct in every particular, but I prefer Mr. Blank's article. It is more favorable to us. If they both came out in the American press at the same time it might produce a bad impression. I will send his first and hold yours for twenty-four hours."

He was also ignorant of current newspaper phraseology in America, and was suspicious of every unusual expression. In one of my stories dealing with the trade unions, I used the expression "labor turnover." He was quite convinced that I meant that there was a tendency towards counter-revolution in the unions, and I had a very difficult time trying to explain away the idea. At the same time, after a while I grew to admire his savage loyalty, his fanatical devotion to Communism, for he was absolutely sincere and single-hearted in his work for the cause, and he never spared himself. Like Chicherin, he lived simply at the Hotel Metropole, never giving a thought to his own health or comfort, and he was a constant sufferer from a serious form of anemia that threatened to develop into tuberculosis.

Besides Rosenberg, I soon made the acquaintance of many other employees of the Foreign Office. They were an interesting lot, many of them trained in the Imperial diplomatic service, others people who had drifted into Russia for various reasons, some who had been involuntarily detained and who preferred service with the Soviet Government to sitting in prison. On the staff of the Western Section was "Joe Feinberg," a well-known Jewish Socialist agitator from London, who spoke English better than he did Russian. He acted as interpreter for the British Labor delegation, and was a red-hot Communist to such an extent that he usually expressed his feelings by wearing a red shirt. Therefore I christened him Garibaldi II.[14] Then there was Rozinsky, also an East Side London Jew, who was interpreter for many of the English and American correspondents. At times, his knowledge of English stood him in good stead

---

14. This is a reference to Guiseppe Garabaldi (1807-1882) who was a military leader and proponent of Italian unification. He was well-known for wearing a red shirt. Feinberg, head of the English section, was briefly arrested in the 1930s, but survived the purges and even WWII in Moscow.

for other purposes than interpreting, as when, for example, in the uniform of a Red Armist he accompanied Mr. Pate and Mr. Walker of the American Relief Administration on their journey from Minsk to Moscow.[15] They had received permission from the Soviet authorities during the Polish armistice negotiations to go to Moscow for a preliminary survey, with a view to undertaking relief work in Russia, and stayed for ten days at my guest house. When they pointed out their escort, telling me that he was a nice little fellow but it was a pity he spoke no English, I was greatly amused.

Second in command to Chicherin was Kharakhan,[16] who was sent, after the signing of the peace treaty, as the Soviet emissary to Poland. He is an Armenian, and is known in Moscow as "Kharakhan the Beautiful" on account of his undeniable good looks. He is one of the new aristocracy among the commissars and lives in the palace of the former Sugar King Kharitonev, where Clare Sheridan, Washington Vanderlip, Arthur Ransome, the English writer, George Lansbury, of the *Daily Herald*, and other foreigners who were especially honored guests of the Soviet Government, lived during their stay in Moscow.[17] He came to the Foreign Office every day in the beautiful Rolls Royce reserved for his exclusive use. Chicherin, on the other hand, used to get a car when he needed one, from the garage of the Central Executive Committee. Once, I remember, he showed up late at a very important meeting because he was unable to get a car.

The Foreign Office is situated in a wing of the former Hotel Metropole, on the square facing the Grand Opera house. The hotel proper, now known as the Second House of the Soviets, is used by Soviet employees and commissars. The offices, mostly converted bedrooms, are crowded and not overly convenient, and a number of the women employees sleep on the mezzanine floor, where are also the offices of the Western Section. There, during the day, credentials and passports of arriving and departing foreigners were examined by Rosenberg

---

15. Maurice Pate (1894-1965) and Herschel Walker were members of the American Relief Administration in Poland who were instrumental in negotiating the administration's role in Russia.

16. Lev Mikhailovich Karakhan (1889-1937) was deputy commissar for Foreign Affairs for more than nine years and a specialist on Asian affairs.

17. Clare Sheridan (1885-1970) was a British sculptor who was in Russia in 1920 to make busts of Bolshevik leaders. Washington B. Vanderlip (1867-1943) was a mining engineer and explorer, often confused with the financier Frank Vanderlip, who had, in the 1890s, explored and then written about Siberia. In late 1920, he negotiated a 60-year coal and oil and fisheries lease to Kamchatka, but the effort fell apart when the new U.S. administration (Warren G. Harding) decided not to recognize Russia or establish trade relations. Arthur Ransome (1884-1967) arrived in Russia in 1913 to study its folklore and reported on World War I and the Bolshevik Revolution. George Landsbury (1859-1940) was a newspaper editor and British member of parliament for several terms as a member of the Labour Party.

and his assistant. They actually obtained leave to depart or a *"permis de sejour,"*[18] from another department presided over by Yakobovitch, whose pretty secretary, Mlle. Lov, is half English. From six until nine or ten in the evening the office was closed, and at about eleven o'clock the press correspondents began to gather and wait, gossiping meanwhile, for the official Soviet bulletin in French, which appeared at midnight. If we had had any interviews or collected any information during the day, we brought our finished stories at that time and submitted them to Rosenberg for his approval, otherwise we waited for the news bulletin, which was a translation of the most important items and leading articles in the daily papers, together with the text of Chicherin's notes and military bulletins from the Polish and Wrangel fronts.[19]

We sat in a small room, the floor of which was covered with a superb oriental rug much too large, furnished with a nondescript collection of chairs and sofas taken from rooms of the hotel, and a big deal table. Later we were given the room next door, formerly the sitting room of a suite deluxe. It possessed a marble top table, an ornate Florentine mirror, gilded pseudo Louis Fifteenth furniture covered with green brocade, and a boudoir lamp with a yellow silk shade. Into these incongruous surroundings we brought several broken down typewriters from the next room and typed our radio messages. At twelve o'clock a samovar, glasses and Soviet tea were brought in. I sometimes contributed real tea, other correspondents brought sugar, and we often had very jolly midnight parties. Among the correspondents in these early days were Griffin Barry, an American who was writing for the *London Daily Herald*, a man from the *London Chronicle* who was doing Russia because he had been told to do so, and was bored to death with the whole business; John Clayton of the *Chicago Tribune*; Lambert of the *London Express*, and George Lansbury, owner of the *Herald*. Mr. Lansbury was a charming, but most credulous old gentleman. His Communism, which was based on a literal interpretation of the teachings of Christianity, rather than on the principles of Karl Marx, was of the idealistic type. He believed implicitly everything that was told him, and surrounded it with a little halo of his own making. Poor Lansbury, who was a very good friend of the Soviet Government, was made fun of behind his back by the more materialistic Communists; a quotation from a speech he made after his return to England in which he was

---

18. Residence permit.
19. Peter N. Wrangel (1878-1928) was a commander in the White Army during the Russian Civil War (1918-1920).

reported to have said, "All is well with Russia, the churches are still open," caused great merriment at the Foreign Office.

Our dispatches to our papers, after being read by Rosenberg, who often made changes or erasures, were sent to Chicherin for approval, with the result that there were sometimes further cuts. Then they had to pass the "Military Censorship," which meant in plain English that they were subjected to the scrutiny of an agent of the Extraordinary Commission, after which such portions as were considered fit to print were sent out by the government radio, to take their chances, if favorable to the Soviet Government, of being picked up and intercepted by various governments en route. The Soviet Government is not entirely to blame for the fact that so little of the truth has gotten out about Russia. In many instances perfectly fair dispatches, giving absolutely truthful accounts of actual conditions, are intercepted, marked secret and filed in the records of Downing Street, the Wilhelm Strasse or the Quai d'Orsay. From the Russian end it was impossible for us to write anything except straight news or interviews, unless we went in for tendential stuff favorable to Communism. The Foreign Office told us quite frankly, and unfortunately there was some truth in the statement, that fair messages were often garbled and changed so as to be violently anti-Bolshevik propaganda.

After some time I acquired a better knowledge of Russian, and I found that through the Rosta, the Russian government news agency, I could get bulletins of the news items to appear in the next morning papers, thereby beating the other foreign correspondents by twenty-four hours on spot news; and, having received permission from Chicherin, I went to the Central Office of the Rosta in the Lubyanka,[20] copying and translating anything that might be of interest to the outside world. There, too, I got an insight not to be had in any other way of what was going on in various parts of Russia. The Rosta has agencies in every town and city and receives full reports of local happenings all over the country. There were often accounts of strikes, peasant uprisings, meetings and events unimportant in themselves, but straws pointing which way the wind in the provinces was blowing, which were either suppressed for various reasons, or not printed for lack of room in the next day's papers, and I was able to read them all. I fancy that this was one of the activities which later made me unpopular with the Extraordinary Commission.

---

20. The Lubyanka was the headquarters and prison of the secret police in the Soviet Union beginning with the Cheka. The building was built in 1898 as the headquarters of the All-Russia Insurance Company.

The Rosta, which derives its name from its official title, The Russian Socialist Telegraph Agency, is undoubtedly the most remarkable organization of its kind in the world. It is not only devoted to the collecting and collating of news, but to educational and cultural work, and it is the chief arm of the Communist propaganda system. I obtained an excellent idea of the tremendous scope of the work of the Rosta from my visit to an exhibition in the Kremlin, which was intended only for the members of the Ninth Communist Convention then in session. I went with Francis McCullagh, a well-known English journalist, who had been with General Knox's Mission in Siberia,[21] as an Intelligence Officer, and had been caught at Omsk in the Kolchak retreat,[22] where he resumed his civilian status and came to Moscow as correspondent of the *Manchester Guardian*. I shall later tell how Mr. McCullagh and I both got into prison at the same time, owing to our prying proclivities.

We had met Kerzhentsev,[23] head of the Rosta, at the office in the Lubyanka, and he had told us of the exhibition. By using his name we felt sure that we would have no difficulty in getting into the exhibition if we could once get to the Kremlin. Admission to the Kremlin was exceedingly difficult to obtain, and no one, from the most important commissar to the humblest peasant bringing in food supplies, can get through one of its well-guarded gates without proper credentials. I had been there once, however, to see Radek; so, when I applied at the gate, Mr. McCullagh and I showed our credentials as foreign journalists, stating at the same time that we had an appointment with Radek. The girl who issued permits, at the gate said that she would call him up. If she had succeeded in getting him I had determined to tell him that I wished to discuss some points in our previous interview before sending it out. But I was banking on the fact that it was very difficult to get telephone connections and that she would probably become discouraged and let us in anyway.

This was exactly what happened. We soon found ourselves inside the sacred enclosure and located the exhibition in one of the rooms of the Commissariat of Justice.

The walls were covered with charts and diagrams showing the branches of the Rosta all over the country. Articles were tabulated and classified, showing the

21. Major General Alfred W.F. Knox was the chief of the British military intervention in Siberia during the Russian Civil War (1918-1920).

22. Alexander Kolchak (1874-1920) was a naval commander for the Whites in the Russian Civil War (1918-1920).

23. Platon Kerzhentsev was the head of Rosta and wrote a book, *Creative Theatre*, in 1918, on Proletkult theatre.

results produced. The name of every correspondent was given with the number of his published articles, and his efficiency was estimated according to a scientific percentage system. The Rosta, from its central office in the Lubyanka, issues all the press matter used in Russia; its activities embrace not only the principal newspapers, such as the *Pravda, Izvestia, Economic Life, Communistic Work, Byednota*, but the innumerable provincial papers, and the wall newspapers, of which there are over four hundred. The last named are pasted in railroad stations, government offices and public places and are usually devoted to special propaganda. There were also propaganda issues of the principal papers written to produce a certain effect at a given time. Provincial correspondents of the Rosta send in their news items by radio. These are edited and colored with the necessary propaganda tint and returned for local publication. Foreign news is dealt with in the same manner, and the morale of the people is largely kept up by systematic reports of revolutions and labor crises in other countries, designed to produce the impression of the unity of the world proletariat.

One of the activities of the Rosta is the oral newspaper. This is used in country districts where the peasants are still for the most part illiterate. On certain days at an appointed time, an agent of the Rosta reads aloud to the assembled peasants the important news of the day, interpreting it after his own fashion. These agents are invariably Communists and trained propaganda workers. Among the journalists who write for the Rosta are many old Russian newspaper men. In addition, it employs the services of a great many former lawyers, and some of the best technical and professional men in the country. As a rule, these men are poorly paid, and they are obliged to have several jobs in order to earn a living. I knew a former newspaper man in Moscow who worked as one of the night editors at the Central Bureau of the Rosta. In addition, he gave lectures on journalism in the courses of the Proletcult,[24] and wrote propaganda pamphlets for the Centro Pechati, the central government printing bureau, under the Department of Education. By this means he managed to make enough, working fourteen or fifteen hours a day, to keep body and soul together.

The Soviet newspapers are usually very serious affairs. There are no sensational stories, no accounts of murders or conjugal infidelities. They are conducted first with a view to propaganda, second with a view to education, culture and technical information. The headlines are often extraordinarily effective. For example the section devoted to economic reconstruction is headed

----

24. Proletcult was the Proletarian Culture (*Proletarskaya kultura*) that existed between 1917 and 1925 to produce proletarian art.

"The Working Front." Among the most popular of the means employed by the Rosta for the spread of Communist propaganda are cartoons illustrating current events. They are posted weekly in all large towns and cities and at several points in Moscow. They are done with water colors, in crude tints on enormous sheets of wrapping paper, and are somewhat Cubistic in character. Underneath each cartoon are pungent comments and witticisms that everybody can understand.

The Bolsheviks will undoubtedly have to get out a dictionary in the near future. They have made excellent and important reforms in spelling such as inaugurating the use of only two forms of the letter "i," where formerly four were used; one letter "e," instead of three, and they have abolished the "*tvyordy znak,*" the hard sign formerly used after words terminating in hard consonants. In many instances they have also simplified spelling. For this all Russians and all foreigners who study the language certainly owe them a debt of gratitude. On the other hand, they have instituted a number of abbreviations for the names of commissariats and governmental departments which make it almost impossible for the uninitiated to read the newspapers. I will give a few examples. The Commissariat of Public Health, "*Narodny Kommissariat Zdravookhraneniya,*" is called "Narkomsdrav"; the Food Commissariat, "*Narodny Kommissariat Prodovolstviya,*" is "Narkomprod." Its provincial branches are the "Gubprodkoms," "*Gubyernsky Prodovolstvenniye Kommitety.*" The Supreme Economic Council, "*Vyshche Soviet Narodnovo Khozaystva,*" is the "Sovnarkhos."

News is distributed by radio or wireless telephone. The transmitting station for sending news abroad and to the provinces is the great wireless station at Khodinka, in the suburbs of Moscow, which I visited with Nikolayev, the superintendent, who was formerly employed at the Eiffel Tower in Paris. There I saw a splendid apparatus in perfect working order, in communication with four hundred and fifty radio stations in Russia, with Copenhagen, Nauen, Paris, Peterhead, Bologna and many other stations throughout the world. New radio stations were being constructed all over Russia and the system when completed will comprise eight hundred and fifty stations.

Incoming messages were received at Dyetskoe Selo, the new name for Tsarskoe Selo,[25] a suburb of Petrograd, formerly the summer home of the Imperial family, and from there passed first through the military censorship, then to the office of the Rosta and finally all over Russia. The antennae of the wireless station at Dyetskoe Selo are synchronized so as to pick up messages

25. Renamed Pushkin in 1937, on the 100th anniversary of the poet's death.

from the wireless stations of any country, and it employs a corps of experts who are able to decipher practically every code in use at the present time.

Outgoing messages were treated in the same manner. Many local messages were handled by wireless telephone, which the Bolsheviks have developed extensively during the last few years. While at Khodinka I was allowed to talk to the operator in Tashkent, eight hundred versts from Moscow.

When I had finished my work for the night at the Foreign Office I returned to the Kharitonevsky on foot, frequently alone, rarely earlier than two or three in the morning. I continued to do this with few interruptions for eight months, and during that entire time I was never once spoken to or molested in any way on the street, nor did I ever see anyone else stopped or interfered with. Order was absolutely preserved by the militiamen who patrolled the streets, instead of policemen, with rifles instead of revolvers. At first I often heard shots and imagined that they were fired at nocturnal marauders, but I later discovered that it was the militiamen's way of signaling to one another, replacing the policemen's whistles in use in other countries. Robberies on a large scale were very rare, though there was a great deal of petty thievery, particularly in the markets.

After getting home in the wee small hours, we were often hungry, and adjourned to my room, where I made scrambled eggs on a little coal oil stove, tea, and occasionally when someone had recently arrived from abroad, cocoa. Our Russian friends used to join us at these parties, and we frequently talked till it was nearly light, discussing everything under the sun. The Russians are great all-night sitters, and everyone falls naturally into the same habit in Russia.

CHAPTER VII
The Gods and Their Machine

*D*uring my first weeks in Moscow I did very largely the things that are done by every other foreigner, visiting Soviet institutions, particularly schools, hospitals, Soviet stores and public dining rooms, and getting a very good idea of the educational, public health and rationing systems. Later I made some unofficial visits to these places on my own account and supplemented what I had learned from official sources by my own observations, and conversations with private individuals.

It happened that during the first part of my stay there was a succession of public meetings and congresses, which gave me an insight into the workings of the Communist Party machine. Shortly after my arrival, the elections for the Moscow Soviet took place, resulting in a Communist membership of over twelve hundred out of the fifteen hundred members. One hundred and forty-eight Mensheviks were elected, and the remainder were non-partisans. There were no independent party lists except that of the Mensheviks. Voting, which was conducted under the Soviet industrial franchise system, was by acclamation, and such was the domination of the Communist element that few people dared to hold up their hands against the Communist candidates. Those who were particularly strong minded simply refrained from voting, that was all. In order to secure an overwhelming majority for the government, offices where there were a number of non-partisans or opposition Socialist voters were grouped with others where Communists predominated. For example, employees of the Moscow Food Administration voted with the employees of the Moscow branch of the Cheka, the Extraordinary Commission.

At the open meeting of the Moscow Soviet, which was held in the Opera House, I had my first glimpse of Lenin, who made the opening address.[1] It was devoted to the government's program for reconstruction, which was then occupying attention to the exclusion of nearly everything else. He told of the organization of the Working Army, of the project of the government to institute one-man control by experts in factories instead of the Work Councils, and gave a clear, impartial picture of the exigencies of the economic situation. When I saw him come out on the stage, my first feeling was one of disappointment. He is a short, thick set, unimposing looking little man, with colorless hair and complexion, a small, pointed beard, piercing gray-blue eyes, and a quiet, unemotional, almost monotonous manner of delivery. He wore a suit of rough English tweeds, and looked like nothing so much as a fairly prosperous, middle class businessman. After the first few words, however, I, like everyone else, began to listen attentively. It was not magnetic eloquence that held me, it was the impression of tremendous sincerity, utter self-confidence and quiet power that Lenin creates. He is so absolutely sure of himself and of his idea, so utterly logical in his deductions. In his writings and brochures, Lenin is often dry and tedious, and uses unusual words and involved expressions, but when he speaks to the people he has a talent for picking out the simplest possible words to express his meaning, without, however, degenerating into colloquialisms. Of all public speakers in Russia, he is the easiest for a foreigner to follow and understand.

The Soviet meeting was planned with the instinct for dramatic effect which is strong in every Russian. Red flags were everywhere; the motto of the Red Republic, "Proletariat of the World, Unite," written in half a dozen languages, appeared on a multitude of banners which decorated the stage, at the back of which was an enormous allegorical backdrop representing the triumph of the world proletariat. Portraits of the triumvirate, Lenin, Trotsky and Karl Marx, surrounded by garlands, appeared everywhere—on the stage, in the lobby, over the boxes. I do not object to Lenin and Trotsky, but from the first I had a spite against Karl Marx. He was omnipresent, and he always had the same ruminative, *echt Deutsch*,[2] stolid expression. Nothing will ever make me believe that that man was as clever as his apostles believed him to be. I shall always have a suspicion that he was just a pedantic old German professor. If he had lived a

---

1. Vladimir Ilyich (Ulyanov) Lenin (1870-1924) was the founder of the Bolshevik Party which led the Russian Revolution in October 1917. By the Opera House, Harrison means the Bolshoi Theater.
2. "True (or pure) German."

bit longer, I am sure he would have proved a great drawback to the execution of his own theories. Above all I despised his benevolent looking beard. No man who advocates brute force exercised by a minority on the majority has the right to a benevolent expression and a grandfatherly beard.

The grand opera orchestra, which is one of the finest in the world, played the "International" at the beginning and end of each speech, and as it is always sung standing, we were continually bobbing up and down.[3] I soon learned the chorus, and used to join in vigorously. The members of the Soviet were all seated on the ground floor, the Imperial box was reserved for People's Commissars and members of the Central Executive Committee; others for representatives of the Central Council of Trades Unions, and the unions themselves, representatives of the Red Army, foreign delegations and press correspondents, while the proletariat occupied the less desirable boxes and the galleries. Admission was by card only, armed guards were stationed in all the corridors, and the space in front of the Opera House was roped off and guarded by Red Army cavalry and infantrymen. These precautions are always observed whenever Lenin and Trotsky appear, and have been in force ever since the attempt on Lenin's life in the autumn of 1918.[4]

Trotsky also spoke at the same meeting. As it was the first time I had seen him, I was very curious as to the impression I would receive of his personality. When he appeared, he was greeted, as usual, with a tremendous ovation. Until it was time for him to speak, he sat at the long red table on the stage with members of the praesidium, or presiding body, of which Kamenev was the chairman. He sat with his head bent, scribbling industriously on a pad in front of him, and I could only see his high forehead with its mass of dark, curly chestnut hair and the sharp line of demarcation between the upper part of his forehead, which had been protected by a cap, and the lower part of his face, which was tanned by life in the open with the Red Army. When it was time for him to speak he pushed back his chair with a quick, restless movement and advanced to the front of the platform. I saw a broad-shouldered man of middle height, slightly

3. The *International* or the *Internationale* was the song of the international socialist, communist and anarchist movements in Europe in the nineteenth and early twentieth centuries. Eugene Pottier, a member of the Paris Commune, wrote the words to the song in 1871.
4. There were actually two attempts on Lenin's life in 1918. The first was on January 14, 1918, when gunmen opened fire on his car, to no effect. The second, on August 30, 1918, was nearly fatal. Fanny Kaplan, a Socialist Revolutionary, fired three shots at Lenin from point blank range. One hit his arm, a second his jaw and neck. The third missed. The bullets were not removed and Lenin's health was reputedly never the same. The assassination attempt, and the murder the same day of the head of the Petrograd Cheka, Moisei Uritsky, led to an intensification of the Red Terror.

inclined to stoutness at the waistline, but erect and military in his bearing. He had gray-green eyes, a prominent chin, brought still more into relief by a dark chestnut goatee, and close-clipped dark mustache.

The line of his mouth was hard, cynical, almost forbidding, until he began to speak, and then I suddenly realized that there was something magnetic and compelling about the man's personality. Squaring his shoulders, he stood with his hands behind his back and spoke in short, terse, pithy sentences, interspersed with real flashes of humor. He understood the art of drawing and riveting the attention of the public. There was something almost exultant in his expression as his eyes swept the enormous crowd in front of him, and it seemed to me that subconsciously it was mingled with a certain amount of racial pride. I could almost imagine him saying, "For the first time since the days of the Maccabees, I, a Jew, am the head of a great army." Later, when I heard him speak before the graduating class of the general staff school, and at the military parade in honor of the Third International, the same idea obtruded itself on my imagination.[5]

While I never had a formal interview with Trotsky, I had an informal talk with him, which was much more diverting. Interviews with Lenin and Trotsky are usually very disappointing affairs. Correspondents are, as a rule, required to make application in writing, giving a number of questions to which they wish to receive the answers. These are prepared by the secretary and handed out at the interview, the great man adding a few words along the same lines, but that is all. My conversation with Trotsky, however, was quite a different matter.

After my visit with Mr. McCullagh to the exhibition of the Rosta in the Kremlin, we strolled around looking at the historic buildings and convents, wandering unmolested in and out of courtyards and passageways. Everything was much the same as in the old days. The Imperial Palace, to which admission may be had on Sundays, and the churches, which are also shown on Thursdays to those armed with permits from the Foreign Office or the Commissariat of Education, have been kept intact. The meetings of the Third International are held in the audience chamber of the Imperial Palace. As we were crossing the great square between the building which is now the Commissariat of Justice, and the Cavalry Corps, the former quarters of the officers of the Imperial Guard, now the residence of several of the People's Commissars, I saw a familiar figure just ahead of me, walking quickly in the direction of the latter building.

....

5. The Third International, also known as the Comintern, was founded in Moscow in 1919 to promote socialism throughout the world, by all available means, including armed force. The chairman was Grigory Zinoviev (1883-1936) who held many other positions in the Soviet government until the mid-1920s before he ran afoul of Stalin and was eventually executed in 1936.

Vladimir Lenin, July 1920

Leon Trotsky exhorts the troops

"That's Trotsky," I said to Mr. McCullagh. "I am going to speak to him," and I started off at a run. When I was within speaking distance I called rather breathlessly:

"Citizen Commissar, may I speak to you for a moment?" Citizen, by the way, is the correct form of address at present in Russia. The word *tovarishch*—comrade—is only used between party members or in the army.

He turned around, evidently very much astonished at being halted in such a manner by an unknown, and evidently foreign, female; but he did not look at all forbidding. I told him that I would like to have him tell me something of his plans for the Working Army; that I could speak Russian very badly and would prefer to talk in French, English or German. He chose the first, which he speaks exceedingly well, to tell me that it was impossible for him at that time to give out anything for publication, but he added that he believed that the project would receive the unanimous support of the army, and that the men were impressed with the fact that winning the economic war was of equal importance with victory over Kolchak, Yudenich or Denikin. He did not anticipate any trouble in holding the men after the cessation of hostilities.

Then he asked me a few questions about conditions in America and my impressions of Soviet Russia. While we were talking, a messenger, who evidently did not recognize the People's Commissar for War in the genial looking officer with whom I was chatting so informally, stopped to ask him the way to the quarters of one of the commissars. "Excuse me for a moment," he said, and took the trouble to explain to the boy in detail how to get there, even pointing the way. After which he turned to me, expressed pleasure at having had a little chat with a bourgeois who had braved the discomforts of life in Soviet Russia to see what was going on in there. I held out my hand. To my amazement he took it, kissed it, like any conventional Russian of the old regime. "*Au revoir*, and a pleasant visit, Madame," he said. Then, with a military salute, he turned on his heel and was gone.

Among my friends in Moscow was a lady, a violent monarchist, by the way, who happened to be living in the country not far from a communal farm to which Trotsky was to pay a visit of inspection. The agricultural expert in charge of the work, wishing to entertain him properly on his visit, and being unmarried, asked her to act as hostess for him during Trotsky's stay. "What, talk to that brutal Bolshevik?" said my friend, "never." But finally curiosity got the better of prejudice and she went.

At dinner, for she was an exceedingly pretty woman, he devoted himself to her, talking conventional small talk so delightfully that she forgot entirely, as she told me, that he was her natural enemy.

"Actually, he was just like any other civilized person," she said in wonderment.

Trotsky's adventures are the source of considerable entertainment in Moscow, and many stories are whispered about him in and out of Soviet circles. On the part of his inamorata they are not always disinterested, a fact of which the great commissar is well aware. In prison I met a young Ukrainian girl of great beauty and charm who had been his mistress for a few weeks when he was directing the campaign against Petlura in 1919.[6]

"Trotsky told me once," she said, "that I was the only woman with whom he had had an affair who never asked him for food supplies."

To return to the Congresses. The meeting of the Moscow Soviet was followed by the annual Communist Party convention, to which I secured admission through Angelica Balabanova,[7] then secretary of the Third International. I sat on the stage with the Russian journalists and a few correspondents of foreign Socialist papers, and I was the only non-Socialist present, a fact which was scored against me at the Cheka, as I afterwards discovered. From a journalistic

6. Symon V. (Petlura) Petliura (1879-1926) led Ukraine's independence movement during the Bolshevik revolution.

7. Angelica Balabanova (1878-1965) joined the Bolshevik Party in 1917 and served in the Comintern from 1919 to 1920. She broke with the Bolsheviks and left Russia in 1922 to support the Italian socialists.

standpoint, the meeting was not of particularly great interest, as the really secret things were not discussed openly, but in committee, and the foreign policies of the party played a minor role in the debates. The most important matters discussed were the inauguration of the one-man system in factories, the working army, and the possible question of the nationalization of the land. It was easy to see at that time the tendency in the Communist Party to split on these questions, all hinging on centralization or decentralization. One-man control of factories and the control of the industrial forces of the country through mobilization were opposed by many Communists who believed in the vesting of the principal power in the Soviets and trades unions, but the Centralists were the victors.

Later, at the meeting of the All-Russian Council of Trades Unions, I had an opportunity to see how party discipline worked. The unions nominated on their praesidium, or executive body, a majority opposed to one-man control of factories. These candidates would have undoubtedly been elected, but before the elections the council was told that the Central Executive Committee of the Communist party did not approve its ticket. A majority in favor of the new policy would have to be on the praesidium. Otherwise the council would be dissolved pending reorganization. This policy was actually carried out with regard to the Printers' and Bakers' Unions, which struck a little later. Their executive committees were arrested and the unions reorganized along Communist lines.

From my standpoint, one of the most interesting illustrations of the workings of the Communist Party machine was in connection with Lord Robert Cecil's proposal to send an investigating committee to Russia from the League of Nations.[8] It was much discussed in government circles, and a number of influential liberals in the party were in favor of permitting the visit of the committee. Therefore, when it was announced that the matter would be debated at a meeting of the Ispolkom, the All-Russian Central Executive Committee, of about two hundred members, which is the actual governing body of the country, and that press correspondents were to be present, I anticipated a very interesting time. The meeting was to be held in the assembly hall of the Commissariat of Justice in the Kremlin at six in the evening. I arrived early, took a front seat, and awaited developments. Six o'clock came and only about forty members were in their places. There was no sign of Lenin, Trotsky, or any of the others, and a few minutes afterwards Chicherin appeared on the platform, accompanied by

....

8. Lord Robert Cecil (1864-1958) was a British politician and one of the architects of the League of Nations. He proposed sending a team to investigate the Russian Revolution. It was never sent.

the secretary of the Ispolkom. He announced that at a meeting of the Central Executive Committee of the Communist Party, held an hour previously, the text of the reply to Lord Robert Cecil had been drawn up and approved. He would read it to the Ispolkom and ask for their sanctioning vote. The note was read, approved without discussion or debate by the few members present, and the proposal of the League of Nations was officially turned down.

The most picturesque of the many congresses at this time was that of the Red Cossacks,[9] which was held at the headquarters of the All-Russian Council of Trades Unions, in what was formerly the meeting place of Moscow's Assembly of Nobles. There were about three hundred and fifty delegates, from all parts of Russia and Siberia, and it was a most colorful gathering. The Cossacks wore their high, peaked caps, long caftans of black, brown or blue, with hoods lined with brilliant color thrown back over their shoulders; gold chased cartridges were stuck in the bandoliers which crossed their chests, and most of them wore daggers in their belts and wonderful swords inlaid with gold and precious stones. They were a tumultuous, noisy gathering. Few of them impressed me as having any clear idea of the principles of Communism; what appealed to them was the assurance that, under the new government, they would be able to maintain their ancient boast of being the "free people."

Through their sympathy with and understanding of the local nationalistic feeling of Russia's conglomerate population, the Bolsheviks have secured the loyalty of numbers of distinct racial groups. The "Federative Republic" is not a mere figure of speech. Counting the Ukraine, which is by far the largest, it actually includes nineteen autonomous republics. The Cossacks have not as yet received autonomy owing to the fact that there has been, and still is to some extent, civil war in the Donskoy Oblast,[10] where the majority of the Cossack population is concentrated, and many of their leaders are still counter-revolutionary. If the Cossacks should decide to support the Communist Government, they would have great weight in stabilizing political conditions in Southeastern Russia, as they are better educated, more vigorous and energetic and more intelligent than the Central Russian peasant population. The great majority of them are professional soldiers, and, should their loyalty be secured, they would undoubtedly support the militaristic wing of the Communist party.

---

9. Cossacks are military groups in southern Russia dating back to the fifteenth century who were there to defend the frontier. During the Russian Civil War some Cossacks supported the Whites and others supported the Reds.

10. Donskoy Oblast, or Don Province, along the Don River southeast of Moscow where many Cossacks lived.

One of the features of the Congress was a Cossack exhibit, which presented in a most attractive form a complete survey of agriculture, industry, education, and social conditions among all the Cossack tribes in Russia. It was illustrated with a number of diagrams in color, and, of course, showed most advantageously what the government had done and was doing for the Cossacks since the Revolution. Then there were a number of inspiring revolutionary posters and a newsstand where propaganda literature was distributed. One of the most original devices was an electric sign board, furnished with plugs over which were printed the questions the average person asks about the Soviet form of government. "What is a Soviet?" "How are the Soviets elected?" "What is the dictatorship of the proletariat?" "What are the aims of the world revolution?" By pressing the button below any question the corresponding answer was flashed on the board in letters about three inches high, and not only the inquirer but all who happened to be passing by could read it.

I often went to the Trades Union headquarters, the "Dom Soyuzov,"[11] where, in addition to the Cossack Congress I have already described, I attended a number of meetings and concerts. It was there that I heard Krasin make his first public report on the progress of negotiations for the reopening of trade with England, and at the same meeting I heard a speech by Kalinin, president of the All-Russian Council of Soviets.[12] While not as well known outside of Russia as many of the other Bolshevik leaders, Kalinin, who is a peasant himself, is probably better known personally to the peasants – who make up ninety percent of Russia's population – than any of the Soviet oligarchy, not even excepting Lenin and Trotsky. He spends very little time in Moscow, living for the most part on his special train, on which he goes from one section of the country to the other. Whenever there is trouble among the peasants, Kalinin is always the man to straighten it out, because he understands peasant psychology. He is a loose-knit, scraggly man with an unkempt blond beard, gentle blue eyes, and speaks with a rough eloquence that compels confidence. He and Krasin formed an incongruous pair—the former a thorough cosmopolitan in his correct suit of English tweeds, with his close-clipped beard and well-groomed appearance, his concise, well-balanced phrases and the air of a prosperous business man.

---

11. House of Trade Unions.
12. Mikhail I. Kalinin (1875-1946) was a leading Bolshevik who was the head of state of the Soviet Union from 1919 to 1946. He was also a member of the Politburo from 1926 to 1946.

Dom Soyuzov in the mid-1930s

Losovsky, president of the All-Russian Council of Trades Unions, and
Melnichansky, the secretary, are two equally contrasting types.[13] Losovsky,
whom I knew very well, is a Russian revolutionary of the old school. He spent
many years in exile and in Siberian prisons. He is an incorrigible idealist, and
a man of broad, general culture. Melnichansky, on the other hand, belongs
to a type of the younger generation of Communists which is often met with
in Russia. Emigrating to the United States when a mere boy, he worked in
American factories and absorbed American initiative and business methods.
His radicalism is of the American stamp. Under the name of Melchner he
was one of the ringleaders in the Paterson strike some years ago, and returned
to Russia at the beginning of the Revolution to introduce American union
methods of organization.[14]

He was very proud of his system for registering the trades union membership,
which is now over five million in Russia, and he showed me all the departments
of the Trades Union Bureau, which seemed to be working with order and

....

13. Alexander Lososvky (Solomon A. Drizdo) (1878-1949) joined the Bolsheviks in 1903 when he served
    as an editor for several publications. He would head the Council of Trade Unions. He was executed in
    1949 during one of Stalin's later purges. Grigory N. Melnichansky (1886-1937) joined the Bolsheviks in
    1903 and served in several party positions. In 1920, he was secretary of the Council of Trade Unions. He
    continued to serve in many positions in the party until his arrest and execution in 1937.
14. The 1913 Paterson Silk Strike in New Jersey began in February 1913 and ended six months later. The
    Industrial Workers of the World (IWW), led by Bill Haywood, wanted an eight-hour work day and other
    workplace improvements. Nearly 2,000 workers were arrested.

dispatch. In the great banquet hall of the Dom Soyuzov, he arranged during the summer a remarkable historical, technical and scientific survey of the trades union movement in Russia, illustrated with splendid diagrams and enlivened by vivid propaganda posters.

The meetings at the Dom Soyuzov took place in the great ballroom where the nobility of Moscow gave its superb fetes in the old days. It is a beautiful room, decorated in white and gold, and hung with huge crystal chandeliers. Around the dancing floor is a row of boxes upholstered in crimson brocade. Behind are luxurious dressing-rooms and a special suite reserved for the Czar and his family when they attended these functions. Now it serves as a meeting and recreation hall for thousands of plain workmen. The mirrors in the magnificent foyers reflect linen blouses, frieze coats and cotton frocks, instead of gold lace, velvets and satins. In the former gaming room a corps of clerks is busy filing records, and the Holy of Holies, the room where the nobles held their meetings, is reserved for the sessions of the Executive Committee. In the chairs around the huge round table, on the back of which are still the inlaid coats of arms of the great nobles with hereditary rights to sit in the assembly, metal workers, textile and transport workers hold their deliberations.

CHAPTER VIII
The Woman's Part

$\mathcal{N}$aturally, when I arrived in Russia I was much interested as a woman in finding out all I could about the position of women in the Soviet Republic, and one of the first persons I met was Alexandra Kollontai,[1] the only great woman publicist among the Communists. As a rule the Communist women, wives of commissars and other prominent individuals devote themselves rather to constructive and educational work than propaganda, but Balabanova and Kollontai are the exceptions. I found them both very attractive personalities. Strangely enough, they are both bourgeois by birth. Kollontai is the daughter of a noted imperial general, and is a lady to her fingertips. When she is in Moscow, she lives at the National Hotel, where I found her in her room recovering from a recent severe illness. She was wearing an exquisite boudoir gown of green velvet trimmed with sable, her little feet were encased in velvet slippers of the same shade, and she was altogether chic and charming. Evidently, she has great regard for her personal appearance, and although not young, she is still an extremely pretty woman of the rather fragile blonde type. We talked principally about the education of children, which is her chief hobby.

Like many other thoughtful Communists, she believes the present generation is hopeless so far as making conscious Communists of the masses is concerned and that, as the Communists express it, "the children are our future." She told me that she considered family life absolutely subversive to the interests of the Commune, that children should from birth be regarded as the property

1. Alexandra Kollontai (1872-1952) joined the Bolsheviks in 1914. In 1919, she helped found the Zhenotdel ("Women's Department"). She served as ambassador to Norway, Mexico, and Sweden. She was the world's first female ambassador.

of the State, that they would develop a much more genuine sense of social responsibility in the atmosphere of the institution reproducing the Commune than in the home, which is under the influence of the patriarchal system. As regards the relationship of the sexes, she felt that it should exist merely for the purpose of reproducing the race, without restraints except those imposed by observance of the laws of eugenics.

In pursuance of her theories, she has planned a new system of motherhood endowment with pre-natal and post-natal care for mothers and babies. It was all very interesting, though I mentally took issue with her on every point. She also told me something about educational work among women, which she found rather discouraging, and of her page in the Sunday *Pravda*, which was devoted to women's work and interests. While acknowledging that much must be done in the way of civic education among women, Kollontai was not inclined to treat the participation of women in politics as a separate problem. "We have organized political propaganda work among women," she said. "Here in Moscow there are weekly meetings of women delegates from the large factories. But women are encouraged to go to all political meetings and to work in conjunction with and on equal footing with men." This is quite true—there is no feminism in Russia, there are no laws, disadvantages, or disabilities operating against women.

I first had an opportunity of observing large masses of women together on March 8, International Women's Day. In Moscow, all offices employing women were closed at two o'clock in the afternoon, there was a special edition of the *Pravda*, devoted entirely to women's interests, and women's mass meetings were held in every section of the town. I went to two with Angelica Balabanova, who was the principal speaker at both.

The first meeting was at the Kremlin, in the amphitheater of the Palace of Justice, a beautiful room in the style of the late eighteenth century. Originally the walls and columns were pure white, but the interior at present suggests a confectionery store at Christmas time more than anything else. The columns have been turned into huge candy canes by diagonal wrappings of red bunting and the spaces between into red and white striped lozenges by means of strips of the same material stamped with revolutionary mottos. It was filled with women employees of the government offices in the Kremlin, wearing the inevitable bright-colored shawl wound tightly around their heads, with an end thrown over one shoulder. I have often wondered if the Russian women sleep in their shawls. Our little maid was never without hers, and one day when I visited the women's ward of a large hospital, practically every patient was wearing one in bed.

When we arrived, a government official was in the midst of a long, tedious speech. The women were listening with the patience characteristic of Russian audiences, but it was evident that they were bored. Many were half asleep, others staring at the walls and ceiling, still others trying to quiet their restless babies. The instant Balabanova stepped on the stage, there was a slight rustle as everyone leaned forward to get a closer look, for hers is a personality that compels attention.

They saw a dumpy little woman, slightly bent, wearing a man's coat many sizes too large, the big fur collar touching the edges of an Astrakhan cap pulled far down over her ears, and carrying a long ebony cane with an ivory handle. Little else about her was visible except a pair of wonderful dark eyes. Throwing off her coat and tossing her cap on the table, she started to speak, and every woman in the hall was galvanized into instant interest. She talked not about the doctrines of Communism but of its practical application to their immediate problems, explaining the reasons for the many hardships they are enduring at present and describing what the Soviet Government is trying to do for them and their children.

"You all remember the days when a washerwoman was a washerwoman and nothing more," she said. "She could never be anything else. Now she can be anything she pleases. The working women of Russia have come into their kingdom." Finally, she outlined in the simplest possible words the principles of the International.

As she walked up and down the platform, her hands in her pockets, her head thrown back, her tired face with its sensitive mouth and luminous eyes aglow with enthusiasm, she was a curiously moving figure, and even the fact that her hair came down and fell in two long braids over her shoulders did not detract from the dignity of her small person. Something of her spirit seemed to catch the audience, for there was much applause when she had finished, but that the response was emotional rather than intellectual was shown by the notes written by women in the audience and sent to the platform during her speech. There were some intelligent questions, but the majority were queries such as, "Where can I get a pair of shoes?" "When will we get more bread?" or "Why are there so many churches in Moscow?" She shook her head as she read them over.

"It is hard to make women appreciate ideals when they are cold and hungry," she said, "especially women of this type —unskilled workers, former servants

Alexandra Kollontai

Angelica Balabanova

and members of the small bourgeoisie. You will see a different attitude among
the industrial workers."

I found this to be true at the next meeting, held at the famous Prokorov
factory, where the revolution of 1905 started in Moscow. Formerly, it was one of
the largest textile plants in Russia, with a yearly production of over 13,000,000
pieces of cotton goods—enough, as the foreman told me, "to wrap the world
around three times." At that time, the factory had some raw material but no fuel,
and except for a small force employed in putting the machinery in order, work
was at a standstill.

When we entered the factory dining room where the meeting was to take
place, it was already half full, though it was nearly an hour ahead of time,
and while waiting we had a chat with the chairman, herself a factory worker.
Following the modern revolutionary fashion, she wore her hair cut short like
a man, but there was a feminine touch in her rhinestone earrings that seemed
singularly out of place, emphasizing her rather masculine features. She had a
fine, intelligent face, a keen, alert manner, and she conducted the meeting in
a way that showed a thorough knowledge of parliamentary procedure. The
audience was responsive to every word, and there was none of the apathy I
had noticed in the meeting at the Kremlin. Several of the speakers were factory
women, and they handled their subjects in a way that would have done credit
to a college graduate. As we left the meeting, I noticed that Balabanova seemed

utterly exhausted, and I found out that she had not eaten anything since breakfast. "I never thought about it," she said simply.

Like most of the women workers in the Communist Party, she never spared herself, often speaking at three or four meetings a day, besides working several hours at her office. In addition, she found time to keep up with current events in Italy, where she spent more than twenty years, and also acted as interpreter for foreign labor delegations.

The wives of most of the People's Commissars are doing constructive work, among them Trotskaya, who is in charge of all the museums in Moscow and arranges popular exhibits; Lunacharskaya, who has the supervision of a number of children's homes; Semaskaya, wife of the Commissioner of Public Health, who works as a nurses' aid in the Novo-Alexandrovsky Hospital, and Krupskaya, the wife of Lenin, who is directing the work of primary education in Russia and founded the rural colonies for children.[2]

While there are trained women workers in all political parties in Russia, religion still plays a great part in the lives of most Russian women, and they are politically apathetic. The proportion of illiteracy is far greater among women than men, and they have not the opportunities of overcoming this handicap, which are given every man in the Red Army. The women of the former bourgeoisie naturally hold aloof from politics. The vast majority of working women are still densely ignorant and too much absorbed in their immediate problems to be susceptible to educational propaganda. When you work from six to eight hours a day, spend three or four standing in line outside one of the cooperatives waiting for food and clothing issued on cards, or dragging a hand sled loaded with wood for several *versts*, cook your own meals, feeding four mouths where there is enough for two, you have little time for anything else. In many cases, the male members of the family are in the army and the entire responsibility devolves onto the mothers and wives. The women of Russia have borne the brunt of the war, the blockade and the economic crisis. Until normal conditions are restored, there can be no extensive development of the work of training them for citizenship.

There has been much talk in America and Western Europe about the immorality and sex demoralization brought about by the Revolution in Russia. As a matter of fact, the aristocracy and the intellectuals were always

....

2. Natalia I. Sedova (Trotskaya) (1882-1962) was Leon Trotsky's second wife. The rural colonies for children were orphanages outside the major cities for the millions of *bezprizorniki* – children made homeless and orphaned by World War I, the Revolution and Civil War.

extraordinarily liberal with regard to sex relationships; among the former, divorce was far more common than in any other European country, and among the latter, irregular relationships entailed no loss of social standing. As is well known, an enormous number of professional prostitutes existed in Czarist Russia, under government regulation, with their famous "yellow tickets." This class has been entirely abolished by the Soviet Government. At first these women were summarily dealt with. Large numbers, who were hopelessly diseased, were shot as the easiest form of prophylaxis, others were isolated, still others put to work. Those belonging to the aristocracy of the underworld made their escape to foreign countries. As a result, there is no open soliciting in the streets of Moscow. What might be characterized as predatory vice has also disappeared. Painted ladies no longer maintain luxurious establishments, or lay their decoy nets—the women of the lower classes are all workers, self-supporting and independent, with the same wage scale as men. Types, such as the old roués and the gilded youth who haunted the cafes and boulevards in former days, are nonexistent, but to a certain, though lesser extent, a new type has arisen to take their place.

Every department of every commissariat contains many of these gentry who constitute what has often been spoken of as the New Bourgeoisie. Some of these men manage to live within the law or to keep from being found out, others are adept at bribery or blackmail, and enjoy immunity, for a considerable time, at least. Often they are Jews, occasionally former bourgeois who have been clever opportunists, and who have managed to construct a fair imitation of their former life. These men have plenty of money, hoards of Nikolai rubles, gold and jewels tucked away in safe places—above all, they have access to inexhaustible food supplies.

The girls who work in Soviet bureaus have none of these things. Often they have non-workers to support on their scanty pay and scantier rations, they need food, clothing, fuel, and they have the irresistible feminine love for pretty things. The rich speculators can give them everything they want— it is the same old story of economic pressure about which such hue and cry is raised in capitalistic countries, that drives them to irregular relationships with their associates or department chiefs. The number of kept women in the Soviet offices is enormous, but as a rule these liaisons are more or less permanent affairs, and there is not much promiscuity.

Numbers of girls with whom I talked were engaged to the men with whom they were living, and they were waiting for better times before getting married.

It was difficult to find living quarters—perhaps the man had an old father and mother to take care of, the girl several brothers and sisters. It was impossible to set up a separate establishment, therefore they both lived at home and met whenever they could. Many women told me frankly that they did not want a home or children under present living conditions.

On the other hand, I ran across a peculiar form of graft, if it can be called by such a term. There are a number of women among the lower classes who deliberately have as many children as they possibly can because of the special privileges they enjoy. They receive a special diet after the first few months of pregnancy, which is continued for some time after the birth of the child. They also enjoy a holiday of three months with full wages and rations and receive thirty *arshins*[3] of material for the baby's outfit. If they do not care to keep the child, it can be put in an institution. As these women are usually healthy animals, they do not mind the physical discomforts, and the State relieves them of any moral responsibility for their offspring. It is an easy way of making a comfortable living.

In the foyers of the vaudeville theaters where the rich commissars and their mistresses congregate, I saw wonderful jewels and superb costumes. The women were often marvelously bedizened and painted, but they lacked the chic of the professional courtesan. I saw few who appeared to belong definitely to this class. Many of them were obviously working women who were apeing the manners and morals of their former employers. I once heard a rather amusing story in this connection.

A Red workman in Petrograd took a seat in a trolley car next to a gorgeously gowned, highly perfumed lady who fairly exuded luxury. He began to reproach her for being a bourgeoisie, accusing her of belonging to the class that had lived so long on the blood of the proletariat.

"And you are still at your old tricks," he cried, "still managing to keep your furs and fine clothes, by crooked means, no doubt, while honest working women in Petrograd are going without coats and shoes."

"Aw, keep your mouth shut," she answered in the Russian vernacular, "I'm the mistress of a fool of a workman like you!" On the whole, however, except for juvenile immorality, of which I shall have something to say in another chapter, I am inclined to think that the Revolution had rather more a stabilizing effect on morals than otherwise. The often repeated story of nationalization of women is regarded as a joke in Russia by those who have seen articles published

....

3. An *arshin* is a unit of measure equal to approximately 28 inches.

abroad on the subject. The vast majority of the people stare at you in blank, uncomprehending amazement if you allude to it. The theory was advanced in a little newspaper published in Saratov by a small group of Anarchists, but purely as a speculative fancy, and even they did not take it seriously.[4]

4. The "nationalization of women" was a rumor that alleged the Bolshevik regime would "seize" bourgeois women for a variety of functions throughout the new state. The rumor persisted for decades despite the writings on women's independence by Kollontai and Krupskaya.

CHAPTER IX
Soviet Weddings

$\mathcal{A}$s a matter of fact, people get married and divorced by Soviet decrees in Russia very much as they do in any other country. The government recognizes only civil marriages performed before a magistrate, and the fact of such a marriage entitles the married couples to mutual legal rights. For example, in case a husband and wife wish to separate, they must appear before the magistrate, state the reasons, arrange for an equable division of their personal effects, for the disposition of the children, who, if they are not of an age to choose for themselves, may be awarded to either parent or committed to one of the children's institutions at the discretion of the magistrate. Questions, such as to which one shall occupy the apartment where both have been living together, are also settled before the magistrate.

It is very simple to get married and equally simple to get divorced. Persons desiring to be married appear before one of the judges of the People's Court in their "Rayon," or police district, bringing two witnesses who certify that they have known the contracting parties for some time and that there is no obstacle to their marriage. Then they are registered by the magistrate as man and wife. In most cases the wife retains her maiden name. This is partly because the women consider it a sign of independence, partly because there are regulations forbidding husband and wife to work in the same bureau. The wives of the great commissars are usually known by their maiden names; thus the wife of Lenin, who is much interested in the organization of the children's colonies, is known as Krupskaya; Gorky's wife was Peshkova.[1] Kollontai has had any

---

1. An error on Harrison's part. Peshkov was actually the birth name of the writer who used the pen name Maxim Gorky.

number of husbands, the last being a soldier twenty years younger than herself, who recently deserted her, but she has always kept her own name.

A divorce may be obtained in the same manner before a judge of the People's Court in a very short time—three weeks, with the consent of both parties; in six months if one of the parties disagrees. There are no legal disabilities attached to illegitimate children, and the father is forced to assume the responsibility for them should the occasion arise. Neither is an irregular relationship looked upon askance.

Among the lower classes, however, old-fashioned ideas still prevail. I had an illustration of this one day when I was walking along the Tverskaya. There was a great commotion in a side street, and a woman came running out, her hair down, her face scratched, screaming like a maniac. She was pursued by a good-sized crowd, in the center of which was another woman, the embodiment of one of the furies. She and the rest of the crowd were sending showers of stones after the fugitive. I ducked one that came perilously near me, then, retiring to the shelter of a doorway, awaited developments. The first woman ran straight into the arms of a militiaman, who halted the entire mob, and began to ask questions of the second woman, who was evidently the aggressor. "Paugh," she said, spitting violently, a habit of the Russians when either frightened or angry, "she is a worthless wench. I go out to work and I come home and find her with my husband. I will tear her to pieces; let me get at her," and she made a threatening gesture, cheered on by the crowd, which was entirely in sympathy with her righteous indignation. The militiaman was impartial and led them both off to settle their differences in the People's Court.

There are still many church weddings in Moscow. I often used to drop in at various churches while weddings were going on, and once I was a guest at a regular old-fashioned Russian wedding. It was at the home of a Mme. B, whose husband was formerly one of the most fashionable tailors in Moscow. He had been arrested nearly a year before I made their acquaintance, because, in a raid on the apartment in which they lived, a circular letter written in Kerensky's time, recommending the Moscow merchant tailors to organize in order to combat the excessive demands of the workmen, had been found among his papers. He was held for two months in the Cheka, where he died of typhus before his case came up for trial. Taking advantage of the decree, which, with variations, has always been in force, permitting the existence of small "artels," or workshops, consisting of from ten to fifty individuals, all of whom worked together on a cooperative basis, and being over the legal working age himself, he had maintained his business in a small way and managed to support his family very comfortably.

The business was carried on after his death by Mme. B, her two nieces and her son, who was serving his term in the Red Army, but had managed through pull to secure an assignment to duty in the War Office at Moscow, where he served for only a few hours each day, being free the rest of the time to devote his attention to the workshop. They had a great many orders from rich commissars, who do not purchase all their clothes from the Soviet stores by any means. One day when I dropped into the shop I saw a good-looking young man being fitted for a suit of English tweeds. When he left, Mme. B told me that he had ordered nine suits, an overcoat and a fur-lined ulster for his trousseau, as he expected to be married very shortly.

Mme. B's niece was to be married in a few weeks, and I was invited to the wedding, which took place at five o'clock in the afternoon at a large church not far from her apartment on the Povarskaya, formerly one of the most fashionable residence streets of Moscow. I went to their home and walked to the church, which was only a short distance away, with an elderly friend of the family. The bridal party was driven in carriages. My escort was very correct in a frock coat of somewhat antiquated pattern, it is true, and the cousin of the bride was smart in an English morning coat and striped trousers, with a white boutonniere in his buttonhole. The same costume was worn by the groom, a prosperous young engineer, and his best man.

On entering the church, the bride, with her attendants, ten pretty bridesmaids in white frocks carrying large bouquets of phlox, accompanied by the members of her family and intimate friends, turned to the left of the door and waited. The family of the groom occupied the lower right-hand corner of the church. In a few minutes, the doors of the sanctuary, flanked by innumerable pictures of saints which take the place of an altar in the Greek church, opened to admit the priest, who advanced down the main aisle of the basilica. He was an imposing old man with a long, flowing grey beard and a fine patriarchal face. He wore a gorgeous robe of green and gold brocade, and carried a superb prayer book in his hands. On his head was a curious miterlike headdress of gold galloon, encrusted with real or imitation stones. He advanced to where the groom was standing with his best man, took him by the hand and led him across to the bride, placing his hand in hers. Then, turning, he led the way to the sanctuary, followed by the bridal couple, the attendants and family, among whom I was included, while a wedding march was chanted by the choir. In the Russian churches there are no organs, but the unaccompanied Gregorian chant is often very beautiful, and it was superb on this occasion, for this particular church had one of the finest choirs in Moscow.

The ceremony was long and exceedingly complicated. During the entire time, the best man and maid of honor held huge gilt crowns over the heads of the bride and groom, there were many prayers and a short homily on the married state by the priest. Then, followed by the bridal couple and their two attendants, still holding the crowns over their heads, he marched three times around the huge Bible on a gilded lectern that stood in the center of the church just outside the sanctuary rail. During the entire ceremony, the guests and spectators remained standing, for there are no pews or chairs in Orthodox churches. There were many places in the service where they all bowed and crossed themselves several times. After the final blessing everybody present kissed the priest's hand, and the Bible, filing in line before the lectern, then the priest and all the guests kissed the bride and we all went home to a beautiful wedding supper.

It consisted of cold meats, delicious Russian salad, hot meat croquettes with fried potatoes, white rolls, elaborate cakes of all kinds, bonbons and fruit, followed by coffee. We drank *kvas*, a plebeian drink, something like a cross between poor beer and cider, which is the Russian 2.75 in a country of prohibition.[2] There had been much discussion before hand as to whether we should have champagne, but as there were at least fifty guests, and the price of champagne, plenty of which could be bought from Soviet bootleggers, was about 35,000 rubles a bottle, it was decided that it would be an unjustifiable extravagance under the circumstances.

We were seated at a long, narrow table extending around three sides of Mme. B's handsome dining room, beautifully decorated with bowls of cut summer flowers. The bride looked very pretty in a real white satin gown with white silk stockings and white kid slippers. There were innumerable speeches, the bride's health was drunk in *kvas*, then the table was taken away by the young men of the party and we danced to the music of a graphophone, alternating with French waltzes and Russian dances played on the piano by one of the guests, and the party did not break up until long after midnight.

In view of the high prices and scarcity of everything in Revolutionary Moscow, a rough estimate of the cost of the party is rather interesting. To

---

2. *Kvas* is a traditional Russian drink based on fermented rye bread with such a low alcoholic level as to be classified as non-alcoholic. The 2.75 term is a reference to the alcohol percentage limit placed on beer by U.S. President Woodrow Wilson in early 1918, just before the 18th Amendment to the U.S. Constitution took effect in 1919.

begin with, there was the bride's costume. Her satin frock was homemade, but the material cost about eighty thousand rubles, the silk stockings eighteen thousand rubles a pair, the kid slippers forty thousand. The bridesmaids' frocks, also homemade, and of silk mull, cost about thirty thousand rubles apiece, their bouquets five thousand each, and the flowers on the table represented roughly twenty thousand rubles. The priest received ten thousand rubles as his fee, the choir about the same and then there was the expense of lighting and cleaning the church and the verger's fee, which amounted to several thousand rubles more. The supper, Mme. B told me, cost over half a million. In all, she calculated that she had spent nearly a million rubles on the wedding. She had not had to buy a dress for herself, as she had many costumes left over from the old days that could be made over.[3]

Among the guests at the wedding was a pretty young girl who was a student at the Moscow Conservatory of Music. Her father, who was a well-known general, had died some years previously, and her three brothers, all guard officers, had been shot at the beginning of the Revolution. She and her mother lived in one room and kept themselves from starving by selling their old clothes, household linen and jewelry, though they did the latter at considerable risk, as selling gold or precious stones is illegal. Nevertheless, her hair was waved and arranged in a tousled mass of curls, Russian fashion; she wore a black velvet dress that had seen better days, and a handsome white fox around her neck, though the wedding was in midsummer. Such incongruities are features of Soviet fashions. People wear what they have, irrespective of the seasons, and it is no uncommon sight to see women wearing superb sable furs in midsummer, covering ragged gowns, and silk frocks during working hours in government offices.

The young couple were given a bedroom and sitting-room in Mme. B's seven-room apartment, which she had managed to keep intact through personal friendship with the chairman of the housing committee. They took no wedding trip. It is impossible to secure permits to travel in Russia without all sorts of passes, and unless they were traveling on official business it would not have been possible for them to secure accommodations in government hotels, so they just said goodnight to the guests and settled down in their rooms, which had been painted and repapered for them by Mme. B.

....
3. The exchange rate was quite volatile at this time. In 1922, the Soviet government exchanged the "old" rubles for "new" rubles at a rate of 10,000 to 1. The exchange rate for U.S. dollars to rubles was one dollar for 2,500 rubles. Thus the cost could be estimated at around $400 in 1920 dollars, or anywhere from $4-10,000 today, depending on what price index one chooses to use.

Novodevichy Convent, 1920s

It is hard to live in Russia at the present time, but it is equally hard to die decently, as I found out upon the death of the father of one of my friends, a former Imperial general of an old and historic family. Great commissars and party leaders are accorded magnificent funerals, like that of the Commissar of Posts and Telegraphs, whose obsequies I have already described, for in such cases reverence is accorded to the idea and not the person. But in the case of ordinary individuals, the dead are disposed of like so much waste paper. When the general died, his family were most anxious to have him buried according to the rites of the Orthodox Church, and this entailed no end of red tape and trouble. In the first place, after obtaining the certificate of death, they had to secure permission to keep the body in the house beyond the fixed period of twenty-four hours after his decease, and they were obliged to procure special permission to hold religious services in their apartment. Ordinarily, officials from the Department of Health would have come to their home, placed the body in a rough board coffin, and carried it on a dray with the bodies of other persons who had died during the preceding twenty-four hours, to one of the public cemeteries. There it would have been dumped in a common grave and the coffin, in all probability, saved to do service again. All this would have been done without any expense whatever to the family. As it was, the State provided nothing. The general's daughter was obliged to go out, buy boards for a coffin, find a carpenter to make it, and bring it to their apartment on a pushcart. Then a cart and horse had to be hired to take the body to the cemetery, a man found to dig the grave and permission secured from the authorities for separate burial. All this took eight days and cost the family over a hundred thousand rubles.

I saw several cemeteries in Moscow, among them the cemetery of Novodevichy, where the composer Scriabin, Chekhov the playwright, the members of the Stolypin family and many other noted Russians are buried. Here the anarchist prince, Peter Kropotkin, who died during my stay in Moscow, was buried in consecrated ground.[4] I also noticed the graves of a number of Communists within the enclosure, distinguishable from the others only by the fact that they lacked the Greek cross that forms the headstone of every Orthodox grave. The cemetery was in good condition, none of the graves had been disturbed in any way, and many of them were decorated with growing plants and flowers. In this as in many other respects, the Russians are slow to abandon tradition, and no amount of materialistic teaching will ever stamp out their reverence for their dead.

---

4. Novodevichy Cemetery is attached to the convent of the same name that dates back to the sixteenth century. It contains graves of many famous artists and politicians. More recently it includes the graves of Svetlana Alliluyeva (Stalin's second wife), Nikita Khrushchev, Raisa Gorbacheva, and Boris Yeltsin. It was closed to the public until 1994. Alexander Scriabin (1872-1915) was a Russian composer and pianist. Anton P. Chekhov (1860-1904) was one of Russia's most famous writers. Peter Stolypin (1862-1911) was a controversial Prime Minister of Russia from 1906 to 1911. He was assassinated in Kiev (where he is also buried). Peter Kropotkin (1842-1921) was a Russian anarchist who believed workers should live in voluntary associations.

CHAPTER X
Bourgeois

*A*fter I had been in Moscow for a few weeks, I got tired of doing purely official things, made friends outside the narrow circle of the Foreign Office around which the life of most correspondents revolves, and began to get an idea of how the average family lives in Russia.

The people who lived best in Moscow were the big speculators. They were quite different from the small fry that haunted the markets or engaged in house-to-house trade. There was a certain class that dealt in foreign exchange and Tsar rubles, turning over millions every day. You could get a quotation on almost every sort of foreign currency, the exchange fluctuating according to the political and international situation. Before the departure of large repatriation echelons, francs, pounds and dollars were always greatly in demand and increased in value accordingly.

Many persons were engaged, in cooperation with Letts and Estonians, in smuggling rugs, paintings, jewels and bibelots out of the country. This was comparatively easy to do, as Lettish and Estonian subjects, under the terms of the peace treaties, had the right to take their personal belongings with them, and they could claim as their own articles later to be sold in Reval[1] or Riga, the money to be deposited in a bank to the credit of the Russian owner after the middleman had deducted his commission. I knew a woman in Moscow who made over two millions a month in this business.

Other people, fantastic as it may seem, bought and sold real estate, on paper, of course, for future delivery when the right of private property would be re-

---

1. Reval is another name for Tallin, capital of Estonia.

established. A flourishing trade was done in passports to foreign countries, permits to travel on the railroads, food cards and Soviet food supplies.

While official demoralization is undoubtedly widespread in Russia I do not think it quite fair to attribute the corruption in official circles entirely to the Bolshevik regime. It was an accepted fact under the old regime that bribery played an important part in all business or official transactions, and things have remained very much the same.

To live on Soviet rations was next to impossible, but nearly everyone in Moscow had other sources from which to buy food supplies. Few people had the right sort of food, however, and the shortage of fats and sugar caused a great deal of anemia and under-nourishment. On the whole, I believe that during my stay in Moscow, while many people were half starved, there were no actual deaths from starvation, and the available food supplies were equably distributed. There was never a time when people who had money could not buy practically everything they wished.

One day, quite by accident, I dropped into one of the many little mushroom shops that had sprung up in Moscow, where *varenets*, or curdled milk, could be bought in glasses, and white rolls and pastry were sold at fabulous prices. The man who waited on me was a distinguished looking old gentleman, evidently very superior to his present job. I began to talk with him and found out that he was a former Colonel in the Russian Army. Being above the age limit, he was not obliged to work in a Soviet office, and he had agreed to keep shop a certain number of hours each day for a Jew who was running the place. He invited me to his house, where I was afterwards a frequent visitor.

His wife worked in one of the branches of the Department of Education, his only son had just taken his degree in medicine at the University of Moscow and was a Red Army physician. His daughter was employed as a clerk in the "GlavKozh," Leather Central, a branch of the CentroSoyuz,[2] which controls distribution in Russia. Between them, therefore, they had three *payoks*, or food rations. The son was drawing Red Army rations, which were about double those obtained by civilian employees. They were living in their old apartment of six rooms, four of which they occupied, two being assigned to other persons. That they had so much room was due to the fact that the Colonel's wife was chairman of the "Housing Committee," which exists in every dwelling and apartment house in Moscow, under a department of the Commissariat of Labor. According to the regulations of the Central Housing Committee, each citizen

2. Ministry of Light Industries.

is allowed a certain number of cubic feet for his lodgings, but these regulations are often honored more in the breach than the observance. Those who know how to get on the good side of the regional commissar, by bribery or otherwise, are frequently allowed to keep their old quarters, and if they give up any of their rooms, to choose their own tenants, and this was the case with my friends.

They kept no servant, the mother and daughter doing all the cooking. They received their food rations through the offices where they worked, supplementing them by selling off their clothes, furniture and jewelry. They had to make all the repairs themselves in this apartment. If the plumbing system broke down, the father had to mend it; if a window was broken, it had to be patched with paper. They had managed to buy enough wood to keep fires in the kitchen and in two of the rooms, the wood assigned them – which they were obliged to go some distance to get and bring home themselves – not being sufficient to keep one stove going for more than three months of the year. It was given them in the form of logs, which the father or the son had to saw into the proper lengths in the courtyard of the apartment and carry up four flights of stairs, as no elevators have run in Moscow for several years. To procure the wood was a matter of time and endless formalities. First, it was necessary to have a *Trudovaya Knizhka*, or workers' book, showing where the applicant for wood was employed. Everyone in Moscow between the ages of sixteen and fifty must be provided with one of these books, otherwise it is not only impossible for him to obtain lodgings, food or clothing from the government stores, but he may be arrested at any time as a work deserter and condemned for a period of months to compulsory labor.

Until recently it was not possible for workers to choose their place of employment. They were registered at the Work Exchange and assigned to work where they were most needed. Often this system caused great hardships, as in the case of a friend of mine, a widow with one child, who was assigned to work in an office at least six *versts* from her residence. As she had no relatives with whom she could leave him, and was unwilling to put him in a children's home, she endeavored to find work in an office nearer her lodgings, and secured a tentative offer from a Soviet official for employment at a higher salary than what she was then getting, provided she could be released from her old position. Not only was release refused her, but she was arrested on a charge of insubordination and condemned to six months of compulsory work, which consisted of cleaning toilets in government offices. She was a highly educated person and could speak five languages, but she was obliged to do this disgusting work as the price for her temerity. In addition to the workers' book, it was also necessary, in order to secure wood, to have an order from your place of employment, which was to be presented at the regional office of the Moscow Fuel Committee and exchanged for an order signed by the committee, after which you had to wait until there was a distribution of fuel in your region, then go to the appointed place, stand in line and wait your turn for fuel. Sometimes, if you were not early, the supply gave out and you were obliged to come back another day.

The same process must be gone through in order to purchase shoes, clothing or household utensils or furnishings, and to draw the weekly food rations on cards. Actually, this system did much to hinder the efficiency of government offices, as the employees lost a number of days in each month collecting their supplies and rations.

My friends told me that frequently supplies assigned on cards were either not given out at the appointed time or that all were gone, and if they needed anything at once they were compelled to go to the Sukharevka, Moscow's illegal market, and purchase them at speculative prices.[3] Once they received no bread for seventeen days from their local distributing center, while people in other parts of Moscow were receiving their regular ration. During this time they were obliged to buy bread in the open market for five hundred rubles a pound.

The working hours of the mother and daughter were from ten till five daily, until two o'clock on Saturdays, with Sundays free. The daughter was studying dancing at the Moscow Ballet School, receiving her tuition free, and she attended her classes after office hours. The mother did all the housework and cooking, the daughter did the laundry work in her odd moments, but they both managed to keep well, even elegantly dressed, and still used silver on their table, which they carefully secreted whenever there was a raid on the apartment, which happened occasionally. The Colonel had also managed to conceal his commission, his sword and many relics of army days. They had few pleasures, occasionally receiving tickets for the theater from the office where they worked, but they were usually too tired to go out at night. They could go to a public library to read and could take out books for home reading if they pertained to the work of their department, but they could buy no books or other reading matter. The mother and father lived mainly in the past. The daughter belonged to a club in her office, which sometimes gave dances and informal parties, spent her meager salary on perfumes, and powdered her nose like any New York stenographer.

. . . .
3. Harrison discusses this in some detail in Chapter 15.

I was often a guest at the five o'clock dinner which was their only real meal during the twenty-four hours. A typical menu was potato soup, black bread, *kasha*, butter and tea. They had a little real tea, which they hoarded very carefully. Usually there was no sugar for tea, and they substituted raisins. Salt herrings, prepared with artificial vinegar, cucumbers and potatoes were luxuries. One day, when I arrived at dinner time, they told me that they had a real treat for me, and the daughter produced a pound of butter which she had bought in exchange for a pair of silk stockings and a tiny piece of chocolate given to her by the chief of her department, with whom she was on very good terms. They were all officially *bezpartiniye*, nonpartisans, but they spent their time abusing the Soviet Government and bemoaning the past. They were absolutely without patriotism or national feeling, hoped the Poles would begin active hostilities and take Moscow, had a fairly superstitious reverence for all foreigners, and a humility that was almost servile and which I found rather repulsive. This is typical of the attitude of the middle class bourgeois Russian.

A favorite expression of these unhappy bourgeois with regard to present-day conditions in Russia was *koshmar*, a corruption of the French word, "*cauchemar*"—nightmare. Many of them felt that they were indeed living in the midst of a terrible dream.

Through them I met General Brusilov,[4] whom I found to be of a very different stamp. I often visited him and his wife at their apartment at number fourteen Mansursky pereulok. While the career of Brusilov since the Revolution has been the theme of much speculation, and of many absurd articles in the foreign press, very few people outside of Russia have any idea as to what he has been doing. People who followed the war news on the Eastern Front remember him as the leader of the brilliant Galician offensive in 1916, which annihilated the Austrian Army on that front and made active assistance to Germany from that quarter impossible. With the exception of the few advantages gained in the East Prussian campaign at the beginning of the war, it was the only substantial military success achieved by the Imperial Army. Much of the territory acquired during Brusilov's advance was lost later, owing to lack of arms and ammunition and the increasing demoralization in the army. Brusilov himself told me of those terrible days, when he realized that the army was going to pieces, and sent frantic telegrams to the War Ministry at Petrograd, asking for the help that never came. His enemies claim that he was and always has been an opportunist,

----
4. Alexei A. Brusilov (1853-1926) was a general in the Russian army who in 1916 led Russia's most successful offensive in World War I. He was considered a hero even in Soviet Russia.

that he was one of the Tsar's boot-licking sycophants, that he afterwards curried favor with Kerensky and later with the Bolsheviks, and it is undoubtedly true that he is despised by the old monarchists and members of the Cadet party,[5] who loathe him as a traitor. Some day he intends to write his memoirs in justification and explanation of his conduct; meanwhile this is his story as he told it to me.

He had always been inclined to sympathize with the Cadets who supported the idea of a constitutional monarchy in Russia, and was intimate with many of their leaders in the Duma.[6] During the dark days at the end of 1916, he became convinced that Russia could not stay in the war under the utterly incapable, weak and vacillating rule of Nicholas II, and when the March Revolution came, actuated solely by patriotism, he offered his services to Kerensky. He remained in command of the Eighth Army until shortly before the October Revolution, when he was removed on account of difference of opinion with Kerensky, who was yielding to the demands of the French, and the English Ambassador, Sir George Buchanan, to keep up the war and continue sending mutinous, unarmed, half-naked men to stop German bullets.

At the end of the October Revolution, he was living quietly in Moscow and was wounded by a bomb dropped by an aeroplane, which fell in his apartment. He was taken to the hospital at the Kremlin, where he remained for several months, after which he was placed under arrest and held for six months in the Kremlin prison, being treated, however, with every consideration, owing to his weakened condition. Subsequently, he was allowed to return to his home but was kept under house arrest until the late autumn of 1919, when he agreed to accept a position in the archives office of the Red Army staff, supervising the compilation of a history of Russia's part in the Great War. He was living on his pay of three thousand five hundred rubles a month, supplemented by the Red Army ration and occasional gifts from his old soldiers, many of whom were prosperous peasants living near Moscow, and they never came to town without bringing him butter, honey, milk, or sour cream, of which the Russians are inordinately fond. I happened to be dining with them one day when they received such a windfall. We had sorrel soup with sour whipped cream floating on top, *kasha* with butter, black bread and tea with honey instead of sugar.

. . . .

5. The Cadet (Constitutional Democratic) Party was formed in 1905 after the revolution that prompted Tsar Nicholas II to issue the "October Manifesto." They wanted a constitutional government and were successful in Duma (parliamentary) elections before the First World War. They were considered a middle-left political party.

6. The Duma was a consultative assembly created in 1906 after Tsar Nicholas II signed the "October Manifesto" in 1905.

Brusilov's attitude towards the Soviet Government was frankly antagonistic, as far as the principles on which it was based were concerned, but he was intensely nationalistic in feeling and violently opposed to intervention.

"We got ourselves into this mess," he often said to me, "through our own indifference and selfishness and corruption, and our utter inability to read the signs of the times. It is up to us to get ourselves out of it. If we are unable to do this, we deserve any form of government that may be imposed upon us."

He despised the emigrants who were always hatching outside plots, safely ensconced in London, Berlin or Paris, and when the Poles began their offensive he wrote the famous letter to the Commissariat of War offering his services to the Government.

He was made chairman of an advisory commission to the General Staff, of which Polivanov, former Minister of War, and General Klembovsky were also members. They were never trusted by the Red Army General Staff, however, and their activities were confined to advising measures to facilitate transportation of food supplies and troop movements from the reserve bases to the fighting

General Alexei Brusilov, 1916

front. They also received and made recommendations on thousands of letters from former Imperial officers who were in internment camps offering to serve in the Red Army against the Poles.[7] General Brusilov estimated, at the

----

7. Alexei A. Polivanov (1855-1920) was a general in the Russian army during World War I, was briefly arrested after the revolution, then went on to play a leading role in the war against Poland. He died of typhus while in Riga negotiating the end to that war. Vladislav Napoleonovich Klembovsky (1860-1921) was a field general in the Russian army during World War I. He was dismissed from his post in September 1917, when he refused Kerensky's orders to remove General Kornilov from his post and

beginning of the Polish offensive, that approximately 100,000 former officers were interned. Most of them were actuated by nationalistic feeling, but there were undoubtedly numbers who hoped by this means to bring about a counter-revolution. Brusilov himself never believed in this possibility, and I know for a fact that he steadily refused secret offers to place himself at the head of such a movement. Something of the sort was actually organized, culminating in the late summer of 1920 in the arrest of an entire department of the General Staff and a number of distinguished officers, among whom was General Klembovsky.

While not trusting Brusilov to the extent of giving him any real responsibility, the government did not hesitate to make use of him for furthering enlistment propaganda against the Poles. Dispatches stating that Brusilov was at Kiev, on the Berezina, or at the Wrangel front were published in *Izvestia* or *Pravda*, often on the very day when I was having tea with him and his wife in their apartment in Moscow, and we used to laugh about it together. "Actually," he said, "I probably know less about the situation on the front than you do, for you hear the gossip at the Foreign Office."

Madame Brusilov, who had a sister in America, Mrs. Vera Johnston of Brooklyn, and who was a niece of Mme. Blavatsky,[8] enjoyed hearing my accounts of life in America, and I spent many happy hours at their house. I was also an intimate friend of the wife of their only son, a young officer who had joined the Red Army and who disappeared on the Denikin front in the summer of 1919. They had never heard a word as to his fate. The Red Army authorities simply reported him as missing, but there were many rumors with regard to his disappearance. Some people asserted that he had attempted to pass over to the Whites and had been killed by the Bolsheviks, others that he had been taken prisoner and executed by Denikin, still others that he was fighting with Wrangel under an assumed name. Young Mme. Brusilov was herself employed in the War Department and managed to live very comfortably, supplementing her rations by selling the many beautiful things she had inherited from her grandmother, who belonged to one of the oldest and richest families in Moscow. She kept an apartment of two rooms, kitchenette and bath in what was formerly her grandmother's home, part of the house being used by a section of the Commissariat of War, and the remaining rooms occupied by M. Ugrimov, a distinguished Russian engineer and an old friend of the family.

---

become senior commander. He was imprisoned by the Soviets in 1918, released during the Polish War, then arrested again in 1921. He died in prison after a brief hunger strike.

8. Helena Blavatskaya (1831-1891) was the Russian born founder of Theosophy and the Theosophical Society.

She very often gave informal parties, at which there were wives of former generals, professors and army men. Many of her friends were in prison and she spent much of her time taking food packages to the Cheka, the Butyrki,[9] and other prisons. One of them was Professor Yakovlev of the University of Petrograd, who had been condemned to death in connection with a counter-revolutionary plot at the time of the Yudenich offensive, but had not been executed owing to the fact that he was desperately ill with a heart affection. His wife, whom I often saw at the house of Madame Brusilov, was arrested late in the summer because she lived with Mme. Rodzianko,[10] whose husband was, and still is, very active in fomenting counter-revolutionary plots in Poland against the Bolsheviks. Mme. Brusilov's uncle, Professor Kotlyarevsky of the University of Moscow, was arrested later and placed on trial for his life in connection with the activities of the so-called Tactical Center, a nonpartisan organization which had for its avowed object the fight for free speech, free press and free party activity in Russia.[11]

I attended the trial, which was most dramatic, with Mme. Brusilov. It was held in the amphitheater of the Moscow Polytechnic School and the public was admitted. It lasted for four days. The three judges sat at a plain deal table covered with red bunting on the stage facing the audience. The accused, twenty-eight in number, were placed in the space usually occupied by the orchestra at theatrical performances, separated from the audience by two rows of vacant seats, which had been roped off and were guarded by a detachment of the militiamen of the Extraordinary Commission. The public prosecutor, Kirilenko, a brilliant speaker, was also one of the judges, which seemed to me a most unfair arrangement. Each prisoner was allowed to make a speech in his own defense, and they were represented by M. Muraviev, head of the Political Red Cross, a former well-known lawyer in Moscow.

Among them were many notable persons, including Chepkin, a well-known leader of the Cadet party, whose brother served on the recently formed and almost as promptly dissolved Russian Famine Relief Committee; Prince Urosov, at whose house, as nearly as I can recollect, the murder of Lenin was attempted;

---

9. The Butyrka Prison had a long history (back to the 18th century) as a harsh prison. The Soviets used it as a transit prison for inmates who were being sent into exile in Siberia.

10. Mikhail V. Rodzianko (1859-1924) was one of the founders of the moderate-right Octobrist Party in 1905. He served as Chairman of the Duma from 1911-1917.

11. In the August 1920 Affair of the Tactical Center, 19 persons were sentenced to death for writing and proposing political changes that were not based on Soviet ideology. Though all the sentences were commuted to lesser punishments, many of the accused succumbed in prison or subsequent purges.

and Alexandra Lvovna Tolstoy, youngest daughter of the great novelist. Professor Kotlyarevsky, who was intensely nervous throughout the trial, broke down under the grilling of Kirilenko and made a full confession. He was sentenced to three years' internment, but was released on parole immediately after the trial.

Alexandra Lvovna Tolstoy made a brilliant speech in her own defense, stating that she had joined the movement not as a counter-revolutionary but as a believer in her father's doctrine of pacifism. She opposed the Soviet Government on these grounds, and also as an individualist, in favor of majority rule and against the dictatorship of any minority. She then added, with a fine gesture, that they might do what they pleased with her body, that she would always be free morally and spiritually, no matter how long she might be kept in prison.

One of the other prisoners, a man named Morozov, in his defense expressed the opinion of a number of the intellectuals who have remained in Russia throughout the Revolution. He said that unfortunately he had spent most of his time in prison since the Revolution and was therefore not able to carry out his intentions, but that if released he would be willing to devote his energies to working with, though not for, the Soviet Government out of love for Russia, because he realized that cooperation with the existing administration was the only way to prevent the utter collapse of Russia's economic and industrial system, and untold misery to the Russian people. There are thousands of nonpartisan workers in every department of the Soviet administration today who share the same views. They admit that the political domination of the Communist party is absolute and complete, but they foresee an eventual political change following the inevitable economic breakdown.

They believe that they can best serve their country by keeping the work of the various governmental departments going, so that when the change comes there will not be utter demoralization and anarchy. All public improvements which are possible under the present regime, all schemes such as the electrification of the villages, reconstruction of railroads and bridges, installation of new power plants and factories, new and scientific methods in the departments of public health, agriculture and education, are being carried on principally by these men. They regard it as no disloyalty to do this, believing that they can be of more use to their country at the present time by doing such work than by engaging in useless counter-revolutionary activities.

Although an attempt was made to prove that the Tactical Center was counter-revolutionary, it served merely for the interchange of ideas between men and women of this type, and the government was, I believe, fully aware of this fact, but it suited the purpose of the Cheka at the time to hold a trial and make an apparently generous gesture by releasing all the prisoners, knowing all the while that it was perfectly safe to do so. If they had been really dangerous conspirators they would have had short shrift and a secret trial. The maximum sentence imposed was ten years in an internment camp for the four alleged leaders, and all were released on parole within a short time.

I had met Alexandra Lvovna Tolstoy before her arrest at the home of Vladimir Chertkov,[12] a charming old gentleman, who was a close friend of Count Tolstoy, who had made him his literary executor. A family quarrel had arisen over this matter, Count Ilya Tolstoy, the eldest son, and his other children maintaining that Chertkov had no right to renunciation of all rights of publication of Tolstoy's works and the royalties therefrom, which Chertkov had made in accordance with the wishes of his friend. Chertkov is today the leader of the remnant of Tolstoyans[13] in Russia, and the head of a nonsectarian league, composed of various denominations, all of whom are pacifists.

They had until recently an office on the Pokrovka in Moscow and were left undisturbed until they became active in supporting conscientious objectors to army service, of whom there are a considerable number in Russia. For a time, Chertkov acted as head of an advisory board to the General Staff to pass on such cases, for the Soviet Government recognizes the validity of the claims of conscientious objectors if based on the tenets of the religious sect to which they belong; but Chertkov wished to push the matter further and secure the recognition of cases of individual objectors. He had many tilts with the War Office over this matter, but his age and his friendship with Tolstoy, for whose memory even the Communists have considerable veneration, secured him immunity.

He and his wife were desperately poor, for they lived on the utterly inadequate ration given to persons over the legal working age, and I really believe that they would have starved to death if it had not been for the gifts of the peasants from Tolstoy's estate near Kolomna, about sixty *versts* from Moscow, who came all the way on foot to bring them enough food to keep them alive.[14] Chertkov was constantly working on some Utopian scheme or other, and he managed

....

12. Vladmir C. Chertkov (1854-1936) was a Russian writer and secretary for Russian writer Leo Tolstoy for many years. He was the founder of the Tolstoyans.

13. These were followers of the philosophical and religious views of Russian writer Leo Tolstoy (1828-1910).

14. Tolstoy's estate was actually at Yasnaya Polyana, 14 km southwest of Tula, while Kolomna lies to the northeast of Tula, and considerably closer to Moscow.

to publish some pacifist brochures, which he distributed among the militia and members of the Moscow garrison. He was always running about Moscow on some such errand, and was also working on a new and revised edition of Tolstoy's works to be published by the Commissariat of Education. At his house I renewed my acquaintance with Paul Biryukov,[15] Tolstoy's biographer, whom I had known in Switzerland. He and his wife and son returned to Moscow during the summer and the son became a Communist, but Biryukov, like many another old revolutionary, was bitterly disappointed in the Revolution.

---

15. Pavel Biryukov (1860-1931) was a long-time secretary and friend of Russian writer Leo Tolstoy.

CHAPTER XI
Under Suspicion

$\mathcal{M}$y first arrest, which occurred on Good Friday, April 4th, was not, I must confess, entirely unexpected. At this time the political situation, which had been much improved when I first arrived, was growing more unstable day by day. It had been confidently expected that the secret armistice with Poland would develop into a formal cessation of hostilities, followed by peace negotiations. The death penalty was abolished; arrests by the Cheka had been much less frequent, people thought less about plots and spies, and more about reconstruction. Denikin was defeated, the Seventh Army, the Third Army and many other individual army units had been turned into working battalions. The papers published dispatches every day from the "bloodless front"; there was much talk of the rebuilding of industry, public improvements, and the Russians were just beginning to breathe more freely and react from war psychosis. The underground organization of the Right and Left Social Revolutionaries was beginning to function, the Mensheviks were seeking more recognition for the trades unions and a modification of Communist tactics, when it became evident that the Poles, backed by France, were about to start an offensive. Repressive measures were immediately taken, the attitude of the government towards its political opponents became more severe, arrests of all persons who had recently arrived from Poland began, and I was one of them.[1]

In addition, I had committed many imprudences. In the first place, I had associated openly with people who were known to be hostile to the Soviet Government. I had rendered myself absolutely independent of the Foreign

1. In April 1920, Polish General Josef Pilsudski launched a major offensive into Ukraine where he was supported by Ukrainian independence fighters. The Red Army launched a successful counterattack.

Office and its interpreters, I had changed foreign money illegally to get the advantage of the higher rate of exchange, I had attended the Communist party conference where I had no earthly right to be, and had gone with Mr. McCullagh to the secret exhibition of the Rosta in the Kremlin which was meant only for delegates to the conference. For some time I had been given suspicious freedom of movement and I had several times felt that the Cheka was only giving me rope to hang myself.

About a week before my arrest and that of Mr. McCullagh, which took place on the same night, Dr. Karlin, he and I were moved from our comfortable quarters in the Kharitonevsky on the pretense that it was to be used by the English Labor delegation, not due until June, to the Savoy, also a government guest house. The Savoy, which was formerly one of the largest hotels in Moscow, was a place where arrests were frequently made and it contained a number of strange foreign guests, many of them like ourselves under suspicion. An arrest in a large place like the Savoy is apt to pass unnoticed and causes less comment than in a small place like the Kharitonevsky. We rather suspected something was wrong when we went there, but at first it was rather amusing.

My room was large and cheerful, well heated, but in a shocking state of disrepair; there was a comfortable mattress, but no sheets on the bed, which was infested with hosts of insect pests, against whom boiling water and kerosene were powerless. The plumbing was out of order and there were no bathing facilities. Nevertheless I was so much diverted by the strange conglomerate company among which I found myself at meal times in the dining room, where our fare was very similar to that in our former quarters, that I forgot to fuss over the increased discomfort or trouble my head over the suspicious circumstances of our transfer.

The Savoy was very convenient, being close to the Foreign Office, and I did not have the long half-hour walk home in the wee small hours, which was rather pleasant.

One night I had stayed there very late as usual, and was crossing the broad theater boulevard between the Metropole and Rozhdestvenka where the Savoy was located, when a soldier stepped up to me and asked very politely:

"*Vasha familia*? – your name?"

"Garrison," I answered, that being the name by which I was known in Russia as the Russian language has no letter "h."

"Your Christian name?" he continued.

"Marguerita Bernardnova," I answered.

"You're arrested," he announced cheerfully, much in the same way he would have told me I was taking the wrong turn in the street had he been a London bobby instead of a Moscow Chekist. I accompanied him to the office of the secret section of the Cheka at Lubyanka 2, [2] where I was placed in solitary confinement and put through two rigid cross-examinations during which I was grilled about my friends in Moscow, my Polish connections and various other matters.

Meanwhile Dr. Karlin and Mr. McCullagh had been arrested at the Savoy. My room had been searched and all my baggage and papers seized. I will not enter into my experiences during my first sojourn in the Cheka, as I shall describe conditions at the Lubyanka more fully when I tell of my second arrest. The upshot of it all was that as I had taken no part in any party activities or plots against the Soviet Government, and convinced the praesidium that I was not a Polish spy, I was released after being detained for forty-eight hours, allowed to return to the Savoy and given back all my baggage and my typewriter. I was told that I would be free to pursue my work, but that permission to leave the country could not be given me for any definite period, certainly not until the Polish situation cleared up. This was a measure of ordinary prudence under the circumstances, for had I so chosen, if permitted to leave the country, I could have undoubtedly furnished valuable information to the Polish Government.

I promised at that time to avoid certain places and people and to do certain things. These promises, candidly, I could not and did not keep. This furnished full justification for my arrest six months later. I never had any personal feeling against the Cheka or the Soviet Government for their action with regard to me. Beset as they were at that time by enemies on all sides within and without, it was quite natural to anyone who understood their methods and psychology. Many other foreigners who had come to Moscow with the full permission of the Soviet Government were arrested on much more trivial charges.

The day after my own release I was rejoined by Mr. McCullagh, whose real identity had not been discovered by the Cheka. I first met him in March when he arrived from Siberia with a safe conduct from Jansen, Soviet Commissar at Omsk. He had convinced them that he was merely a harmless newspaperman of unpractical, dreamy tendencies with a proclivity for getting himself innocently into awkward situations. A mass of notes, distinctly unfavorable to the Kolchak regime, which he had made during his trip across Siberia, helped to bolster

2. The Metropole and Savoy are located easy walking distance from Lubyanka Square, the headquarters of the Cheka (and later KGB).

up his case, and he was hoping to make a quick getaway under the pretext that it was very important for him to get his book on Kolchak out as soon as possible. He also had an enormous amount of interesting matter with regard to the murder of the Tsar and the Imperial family at Yekaterinburg, all of which, like many other data, he had not written down fully in his notes.[3] An English echelon of civilians and prisoners of war released under the Litvinov-O'Grady arrangement was leaving very shortly, and he planned to leave at the same time.[4]

With this end in view, he was a frequent visitor at the home of the Reverend Frank North,[5] the Anglican clergyman at Moscow who had been unofficially in charge of the interests of British citizens, and of British Red Cross work for political prisoners and prisoners of war, since the rupture of relations between Great Britain and Russia in the latter part of 1918.

With only a few supplies from England, he managed to look after all the English prisoners and a number of dependent civilians, collecting large sums to purchase food in Moscow by the following method: He took from English and Russian subjects Soviet or Czar or Kerensky rubles, giving them receipts payable in sterling at the Bank of England at a fixed rate of exchange. The Russians took chances on hiding these receipts and smuggling them out of the country. Some of those who did business with Mr. North in this manner were caught and paid the penalty in terms of imprisonment, but the majority escaped, and I know of several instances in which very considerable sums were transferred to safety in this manner. The Britishers at first hid their receipts also and took them out of the country, but at the time of the departure of the last two echelons, searches were growing more strict, and Mr. North advised them to remember the amounts and destroy them, promising to furnish them with duplicates as soon as the Finnish frontier was crossed. The officers of General Knox's Siberian Mission who were captured at Omsk, whom Mr. North kept well supplied with comforts and even luxuries, were in the Andronovsky prison camp.

They were allowed a considerable amount of freedom, several of them coming in every Sunday to service at the British church. One afternoon, by invitation, with the permission of the Foreign Office, I went to tea with the officers in the camp. The Andronovsky, which was formerly a monastery, is the

---

3. After Nicholas II abdicated the throne in March, 1917, he and his family were eventually put under house arrest in Yekaterinburg. In July 1918, the Bolsheviks executed the entire family.
4. The Litvinov-O'Grady Agreement was made in early 1920 between the British and Soviet governments in order to repatriate prisoners.
5. Frank North was an Anglican priest at St. Andrew's Anglican Church in Moscow. He was expelled later in 1920 by the Bolshevik government.

place where many of the American prisoners were confined.[6] It is a picturesque agglomeration of buildings on a high hill on the right bank of the Moskva river, which divides the city into two parts. Around the enclosure runs a high white wall, for all monasteries were built in a semi-fortified manner, at first to protect them against the ever present menace of Tatar and Polish invasions, later to guard them and their treasures against internal disturbances. Inside there are large grounds with old fruit trees and the remains of flower and vegetable gardens. In the center court where the prisoners take their exercise are the tombs of the former monks with their ornate iron crosses. Entrance to the court is through an imposing gateway with beautiful wrought iron gates, crowned by a tall bell tower. On the right is the church, on the left what was formerly the residence of the Abbot, now the office of the Commandant.

We presented our permits at the wicket, and were shown into the courtyard by the Red soldier on guard. The officers' quarters were in a long building on the left side of the court, which had served as living quarters for the monks. Their beds were in a spacious dormitory on the second floor. They had their own stove, for which they cut the wood themselves, and they did their own cooking. Adjoining the dormitory was a large recreation room where there was a piano. On Sunday afternoons they were allowed to receive visitors, and many Russian girls as well as members of the English colony used to gather there for informal tea parties. I was allowed to talk to the officers quite freely, though always in the presence of the representative of the Foreign Office who accompanied us, and I was given good English tea with white bread and butter and English cigarettes. The officers told me that, all things considered, they were very comfortable.

Once a week they were taken in a big motor lorry to the opera or the theater, and they were frequently permitted to go into Moscow with an escort in groups of twos or threes to do their shopping or to visit Mr. North at the Rectory. They were not supposed to visit their friends in private families, but as a matter of fact they often did so, and stayed to supper if they happened to have an obliging guard. The other prisoners in the Andronovsky, political prisoners and hostages, among whom were a number of Hungarian officers, were not allowed as much liberty as the British officers and occupied different quarters. At that time there were two Americans there, Dr. Lambie, a well-known Moscow dentist, who had

---

6. Andronnikov Monastery, on the left bank of Moscow's Yauza river, was founded in 1357 by Metropolitan Alexey and named for the monastery's first Father Superior, Andronika, a student of Sergey Radonezhsky. The monastery was shut in 1918 and the grounds and buildings turned into one of the first Soviet prison camps. During 1922-28, it was turned into an institution for homeless children. In 1928 it became housing for workers. Its Savior's Church is the oldest surviving church in Moscow.

lived in Russia for nearly thirty years, and Alfred Hipman, formerly doorkeeper at the American Consulate. They declared that they were held as hostages; the Bolshevik authorities insinuated that they were held for speculation. No charges were ever preferred against them, however, and after three months both were released.

I was also once invited to meet the British officers at the opera where they occupied the former Imperial box. Before the departure of the English echelons, I spent much time at the rectory, doing typewriting for Mr. North, making out receipts for the money he had received from private individuals, and lists of the passengers. After many delays the last train finally left early in May. Mr. North and his wife, before leaving, were subjected to a rather disagreeable ordeal in which they were compelled to appear several times before the Cheka, on the charge that he had handled some of the money alleged to have been spent in counter-revolutionary activities by Paul Dukes,[7] but he always claimed that he had no knowledge whatever of the uses to which these funds were to be put. The Cheka, however, was very anxious to discredit Mr. North, and being unable to get anything incriminating from him, published an alleged confession of Mrs. North, in which she was said to have revealed her husband's connection with Dukes. They were satisfied with instituting a civil suit against Mr. North, and allowed him to leave the country before the case came to trial. The English Rectory was taken over by the Foreign Office and subsequently assigned to the Danish Red Cross.

Dr. Karlin was detained for about a week after which she spent a short time with me at the Savoy and then, having secured an appointment as a Red Army physician once more, she left for the Polish front and I never saw her again. I remained at the Savoy for several weeks and took up my old life just the same as ever. An indefinite stay in Russia was opening before me, but I was determined to make the best of it and accept the inevitable. Besides, life was intensely interesting and by no means devoid of excitement and amusement.

The official host at the Savoy was an employee of the Foreign Office, Sabanyin by name, a man of very good family, who had formerly been in the Tsar's diplomatic service. Other employees of the Foreign Office who lived there were a Soviet courier, who made the trip several times a month from Moscow to Murmansk, and Dmitry Florinsky, a Russian of cosmopolitan experience, who had been at one time in the office of the Russian Vice Consul in New

---

7. Paul Dukes (1889-1967) was a spy for Great Britain before World War I. He helped many prominent White officials escape from Bolshevik prisons in 1920.

York and had many friends in America. His father, a Ukrainian nobleman, had been shot at Kiev at the beginning of the revolution. While spiritually converted to Communism, so he averred, Florinsky was in appearance a typical boulevardier. He was always dressed in the pink of perfection, with matching ties, handkerchiefs and socks; his life was miserable until he discovered a Chinese laundry where he could have his collars done at three hundred rubles apiece. He was very fond of a hand of bridge or a good game of poker, and he never got up until eleven or twelve in the morning. Then there were a solemn Czech Communist who was writing a book on Soviet Russia, several Swedish business men, a German working men's delegation, Dr. Barrakatula,[8] a well-known Hindu professor, who later departed on a mysterious mission in the direction of Bukhara and Khiva, where a revolution shortly after occurred; a Hindu nationalist, Dr. Mansur, whom strangely enough I had seen and heard speak at a meeting in Berlin during the previous year, and a former Austrian general staff officer, Meyerhoeffer, who was in Russia to negotiate an agreement for the repatriation of Austrian prisoners of war. There was also a mysterious Russian gentleman who said very little but looked and listened a lot. I afterwards made his acquaintance in the Cheka.

Some weeks later I got back my room at the Kharitonevsky. There I found several new guests, among them Dr. Alfons Goldschmidt,[9] a German publicist, who was compiling a book on trades unions in Russia; and a Japanese journalist, Fusi of the *Osaka Mainichi*, who had come to Moscow with permission of the Soviet Government but was regarded with grave suspicion on account of the fact that he had, before the Revolution, been attached to the Japanese embassy in Petrograd as an Intelligence Officer. He was placed under house arrest only, thanks to the intervention of the Foreign Office, which is not always able to protect its guests against the Cheka. Fusi was occasionally allowed to go out with an escort, but almost all of his information was based on what he read in the papers. Apropos of the news furnished by the Soviet papers the Bolsheviks themselves have a saying which I often heard repeated with great gusto. The two leading papers in Moscow are the *Izvestia*, which means "news," and the *Pravda*, meaning "truth." The saying is, "There is no news in the truth, and no truth in the news."

....

8. Barrakatullah or Maulana Barkatullah (1854-1927) was a fierce anti-British Indian nationalist who visited Moscow in 1921 while Harrison was in prison. The chronology of events here seems to be a bit out of sequence.
9. Alphons Goldschmidt (1879-1940) was a German journalist and professor who was in Russia in 1920, where he co-founded the Artists Help for the Starving in Russia.

At this time the situation in the Near East was very interesting. Georgia and Azerbaijan had gone Red; the nationalist movements in Anatolia and Northern Persia were well under way; the Siberian Far Eastern Republic had just entered into existence; a Pan-Mohammedan Congress was being held at the Foreign Office. The proceedings of this Congress were shrouded in mystery, but they concerned the vast Asiatic nationalist conspiracy, sponsored by the Bolsheviks, of which I saw many evidences during my stay in Russia.

Consequently I was often obliged to go to the Eastern Section of the Foreign Office for news and information. When I first arrived in Moscow it was in the charge of a Left Social Revolutionary, named Vosnesyensky. He was an experienced diplomatist, trained under Nicholas II, and had spent most of his time when not in prison for his revolutionary activities, in diplomatic posts in India, China and Japan. He spoke four or five Eastern languages and several dialects fluently; there was even something oriental about his mask-like, impassive face with its parchment skin, and high domed forehead and deepset grey eyes. He was always at loggerheads with the government, but Chicherin employed him because he could not find anyone who was as well fitted for the position.

Vosnesyensky dreamed of a Soviet imperialism that would make Russia mistress of all Asia. He had a propaganda map, which he once let me see, in which centers of Bolshevik agitation were marked with little red circles. They extended all over Asia and there were even several of them in the Philippines. Under his supervision men were trained and sent out to each of these countries, and he supervised the publication of an immense amount of propaganda literature in every oriental language. Vosnesyensky was frankly a militarist. He believed in taking the offensive against Japan and backing open revolt of the nationalists in Persia, India and Asia Minor; he favored supporting the southern Chinese government, and stimulating a revolution in Korea.

"If my plans are followed," he said to me once, "within a year all Asia will be aflame." They were not followed, however. The policy of Chicherin was too subtle and opportunistic for Vosnesyensky; he failed to take the economic situation of Russia into account in his calculations. Finally he got himself so hopelessly embroiled with the Foreign Office that he was threatened with arrest but was eventually allowed to resign and retire to the country where he was living with his wife at the time of my second arrest. Like many other Soviet intransigents, I firmly believe that Vosnesyensky was an unconscious nationalist; his aim was to see the Slav and Slav influence predominant in Europe and in Asia.

It was in Vosnesyensky's office that I met Krasnoschokov,[10] the head of the Far Eastern Republic. Krasnoshchokov was quite well known in America. He lived for many years in Chicago under the name of Tobelson, where he was the head of a Jewish orphan asylum and I believe practiced law as well. He was a man of extremely liberal views, recognizing the fact that a coalition government in Siberia was absolutely necessary, and he fought the matter out successfully with Moscow. Krasnoshchokov is a man in the late forties, a Jew of the blond type, smooth-shaven, with a firm, square jaw and keen grey eyes. Naturally he speaks English very well. He believed it would be a long time before the majority of the population in Siberia would come to accept a Soviet Government based on strictly Communistic principles, and considered that it was wiser to first build up the resources of the country under a modified capitalistic system.

Personally I believe that Krasnoshchokov is an extremely good politician and something of an opportunist. He will steer a middle course in Siberia as long as he can, then swing to the right or left, according to the state of the political barometer.

The Commissar from Omsk who succeeded Vosnesyensky as head of the Eastern Section of the Foreign Office was a very liberal man and he was responsible for safe conducts issued to many Americans and Englishmen who later arrived in Moscow with his permission and were decidedly unwelcome guests of the Soviet Government.

Occasionally I had fantastic experiences which gave me queer glimpses into the underworld of intrigue and propaganda in Moscow. Once I was called on the telephone by a mysterious person who asked me if I would be willing to translate an article from an English magazine into German.

"Certainly," I answered, "but before I can state my terms, I must see the article and know with whom I am dealing."

"My principal cannot tell his name," was the answer.

By this time my curiosity was aroused, so I told the man to bring me the article. It proved to be an article on the ciphers in use in the British War Office and the publication in which it appeared was the *British Army Journal*. I cannot imagine what use it would have been to the owner, as the British certainly do not publish the keys to their most secret ciphers, but there was evidently some reason which I could not fathom. I put a prohibitive price on my services and never heard anything more from my mysterious German friend.

....

10. A.M. Krasnoschokov (1880-1937) joined the Bolsheviks in 1917 and served in the Foreign Office. He was arrested in 1937 and died in prison.

Among my acquaintances was a German aviation officer who had flown to Russia in the autumn of 1919 with the first drugs and medical supplies brought from Germany. His plane had fallen near Vitebsk and he had been badly injured, but after his recovery he remained in Moscow for many months, well treated and apparently on a mission from the German junkers who were undoubtedly intriguing with the Soviet Government at the time of the Kapp Putsch in Berlin.[11]

I also met a Hungarian, posing as the agent of the Red Cross, universally condemned as an international crook and speculator, and yet he seemed to enjoy peculiar immunity, coming and going between Russia and Berlin with great frequency. The German officer lived at his apartment. Such clues picked up from time to time were very interesting to me. I wondered if, after all, the Allies had only scotched their snake, not killed him. Many stray bits of evidence seemed to point to the fact that Pan-Germanism is slowly and painfully beginning to blaze a new trail from Berlin to Baghdad, via Moscow and Tashkent.

Once I had a telephone message from a Russian who refused to give his name and asked me to meet him at an appointed time on a certain street corner. Curiosity got the better of prudence and I went. There I found a young man exceedingly well dressed, of rather prepossessing appearance. He had a short, curly beard, and when I looked at him more closely I saw that it was false. This at once aroused my suspicions. He proceeded to tell me, with an apparent amazing lack of caution, without stopping to find out my own political opinions, that he was a counter-revolutionary, in fact a Monarchist. His father and two brothers had been shot, he told me, under the most brutal circumstances, and his one thought was revenge. He was connected with a counter-revolutionary Russian group in Berlin, of whom the head was a man whose name, as I recall it, was General Bitkopsky; he would be undyingly grateful to me if, on leaving Russia I would agree to take a letter through to the general.

I told him that his confidence in a stranger was overwhelming, to say the least. "Moreover," I added, "if you are trying to conceal your identity you should be a little more careful about the way you put on that false beard." He was nothing more or less than an agent of the Moscow Cheka who had been sent to test my political opinions.

---

11. The Kapp Putsch in Berlin was an attempted coup to overthrow the Weimar Government in 1920 in protest of the conditions of the 1919 Treaty of Versailles.

CHAPTER XII
Bureaus and Bureaucrats

*E*ndless visits to commissars, commissariats and Soviet institutions form part of the regular routine of foreign correspondents in Moscow. They usually take up a tremendous amount of time and energy, owing partly to the fact that no Russian has the faintest value of time and partly to the enormous distances to be covered. The street railway system does not operate between October and the end of April, and when the cars started running they were always so crowded that it was as much as one's life was worth to get on, much less secure a seat, as there was a tremendous car shortage. *Izvozchiks*[1] were outrageously expensive. I never understood why, in view of the utterly inadequate transportation facilities, the Soviet Government did not nationalize the cabbies. They were the most brazen profiteers in Moscow. It was impossible even after bargaining for at least ten minutes to induce one to take you anywhere for less than fifteen hundred rubles, this at a time when a ruble was twenty-five hundred to the dollar, and a trip of any length cost from ten to twelve thousand rubles. Occasionally we were promised a government automobile, but it frequently failed to show up altogether or arrived an hour or two late. Kerosene was the only motor fuel, all cars were in bad condition, and we often got stuck in the snow, or broke down by the roadside. Consequently I made most of these excursions on foot.

It often happened that commissars forgot their engagements or absented themselves without a word of apology as in the case of H. N. Brailsford,[2] the distinguished English journalist, who stayed at my guest house. Although he

1. The Russian word for cabbies.
2. Henry Noel Brailsford (1893-1953) was a well-known left-wing British journalist who was in Russia in 1920 and 1926.

was writing for the *London Daily Herald*, which was said to be subsidized by the Soviet Government, he left Russia without seeing either Lenin or Lunacharsky, the two men he particularly wished to see, with both of whom he had engagements which were broken at the last minute. I was more fortunate, owing to the fact that I spent a much longer time in Russia than most correspondents, and was able to accommodate myself to Russian habits of procrastination.

Perhaps the most interesting of my interviews with various commissars was one with Dzerzhinsky,[3] Commissar of Internal Affairs and Chairman of the Extraordinary Commission, popularly known as the Cheka, who, as it

Felix Dzerzhinsky

afterwards proved, was my jailer for nearly a year. He was probably meditating locking me up when I called on him in the early spring at his office in the headquarters of the Extraordinary Commission, a ramshackle building on the Lubyanka. I arrived at the appointed time, and was escorted up a narrow stairway into a rather gloomy room with two windows looking out into a small court. There was apparently only one door, that by which I had come in, two sides were lined with bookcases reaching almost to the ceiling. I was told by a clerk that the Commissar would see me in a few minutes. In a little while a desk telephone rang, the clerk got up, and much to my amazement, opened the door of one of the bookcases and asked me to walk in. It was a secret passage leading to Dzerzhinsky's office, a tiny cabinet with one window. Seated at a huge desk was a mild looking little blond man, whom I at first took for Dzerzhinsky's secretary, and it was at least a minute before I realized that I was talking to the most feared man in all Russia.

Dzerzhinsky is a Pole of very good family and inherited estates near Svenchyany[4] in the province of Vilna. He has been a Revolutionary since before the Revolution of 1905 and spent eleven years in prison under Nicholas II. As I looked at him I recalled what I had read of the frailty and refinement of Robespierre. He is slender, slightly under average height, with fair hair, rather thin around the temples, a small, pointed beard, clean cut, aristocratic

---

3. Felix Dzerzhinsky (1877-1926) was a professional revolutionary since the nineteenth century. He was the first chief of the Cheka. He held numerous other positions in the early Bolshevik government. He died of a heart attack in 1926.
4. Today it is referred to as Svencionys in Lithuania.

features, skin as smooth as a child's and cheeks flushed with hectic color, for he contracted tuberculosis while in prison. I had dozens of questions to ask him, but he forestalled them all by describing to me the activities of the Extraordinary Commission since its creation in the early days of the Revolution, stating quite frankly that it was an organization duplicating in many respects, the Okhrana, the Tsar's secret police, but that it was both justified and necessitated by post-revolutionary conditions. He claimed, and I believe this to be substantially true, that the majority of executions in Russia at the present time, are not political, but chiefly for banditism, speculation, espionage and army desertion.

It is perfectly true that the Cheka has succeeded in restoring order in the great cities. Moscow and Petrograd are safer for the average citizen, as far as highway robbery and lawlessness are concerned, than any of the large cities of Europe or America, but, on the other hand, he is never safe from arrest.

Two stories which came to my personal knowledge will serve to illustrate the methods of the Cheka. A commissar in charge of issuing food cards devised a scheme, with the cooperation of six of his employees, of issuing three hundred food cards to fictitious individuals. The supplies collected in this manner were sold by the gang on the open market, the commissar receiving sixty percent of the proceeds and his confederates the remainder. In time of partial famine, such as actually then existed in Moscow, there could be no greater crime against the community. The man was detected by the Cheka and shot. He certainly richly deserved his fate.

On the other hand, I knew of two brothers who were arrested for counter-revolutionary activities. They had no accomplices and the only way to convict them was to get one to implicate the other. After repeated cross-examinations the examining judge found that the elder brother was of a far more nervous temperament than his junior, so he resorted to strategy. He informed him that his brother had been shot and that the only way for him to save himself was to confess his part in the affair. The man refused to believe him.

"Very well," said the judge, "we will show you his dead body."

Meanwhile he compelled the younger brother to undress and had ordered his clothes put on the body of a man who had really been shot. It was placed in a dimly lighted room, the face of the corpse being purposely disfigured by gunshot wounds, that would make identification difficult, but the two men were very similar in build. Being completely unnerved the elder brother was not disposed to be too minute in his examination of the body and believing it to be that of his brother he made a full confession. He was then taken to his cell where he awaited his release. After three weeks he was summoned by one of the Cheka guards and taken to a courtroom of the Revolutionary tribunal where he was confronted with his brother against whom he was the principal witness.

With regard to shootings which actually occurred in Moscow during my stay, I believe the monthly statistics published by the Cheka to be approximately correct. There were several hundred each in March, April and May, increasing to about six hundred in June, and eight hundred in July, owing to the Polish offensive. Few people were shot as counter-revolutionists, the majority being committed to internment camps. No one is shot at the present time on sight, so to speak, and all accused prisoners go through some form of trial either before the Revolutionary Tribunals or the Presidium, the governing body of the Cheka. People were arrested and often held for months for the most trivial reasons, frequently as witnesses or again simply for the purpose of isolation during political agitations. The whole system is bad in theory, in practice it is subject to many abuses, and often misused for the gratification of personal grievances. But terrorism as we understand the word does not exist except in provincial prisons, where cruel or unscrupulous officials often order unjustified executions without the knowledge or sanction of Moscow. Many liberal Communists are much opposed to the Cheka and it is planned to eventually abolish it altogether, putting the entire administration of justice in the hands of the People's Courts, with right of appeal to the Central Executive Committee sitting as the Supreme Court. But the Cheka has a strong hold and is supported by the ultramontane elements[5] in the Communist party. Whenever there is an agitation for the abolishment of the Extraordinary Commission or curbing its power to inflict the death sentence, the *Pravda* and *Izvestia* are filled with accounts of dangerous conspiracies frequently said to be instigated from abroad. Unfortunately there is just enough truth in them to support the claim of the Cheka that it is a necessary institution.

Kursky,[6] the Commissar of Justice, formerly a well-known lawyer, who is in charge of the People's Courts, told me that he was working on a scheme for a code of laws based on the decrees of the Council of People's Commissars and other administrative bodies, which for the present take the place of laws. They are constantly changing and are frequently innocently violated by people

---

5. Ultramontane: a term that refers to a movement in the Roman Catholic Church that favors the centralized authority and influence of the Pope as opposed to local independence.
6. Dmitry I. Kursky (1874-1932) joined the Bolsheviks in 1904. He served as the Commissar of Justice from 1918 to 1928.

who have not had time or who are unable to read them as published in the newspapers pasted on the walls, which are their only source of information.

Once I took an all day trip with Rykov,[7] then Chairman of the Supreme Economic Council, to inspect a new electric power plant in process of construction some sixty *versts* from Moscow. In our party were Losovsky, Chairman of the All Russian Council of Trades Unions, a number of engineers and several foreign correspondents. On the train I had a long conversation with Rykov, who was formerly one of the heads of the cooperatives. He told me something of the organization of the Supreme Council, which at that time had fifty departments controlling nearly five thousand nationalized industries, and all the cooperatives, comprising the entire machinery of production and distribution in Russia.

He was a delightful host, but he struck me as being a rather vague and unpractical person. The plant we visited was one of the links in the vast scheme for the electrification of Russia, planned by the great engineer Kryzhyanovsky, which if it is carried out, will perhaps in twenty-five years' time supply light and power to every city, town and village in Russia. Railroads, plants and factories will be operated by electricity and such a tremendous saving of labor will be effected that no one will have to work more than three or four hours a day. Rykov explained all this to me with enthusiasm while showing us around the plant.

It was being built close to large peat deposits which were to supply the fuel and where machines for cutting and drying peat were already installed. The powerhouse, which was to furnish seven thousand kilowatts daily, was nearly finished, and as they were not able to get turbines, the constructing engineers had utilized two turbines from dismantled battleships at Kronstadt.[8] A short distance away was a model workmen's village with attractive wooden cottages, a large community dining hall, a splendid schoolhouse and a recreation center. It was a Utopian scheme in miniature.

Meanwhile Rykov was actually facing a shortage of fuel, raw material and labor, which had closed practically all the factories in Russia except the most essential industries. The cumbrous departments of the Supreme Economic Council were overburdened with red tape, the cooperatives were unable

....

7. Alexei I. Rykov (1881-1938) joined the Bolsheviks at the turn of the twentieth century. He served in several positions in the early Soviet government including the Chairman of the Supreme Economic Council also known as the Higher Council of National Economy. He was executed under Stalin in 1938.

8. Kronstadt is a Russian seaport town on Kotlin Island in the Gulf of Finland that served as a key naval installation.

to supply the needs of the people, the transportation system was utterly inadequate, but Rykov and his associates with characteristic Russian idealism were dreaming of a future millennium.

I found the same attitude of mind on the part of Sereda,[9] Commissar of Agriculture, whose pet scheme is the organization of the rural farm communes which so far have not proved a success. The wonderful propaganda and educational work of the Commissariat is overbalanced by the fact that they lack the practical arguments, seeds, agricultural implements, and farm machinery to convert the peasants to Communist methods and to stimulate agricultural production.

Schmidt,[10] the Commissar of Labor, is quite an able man and a German by birth. He lives in the Kremlin and his mother, who was formerly a cook in the palace of one of the Russian Grand Duchesses, says that she doesn't know much about the Revolution, but she knows that her boy has certainly got a fine position. Her favorite amusement is to sit at her window on the ground floor of her apartment and hand out homemade cakes to passing Red Army men.

Every Russian citizen between the ages of eighteen and fifty for men and eighteen and forty for women, must be a worker and must register through the work exchange of the Commissariat of Labor, which acts in cooperation with the Trades Unions. Efficiency of industrial labor has been tremendously decreased owing to living conditions, conscriptions for the army, exodus of skilled workers to the country, where they obtain better food and pay, and the influx of unskilled peasant workers who have no means of cultivating their land. Many of the best factory workers are Communists and are excused to do propaganda work.

In the Commissariats there is much sabotage, much padding of payrolls and much inefficiency, largely due to the complicated bureaucratic system, and there is an enormous amount of official corruption, an inheritance from the old regime. One of my friends at the Foreign Office was the head of the financial section. He was a middle-aged man with a taste for old porcelain and furniture. One day when I was in his office to collect a draft sent me by radio from the office of the Associated Press at Copenhagen, he showed me all his treasures, comprising two beautiful Sevres vases and a silver-inlaid musket, which had belonged to Peter the Great. The next time I inquired for him I was told he was

---

9. Semen P. Sereda (1871-1933) served as Commissar of Agriculture from 1918-1921.
10. Vasily V. Schmidt served as Commissar of Labor from 1918 to 1928.

out, and I afterwards discovered that he had been arrested, convicted and shot for speculation.

In several Commissariats, such as that of Posts and Telegraphs and that of Ways and Communications, which handles rail and water transportation, the old personnel has remained to a large extent. In the former, the same employees in the Foreign Mail Censorship department who examined all outgoing letters for the Tsar's Okhrana are performing the identical service for the Cheka.

One of the most efficient Commissariats is that of Public Health, under Dr. Semashko,[11] who is a remarkably capable, hard-working man, and he has done wonders with the limited means at his disposal. He is tremendously handicapped by the shortage of physicians and medical and surgical supplies. All physicians are nationalized and the best have been taken into the army sanitary service. A feature of the work of the Public Health department is its educational campaign. It gets out an enormous amount of literature in popular form. One of the most amusing of its pamphlets was one written in verse, in which it described how disease is spread by vermin. A number of disinfecting and delousing plants have been constructed in Moscow, Petrograd and other cities, and periodical "Weeks of Cleanliness" and "Bath Weeks" are held, but sanitary conditions in all Russian cities are bad, owing to the complete or partial breakdown of plumbing and water supply systems, lack of repair material, skilled workmen and the utter disregard by the majority of the people of the observance of ordinary rules of cleanliness or decency. I doubt if they are much worse in this respect than they were in the old days.

The most interesting of all the Commissariats to me was the Commissariat of Education, which is indirectly one of the most important political factors in Russia at the present time. It has done more than anything else to keep up the morale of the people during a period of intolerable suffering and privation and it is teaching the people of Russia to think for themselves. Until its work is accomplished, there can never be any form of genuine popular government in Russia.

Lunacharsky, Commissar of Education, is an extremely cultivated man, who speaks nearly all European languages fluently. Although a Communist by training he is far more of a Maximalist[12] by instinct, and an artist and individualist to his fingertips. When I saw him in his apartment in the Kremlin,

11. Dr. Nikolai A. Semashko (1874-1949) was an early Bolshevik and served as the Commissar of Public Health from 1918 to 1930.
12. The Maximalists were a terrorist faction of the Socialist Revolutionary Party that claimed hundreds of lives from 1905 to 1907.

in a seventeenth century palace, alluringly christened the "Palace of Little Pleasures," and formerly the residence of the commander of the Kremlin, he talked to me chiefly of the Proletcult, his great scheme for making world culture accessible to the masses of the people, and little of the general plan of education.

He was enthusiastic about the formation of dramatic clubs for workmen and sent me to the director of this department, through whom I later saw some very interesting performances of this character. Lunacharsky told me that he believed the best of the world's dramas and literature should be placed within the reach of the people, without any intermediate preparatory stage, trusting to what he is convinced is their own unerring and uncorrupted aesthetic sense. In some cases his theories have worked out with startling results, though not always in the way he intended. For example, he had an idea that the peasants would enjoy the ballet, and sent the ballet from the Grand Opera House in

Anatoly Lunacharsky

Moscow to make a provincial tour in small towns where nothing of the sort had ever been seen before. Instead of being entranced by the beauty and color of the thing, the peasants were profoundly shocked by the display of the bare arms and legs of the coryphees and left the performances before they were over, thoroughly disgusted.

While I was talking to Lunacharsky, his two children, a boy and girl about nine and twelve years old, respectively, came in, asking permission to go to a performance at the children's theater. I found that they did not live in one of the many children's homes, but with their parents, and attended day school like any other children in capitalist countries. Contrary to general opinion, the placing of children in homes or other institutions is not compulsory in Russia, but it is easier for the average parents who are compelled to work all day and who find it difficult to take proper care of their children and to go through the red tape necessary to collect the rations and clothing given out on cards. The public school system in Russia is magnificent in theory; according to the general plan of education, every Russian citizen will eventually be able to obtain an education absolutely free, under a uniform school system, extending from the kindergarten grade to the most highly specialized technical or professional training.

At present it is hampered by material difficulties. I knew of many children who were not able to go to school at all, owing to the fact that they had no shoes or clothing; others who lived in districts where the schools were closed on account of disrepair or lack of fuel for heating purposes. Hundreds of them spent their days in the streets, speculating or stealing, while their parents were at work, and the amount of juvenile immorality among children of this class was appalling. Thousands more lived in the children's homes, which, as a whole, were very well run and exceedingly interesting. They were usually in the former residences of rich bourgeois and were organized on the cottage plan, not more than twenty children to a house. They were of both sexes, ranging in age from three to sixteen, in order to give the atmosphere of normal family life. The boys and girls slept in separate rooms, the little ones being taken care of by the larger ones, who did most of the manual work. The older children went to school, the little ones being taught at home, often in a thoroughly modern manner, by teachers trained in the Montessori system. Great attention was given to developing originality and initiative, and of course the authorities saw to it that they received thorough grounding in the principles of Communism. If the Soviet Government remains in power for some years it will be very interesting to see what hold the Communistic idea gets on the younger generation, starting out without any preconceived ideas or prejudices. In one of the homes I saw a little girl about five years old playing with a doll.

"What a pretty dolly," I said. "Is she yours?"

"Oh, no," was the quick reply, "she isn't my dolly, she's our dolly."

In another home I saw an impromptu performance of one of the fables of Krylov,[13] the Russian La Fontaine, by tots between four and six. Each child wore a crudely painted muslin mask representing one of the animal characters. Not one forgot or stumbled over a line, and the way they entered into the spirit of the thing was remarkable. The wolf was ill-natured and snarling, the bear delightfully clumsy, the little fox had just the right mixture of servility and cunning, and the lamb was appropriately meek and terrified in such strange company.

In the suburbs I saw a well run home for tubercular children equipped in a thoroughly up-to-date manner, a home for orthopedic cases and a sanatorium for children physically under par, where they received particularly nourishing

13. Ivan Krylov (1769-1844) is one of Russia's best-known writers of fables.

food and spent part of each day during the Summer lying naked in the sun. There was also a fascinating school in Moscow for children who showed unusual aptitude for music, drawing or dancing. Dancing was taught by the Dalcroze[14] method and some of the little pupils gave really remarkable exhibitions of interpretative dancing. I also saw a splendid home for defective children. The food in these institutions and in the primary and secondary schools, where every registered pupil gets one hot meal a day, is far above the average of that obtained in adult dining-rooms, though it is not sufficient by any means. It varies greatly, depending upon the supplies on hand in the Moscow Food Administration and the honesty of the individual superintendent. One day I dropped in unannounced at two dining rooms not far apart, where the rations for the day should have been similar. At one the children had a good thick soup, roast pork with kasha, and a large piece of black bread; at the other they had a soup like warm dishwater, a small portion of kasha, and nothing more.

Registration in the University of Moscow was enormous, amounting to about five thousand pupils, but the attendance was relatively very small, owing to the fact that the buildings could not be properly heated. I found many of the old professors in charge of the courses, and they fared tolerably well as they obtained the academic *payok*, a food ration superior to the average. They were terribly handicapped in many cases by the lack of textbooks and laboratory material. The students were, as a rule, not actively interested in politics, in distinct contrast to the old days, and if they had any political opinions at all they were inclined to be reactionary rather than otherwise.

The working schools, which are run in connection with the public school system, where the children receive practical vocational and technical training, are very interesting. I saw some of the concrete results of this training at an exhibition at the Stroganov Institute,[15] where there were some excellent samples of textile designing and weaving, pottery, woodcuts, lithographs, toys, furniture and mechanical models made by boys and girls from twelve to sixteen.

I have already spoken of the classes for adult illiterates in the Red Army. These have been extended to the civilian population and are part of the Communist propaganda, many party workers volunteering as teachers in clubs or factories.

Many of the teachers in Soviet schools and institutions are non-Communists. Numbers of them have been engaged in educational work for many years.

....

14. This is a dance method based on the teaching of Swiss composer Emile Jacques Dalcroze (1865-1956).
15. The Stroganov Institute is one of Russia's oldest schools of art and design, founded in 1825 by Sergei G. Stroganov.

While bitterly opposed to the Soviet Government on principle, they are absorbed in their work and very happy in being able, even with the tremendous material difficulties existing at the present time, to carry out their theories and ideas, for in all matters connected with art, science or education, the Soviet Government is remarkably, often exaggeratedly, liberal. It is always willing to try new methods; many of those in practical operation at the present time were thought out by idealists many years ago under the Czar's regime and cherished in secret. Altogether, the new system of education in Russia is admirable in theory. "But," the average foreigner will ask, "to what extent are the Bolsheviks putting it into practice?" Roughly speaking, I should say that in the parts of Russia where reasonably normal conditions exist, possibly forty percent of the children are receiving an education. In Moscow and Petrograd the percentage is much higher; in the country districts very much lower as a rule.

CHAPTER XIII
Icons and Anti-Christ

One of the facts that struck me most forcibly in Moscow was that the churches were invariably packed to the doors at the services. I often dropped in at vespers or high mass on Sunday at churches in various parts of the city, and there was always an enormous congregation. It occurred to me that it would be extremely interesting to find out about the position of the church from other than government officials. So, having learned from some of my Russian friends that the Patriarch Tikhon[1] was living in Moscow under house arrest in the palace of the former Metropolitan Bishop, I went to call on him, accompanied by Francis McCullagh.

The Metropolitan's palace, which is tucked away behind one of the boulevards, was hard to find, but we managed to locate it by means of a street map, rang the bell and were ushered in by an ancient flunky in faded dark blue knickerbockers and coat adorned with gold lace, and wearing worn-out buckled slippers, to the office of a deacon who was acting as his secretary. At first the latter was not at all inclined to even take in our names to the Patriarch, but when he found that Mr. McCullagh was a Catholic, and was leaving shortly for England, he consented to ask him if he would receive us. The Patriarch, even in the old days, was known as a man of exceedingly liberal views, and one of his dreams has always been a federation of the three great Christian denominations — Orthodox, Anglican and Catholic churches. He believes that only by some such cooperation can Christianity be saved and the present wave of social unrest be stayed in Europe and America.

....

1. Patriarch Tikhon (1865-1925) was a well-respected head of the Russian Orthodox Church who was later arrested and died in 1925 under suspicious circumstances.

After a short absence the deacon returned to say that the Patriarch would see us, and we were shown upstairs to the Metropolitan's audience chamber, a once beautiful room with walls of pale blue brocade adorned with portraits of former Bishops and church dignitaries, with rococo gilt furniture upholstered in the same delicate shade, but a bit down at the heel like the old retainer and everything else in the house. There was evidently not enough coal to heat the building, for we could see our breath as we sat on a sofa at the end of a long gilt table with a superb inlaid top and waited for the Patriarch.

In a few minutes the ancient retainer, who seemed to constitute the Patriarch's sole retinue, flung open the door at the end of the room with a low bow, and Tikhon came in, looking every inch a prince of the church and showing no ill effects from his confinement. He was dressed in a long cassock of rich black silk. Around his neck was a jeweled chain terminating in a superb cross, on his index finger was his ring, which Mr. McCullagh kissed devoutly. He wore on his head the traditional headdress of the Greek church, a close-fitting helmet-like cap of white velvet beautifully embroidered in seed pearls, with long rounded tabs that fell on either side of his full grey beard, and surmounted by a gold cross studded with diamonds and rubies. Such ceremony seemed rather futile under actual conditions, but I could not help admiring the old gentleman's fine spirit and his insistence on keeping up the semblance of pomp and circumstance.

He greeted us in Russian, apologizing at the same time for the fact that he had forgotten most of his French, and was much relieved when he found we understood the Russian language.

"I also once spoke a little English," he added, "but that was many years ago when I was Bishop of Alaska, and I remember very well visiting Minneapolis when it was a small town. I suppose it is a great city now."

We asked him to give us an idea of the position of the Orthodox Church and its relation to the Soviet Government. He told us that while he was a constitutional Monarchist, and on those as well as on ecclesiastical grounds, bitterly opposed to Bolshevism, he believed that the Bolsheviks had done one good thing for the Russian church, by bringing about the separation of church and state. Formerly the priest was merely a government functionary, working as such, generally without any sense of particular fitness for his vocation.[2] Sons of priests inherited the right to go to seminaries and become candidates for the priesthood. Most of them were lazy, inefficient; they were often immoral and

---

2. Peter the Great (1682-1725), effectively made the Russian Orthodox Church a part of the government, with limited independence from state control.

great drunkards. Discipline of the clergy by the church itself was very difficult if a priest happened, as was often the case, to have the protection and patronage of one of the great nobles. The people were compelled to support the priest, and his parish visits were made mainly with the object of collecting his tithes in kind and money. Now, the people, when they supported their priest, did so voluntarily and at great personal sacrifice to themselves. He had to give them of his best, and be a very superior sort of man at that in order to keep his parish.

The Soviet Government allowed in each parish as many priests and churches as the parishioners were willing to support, and had left all the churches in possession of their icons, robes and sacramental vessels, many of which were of

great beauty and represented untold millions in value, although it had dispossessed the church of all its lands and revenues. The church treasures were technically the property of the state, but were held in trust for it by the priest. Duplicate lists of the contents of every church were made by a commissar acting for the Soviet Government, one copy being retained by the priest. Once a year the list was checked over by the priest and commissar to see that nothing was missing. A number of priests had been arrested for counter-revolutionary activities and, as far as he had been able to compile a list, which was difficult owing

Patriarch Tikhon

to poor facilities for communications, three hundred and twenty-two bishops and priests had been executed since the beginning of the Revolution.

At the moment, the Patriarch believed that the influence of the church on the lives of the people was stronger than it had ever been in all its history, but he was dubious as to its future if the Communist dictatorship kept up too long. In the first place, he said, it was impossible to hold convocations of the clergy for the purpose of ordaining priests or bishops to take the places of those who died or were arrested or executed, as priests and ecclesiastical dignitaries were not permitted to travel. Secondly, all the seminaries and theological schools had been closed and there would be no new generation of priests to take the place of the others. Then the church was obliged to give up all its parish schools and the Soviet administration was conducting a strong anti-religious propaganda among the school children. Parents, however, could instruct their children in religion and send them to the priests for individual teaching.

As regarded his own part in the movement against Bolshevism, I gathered that he was content for the time at least to rest on his laurels. He had, about a year before, gotten out an encyclical against Bolshevism, but he realized, like the intellectuals, that the time for active propaganda was not ripe, and that any conspiratorial action would not only be quite useless, but would remove from the people one of their great sources of strength and consolation. My estimate of him was that he was absolutely sincere, with a fine conception of the dignity of his office and his mission, but a man of limited intellectual capacity and rather passive in character. He spoke to us with the enthusiasm of an idealistic dreamer about the union of the churches. As to his treatment by the Soviet authorities he said that he had nothing of which he could complain, and he was rather inclined to be reserved about anything touching on political matters.

My own observations bore out his assertions, though I believe that he rather underestimated the strength of the religious movement in Russia at the present time. In the provinces as well as in Moscow the churches were always crowded, and I talked to a number of provincial priests, who told me that they had never lived so well on tithes as they were then living on the voluntary contributions of their parishioners. In the Church of St. Khariton, just across the way from my guest house, several artists from the Moscow Grand Opera sang in the choir. I was often astonished at the piles of five hundred and thousand-ruble notes heaped on the plate during the offertory. Sometimes, standing during the long services, I was struck by the rapt devotion on the faces of the people around me, many of whom were Red Armists in uniform. In the children's homes run by the Soviet Government I frequently noticed icons, or sacred images, tied to the heads of the beds. In the churches, in spite of the high price of kerosene and the fact that many homes in Moscow were actually in darkness on account of the inability of families to purchase fuel for lamps, I saw hundreds of votive candles, and at all hours of the day there were always scores of devout worshipers with votive offerings before the shrine of the Virgin of Iberia[3] at the entrance to the Red Square, in full view of the often quoted sign on the Moscow municipal building, just across the way, that "Religion Is Opium to the People."

I was much interested in the effect produced by the opening of the "*moschi,*" or bodies of the saints, which was undertaken by the Soviet Government some two years ago to prove to the people that their sacred relics were dummies of old

3. A copy of the Iberian Virgin was painted on the Resurrection Gate in Red Square in 1648. The icon was removed to the Cathedral of the Resurrection in Sokolniki when the Iberia Chapel and Resurrection Gate and were torn down in 1929 and 1931, respectively. The gate and chapel were rebuilt at the entrance to Red Square in 1996.

clothes, papier-mache, cotton-wool and straw. It was given the widest possible publicity by pamphlets, newspaper articles and motion pictures, but on the whole produced very little effect. The great mass of the people never knew anything about it, owing to the fact that they could not read, and movies and propaganda workers could not reach the country districts. Some were bitterly disillusioned and turned against the church, others were simply indifferent, and many devout persons believed with touching naivete, as one old peasant said to me, "*Baryshchnya*,[4] our holy saints disappeared to heaven and substituted rags and straw for their relics when they found that their tombs were to be desecrated by nonbelievers. It was a great miracle."

I once had an opportunity of seeing how the dispossessed nuns who still adhere to their vows are living at the present time, when I accompanied young Madame Brusilov to the convent of Novodevichy[5] on the outskirts of Moscow, which was once a fashionable boarding-school, and where she was herself a pupil. A great many of the convents and monasteries have been taken over by the government as internment camps, but there are certain ones in Moscow and throughout the provinces where the monks and nuns are allowed to remain undisturbed in part of their old quarters, the remainder being occupied by working people. This was the case with the nuns at Novodevichy. They were permitted to live in one of the houses inside the huge red wall surrounding the convent enclosure, which shelters five churches, a tall bell tower, and a number of buildings formerly used by the nuns, lay sisters, and boarding pupils.

The mother superior, about twenty nuns and as many lay sisters still occupied the building formerly reserved for the lay sisters only. I had tea with one of the nuns in her little room, which was spotlessly clean. She gave us delicious tea, made on a beautiful old brass samovar, and apologized for not being able to offer us anything but her scanty supply of black bread, which we refused to eat, for we had brought our own bread, and sugar, which we shared with her, for she had none. She was a sweet-faced, gentle-voiced woman, utterly resigned to her fate, utterly uncomprehending of the great movement that had swept away her world, and she lived on a bit bewildered by all the changes, clinging instinctively to the shelter of the familiar walls, her long black robe and medieval headdress. She told me that the nuns were given their quarters free by the Soviet Government, that they were quite unmolested and had excellent relations with

....

4. A term for a young Russian woman.
5. The Novodevichy Convent was founded in Moscow in the early sixteenth century. Later, Peter the Great's half-sister and first wife were forced to take the veil there. It was closed by the Bolsheviks in 1922.

the working people who occupied the rest of the convent buildings, but that they received no food, fuel or clothing rations, and were debarred from work in all government offices or institutions. She particularly regretted being cut off from work among the children whom she loved. The nuns supported themselves, she said, by going out for the day as domestic servants or seamstresses, and doing fine needlework, making underclothes and summer dresses for the wives of the rich commissars. Their former pupils brought them donations of money and food and thus they managed to get along, living from hand to mouth.

In the cathedral of the convent I found all the treasures, including the famous, reputedly miraculous image of the Virgin of Smolensk, absolutely intact, although they represented many thousands of dollars in value. The Virgin of Smolensk is a typical Byzantine madonna of the sixteenth century, and she is fairly engulfed in an enormous headdress of gold wire strung with pearls in an intricate lace pattern, studded with huge emeralds, diamonds, rubies and other precious stones.[6] In the same church are other icons of almost equal value, and over the tombs of many of the Tsarinas, including the wife and two sisters of Peter the Great, are still hung their personal icons, which they used during their lives, several of them exquisitely painted and set in frames studded with precious stones or enriched with the wonderful old Russian enamels. I have often heard it said that many of the stones in the icons are imitation, having been replaced years ago by unscrupulous priests. How true this is I do not know; perhaps the Bolsheviks do; but I saw many superb vessels which were evidently of real silver or gold and which had not been touched.

Among the ecclesiastics in general in Moscow I found many interesting tendencies, for there is now, as always, a great latitude of opinion among the higher clergy. Bishop Turkestanov,[7] one of the most eloquent preachers in the Orthodox Church, was very fearless in his upholding of the old order and his denunciation of the existing regime. Bishop Varnava, an equally well known prince of the church, had declared himself to be a Christian Communist and it was whispered by many people that he was an agent of the much dreaded

6. It is not certain if here Harrison is talking about one of the most revered of Orthodox icons, the Virgin of Smolensk; she may have seen a locally made reproduction. Eastern Orthodox legend asserts that the original icon was painted by St. Luke, and later made its way to the Monastery of the Panaghia Hodegetria in Constantinople, which was built specially to contain it. It disappeared in 1453, during the fall of Constantinople. The Russian Church then claimed that the icon surfaced in the Cathedral in Smolensk, and it was later brought to Moscow on several occasions and Novodevichy Monastery was built in its honor. The icon is believed to have perished in a fire in 1941, during the Nazi occupation of Smolensk.
7. Most likely she is referring to Metropolitan Trifon, who was born Boris P. Turkestanov (1861-1934).

Cheka. An Archimandrite whom I met, Father Arsene by name, consoled himself with metaphysical speculations and the writing of erotic verse, which he read to me with great gusto. Other priests were deeply interested in theosophy and spiritualism, which, in Russia, as in other war-ridden countries, has taken a great hold on the popular imagination.

The Catholic church is also quite strong in Russia. Acting on instructions from Rome, the Catholic clergy have taken no part in any political activities or preached against Bolshevism, and they are allowed to work undisturbed. In Minsk, Vitebsk and in Western Russia I found the Uniates, who are very close to the Catholic church, were steadily but quietly enlarging their membership. There were three Catholic churches in Moscow, all Polish, but in spite of this disadvantage, during the days of the Polish offensive they managed to keep open and escape any suspicion of political activity. I knew the Polish priest of the largest church, in the Maly Lubyanka, within a stone's throw of the prison of the Cheka, very well. He was a delightful man, a hopeless invalid, and a great philosopher. As a Pole he deplored the Polish offensive as a source of great internal danger to Poland through the embarking on a militaristic policy, which he believed would sooner or later lead to revolution, and as the cause of a reinforcement of Bolshevik morale by the creation of intense national feeling. There was also a small Russian Catholic group in Moscow in which I was much interested. It was headed by Father Vladimir, one of the Abrikosovs[8] who were among the fabulously rich merchants of old Russia. His followers, several hundred in number, were known as the Abrikosi, and went back in their observances to the early days of the Catholic church, following the liturgy of the Christian martyrs and practicing an extreme asceticism.

Starting from Galicia, in the days of Petlura, the Catholic church began an active propaganda in the Ukraine which was productive of great results and has not entirely ceased at the present time. That the Bolsheviks still fear this propaganda was shown by the publication last summer of documents alleged to have been discovered in the Ukraine by agents of the Extraordinary Commission, disclosing the existence of a secret agreement between the Pope and Petlura. The story was as follows:

During the war, the Vatican was said to have loaned considerable sums of money to the Italian Government, which the latter was unable to pay at its close,

---

8. The Abrikosov family was an old merchant family dating back to the early nineteenth century in Moscow. In 1908, Anna I. Abrikosova (1882-1936) converted to Catholicism and became the head of the Catholic community in Moscow. She was arrested several times by the Bolsheviks between 1923 and her death in prison in 1936.

turning over instead to His Holiness a large quantity of leftover munitions. Count Tuskievitch, then emissary of Petlura to Rome, offered to take them off the Pope's hands. He agreed, stipulating for compensation to the Catholic church for losses sustained in the Ukraine during the Civil War, the creation of an Ukrainian cardinalate and the right to conduct Catholic propaganda, in addition to a cash sum. Part payment was made, and some munitions were delivered to Petlura, but the contract was never fulfilled in its entirety owing to the fact that Petlura was defeated and driven out into Poland.

Next to the Catholics, the Baptists have made more progress than any other sect in Russia during the past few years. They are very strong in the neighborhood of Saratov[9] and generally in Southeastern Russia, and there are still numbers of Old Believers among the Don Cossacks. There are also evangelistic movements in Moscow and Petrograd and other parts of the country, but these are regarded as counter-revolutionary. A Christian brotherhood organized in Petrograd by a former professor whose name I do not recall at the moment, was dissolved by the Cheka last summer, its leader and a number of members put into jail, and I myself was recently in prison with members of the Russian branch of the Salvation Army.

Added to all these denominational movements there is the inexorable tie of habit and tradition which binds the great mass of the peasants to their religion, the Russian temperament, idealistic and mystical, which holds the better educated in the spell of various fanatical movements, the old love of the supernatural which is as strong in human nature as ever. The peasants have clung to many of their ancient superstitions and legends, particularly the one about the coming of the Anti-Christ, and many of them believe that he is Trotsky. At times all Moscow is vibrating with rumors of mysterious signs and portents seen in the heavens. Last August the people were all agog over a flaming crown said to have rested over the church on the Pokrovka, where the Empress Elizabeth was married. They declared that it was a sign that the monarchy would be miraculously restored.

Then there is the great new religion of Communism, for to its sincere and devoted followers it is a religion for which they are just as willing to sacrifice themselves and their neighbors as the Raskolniki[10] in the days of Peter the Great, who immolated themselves and their families in great *auto da fes*, hundreds at

------

9. Perhaps owing to the fact that the Saratov region was the destination for a great number of Germans, who were invited to settle there during the reign of Catherine the Great.

10. This name, literally, "splitists," was used for Old Believers who were Russian Orthodox followers that rejected the reforms brought by Patriarch Nikon in 1666-67.

a time, the willing sacrificed with the unwilling victims. The propaganda of Communism as a faith has its appeal to the young and imaginative, as well as to the more mature idealists and the fanatics of Marxism. There are many people who take a fierce delight in the renunciation of their individual freedom for the collective good, and there are many features of the Communistic doctrine which, when studied from this angle, have a tremendous appeal.

These dreamers of a new social order based on the religion of Marxism are inevitably doomed, in my opinion, to failure, for economic and political reasons as well as from the fact that the vast majority of members of their own party are not actuated by any such altruistic motives. They are having great success, however, in the organization of the Communist youth, boys and girls of the working classes, who do not see the practical failure of Communism, who are at the age which hopes and believes all things. It will be interesting to see what fruit the purely spiritual and intellectual side of Communism produces in the next generation.

CHAPTER XIV
Radical Anti-Reds

*A*t about this time I began to make the acquaintance of members of some of the opposition political parties, among which were the Mensheviks and the Anarchists. Both of these groups had a semi-legal status, held meetings and had their headquarters, the former having a club on the Myasnitskaya, the latter on the Tverskaya. At the Mensheviks' club I met both the leaders, Martov and Abramovich, who have now taken refuge in Germany.[1] They, being like the Bolsheviks, Social Democrats, were anxious to cooperate with the Soviet Government, but differed radically from the Communists on the question of the status of the trades unions, and were opposed to Trotsky's policy of the militarization of labor. I had great trouble in hunting them out, for they were under suspicion even at that time, and my visit to the club, together with those to Chertkov and the Anarchists, were known and noted against me though I was not conscious of it at the time.

The Anarchists held open meetings every Sunday, and were allowed to preach their doctrines undisturbed, though to tell the truth, at their meetings there was at least one Chekist to every Anarchist or impartial listener, and they held debates with corresponding prudence and due realization of this fact. The Anarchists were divided into two groups, the Communist Anarchists, who believed that Communism was a necessary stage in the evolution of anarchism, and those who wished at once to abolish all government. Numbers of them

1. Yuli O. Martov (1873-1923) worked with Lenin in the late 1890s, but broke with him in 1903 to lead the Menshevik Party until his death in 1923. Raphael Abramovich (1880-1963) worked in various left-wing groups before 1917. He worked to find common ground between the Bolsheviks and other left-wing parties. In 1940, he emigrated to the United States.

had already been arrested, and during my own term of imprisonment a general roundup of all Anarchists was made by the government. The Anarchists were a rather faddy lot, one of their pet schemes being the launching of a new universal language which they claimed to be far superior to Esperanto, and in which letters were replaced by numbers.

They also ran a restaurant on the Tverskaya, open to the public, where a very good meal could be had for thirty-five rubles, astonishingly cheap for Moscow. Undoubtedly many of their supplies were purloined from Soviet stores, for they claimed the right to rob the government, whose authority they did not recognize.

It was at about this time that large numbers of deported American Anarchists began to arrive in Russia. They were not by any means welcome visitors. Many of them were to all intents and purposes Americans, having left Russia as small children, and did not speak a word of the language. Some of them had left their families behind in the United States, others found absolutely no trace of their relatives whom they had left in Russia many years before; nearly all were very poor, and found great difficulty in obtaining work. They soon became bitterly disillusioned about the Soviet Government, and the Russians themselves were not unnaturally indignant at having a lot of what they were pleased to term foreigners, radically disagreeing from them politically, dumped down in their midst. Emma Goldman and Alexander Berkman, who arrived at the same time, and who commanded almost universal respect on account of their personal character and intellectual attainments, established a sort of unofficial employment bureau for these poor people and formed as a nucleus to hold them together a society called "The Russian Friends of American Freedom."[2] They had interviews with Lenin on the subject, and hoped to be able to form a powerful organization of Russians with ties connecting them with America to help promote revolutionary doctrine in the United States, but as it was sponsored chiefly by Anarchists Lenin did not look on it with any great degree of favor and the project was, I believe, eventually dropped.

I saw a great deal of Emma Goldman and Berkman during their stay in Moscow. Berkman lived at my guest house and for several weeks had the room next to mine. He is a quiet little man with a big, domed forehead brought

---

2. Emma Goldman (1869-1940) and Alexander Berkman (1870-1936) were both born in the Russian Empire (Lithuania) and emigrated to the United States. They met in 1889 and were comrades thereafter. By 1900, they were the leading anarchists in the United States. In 1920, they were exiled to the Soviet Union for their anti-war views during World War I. They left the Soviet Union in 1921 and traveled around Europe speaking and writing until their deaths.

Emma Goldman

Alexander Berkman

more into prominence by his baldness, with kindly, somewhat near-sighted gray-green eyes, rather owlish in expression behind his huge horn-rimmed spectacles. Long imprisonment and much thought have given his anarchism a rather speculative, theoretical character, and he is by nature a gentle, exceedingly sweet tempered person. Knowing him as I do, I cannot imagine him trying to blow up Mr. Frick[3] or anyone else with bombs. I think the two subjects on which he feels most strongly are the prison system in general as a form of punishment, and militarism. For these reasons, whatever he might see of good in the Soviet Government was overbalanced by his horror of the Cheka and the Red Army. He told me many stories of the men he had seen turned into enemies of the human race by imprisonment, and he regarded death as a much more humane form of punishment. He admitted that until society reached an ideally altruistic state it would be perhaps necessary to keep some individuals under restraint in reformatory colonies, or under treatment for mental abnormalities not clearly understood at present, and of which he believed much more exhaustive study should be made. He also felt that in an anarchistic state where individualism was given full rein, and people were directly interdependent, this sense of social responsibility would

3. Henry Clay Frick (1849-1919) was an American industrialist and partner of Andrew Carnegie. Alexander Berkman tried to kill him in 1892 for what happened in the Homestead Strike.

develop much more rapidly than is possible under any present system of government. We had long conversations on these subjects, and he told me many stories of his life in the Atlanta penitentiary. In all he has spent twenty-five years in prison, but it has not destroyed his interest in life or influenced his point of view. In his judgments of individuals he is exceedingly charitable, though sweeping in his condemnation of man-made systems. We also had long chats about literature, art and music, in which he has very good taste and a fine appreciative faculty. Long years of imprisonment have considerably undermined his health, and he found Moscow fare, black bread and kasha, very trying.

Finally, his digestive troubles culminated in a very severe attack of intestinal disorder. I helped Emma Goldman heat and prepare special dishes for him on my little kerosene stove, and he found my hot water bottle very useful. I often wondered what my conventional American friends would think if they could see me sitting by the hour in Berkman's bedroom administering medicines and changing hot water bottles. If I had thought about him at home at all I had always pictured him as a wild man with a bomb in one hand and equally explosive literature in the other. As a matter of fact, I found him one of the gentlest, most courteous and kindliest individuals it has ever been my pleasure to meet.

I liked Emma, too. Honesty, good nature and a delightfully refreshing sense of humor are her salient characteristics, mixed with a keen intelligence, considerable shrewdness and great executive ability. The feeling of being a round peg in a square hole wore on her energetic temperament. She hated her enforced idleness, but she was absolutely unwilling to go into any sort of work where she would be directly or indirectly supporting Communist policies. She spoke Russian very poorly and she was desperately and humanly homesick for America. I do not believe for one instant that Emma is any the less a sincere anarchist for her experience in Russia, but I believe that she is a much better American. I am not sure even that she is in her heart of hearts not convinced that it is not such a simple thing to bring about a social revolution and that it would not be well to make haste slowly in the United States. I greatly enjoyed listening to her apt criticisms of leading personages, whose weak spots she picked out unerringly, and her efficient scorn of the loose business methods and administrative incapacity of the Russians.

After oscillating restlessly between Moscow and Petrograd for some time, "looking over the field," as Emma expressed it, she and Berkman finally found a job into which they could enter whole-heartedly – collecting material for a historical museum of the revolution. They were given a private car, with a Red Soldier as an attendant, they stocked it well with provisions, Emma, who is an excellent cook and housekeeper, superintending the stocking up; and they started off for the Ukraine on an extended tour, on part of which they were accompanied by an American correspondent, Henry Alsberg,[4] who was then writing for the *London Daily Herald* and collecting material for a series of articles in an American weekly. It was a source of wonder to us that Alsberg was able to take the trip, for the Ukraine was in a very unsettled state at that time, as indeed it is still, the Polish offensive was on, and no other foreign correspondents were permitted to travel in that part of Russia. The Foreign Office insisted that he had gone without permission, the Cheka outwardly raged and swore that Alsberg had been detained in Kharkov, but as a matter of fact this was camouflage to appease the other correspondents, who did not have Alsberg's pull. He traveled over a large part of the Ukraine tranquilly and quite unmolested, returning to Moscow in his own good time many weeks later.

There was another class of individuals, many of whom would be ranked as radicals at home, but who were, for the most part, beginning to turn against the Soviet Government — the Jews.

That the Jews helped to make the Russian Revolution is a fact too well known to need comment; that they reaped great immediate advantages from it is undoubtedly true; that many of the men who are leading forces in the political and economic life of Soviet Russia are Jews is unquestionable, and these facts have given rise to the general impression outside of Russia that Bolshevism is a movement sponsored by the great mass of the Jewish population. As a matter of fact, the great masses of the Jewish population have gotten less out of the Revolution than any other race or class; they have been crushed, so to speak, between the upper and nether millstones of revolution and reaction. The majority of them, barring the fact that they dread counter-revolution on account of the inevitable pogroms[5] which would accompany it, would be glad to see the overthrow of the Communist dictatorship in Russia.

The immediate result of the Revolution had been to remove the many disabilities of the Jews. For the first time in history the Russian Jew was a

---

4. During the Great Depression, Alsberg was the head of the Federal Writers' Project for Franklin D. Roosevelt's New Deal.

5. A pogrom was an unofficial, violent attack by Russians upon Jews who lived in the Russian empire in the late nineteenth and early twentieth centuries.

free citizen with all rights and privileges. The Revolution also at first brought many material advantages to the Jews. In the general demoralization and disintegration of the bourgeoisie, the old official class was dispossessed and scattered. Many were executed, others joined the counter-revolutionary armies or escaped while there was yet a chance beyond the frontier. Many of those who were left refused to work for the new government or practiced sabotage.

Among the class-conscious Russian proletariat which had taken part in the revolutionary movement there were few men with the education or training to occupy executive or administrative positions. The Jews, as a race, in spite of their many handicaps, were better fitted for such positions than their Russian co-revolutionists. Nearly all of them were from the merchant or small trader class, and had a fairly good education. The percentage of literacy was much higher among them than among Gentiles of the corresponding class. They had never owned land, and in the distribution of land among the peasants they had no share. They were reaping their harvest from the revolution in clerkships and administrative and executive offices.

As far as Petrograd, Moscow and the large cities were concerned, they fared well. Thousands of them were taken into the many departments of the Commissariats, primarily because of their fitness for such positions. In the provinces this was also true to a certain extent, but as the Soviet machinery there was not so complicated and did not require such a large number of paid workmen, the majority were left without employment. The Red Army absorbed some of them, largely in its sanitary service, for the Jews as a race do not take more kindly to military service in Russia than in any other country.

But many, in the sections where there was a large Jewish population, were left without resources or employment. They were not trained as industrial workers – even if they had been, the constantly decreasing factory production owing to the economic ruin produced by the Great War, the Civil War and the blockade, gave them few opportunities in this field; they were town dwellers, and had not profited from the distribution of the land.

At first they did not feel their position. True, their little shops were closed, their supplies requisitioned, but long years of persecution had taught them how to evade the law, conceal their goods and practice illicit trade. They did a flourishing underground business, practiced contraband and smuggling very successfully, and lived well for a time. Then as the central government became better organized, decrees against speculation were more rigidly enforced, numbers of the Jews were arrested and severely punished, in many cases getting the death penalty. Others became frightened, gave up their illicit occupations, or exhausted their reserve supplies, and then began a period of misery and privation for the provincial Jewish population. Many were over age, entitled to receive workers' pensions, but this branch of the Soviet Government has never been well organized and the destitution among old people all over Russia is very great. Others, as I said before, were unable to find employment in their provincial towns and drifted involuntarily into the status of non-workers without the right to draw food rations.

In Moscow I found many Jews occupying important political positions, but in positions of greatest authority Jews were not in the majority by any means, although they preponderated in many of the executive offices of the Soviet Government.

Among the People's Commissars, seventeen in number, there were actually very few Jews, Trotsky being the only one among those I met, about whom there can be no question. Zinoviev, chairman of the Executive Committee of the Third International, is a Jew, and I believe that Jews are well represented on the committee. On the other hand, the predominant influence in the All-Russian Council of Trades Unions is not Jewish by any means. Among the Communist publicists, Steklov, editor of the *Izvestia*, the organ of the Central Executive Committee, is not a Jew, while the editorial staff of *Economic Life*, the fairest paper published in Russia at the present time, is composed largely of Jews.

The Jews registered as members of the Communist party and occupying responsible administrative positions were, in many instances, rank opportunists. There was a far greater proportion of sincere Communists among the real Russians. There were many hundreds of Jews among the "*Bezpartiny*," nonparty members, belonging to the class of intellectuals or professional men who were content to devote themselves to purely educational or executive work, and who were at heart violently opposed for the most part to the dictatorship of the Communist party.

In the opposition Socialist parties, such as the Mensheviks, Right and Left Social Revolutionaries,[6] and even the Anarchists, I found an ever-increasing number of Jewish members. This was especially interesting as regards the

6. The Socialist Revolutionaries existed from 1902 to 1922. They emerged like many groups in reaction to repressive tsarist policies. By 1917, they were fracturing into left and right groups. The major difference was that the left group was more internationally oriented.

Right Social Revolutionaries. The Social Revolutionary party is essentially a peasants' party, and until a short time ago it had practically no Jewish members. At present it has many hundreds. They are purposely holding back, refusing to take any prominent part in the party councils, because, as one of them who was imprisoned with me said, "There is such a prejudice against Jews in general in Russia that we feel we would do more harm than good by openly occupying important positions in the party."

Among my fellow-prisoners was a woman who had been one of the directors of a Jewish Cooperative Artel[7] at Smolensk, one of a number which have been organized by Jews throughout Russia to give work to their co-nationalists. This organization was so successfully managed that it executed large contracts for the Soviet Government, and although in size it was far beyond the limit of fifty individuals prescribed for cooperative industrial enterprises, it was left undisturbed for some time. Finally, after several unsuccessful attempts to nationalize the industry, charges of counter-revolution were made against some of its leading members, they were arrested, and sent to Moscow. I was also in prison with a number of Jewish women arrested for membership in the above-named political parties, and with several members of the insurgent faction of the Bund,[8] a Socialist organization composed entirely of Jewish members, which this year split into two factions, the majority refusing to subscribe to the Third International, the minority going over to the Communists.

The only Jewish political organization as such, which is preponderantly sympathetic to Bolshevism, is the Poale Zion,[9] a league of industrial and factory workers. The Zionists are regarded as rank counter-revolutionaries. At their annual convention in Moscow last year, the entire body, consisting of one hundred and twenty-five delegates, was arrested and put in prison for several weeks.

A significant illustration of the state of public opinion with regard to Jews was shown by the reception given a vaudeville act at the Nikitskaya theater last summer. It was a skit in which a Red and a White officer come out on the stage and engage in a rough and tumble fight for the possession of the throne

....

7. An *artel* was an informal cooperative of workers, usually in a trade or in the mining or fishing professions.
8. The Bund was a Jewish secular labor party in Russia between 1897 and 1920. By 1903 they rejected Zionism and the idea of returning to Palestine, which put them at odds with other Zionist groups at that time.
9. Poale Zion was a Jewish workers' organization that embraced Zionism after the Bund rejected it in 1903. It had members throughout Europe and in New York, but was most active in Russia.

at the back of the scene. After the Red officer has given the Monarchist a good licking, he turns around to take his seat on the throne and finds perched on it a little Jew who has sneaked in meanwhile and taken his seat there. Jibes, catcalls and inelegant, if forcible, remarks from the audience with regard to the Jewish gentleman were allowed to go unchallenged by the police authorities.

There is a Jewish branch of the Commissariat of Nationalities in Moscow where Jewish affairs are handled as those of a separate race, just as those of the Tatars, Cossacks, the German communities, the Ukrainians and other nationalities within the Federative Republic. The attitude of the Soviet government is just as hostile to Jewish as to Russian Orthodoxy in matters of religion.

The facts I have cited above are, I think, sufficient in themselves to justify my belief that Jews as such play no great role in the Soviet Government at the present time. That the Jews had an important part in bringing about the Revolution is undoubtedly true; that the great masses of the Jewish people in Russia have not reaped the advantages they hoped for from it is equally true; and it is also a fact that anti-Semitism, perhaps at times unconscious, is directed against the race-conscious Jews by both Jew and Gentile Internationalists. Added to this is the universal detestation of the Jews by the peasant population, who still do not feel safe from Jewish exploitation, and attribute all the evils of Bolshevism to the Jews. Thus the Jews are getting it going and coming.

The explanation of their part in the Russian Revolution is self-evident. As long as there was a question of doing away with Tsarist Imperialism, they were for Bolshevism, but all their inherited instincts and training are against the Soviet economic and industrial system, as are their religious instincts deeply grounded in the patriarchal or family system. There are, as there always have been, iconoclastic spirits among them running counter to tradition, others whose racial pride is appealed to by the opportunity to exercise widespread political power and influence.

Then there is the trader, or speculative instinct of the Jew, which tells him that there is always the chance to profit through political or economic crises. Now that they have brought about these results, the majority of the educated Jews are running true to their innate conservatism and to the same iconoclastic instinct which has always placed them on the side of the minority. They realize that the political unity of the Jewish race throughout the Diaspora, as they term the Christian world, is not to be maintained by the merging of the race-conscious Jew in the Internationalist. These are the forces that are pushing many of the intelligent Jews back along the road away from Communism. The Jewish proletariat at large has failed to gain either material prosperity or spiritual freedom through Bolshevism, and will probably remain aloof and passive, hostile to Communism but fearing counter-revolution in Russia.

CHAPTER XV
Sukharevka

$\mathcal{F}$or some months I had lived almost entirely on Soviet rations, but I began after a time to feel decidedly undernourished. The food at our guest house, while better than that served in the average Soviet dining-rooms, which I often attended, was not sufficient. At that time it was estimated that the average food ration in Moscow contained only approximately sixty percent of the calories necessary for the human organism. Through legal means, nobody except those receiving commissars, academic and Red Army *payok* obtained anything like the requisite amount of nourishment. So, like everybody else who had the means, except a few absolutely honest and devoted Communists, I began to patronize the markets and the illegal restaurants. Practically everything could be bought for a price at the picturesque stalls on the Okhotny Ryad, within a stone's throw of the Foreign Office, in the Sukharevka or the Smolensky market.[1] I supplemented my rations with milk, fresh eggs, cream cheese, honey and, later, delicious fruits and vegetables, which were very abundant. I always had permission to use the kitchen in the guest house where I was living, and in addition I had my "primus" supplied with kerosene bought illegally for five hundred rubles a quart. I was often hostess at informal supper parties and frequently had my Russian friends, as well as members of the foreign colony, to dinner or tea.

---

1. Sukharevka was a Moscow shopping area dating to at least 1789. It was an active and highly popular goods market from 1812 until the Revolution. By the time of Harrison's visit, the market covered nearly 10 acres of open space in Sukharevka square and was under constant threat of being shut down as a den for speculators and thieves.

It happened that I needed a saucepan in which to do my cooking and so, in order to find out just how the Moscow housewife does her shopping through legal channels, I applied at the Moscow food administration for a permit to buy it through the Soviet stores. Upon presentation of papers proving my identity and my right to live in Moscow as a "correspondent of the bourgeois press," I received an order entitling me to purchase a saucepan. This order was countersigned by three officials in the Food Administration, the process taking an entire day.

On the second day, I exchanged it for an order permitting me to go to the government store, where samples were on exhibit, and pick out the particular kind of saucepan I desired. I chose it by number, whereupon I received another coupon entitling me to purchase it at the government cooperative in the district in which I lived. Then I had to ascertain on what day saucepans would be on sale. On the morning of that day, I was obliged to go early and stand in line until the shop was opened, in order to make sure that all the saucepans would not be sold before I arrived. The entire process occupied a large part of my time for a whole week, but the saucepan was good and cheap, only three rubles. Similar ones sold on the Sukharevka for two thousand five hundred.

It was a wonderful sight to see the crowds on the Sukharevka, particularly on Sundays. Everything under the sun was sold in the wide-open space occupying the center of the boulevard on both sides of the beautiful Sukharev gate, which was built by Peter the Great in memory of one of the loyal generals during the revolt of the Streltsy.[2] To the right was the general market, to the left the food market. The wares were classified in sections, by a sort of unwritten law. At the beginning of the market, in long lines along the pavement, were the peddlers with small miscellaneous wares. Then came the shoemakers with new and second-hand shoes, leather and shoemakers' materials. There were always numbers of Red soldiers in this section, holding under their coats and offering surreptitiously for sale, excellent army shoes purloined from the commissary stores.

A little farther on, in the center, were vendors of household linen, blankets, rugs, underwear and miscellaneous clothing; to the extreme right, the household furnishers with complete stocks of kitchen utensils in tin, aluminum, copper and enamel, china and crockery. Here were also sold workmen's tools, most of

---

2. The *streltsy* were elite palace guard units from the sixteenth to the eighteenth centuries. In the 1680s and 1690s there were several revolts against Peter the Great in favor of his half-sister Sophia, who had served as his regent. The streltsy were disbanded in the early eighteenth century.

Sukharevka Market in the 1920s

them stolen from the government tool factories. On the left was the furniture section, where people brought in huge drays of furniture of every description – beds, wardrobes, massive sideboards, rugs. Often superb pieces of great value were offered for sale, and I saw Oriental rugs worth small fortunes sold for a few thousands. Interspersed among these gentry were the antiquarians, disposing of exquisite old porcelains, bronzes and bibelots of all descriptions; then came the sections where women's clothing was sold, ball gowns, negligees, French lingerie, blouses, street costumes, false hair, cosmetics, toilet articles, in short, everything imaginable for feminine adornment.

Many of the people who did business in the Sukharevka were professional traders, but there were others – members of aristocratic families, wives and daughters of former generals and imperial functionaries, persons belonging to the intellectual class – who came there to sell their last possessions in order to buy bread. Among them I found many charming people and made several close friends. In the very center, between rows of closed booths, stood the vendors of gold and gems, always furtive, always on the alert for spies or for an *blava*,[3] a raid on the market, for while the sale of one's old belongings was legalized, traffic of this sort was strictly forbidden.

There was also considerable mystery about the section where wool and cotton goods were sold by the yard. Legally, anyone had the right to dispose of three *arshins*, an *arshin* being a little over three-quarters of a yard, but larger quantities, frequently purloined from government stores, were constantly changing hands. Numerous people were arrested, but it was a well-known fact that many of the officials of the Moscow Cheka which conducted the raids

3. *blava* – a Russian term for a police raid.

could be "fixed" if you knew how. I knew of a case where a man was arrested with thirty *arshins* of cloth in his possession. He was taken off to the Cheka.

"How many *arshins* were you offering for sale?" demanded the examining officer.

"Three," he answered promptly, with a wink at the official.

"Good," was the reply, "you may have your three *arshins* back." Thereupon he received his liberty and his three *arshins*, the remaining twenty-seven resting in the possession of the official.

Everyone was not so lucky, however. In an apartment where I was a frequent guest, a workman lived with his wife and three small children. They had great difficulty in making both ends meet and one day, when the husband was at work and the children at school, the wife, who was employed for only five days a week in a government office, decided to go to the market to sell six silver spoons which had been part of her little dowry. She never came back, and her frantic husband, after repeated efforts, located her in the Moscow Cheka three weeks afterwards.

The section of the Sukharevka nearest the big gate was devoted to soap and cigarettes. In spite of the universal scarcity of soap, excellent toilet and laundry soap in enormous quantities could always be bought there. Much of it was homemade soap brought in by the peasants, but much was also from apparently inexhaustible hidden stores from the old days. I bought there French soaps of well-known makes. The traffic in cigarettes and tobacco was most of it perfectly legal and quite natural. All Soviet offices give out cigarettes to their employees, often as many as five hundred a month, to smokers and non-smokers alike. In many offices tobacco, of which they had a considerable stock on hand, was given out as part of the workers' compensation, instead of the more necessary food supplies which were not sufficient to go around in all departments. I knew an elderly lady who was employed in compiling weather reports in the Moscow Meteorological Observatory. She received three thousand five hundred rubles a month and two pounds of English smoking tobacco, which represented in value between seventy and eighty thousand rubles. Naturally it was understood that she would dispose of it.

In the food market, the peasants were allowed to dispose of their homegrown produce undisturbed, and bread was openly sold, though the government was supposed to have the bread monopoly. It was next to impossible to tell what was legally placed on sale by persons who received the maximum allowance of two pounds a day, such as the Red Army workers, and those who made it with flour secured through underground channels, or bread stolen from the government bakeries. Regulations governing the sale on the open market of all these things were constantly being changed. One week it would be legal, for instance, to sell meat, two weeks afterwards there would be a decree forbidding the sale of meat and a raid would be made on all meat dealers. It was the same with butter and many other things. In the late spring, the market on the Okhotny Ryad was closed and the booths torn down, but the Sukharevka was allowed to go on undisturbed. Still later, all the small stores were closed, then they were opened and the Sukharevka closed. Finally, in the early part of March 1921, after the decree permitting free trade, markets, stores and street booths were reopened once more. The policy of the government with regard to the regulation of private trade was so vacillating that no one knew exactly what was legal and what was not.

The frequent raids on the Sukharevka were very exciting, and I happened to be in several of them. Often they were directed against a particular class of illegal traders, again they were for the purpose of rounding up deserters or for catching the suspicious characters without a *permis de sejour*,[4] who always abounded in Moscow. You could almost always tell when a raid was about to take place. Warned by a mysterious system of wireless telegraphy, sellers and buyers alike began to grow restless, wares were gathered up in bundles, portable stands were dismounted, their owners scuttling down side streets and vanishing mysteriously into open doorways. Then a panicky movement of the crowd began, the more timid simply taking to their heels and running. Those who were unlucky enough not to make a quick getaway soon found all exits blocked by militiamen, who examined all documents and looked into all packages. Those who were caught with illegal merchandise or who were unprovided with proper documents were herded *en masse*, surrounded by a cordon of militiamen, and marched off to the Cheka, the others were let out one by one. When everything was over, sellers and buyers began to reassemble, cautiously at first, then more boldly, and in half an hour everything was in full swing again. The militiamen were as a rule very correct in handling the crowd and I never saw any brutality or violence. The hundreds of thieves who always haunted the market usually took advantage of the confusion to help themselves and made rich hauls. Once I saw one of them caught in the act. He was pursued by a young militiaman armed with a rifle. Failing to catch up with his quarry, he lost his head and fired

4. Residence permit.

into the crowd after the fugitive, who escaped, but one innocent bystander was killed and two wounded.

The rapidity with which illicit dealers managed to dispose of their wares when warned of any approaching raid was positively uncanny. One morning I wished to buy a pound of butter. There was plenty of fresh country butter on the market, and I was having some difficulty in making a choice. Suddenly word went around that government inspectors were after the butter dealers. In five minutes there was not a pound of butter to be seen. No one had butter for sale, no one ever heard of butter being on the market.

The peasants who came to town with country produce were often very picturesque. I never tired of talking to them or of watching their primitive arrangement for weighing their wares on a notched stick weighted at one end. Many of them were enormously rich, in fact, not being able to count, they did not know how much money they actually had. A friend of mine who was employed in the Commissariat of Agriculture came in close contact with peasants of this class who came in representing their local Soviets to discuss the distribution of seed grain and other matters.

One day one of them asked her to come down and spend the weekend in his village, promising to give her comfortable quarters, milk, eggs and good country food. At first she refused, but finally consented on being promised a large basket of eggs and several pounds of honey to take home. When she first arrived, she was treated as an honored guest, but as she knew there was some motive for their invitation, she waited to see what was coming. On Sunday morning after church she found out the real object of the invitation. Several of the leading peasants came to see her, carrying huge sacks stuffed with what was apparently waste paper. "*Baryshchnya*," they said, "we have a great deal of money. No one in the village knows how much he has, because no one here can count over ten thousands rubles. Will you count our money for us?" She counted all that day and far into the night. Each of the peasants had at least several millions.

For all that the peasants are not contented. Their money will not buy them any of the things they most need – agricultural implements, tools, nails, rope, harness, substantial boots and clothing. Consequently they are either hoarding it or buying useless luxuries such as bedroom sets of walnut and mahogany, silver, fine china, silk gowns and jewelry for their wives, bric-a-brac and graphophones.

There is an enormous graphophone section on the Sukharevka, where dozens of machines and thousands of records change hands every week. To attract attention to his wares, each merchant keeps his machine going full blast, and the medley of popular airs, classic selections, comic operas and ragtime is maddening. I once saw a rather dramatic incident in this connection. One man, intentionally or unintentionally placed on his machine a record of the old national anthem, *God Save the Czar*. As the first bars sounded through the crowd, the effect was electric. Everyone within hearing stopped short. Most people were visibly terrified, a few openly exultant, some evidently indignant, but all, including the militiamen standing near, were, for the moment, paralyzed. To everyone present, the familiar air brought a host of memories and recollections. The first person to recover from the shock was an officer in the uniform of the Red Army. Walking up to the merchant, he quietly requested him to stop the machine, the crowd drew a long breath, recovered its balance, and life went on as usual.

The open air restaurants on the Sukharevka, and there were hundreds of them, were always liberally patronized, in fact, I often patronized them myself. There you could get white rolls with butter, beefsteaks, more often horse than not, excellent meat cutlets, hot dogs, *pirogi*, or rolls stuffed with forcemeat or chopped hardboiled eggs, tea, coffee, milk by the glass, cakes and tarts of all descriptions, kasha, *varenets*, which is similar to our junket;[5] *kissel*,[6] cranberry juice thickened with potato flour, and many other Russian dishes. Prices ranged from five hundred rubles for a glass of tea or coffee with a white roll, to nine hundred rubles for a piece of delectable pastry. Beefsteak or cutlet with potatoes was from five hundred to seven hundred and fifty rubles, a bowl of kasha or mashed potatoes with chopped up carrots and onions was from a hundred to two hundred and fifty rubles.

At the illegal restaurants, which were chiefly in private houses where no one could go without an introduction from a patron, delicious dinners were served at prices ranging from three to five thousand rubles. I was taken to one of these, of which later I became a habitue, by an employee of the Foreign Office. It was in a very pretty house on an out-of-the-way street. The hostess, who waited on us herself, assisted by her daughter and an old family servant, was an extremely elegant, very pretty woman of a distinguished Georgian family. Her husband was a trusted employee in a government office. The table appointments were all most attractive; we had delicious meals and most congenial company. Dinner, which was served from three until five, consisted of a good vegetable soup,

---

5. *Varenets* and junket refer to a traditional warm milk drink.
6. *Kissel* is a thick fruit drink that is usually served as a desert.

followed by roast meat, cutlets, or chicken, with two vegetables. Real coffee, white rolls, cakes and tarts, of which she always had a great variety, and ices were extra.

Another restaurant to which I often went was frequented by theatrical people, and there I met many of the best known artists in Moscow. The actors were also allowed to run a semi-legal restaurant not far away, where much better meals than those furnished in the Soviet dining rooms could be obtained at moderate prices. In June, when the American committee from the Joint Distribution Committee[7] came to Moscow, I often went with one of its three members to an excellent Jewish restaurant where we had "gefullte" fish,[8] roast goose with apples and onions and other Jewish delicacies. Occasionally these places were raided, their owners arrested and their supplies confiscated, but others were always springing up to take their places.

---

7. The American Jewish Joint Distribution Committee was founded during World War I to ameliorate the affects of the War on Jews living in the Pale of Settlement and those resettling to Palestine. Its humanitarian work continues to the present day.
8. Gefüllte or gefilte is a traditional Jewish fish dish.

CHAPTER XVI
Moscow Foyers and Salons

$\mathcal{F}$or some time I only patronized daytime restaurants, but I soon discovered that there were after-theater restaurants where you could get coffee, cakes and ices. One of these was the "Domino," the poets' club on Tverskaya, where the new poets read their latest effusions nearly every evening and there were long debates on the relative merits of the rather artificial post-revolutionary schools. I met a number of them, among them the famous Demyan Bedny,[1] chief exponent of the proletarian poets, who are a direct outcome of the revolution and represent the only vital, really interesting literary movement in Russia at the present time, and knew Mayakovsky,[2] a Futurist and poet laureate of the Red Army. All these men practice poetry on the side as it were, for no one can live in Russia by being merely a poet. Bedny is employed in the Communist propaganda service. He is a bluff, good-natured, wholesome individual, who is immensely popular with the masses and makes stirring revolutionary speeches. Mayakovsky is a Red Army officer. Two other literary friends of mine, Bobrov[3] and Aksyonov,[4] were employed, respectively, in the statistical section of the Commissariat of Posts and Telegraphs, and in the Foreign Office.

---

1. Demyan Bedny (1883-1945) was a poet and a fierce defender of the Bolshevik agenda from 1912 until his death in 1945.
2. Vladimir V. Mayakovsky (1893-1930) was one of the best known Bolshevik poets. He later became disillusioned by the regime and killed himself in 1930.
3. Yevgeny Bobrov (1867-1933) was prominent Russian philosopher.
4. Ivan Alexandrovich Aksyonov (1884-1935) a constructivist poet, literary and art critic and translator. A close friend of the poets Nikolai Gumilyov and Anna Akhmatova, as well as the director Vsevolod Meyerhold. Distinctively anti-ideological, he was very internationalist in orientation and, as Harrison notes, a lover of Shakespeare and Elizabethan poetry more generally.

Aksyonov, who was official host at our guest house on Kharitonevsky, was frequently assigned the task of personally conducting foreign visitors, as well as of acting as intermediary between the Cheka and the Foreign Office in the case of the arrest of foreign subjects. He comes of an old and very distinguished Russian family. Before the Revolution he was an officer of the Imperial Cavalry, and also, I have heard it rumored, chief at one time of the Okhrana or secret police in Kiev. He later served as an officer in the Red Army in the Petlura and Denikin campaigns. He is a poet of no mean ability, lived for many years in Paris, is a connoisseur of French art and literature with fine critical perceptions, and a great lover of Elizabethan literature. One of his fads is the translation of Ben Johnson, on which he was busily engaged when I first made his acquaintance. He is professedly a devoted member of the Communist party, and the real object for which he is employed is to keep tab on all foreigners, reporting their exact state of mind and their attitude towards the Soviet authorities.

I sometimes went with him to the concerts of the Moscow Symphony Orchestra, which has kept up its high standard under its old director, Koussevitzky,[5] who was invited to take the direction of the Boston Symphony Orchestra many years ago. At present he is directing concerts in Europe, getting in touch with musicians and buying music for the use of the Conservatory under a *kommandirovka*[6] from the Soviet Government. Like most musicians and artists he has carefully kept out of politics. The concerts at the Conservatory—and there were a great many of them—were always a delight. The programs were extremely varied, many of them being most interesting in character, particularly a series of historical concerts of Russian music, and a series of Scriabin[7] concerts given on the occasion of the fifth anniversary of his death. With Aksyonov I also attended several concerts of what is perhaps the most wonderful chamber music quartet in the world. It is composed of four of the finest musicians in Russia, and the instruments are all Stradivarii[8] of the first order, taken from private collections. The tone is positively luscious, and I have never heard anything more beautiful than the perfect ensemble of these wonderful instruments in the hands of expert musicians. Besides these concerts, there were many interesting

....

5. Sergei A. Koussevitzky (1874-1951) was a famous conductor in Petrograd during World War I who left Russia in 1920 for positions in Berlin and Paris. In 1924, he emigrated to the United States.

6. A bit of a misnomer on Harrison's part. A *kommandirovka* is a business trip.

7. Alexander Scriabin (1872-1915) was one of Russia's most influential composers and pianists.

8. A stradivarii is a stringed instrument made by a member of the Stradivarius family, especially Antonio. They are supposed to be the finest instruments in the world.

recitals at the Conservatory and elsewhere, and I heard several very fine choral concerts of Russian folk music.

I also attended an exhibition of the new school of Russian artists which has developed since the Revolution. To apply any name to this school would be impossible; its protagonists are not Cubists, Symbolists or Futurists, but wild individualists, and some of the canvases I saw at their salon looked to me more like the efforts of first year kindergarten pupils than anything else.

Amazing conglomerations of the colors of the spectrum, applied in cubes, half moons, circles and streaks, were supposed to represent the Spirit of the Revolution, the Genius of Electricity, the Triumph of the Proletariat, or portrait impressions. There was one clique which employed as a medium only black on white, or white on black; another which produced so-called paintings by means of wiggly lines of black varnish on a dull black background. Connoisseurs of the new movement professed to find great merit in these extraordinary productions. They seemed to me either utterly childish or monstrously decadent. The vigorous propaganda posters of the Tsentr Pechati, the government printing office, and the Rosta cartoons were much more wholesome and interesting.

It was the same with regard to sculpture. Most of the squares in Moscow were adorned with preposterous statues of Revolutionary heroes and prophets of the new social order, such as Lasalle, Marx and Bakunin;[9] in the Soviet square was an obelisk commemorating the October Revolution. The only commendable thing about these productions was that they were modeled in plaster or coarse-grained concrete, owing to the impossibility of chiseling or casting in Russia under present conditions, and therefore bound to crumble within a comparatively short space of time.

Most of the good artists in Russia have been compelled from necessity to give up purely creative work and go into the designing of posters for the government. For this they are fairly well paid, and receive all their materials from the government stores, as well as ateliers to work in, but many of them, who cannot adapt themselves to this work, are very poor and suffer terrible privations.

The same thing is true to a large extent of the poets and authors. The government spends nearly all its energies on the publication of propaganda literature. It is almost impossible for an author to have a purely imaginative work published, for there are no private printing presses, and paper is very scarce.

9.   Mikhail A. Bakunin (1814-1876) was a revolutionary writer who was the primary advocate of anarchism.

The Moscow authors have a club on Prechistenka, where they hold frequent meetings and read selections from their works, but this is necessarily before a very limited public. They also have a small bookshop of their own, where they sell the few volumes they are able to put in print, and valuable books from their own libraries with which they are compelled to part to buy the necessities of life. Famous authors take turns keeping shop. It is a cooperative enterprise and the proceeds are divided between them. The poets have a similar establishment opposite the Art Theater in the Kamergersky Pereulok.[10] To these places the superannuated members of the "intelligentsia" bring their cherished libraries to be sold on commission, for though this traffic is technically illegal, all books being theoretically the property of the state except those allowed individuals for use in their special work, it is impossible to control such sales.

One of my favorite recreations in Moscow was frequent trips to galleries and museums. All of the old galleries, such as the Shchukin and Tretyakov,[11] have been preserved intact, and many private collections which were inaccessible to the general public before the Revolution have been thrown open for everyone to enjoy. The famous Rumyantsev Museum,[12] with its historical paintings, its fine library and its remarkable ethnographical section, is well kept up. It is not always safe to indulge, however, even in such harmless amusements as visiting museums in Russia. A lady whom I knew very well was caught in the Rumyantsev Museum during a raid of the Cheka. Some of the officials, it seemed, were suspected of counter-revolutionary activities, the building was raided and all the visitors were arrested and held for six days in the Cheka as witnesses.

The Tolstoy museum[13] was open, as was the house of Herzen,[14] which has been turned into an interesting exhibit of original manuscripts and documents on the early history of the Socialist movement among the intellectuals. One

---

10. Kamergersky Pereulok is now a pedestrian area near Tverskaya Street in the center of Moscow.
11. The Shchukin Gallery was one of the world's first museums of modern art (primarily Western impressionists, Cubism, etc.) and was opened in 1909 by the wealthy Shchukin brothers (Sergei, Peter and Dmitry). In the late 1920s and early 1930s, the collection was combined with the Morozov collection. Later, most pieces ended up in St. Petersburg's Hermitage Museum and Moscow's Pushkin Museum. The Tretyakov Gallery was founded by industrialist Pavel Tretyakov in the nineteenth century based on primarily private collections of the Tretyakov family. It is best know for its icon collection.
12. The Rumyantsev Museum was located next to the Kremlin in the late eighteenth century after being transferred from St. Petersburg. In 1925, it was dissolved and its collection was spread among other museums. Later, the V.I. Lenin State Library was located on its site.
13. This was a museum to honor the famous Russian writer Leo Tolstoy.
14. Alexander Herzen (1812-1870) was known as the father of Russian socialism. He spent most of his life in exile in England publishing several socialist periodicals.

of the most delightful collections recently thrown open to the public was the famous Morozov collection of paintings, bibelots, old porcelain and furniture.[15] Then there were the Historical Museum on the Neglinnaya,[16] the peasant art, or Kustari exhibit in the Leontyevsky Pereulok[17] and many others.

In addition, a number of new museums were established. One of these was a Historical Exhibit of Russian Army Uniforms from the earliest times. It was being assembled in the former home of Prince Yusupov,[18] the man who murdered Rasputin. The palace, which was a gift of one of the Tsars to the Yusupovs, is a picturesque pile of buildings in a large garden surrounded by a superb wrought iron rail. The oldest portion was built in the seventeenth century, and is typical of the Russian architecture of that period. It is flanked by a semicircle of picturesque one-story outbuildings, formerly used as officers' and servants' quarters. During the imperial war it was turned over to the British Red Cross, and for some time after the Revolution a number of British officers were interned there. The proletarian museums, of which there are several devoted to applied arts and technical subjects, were also most interesting.

The theatres were an unalloyed pleasure to me, beginning with the Grand Opera, where I was usually able to get a seat once a week or oftener in the box reserved for the Foreign Office. While nothing new has been put on within the last few years, the repertoire of operas and ballets is but little below the pre-war standard, though of the former stars none are left but Geltser,[19] whose dancing is perennially delightful, in spite of the fact that she is nearly fifty, and Nezhdanova,[20] the leading soprano, who has a really exquisite voice. Much gossip is current about Geltser, who is reputed in Moscow to be an agent of the Cheka, her special function being said to be denunciation of those who still have jewels or money in their possession or who are trying to secretly dispose

---

15. Ivan Morozov (1871-1921) was another Moscow industrialist (textiles) with a great passion for French impressionism. His collection, however, was private until it was nationalized in 1918.

16. The Neglinnaya is a river that runs through Moscow, most of it now underground.

17. The Russian word "*kustar*" means handicrafts. The Museum of Russian Handicrafts was opened by Savva Morozov (1862-1905), an industrialist and great patron of the arts, at Leontyevsky pereulok 7.

18. Prince Felix F. Yusupov (1887-1967) participated in the killing of Grigory Rasputin in 1916. His family was one of the wealthiest in Russia before the revolution with palaces in both Moscow and Petrograd. The Moscow house, at 21 Bolshoi Kharitonevsky pereulok actually dates to the 16th century and Ivan the Terrible used to stop over at the house after hunting. The house has recently been beautifully restored.

19. Yekaterina Geltser (1876-1962) was a ballerina at the Bolshoi from 1898-1935. She was awarded the title Peoples' Artist of the Republic in 1925 and a Stalin Prize First Degree in 1943.

20. Antonia N. Nezhdanova (1873-1950) was a famous soprano who performed in St. Petersburg, Moscow, Kiev, and Odessa.

of them, but this has been indignantly denied by the dancer herself and many of her friends.

Chaliapin[21] does not sing at the "Bolshoi Oper," as the Moscow Grand Opera House is called, and is officially attached to the Marinsky Opera in Petrograd. When he comes to Moscow he sings at the Little Opera, as he had a quarrel with the director of the Grand Opera and refuses to appear there. I often heard him in *Faust* and *Boris Godunov*, his favorite roles. His voice has failed considerably, but his acting is as wonderful as ever. He also frequently appeared at the Hermitage, one of Moscow's summer theaters.

The people of the working classes adore him, as there is a story of how from a blacksmith he became a great artist. About two years ago he became a Communist

Fyodor Chaliapin

and his glorious interpretation of such songs as the *Dubinushka* or the *Internationale* is enough to make any impressionable individual run out and register as a candidate for party membership. Nevertheless, he is reputed to be immensely rich in the only concrete wealth in Russia at the present time—provisions. As a government employee, he receives the excellent *payok* and pay accorded to all artists; in addition he gets a premium in food products for every appearance in public and has permission to sing in concerts organized by the trades unions, governmental departments and various Communist organizations. For this he always exacts payment in kind, his price sometimes being prohibitive. I remember one occasion on which he was turned down because his price was too high. The employees of the War Office organized a concert for the benefit of a fund to purchase provisions for distribution among those who were in need of extra rations owing to the number of non-workers dependent on them. Chaliapin was asked his terms, which were as follows: half a *pood* of cocoa (a *pood* is thirty-six pounds), half a *pood* of rice, and a *pood* of white flour. The concert was held without him, but it

21. Fyodor I. Chaliapin (1873-1938) was one of the world's most famous opera singers. He toured extensively throughout Russia and the West. He died of leukemia.

was a great success. I attended with Mlle. Buturlin, daughter of an old Imperial general, and young Madame Brusilov, both of whom worked on the staff of the War Office. After the concert there was an informal dance at which there were many Red Army officers. The girls all wore pretty summer costumes, and it was a very pleasant occasion.

I found the regular theaters in Moscow both excellent and at the same time disappointing. To begin with there was the Art Theater, with Stanislavsky[22] as its head, which was giving exactly the same class of plays as it had always done, with the same perfection of detail and stage settings, the same finished acting. The repertoire of the theater included historical plays, such as *Boris Godunov*, and *Tsar Fyodor*, one or two of Chekhov's comedies, Tolstoy's *Living Corpse*, Gorky's *On the Bottom*, a translation of Dickens' *Cricket on the Hearth*, which was very popular; a translation of Berger's[23] American play, *The Deluge*, a Russian version of Byron's *Cain*, spectacularly staged with wonderful scenic effects quite remarkable considering the difficulties in obtaining materials and technical equipment in Russia at the present time, and an up-to-date version of the old French opera, *The Daughter of Madame Angot*. This, as a revolutionary play, had quite a vogue in Moscow, and its permission by the Soviet authorities was a testimony to the liberal views of the government in artistic matters. It is really a satire on the French Revolution. In one scene the hero comes out and says, "It's fine to live in a Republic. Before the Revolution I was locked up in one prison. Now I go from one prison to another." This sally was always greeted with roars of delight from the audience, as was a remark to the effect that a Republic is the last place in which anyone wants to hear the truth.

The Art Theater has under its direction two small theaters, known as the First and Second Studios, the former in the Soviet square, the latter in the Milyutinsky Pereulok, where new productions are tried out and young artists trained for the main theater. I saw several charming plays there, one a revival of an old Polish legend, *Balladina*, which was given at the First Studio, the other a dream play with a socialistic moral, *The Rose Pattern*. Both were beautifully staged and excellently presented.

The Pokazatelny, or Portable Theater, has introduced rather new and original stage settings, but its repertoire is confined to Shakespearian productions and

22. Constantine Stanislavsky (1863-1938) headed Moscow's Art Theatre as a publicly accessible theatre. He was also an actor and director who famously developed his own system of acting.
23. Henning Berger (1872-1924) was a Swedish writer who briefly lived in the United States. This play was also known as *The Flood*. The more common title for Gorky's play is *The Lower Depths*.

translations of the Goldoni[24] comedies. There were also the Little Theater and the Korsch, where comedies of Chekhov and Madame Gippius[25] were given; the Gabima, where Jewish plays were presented in Hebrew, the most popular being a version of Eugene Sue's *Wandering Jew*, under the title of *The Eternal Jew*; and the Nikitskaya, a comic opera theater where *The Dollar Princess, The Merry Widow,* and *The Geisha,* with time-worn costumes and voices, were the only attraction.

The only really interesting theater from the standpoint of originality was the Kammerny, which was founded several years ago by a group of secessionists from the Art Theater, headed by Tairov and Madame Konen,[26] a delightful artist. Tairov, with whom I had several conversations, has very original ideas about stage production. He maintains that no matter how fine the lines of any play, its immediate appeal is to the vision alone; that the ear is half as quick as the eye to absorb impressions. Therefore he devotes great attention to gesture and pantomime, according them what seems to the theatergoer accustomed to ordinary stage technique a somewhat exaggerated importance. The pantomime of the actor throughout must emphasize every shade of emotion; the inflections of the voice are of secondary importance.

Tairov's stage settings are bizarre, often decidedly Cubistic and somewhat bewildering, but they are all interpretative of the spirit as well as of the actual wise en scene of the play. In *Shakuntala*, for example, attention is not paid so much to reproducing with historical accuracy the costumes of the period as to emphasizing the erotic symbolism of the old Indian legend. Other plays produced by Tairov during the season of 1919-20 were: *Salome, Adrienne Lecouvreur, Pierette's Veil,* a pantomime with new and very interesting incidental music, and *Princess Brambilla*, a satire taken from the *Decameron* of Boccaccio, very cleverly ridiculing the blood and thunder plays of the romantic period. Scribe's *Adrienne Lecouvreur* was interpreted in the same manner. He is the only stage director in Moscow who ignores tradition and expresses something of the iconoclastic spirit of the Revolution.

After I was imprisoned I was told by some of the people in my room in the Cheka that the Nikitskaya Theater, which had existed under private

24. Carlo O. Goldoni (1707-1793) was a famous Venetian playwright. He was best known for his comedies.

25. Zinaida N. Gippius (1869-1945) was a well-known writer who left Russia after the Russian Civil War.

26. Alexander Tairov (1885-1950) was an innovator in theatrical art who was later exiled to Siberia under Stalin. Alisa Koonen (Konen) (1889-1979) was a famous actress in the Art Theatre and then later in the Chamber (Kammerny) Theatre. She and Tairov were married.

management, had been turned into a theater of Revolutionary Satire, and that very clever performances were given there.

A prisoner from Petrograd described to me the lurid plot of one of these satires which she had seen shortly before her arrest. It was called *The Dirty Dog*, and was intended primarily to appeal to the Red Army men. Half of the action of the piece took place in the audience itself. It opened with the session of a produce exchange that dealt in human flesh. A manufacturer and a general wearing a death's head appear and order workmen and men for cannon fodder. The brokers dash into the audience and bring out a young workingman who serves as a sample for the merchandise to be delivered for the human sacrifice to Capital and Militarism. He displays his muscles, makes him show his teeth, feels him from head to foot, declares him sound in mind and limb, and finally drives a bargain at a wholesale price, for so many thousands.

A revolutionary poet jumps onto the stage and protests, threatens to commit suicide and is thrown out by the "bouncers." A sleek "Madam," painted, powdered and befeathered, comes on and picks out a lovely young girl from the audience. She is also bought for a price and carried off to white slavery. Predatory capitalism continues its traffic in lives until the inevitable moment of retribution, when there is a terrific thunderclap, the entire structure of the produce exchange falls, crushing its members and their satellites, and the five-pointed star of the Soviet Republic rises above the ruins.

At the circus in Moscow there is a famous clown called Bim-Bom,[27] who has gotten into trouble a number of times over his proclivities for making fun of the Soviet Government. Once he came out and began wearily to tell how hard it was to live in Moscow, how scarce food was, how next to impossible to get a log of wood or a pair of shoes. Then he sat down on a drum and put his head on his hands quite dejectedly. His interlocutor inquired,

"Well, Bim-Bom, what are you going to do about it?" No answer from Bim-Bom.

"What are you waiting for anyhow?"

"I'm waiting to see what the Russian people are going to do about it," was the answer.

---

27. Bim-Bom was a famous Moscow duo with Ivan Radunsky as "Bim" and several other actors playing Bom over the years – the act existed from 1891 to 1946. They were often censored for their criticism of the government.

On another occasion Bim-Bom came out with a picture of Lenin and one of Trotsky. "I've got two beautiful portraits," he announced. "I'm going to take them home with me."

"What will you do with them when you get them home?" he was asked.

"Oh, I'll hang one on a nail and put the other against the wall," was the quick retort.

Again Bim-Bom propounded a conundrum. "Why is the Soviet Republic like a wheel?" he asked, and receiving no reply, proceeded to give the answer. "Because it is held together by the Cheka," *cheka* being the Russian word for hub, and at the same time the popular abbreviation for the title of the much dreaded Extraordinary Commission.

For these and other remarks of like character, Bim-Bom has spent many weeks in prison, but he is always released after a few days because he is about the most popular entertainer in Moscow and the Soviet authorities fully realize the enormous importance of keeping up the public morale through theaters and amusements.

At the Nikitskaya Circus, a theater where both legitimate drama and vaudeville are given during the summer months, I heard a popular artist sing a song describing the fate of a horse that died in Moscow. First the carcass was sent to the Narkomzdrav, the Commissariat of Health, to discover the cause of death, then to the Narkompros, the Commissariat of Education for anatomical research, then to the "Glavkozh" Leather Administration, for the sake of its hide, and finally to the Narkomprod, Food Administration, to be carved into beefsteaks.

There was a vaudeville theater called The Bat, where excellent vaudeville performances were given and there was a very clever monologist who was almost as daring and quite as popular, with a rather different audience, as Bim-Bom. Between the acts, refreshments such as coffee, cakes and ices were served at The Bat. It was a great rendezvous for the rich speculators and their mistresses.

The motion picture theaters in Moscow were as a rule gloomy and unattractive places, poorly heated, dirty, and for the most part, displaying worn-out films from pre-war days. There were a few theaters where the Soviet news weeklies were shown together with a number of propaganda films, but the government has been terribly hampered with regard to film production by the lack of technical material. The motion picture industry is controlled by the Kino Komitet, a branch of the Department of Education, and it has planned a wonderful program on paper for popular amusement and education through the movies, but at present little can be done.

I have almost forgotten to mention one of the most delightful theaters in Moscow, the Children's Theater, where all last year performances were given on several afternoons during the week and on Sundays, of a dramatization of Kipling's *Jungle Book*, under the title *Mowgli*. It was charmingly acted and the jungle stage settings were quite extraordinary. There were a number of special performances at this theater for child speculators who were picked up on the streets by special agents of the Department of Education and given free tickets to the performance. Between the acts, a woman speaker came out and told them what a mistake they were making, what poor citizens they were, and tried to induce them to give up their illegitimate calling and go back to school. This theater was also used for children's concerts, where the various numbers on the program were explained in terms the children could all understand.

Most of the theaters and vaudeville houses were nationalized, but others such as the Art Theater and the Nikitskaya were run by collectives as cooperative enterprises. They were compelled to turn over a certain number of seats at each performance for distribution among the trades unions and government offices at fixed prices, and their artists were required to give their services for a fixed number of free performances in various institutions and factories, and for the Red Army. Companies were frequently sent to the front or to the provinces under the management of the Department of Education.

It was very amusing to note that ticket speculators flourish in Moscow just as they do on Broadway. In addition to the seats distributed free, a certain number of seats for theatrical performances and concerts are sold at the government ticket office on Petrovka and at the various theaters. These tickets, as well as those received free by workmen and employees, are bought up by the speculators and sold at an advance of sometimes two or three hundred percent. The curbs in front of the theaters were often lined with them before the evening's performance. They were frequently rounded up and arrested, but in a few days the industry was as thriving as ever.

The Art Theater was rather crippled during the winter season of 1920 by the absence of three of its principal artists, Madame Germanova, Madame Knipper and Kachalev,[28] who had gone to Kharkov before it was taken by Denikin in

....

28. Maria Germanova (1884-1940), left Russia in 1922; Olga Knipper-Chekhova (1868-1959) stayed in the Soviet Union and was highly decorated; Kachalev refers to Nina Litovtseva (1878-1956), whose married name was Kachelev. She also remained in Soviet Russia until her death and was highly decorated as an actress.

the autumn of 1919 and had, as many people asserted, deliberately allowed themselves to be captured by the Whites. After the defeat of Denikin they were afraid, so it was reported, to come back to Moscow. They finally returned, in the autumn of 1920, and were allowed to resume their work unmolested. At present they are touring Europe. Stanislavsky, who is getting old, was much disheartened over the outlook. He missed his bourgeois audiences, and did not feel, so he told me, the same enthusiasm about playing before the proletariat. He complained of the scarcity of stage material, of the difficulty of life in Moscow, and was only living for the time when he would be able to take his company out of Russia and tour Europe and America.

In this I think Stanislavsky was wrong. I found everywhere among the lower classes in Russia an intense appreciation, though not always comprehension, of all that was best in art, music and literature. On the whole I think the Russian people have more unerring artistic instincts than any people with whom I have ever been brought in contact. The crowds of the great unwashed at operas, plays and symphony concerts were usually almost reverentially attentive, even if it was at times a bit over their heads. This, of course, applies to the town population only. The peasants were usually mystified, and often frankly bored at efforts made to cultivate them.

CHAPTER XVII
A Provincial Junket

*B*y the end of May, the Polish offensive was in full swing and I witnessed a remarkable change in the attitude of the people towards the government. It aroused a perfect storm of national feeling, somewhat stimulated, it is true, by adroit propaganda, but none the less sincere at bottom. Thousands of former officers volunteered their services against the Poles in perfect good faith; engineers, doctors, and professional men generally rallied to the support of the government. The Mensheviks and Social Revolutionaries voluntarily agreed to suspend all political activities during the period of the war. The common soldiers were lured by the promise of extra food rations and raids into a country where food supplies were more plentiful.

Moscow was plastered from end to end with patriotic placards and posters and some of these were extraordinarily effective. None of them were directed against the Polish people, but all against the Polish Pans, the feudal aristocracy, who, it was alleged, had plunged both countries into war against the wishes of the people. Poles living in Russia, whether Communists or not, were bitterly opposed to the war and saw in it the possible ruin of their own country.

At this time the morale of the Russian people was further strengthened by the visit of the British Labor Delegation, and the Soviet authorities did not fail to make the most of the propaganda possibilities afforded by its foreign guests. In the beginning of June, I accompanied the British Labor Delegation on its trip down the Volga. We went by rail from Moscow to Nizhny-Novgorod, and thence by steamer to Saratov, stopping at Simbirsk, Samara, Kazan, the capital of the Tatar Republic, Marxstadt, the capital of the German Commune, and many villages en route.

Our official hosts were Sverdlov,[1] then actual head of the Soviet Railroad Administration, temporarily replacing Krasin who was in London, and Losovsky, president of the All-Russian Soviet of Trades Unions. In the party, in addition to the members of the British delegation, were two delegates from the British Shop Stewards' Committee, a German Syndicalist, several Swedish Socialists, and a small international group of correspondents. The latter included Mr. Meekin of the *London Daily News*; Henry Alsberg, an American newspaper man, who on the Volga trip as well as in Moscow acted for some time as correspondent of the *London Daily Herald*; Bertrand Russell,[2] the great Cambridge mathematician and Fabian Socialist, who was to write a series of articles on Russia for the *Republic*; Rudolph Herzog, the German publicist; M. Marsillac of the Liberal French paper *Le Journal*, and Signor Magrini from the Italian Serratist organ, *Avanti*. We were furnished with official interpreters by the Moscow Foreign Office, and in the entire party, with the exception of Charles Buxton,[3] who had come to Russia as a member of the British delegation with the specific object of ascertaining whether there were any traces left in the Volga region of the work of the British Society of Friends among the peasants, which was stopped after the Revolution, there was no one who spoke any Russian except myself. For that reason I was able to get a better first-hand estimate of the situation than any of the other foreigners.

Our tour was a most luxurious one throughout, giving no idea of the ordinary hardships of travel in Russia at the present time. We had a special train composed of International Sleepers, with all the former comforts including spotless linen, and electric lights, a dining car where we had three good meals a day, service and appointments being very nearly up to peace time standards. The same conditions were reproduced on our steamer which was one of the best boats of the Volga Steam Navigation Company, whose summer tours were formerly included in the itinerary of every traveler who "did" Russia properly. We had no meals on shore except a superb banquet at Nizhny-Novgorod, beginning with the *zakuski* hors d'oeuvres for which Russia was famous in the

....

1. Yakov M. Sverdlov (1885-1919) joined the Bolsheviks as a young man and went on to become one of its most promeinent leaders. Most sources note his death in March 1919, which is a full year before Harrison notes their traveling together. However, there was some suspicion at the time that he did not actually die in March of 1919. She is therefore likely referring to a much lesser-known assistant in the Soviet Railroad Administration named V.M. Sverdlov.
2. Bertrand Russell (1872-1970) was a British philosopher who was sympathetic to the Bolsheviks, but later grew disillusioned with the Soviet regime.
3. Charles Buxton (1875-1942) was first a member of the British Liberal Party, but later a member of parliament as a member of the Labour Party.

old days and ending with ices. Taking it all in all, the only physical hardship endured on the trip was the absence of vodka, which was particularly trying to those who had forgotten to bring their flasks with them.

At Sormovo, the great locomotive and munition works near Nizhny-Novgorod, a demonstration was arranged in honor of the delegation, with a brass band, red banners galore; the cheering proletariat turned out in force to be told by English and Russian speakers that their troubles would soon be over and that the visit of the British Delegation was the first visible evidence of the united support of the Soviet Republic by the working masses of the outside world. Similar meetings were arranged in all the towns, and it soon became evident to the members of the delegation that they were being used to stimulate the morale of the Russian people and were not getting an insight into real conditions.

When the matter was put up to Sverdlov and Losovsky, they agreed with perfect fairness that this was so, and at once arranged for us to stop at a number of villages, which had not been included in the original itinerary. This was a real sacrifice on their part, because it meant cutting out an elaborate celebration at Kazan, including manoeuvres of the Army Reserve Corps stationed there, which was sixty thousand strong. In the towns and villages, the members of the delegation were given opportunities to talk with the people, but they could only do this by means of interpreters; and as the peasants are by nature secretive, and by training and habit dating back to pre-revolutionary days, suspicious of any official personages coming from the "center," as the capitol is called, they learned comparatively little about the actual situation. Being able to speak a little Russian, I made a point of cutting loose from the official party, and in many small homes and *izbas*, where I was received with the whole-souled hospitality and simple friendliness that are among the many lovable traits of the Russian people, I acquired facts that left no doubt in my mind as to the imminence of coming famine.

Crops in the provinces on both sides of the Volga were average or above, but the acreage under cultivation had been steadily declining since 1916. This was due partly to the fact that most of the young men had been conscripted in the Kolchak or Red Armies and that portions of the country had been devastated during the civil war, but principally to the lack of seeds, fertilizer, farm implements, and the opposition of the peasants to the land tax and requisitioning systems.

The land tax required them to deliver to the government everything they produced in the way of farm and dairy products above a certain quantity fixed at so much per capita and estimated by the government as sufficient to carry them over till the next harvest. There was no incentive for them to raise anything beyond the amount necessary to supply their own needs, and they had no confidence in the promises of the government to give them in return the seeds and implements which would enable them to plant a larger acreage another year, when the existing land tax, which it was understood was only a temporary war measure, would be replaced by one based on the return of a percentage of the harvest, leaving them in possession of the remainder. It was evident that some districts would fall far below the quota in the matter of returns and only one, the Tatar Republic, had a prospect of exceeding the required amount. In many places the peasants had concealed huge quantities of food supplies, the hiding places had been betrayed or discovered and everything confiscated, leaving them face to face with the necessity of buying from their neighbors or starving.

In addition there had been special requisitions for the immediate needs of the Red Army in many districts, and nominally voluntary levies for the children in Moscow and Petrograd. There was an enormous amount of stealing and corruption among the local government officials, so that many people were actually hungry in the early summer of 1920, with the prospect of the continuance of the requisitions. It was evident that there would not be enough seeds to go around in the autumn distribution and that the acreage planted for 1921 would be less than that of the previous season. Many peasants were emigrating to the large towns in search of factory employment.

I also heard reports of a real famine to the east, along the foothills of the Urals, and ran into several large parties of peasants from the Ufa district who told me that there was no bread or work there, and that they were emigrating west in search of employment and food.

At one of the villages between Samara and Saratov where Sverdlov stopped to meet some people on business matters, we met the first party of emigrants. It was late at night when we arrived and the emigrants were camped on the river bank — men in sheepskin coats, high boots and astrakhan caps; women in gaily colored shawls and head kerchiefs were huddled in picturesque groups around their fires, as the spring nights were still cold, crooning weird songs, laughing and shouting to one another or talking in low tones. Their baggage, boxes, bales, nail-studded red chests and bulky bundles were in conglomerate heaps. In the background was a forest of birch and spruce. Over all was the pale light of the spring moon. It was one of the most picturesque sights imaginable.

On the way to Saratov we stopped at the German autonomous commune of Marxstadt, a colony founded in the days of Catherine the Great, which has kept its German character for almost a century and a half. Many of the inhabitants to this day speak only German. Marxstadt was run with true Teutonic efficiency. All requisitions proceeded in the most orderly manner, available supplies were equitably distributed, schools, hospitals and all community enterprises were well administered, and the small local industries were in a relatively flourishing condition. The percentage of illiteracy among the inhabitants was remarkably small for Russia, only fifteen percent. The inhabitants were already perturbed, however, over the fact that their reserve supplies were exhausted, and they told me that, unless the early harvest in 1921 was a good one, the food situation would be very serious.

At Marxstadt we had a small-sized scandal which was the subject of much gossip and no little excitement aboard ship. The German syndicalist, who was a member of our party, asked permission when we arrived at Marxstadt, to make a speech to his fellow countrymen. To the horror of the Soviet authorities he burst forth into a violent denunciation of the entire Communist system, asserting that the people were just as much slaves in Russia as anywhere else and denouncing what he termed the military imperialism of the Soviet oligarchy. He was finally cut short by Losovsky, who was a most tactful and pacific individual. He made the suggestion that as everybody was hungry we had better go to supper.

Across the way from Marxstadt was a village of Old Believers, a primitive Greek sect, of whom there are still several hundred thousands in Russia. They regard all who do not share their faith as unclean, and it is against their principles to use any articles touched by non-believers. Though they invited us to have tea and simple refreshments in their houses they would not serve us from their own dishes, but used those specially provided for the purpose. In this village we saw the Executive Committee of the Soviet in session, and it seemed to be transacting its business affairs with considerable efficiency.

There was a very clean hospital, well equipped, though lacking in some of the most necessary medicines, a good school building, a library and the newly established village museum, of which the inhabitants were very proud. The chief objects displayed in it were some geological specimens, a few antiquated muskets, some caterpillars and a large wasp's nest.

The farm implements in use in the village were of the most primitive description. I saw ploughs which looked as if they might have belonged to

Biblical days, with wooden shares, bound together with thongs instead of nails, and the women did not even have spinning wheels, but spun their wool and flax with a distaff and spindle. In the village cooperative store we found a little salt, a few yards of calico and some kegs of nails. That was practically all the people were getting on cards.

In the towns food was scarce, and the government rations, except those for the Red Army and war industries workers, were exceedingly meager, the bread ration being three quarters of a pound a day, and not always regularly supplied. There was a universal dearth of salt and sugar. Meat was cheap and plentiful in the open market, but this was a bad sign, for it meant that the peasants were killing their cows and horses owing to the scarcity of fodder.

A vigorous "plant more and plant better" campaign was being waged by the government, but it was not backed up by definite prospects of seeds and supplies to insure its being carried out, and the people were fully convinced that a famine was coming.

In Saratov we were treated to the usual rounds of receptions and public functions. I cut them all and went out to talk with the people. I learned that there was already great scarcity of food, citizens were receiving half a pound of bread a day on cards, and very little else. Prices in the markets were lower than in Moscow, but high as compared with the wage scale, which is lower in the provinces.

While walking through the streets, I saw a young Jewish girl dressed in filthy rags huddled on the steps of a house, gazing stolidly ahead in apparently hopeless despair. She told me that she was nearly starving. She was employed for three days in the week in a Soviet dining room, receiving a small stipend, and barely enough food to keep her alive. Her father and mother were dead and she had an old grandfather and grandmother to support, neither of whom received anything from the social maintenance department of the provincial government. In the dining room, she told me, she was constantly subjected to insults from the other girl employees, who taunted her with being a "Yid," and only the day before she had had her face scratched and her clothes torn by several of her companions, who set about to beat her up because she was a Jewess.

At Saratov I asked permission to remain on the steamer on which Sverdlov was proceeding to Astrakhan, as I had been nursing Clifford Allen,[4] a member of the British Delegation, who was desperately ill with pneumonia and not in

---

4. Clifford Allen (1889-1939) was a British politician who as a conscientious objector during World War I.

any condition to be moved. This permission was refused and no correspondents were allowed to go on to Astrakhan. Dr. Haden Guest,[5] Mrs. Snowden[6] and Bertrand Russell remained with Mr. Allen. The correspondents, including myself and the rest of the delegation, returned to Moscow on a special train via Tambov, according to the original plan.

In the Tambov district we saw thousands of acres of uncultivated land, the crops looked exceedingly poor and I was told by a man in the station that in many villages the peasants were actually without bread, and the general bad outlook for the harvest was complicated by the activities of Antonov,[7] the Social Revolutionary leader, under whom a number of small sporadic revolts were constantly breaking out. Altogether it was evident that even under the most favorable conditions at least several millions of people would this year be facing complete or partial famine in the Volga and Tambov districts, and that they were not going to be able to contribute their allotted quota towards the approvisionment of the cities and the industrial population.

On the trip I had many long talks with the members of the delegation. They were divided into three distinct groups, the extreme left represented by Robert Williams[8] of the Transport Workers. Williams apparently saw nothing and believed everything that was told him. He seemed carried away by a sort of romantic hysteria and made many speeches that I am sure he would never have uttered in England. Before he left, he had practically pledged the support of the British Transport workers to the Third International and direct Revolutionary action in England. I am not sure whether the canny Bolsheviks put entire confidence in his Red promises. He was a very popular figure at meetings, however, and he had learned a few words of Russian with which he always brought down the house. With his execrable Russian accent he interlarded every speech with *"Da sdrast vuyet Sovietski Vlast, da sdrast vuyet mirnoe revolutye."* "Long live the Soviet Government, long live the world revolution." Anything else he said mattered very little.

. . . .

5. Leslie Haden-Guest (1877-1960) was the first Baron Haden-Guest, a doctor and a British Labour Party member.

6. Ethell Snowden (1881-1951) was a British socialist and Labour Party member who published *Through Bolshevik Russia* in 1920.

7. Vladimir A. Antonov-Ovseenko (1884-1939) was once associated with the Socialist Revolutionaries, but by 1920-21 he was closer to Trotsky's views. He worked in the Tambov region to quash revolts.

8. Robert Williams (1881-1920s) was a British Trade Union Organizer and helped form the Red International of Labour Unions after his visit to Russia.

Wallhead, leader of the British Independent Labor Party,[9] was thoroughly in sympathy with the aims of the Soviet Republic as far as its own internal administration was concerned, and like all the members of the delegation and the press people who accompanied it he was unalterably opposed to blockade and intervention. He regarded the Communist dictatorship as a wonderful experiment, the success or failure of which could only be fairly determined by giving the Bolsheviks a chance. As a Marxian Social-Democrat, he believed in the dictatorship of the proletariat and the combination of parliamentarianism with direct action, but he resented the dictatorship of the Russian controlled Communist International. He and Lenin had some hot words on the subject when the delegation returned to Moscow, which resulted in the failure of the Independent Labor Party to join the Third International. They proposed to make a revolution in England in due time, but they were not going to have Moscow tell them when to make it or how to make it.

I was much amused on one occasion to detect the underlying sturdy British nationalism of Wallhead, for all his detestation of the capitalistic class. We were talking about the retirement of the British forces in Northern Persia from the shores of the Caspian Sea. A Soviet dispatch announced that the Commander had been forced to retire on account of the bombardment by Red gunboats.

"By God," said Wallhead impetuously, "if we had had one British gunboat there, we could have sent their little tin navy to the bottom of the Caspian." It was the most spontaneous thing I heard said during the entire visit of the delegation.

The right wing of the delegation was from the first opposed to the principles of the Third International.[10] Its favorable disposition towards the Soviet Government as such was considerably changed by the evident intention of its leaders to exploit them, to use them for propaganda purposes, representing them as sympathizers with rather than investigators of actual conditions, and they resented having their time planned out for them and the efforts made to block any independent investigation and interviews with the representatives of opposition parties. Dr. Haden Guest, Shaw,[11] Turner and Mrs. Snowden took

---

9. Richard Collingham Wallhead (1869-1934) was a British Member of Parliament from 1922 to 1934 and at this time Chairman of the Independent Labor Party, as well as a journalist and lecturer.

10. The Third International, also known as the Comintern, demanded allegiance to democratic centralism (discussion and debate amongst comrades, but a united face to the outside world) and adherence to Moscow's leadership. The organization also drew a hard line between loyal communist allies and less reliable bourgeois socialist parties.

11. Most likely a reference to British Fabian (socialist) and writer George Bernard Shaw (1856-1950).

this attitude. Dr. Guest in particular, a former British Army officer and a man close to the coalition government, was the object of much suspicion. It was openly insinuated that he was an agent of the British Government and only the guarantees given the delegation secured him personal immunity from arrest.

Clifford Allen, who was desperately ill during most of his stay in Russia, was the only real Communist in the party, and even he was rather contemptuously looked upon by certain leaders for his pacifism. Bertrand Russell as a Fabian was also profoundly shocked by what he regarded as a tendency to Communist imperialism.

The leaders at Moscow were constantly running up against this sturdy independence on the part of foreign Socialists during the summer, and I believe that when the labor history of the present transition period is written, the year 1920 will be marked as the apogee of Russian influence in the World Revolutionary movement, and the beginning of its decline.

CHAPTER XVIII
Pageants and Plots

*T*he two outstanding events of the summer which dragged on without incident except for the depression caused by the military reverses of the Red Army, were the great festival of the Third International,[1] and the train of local disturbances due to the Polish situation. I was not allowed to attend the congress of the International or to talk with the delegates, but I took part in some of the public celebrations, the most elaborate of which was the great parade held in the Red Square in honor of the delegates. The whole square, bounded on the west by the crenellated battlements of the Kremlin, on the south by the cathedral of St. Basil the Blessed, on the east by the buildings of the great Kazansky Bazaar, where Moscow's trade with the Far East was formerly carried on, and on the north by the Moscow Historical Museum, was transformed into a glorious riot of color by standards hung with red banners and pennants.

All the surrounding buildings were draped with huge posters painted on linen, representing the Triumphal of the World Proletariat and of the Soviet armies. Fraternal greetings to the delegates floated in letters of gold in every imaginable language from innumerable banners and placards. Over the cathedral of St. Basil hovered a flock of sausages and other balloons dripping

1. The Second World Congress of the Comintern (Third International), held July 19-August 7, 1920. At this Congress, Lenin's 21 Conditions were adopted as prerequisites for any group affiliated with the International. They called for the demarcation between Communist parties and other socialist groups, instructed the Comintern sections not to trust the legality of the bourgeois states, and called for the build-up of party organizations along democratic centralist lines. Notably, the 11th thesis stipulated that all communist parties must support the bourgeois-democratic liberation movements in the colonies, yet some delegates opposed the idea of alliance with the bourgeoisie, and preferred to support communist movements in the colonies instead. Many European socialist parties went through splits on the basis of allegiance to or disavowal of the new International.

red pennants and streamers; Red Army airplanes circled overhead all day long, dropping showers of propaganda leaflets. On the west side of the square was a large tribune with an elevated portion in the center for the People's Commissars and the speakers of the day, flanked by seats on the right for the foreign delegates and on the left for the members of the Central Executive Committee.

The delegates were of every nationality under the sun, and the sober costumes of the Europeans and Americans threw in relief the bright spots of color afforded by the Orientals, some of whom wore truly magnificent costumes with jeweled chains around their necks and flashing jewels in their turbans. From the tribune, Trotsky reviewed the great parade, which began at ten in the morning and lasted until nearly five in the afternoon. First came detachments from every branch of the Red Army, including a picturesque regiment of Uhlans,[2] carrying lances with small red pennants; then followed the militia, the armed bands of factory workers, of whom there are thirty thousand in Moscow, and the great mass of the proletariat representing the twenty-three trades unions and every department of the Soviet Government. Each detachment marched with military precision and carried its own banners inscribed with Revolutionary mottos.

The men nearly all had a touch of red somewhere, and the women, of whom there were thousands, wore red head kerchiefs. There were innumerable bands and, when these were lacking, detachments marched by singing the *Red Flag* or the *Internationale*. Thousands of school children and numbers of regiments of boy scouts were in line, representing the Communist youth. One detachment of boys made a particularly good impression. They were members of an athletic organization and marched in swimming trunks only, displaying their sunburned muscular frames to great advantage. It was, on the surface, a wonderful spontaneous demonstration of the power of the proletariat. Later, however, when I discovered that the employees of the Soviet offices were compelled to take part in the procession under threats of various punishments, one of which was that of losing their weekly food ration, I had some doubts about this fact. It was undoubtedly true, however, that the great mass of factory workers entered heart and soul into the mood of the demonstration.

The pageant in the Red Square was witnessed by few of the inhabitants of Moscow except those who took part in it. Admission was by ticket only, all approaches were most carefully guarded by detachments of Red Cavalry and infantry, and every guest's credentials were minutely scrutinized. On either

2. Uhlans refer to Polish light calvary.

side of the tribunal was a military exhibit representing every branch of the Red Army service.

During the afternoon and evening the people of Moscow were treated to a series of open air theatrical performances; special trolleys equipped with portable stage settings were sent all over the city; the services of artists from all the theatres had been requisitioned for the day and comedies, operettas and vaudeville performances were given in all the squares. Accompanying each unit was a Communist propagandist, who talked to the crowd between the acts. At night, under a great arch which forms one of the entrances to the Kitai Gorod,[3] the walled enclosure which lies just east of the Kremlin, I saw a wonderful performance by a workmen's dramatic club of the Greek tragedy of Eschylus, *Oedipus Tyrannus*. There was an even more elaborate pageant, so I was told, in Petrograd, after which the business of the Third International was conducted, in a very sober manner, in the Imperial Palace at the Kremlin.

Another impressive ceremony which took place at about this time was a review by Trotsky, in the Opera Square, of five hundred graduates from the General Staff Officers' School in Moscow. I was lucky enough to meet Kamenev of the Moscow Soviet just before it began and he found an excellent place for me on the steps of the Opera House just behind Trotsky. While we were waiting for the review to begin I had a conversation with another Kamenev, Chief of Staff of the Red Armies.[4] He told me something of the plan of military training. Military service in Russia is compulsory for all citizens between the ages of eighteen and forty. When the army is on a peace footing, the term of active service will be six months, after which the soldier becomes part of the reserves of the Red Army. These reserves are kept in training by compulsory drill of two hours a week. They constitute what is known as The Workers' Militia. Officers' courses in the General Staff school extend over a period of three years. The period of training for line officers in the army and the reserves is from six to eight months. The line schools are scattered all over Russia. At that time, there were nearly four hundred in operation and it was planned to establish at least three hundred more. Working men and peasants as well as men of university education are eligible for these courses if they show special fitness for such training. Kamenev, who was formerly an officer in the Imperial Army, is a middle-aged man of fine appearance, with all the earmarks of a professional

....

3. Kitai Gorod is a business district of Moscow near Red Square that translates as China Town, but this is a misnomer, as the name likely derived either from the Russian word for whale *(kit)* or wall *(kita)*.
4. Sergei S. Kamenev (1881-1936), a commander during the Civil War and Chief of Staff from 1919-1924. A close ally of Trotsky.

soldier, and seems to take little interest in politics, his aim being merely to train a first class fighting machine.

Petrovsky,[5] chief of the Army Political Schools, whom I met at the same time, was, on the contrary, a red hot Communist. He had the supervision of most of the two hundred and fifty thousand Communists, who were mobilized and sent to the front in every branch of the army as political commissars, teachers, officers, Red Cross men and even as private soldiers. I have already told something of the organization of the Army Political Schools as I saw them on the front.

All Moscow was thrilled at that time over the exploits of Tukhachevsky,[6] who was then starting his famous drive on Warsaw, and Budyonny,[7] the great cavalry leader in the Ukraine. Both had had an equally meteoric rise, and from quite different origins. Tukhachevsky was a former Imperial officer, was taken prisoner by the Germans during the Great War, and spent over a year in a prison camp at Magdeburg, finally making his escape to Russia and offering his services to the Red Army. Budyonny was a simple peasant who had been a corporal in the old army. He was retired from service and reenlisted voluntarily to fight against the Whites, after returning to his home in the province of Tambov and finding that his father and two brothers had been murdered in the raid of Mamontov's cavalry.[8]

The young officers whom I saw on the day of their graduation were a rather fine looking lot. There were cavalry, artillery, infantry and engineer officers among them. Their khaki uniforms were exceedingly smart and many of them were already wearing the new pointed cap with a large red star on the front, somewhat resembling the old German helmet. Their oath of allegiance, which was read to them by Trotsky and subscribed to by every man present, standing at salute, was as follows:

1. I, son of the working people, citizen of the Soviet Republic, take upon myself the name of a warrior of the Workers' and Peasants' Army.

2. Before the working classes of Russia and of the whole world I undertake to carry this name with honor, to follow the military calling with conscience and

5. Gregory I. Petrovsky (1878-1958) was later the Chairman of the Central Executive Committee of the USSR from 1922-1938.
6. Mikhail N. Tukhachevsky (1893-1937). In July 1920 he launched a successful counterattack against the Poles that retook Minsk and much of western Ukraine. His August 1920 attack on Warsaw failed, however, leading to Russia's loss in the war.
7. Semyon M. Budyonny (1883-1973) was a career military commander in Imperial and Soviet Russia. He commanded Red Army forces in Ukraine during the Russian Civil War.
8. Konstantin Mamontov was a White military commander in the Russian Civil War.

to preserve from damage and robbery the national and military possessions as the hair of my head.

3. I pledge myself to submit strictly to revolutionary discipline and to fulfill without objection every command issued by authority of the Workers' and Peasants' Government.

4. I undertake to abstain from and to deter any act liable to dishonor the name of citizen of the Soviet Republic; moreover, to direct all my deeds and thoughts to the great aim of liberation of all workers.

5. I pledge myself to the defense of the Soviet Republic in any danger of assault on the part of any of her enemies at the first call of the Workers' and Peasants' Government, and undertake not to spare myself in the struggle for the Russian Soviet Republic, for the aims of Socialism and the Brotherhood of Nations to the extent of my full strength and of my life.

6. Should this promise be broken, let my fate be the scorn of my fellows. Let my punishment be the stern hand of revolutionary law.

That the Bolsheviks intend to make Russia a nation of soldiers is shown by the fact that military training does not by any means begin with the attainment of the age for military service. The Boy Scout movement, which is under the supervision of the remarkable organization known as the Communist Youth, is very widespread in Russia. Boys up to the age of sixteen combine physical and military training in these Scout organizations, and it was interesting to note that they had preserved the fleur de lis, the international symbol of the Boy Scouts, as their insignia. Boys from sixteen to eighteen also receive a certain amount of military training in the clubs of the Communist Youth, or, if they are industrial workers, in their factory organizations. There are a number of Girl Guides, corresponding to our Campfire Girls, and a few women are in the regular militia and the workers' reserve.

The internal situation meanwhile was growing far from satisfactory. The Red Army drive on Warsaw, during which Tukhachevsky extended his army in a long narrow wedge reaching nearly to the German border, was recognized as an impossible tactical position. When the offensive was undertaken, the government was counting on an immediate revolution in Poland. This idea was so firmly rooted in the minds of the Bolshevik leaders that, after taking Minsk, a Polish committee, headed by Dzerzhinsky and Marchlewski,[9] were sent to the occupied territory and published a proclamation proclaiming Soviet

....
9. Julian Marchlewski (1866-1925) was a member of the Polish Socialist Party (*Polska Partia Socjalistycznna*, PPS).

government in Poland. It was expected that the army, supported by the peasants, would mutiny and start a revolution. It turned out that the Communists were misinformed as to the strength of the revolutionary movement, and they miscalculated in this respect, falling as far short of realizing the actual situation in Poland as they did that in Germany, when they signed the peace of Brest-Litovsk.

After the failure of the Warsaw drive, there was much discontent in the army, stimulated by the reduction of the food rations, the lack of equipment, particularly in shoes, and the long drawn out armistice negotiations. In August there was a mutiny in the Moscow garrison, owing to the fact that straw slippers known as "*lapti*"[10] were given out to the soldiers instead of boots. Several regiments on the Western front held meetings and sent a delegation to Moscow to protest against the reduction in food rations. The delegation was arrested and several of the members shot, whereupon the front line regiments arrested their political commissars, threatening to hold them until their comrades in Moscow were released, and this was done. Mass desertions took place among regiments leaving for the front. One regiment passing through Moscow lost over five hundred men between that city and the front. Reserve troops were not given rifles until they reached the front lines, for fear they might start trouble en route. This state of affairs in the army is nothing new, however, and it was one of the difficulties that had to be contended with throughout the Great War.

Wrangel was making some progress on the Crimean front and his raid in the direction of the Caucasus, while not successful, caused an unsettled condition in that part of the country. Moscow seethed with plots of all descriptions. One day in the Petrovka several armed men in an automobile held up a government truck that was transporting three hundred million rubles and got away with their booty. The money was afterwards recovered in a rather curious manner. Some children in one of the suburbs of Moscow were holding the funeral of a pet cat and started to dig the grave on a vacant lot a short distance from their home. They chose a spot which looked as if someone had been digging there a short time before. About a foot underneath the surface they struck something hard. "Hidden treasure," they said, and began to dig harder than ever. It was indeed hidden treasure, for it proved to be the entire sum, which had evidently been placed there during the night by the bandits for temporary safe keeping. The Soviet authorities gave it out that this robbery was political in character and

10. *lapti* are Russian peasant slippers woven from straw.

had been committed by the Social Revolutionaries for the purpose of securing funds for party propaganda.

As the weather was very warm, we often had tea parties in the garden at the Kharitonevsky. One Sunday afternoon at about six o'clock, as we were peacefully sipping tea, we were startled by a series of terrific explosions, developing into what sounded like a regular bombardment. The large plate glass windows in our house rattled like castanets, a dense cloud of smoke could be seen to the northwest, and evil looking little white rings rose in the air bursting with a horrible noise. As the thing grew worse one of our windows went, then we could hear the sound of breaking glass in all directions. Evidently something terrible had happened. A few nervous individuals suggested that the Poles might be coming, for it was then well known that they had pushed some distance east of Minsk in the Berezina offensive, but we at once dismissed this idea as impossible. The telephone was temporarily out of commission; so, curiosity getting the better of us, although there was considerable danger in the streets from breaking glass and bits of cornices dislodged by the concussion, we started for the Foreign Office to find out what was the matter. On the way we met many frightened groups of people, and one or two who had been badly cut by pieces of broken glass. Wild rumors were current, chiefly of a Polish plot to blow up all Moscow. When we arrived at the Foreign Office we found that there had been an explosion at Khodinka, the large munition depot, about eight versts from the city. About fifty persons, chiefly guards, had been killed. Detachments of the militia had been sent to stop the resulting conflagration and prevent the explosion from spreading to a still larger depot, and the aviation station nearby. It was said frankly, that if the fire could not be stopped there would be serious danger to Moscow. Meanwhile the town was put under military law, and people warned to keep off the streets unless on urgent business. All that night the explosions continued and it was only by early morning that their decreasing frequency made us realize that the situation must be under control. The bombardment kept up at intervals until the afternoon of the next day. Hundreds of arrests were made in connection with the affair, which turned out to have been a Polish plot for which three Poles, three Russians and three Jews, were eventually executed.

CHAPTER XIX
A Modern Babel

*A*nyone who imagines that the isolation of Russia from the rest of the world is anything more than a material isolation is very much mistaken. Moscow is probably today the most cosmopolitan city of Europe. I certainly found it so during the summer of 1920. The meeting of the Third International brought delegates from every part of the world, as well as hosts of sympathizers and foreign journalists. There were peace delegations, labor delegations, businessmen, representatives of oppressed nationalities and political minorities, propagandists, crooks and idealists from the four quarters of the globe.

During the Latvian peace negotiations, which took place in June,[1] I met Ioffe, head of the Russian delegation. Ioffe is Russia's professional peace negotiator, having conducted the negotiations with Estonia, Latvia, Lithuania and Poland. He is a Jew, short, thick set, bearded, with keen brown eyes and a rather prepossessing manner, and was a frequent visitor at our house, where his young daughter and his first wife, from whom he had been divorced two years previously, were living. She and her daughter, who was just recovering from an attack of typhus, occupied the two best rooms and had all their meals served in their apartment. When they went out a motor always came for them.

Madame Ioffe was beautifully dressed, she was very pretty, a wonderful musician and distinctly bourgeoise in manner and appearance. It was in her sitting room, where he came for tea practically every evening, that I had my talk

---

1. Latvia's war for independence (1919-1920) involved repulsing both a Soviet-backed government led by Peteris Stucka and backed by the Red Army (which occupied most of the country), and a Baltic German government headed by Andrievs Niedra and supported by German troops. By May 1920, Latvia had won its independence, which it more or less preserved until Soviet occupation in 1939.

with Ioffe. The fact that he had another wife in Petrograd did not in the least disturb their amicable relations.

I found him very alert and intelligent, a born diplomatist. He was interested in all national questions and was particularly enthusiastic about a proposition he had made on behalf of Russia at the Latvian conference for the cancellation of all war obligations and indemnities by the nations of the world. His ideas in this respect, he told me, exactly coincided with those of the English author, Mr. Keynes,[2] whose book he had read with great interest, and he asked me what impression it had produced in America.

I saw a great deal of the members of the Latvian delegation, which stopped at the Savoy where they had an entire floor to themselves. They had brought their own provisions and servants and had their meals served in their own dining room. Every day they were taken in a big motor bus to the home of Kharitonev, the sugar king, on the Sofiskaya Naberezhnaya, where the peace parleys were held. At night they were frequently the guests of the Foreign Office at the theater or the opera, but none of them was allowed to walk in the streets or visit private homes.

They could not receive any visitors unless the latter had special permission from the Foreign Office, and their callers were compelled to register in conformity with the regulations in force in all the government guest houses in Moscow. Every caller at these places must register with the soldier from the Cheka who is on guard at the door, his name, address, occupation and the nature of his business, and show his documents of identity or "*permis de sejour.*" He surrenders these documents on entering, receiving them on leaving the building, when the length of his stay is recorded opposite the information already furnished. These lists are turned in daily to the Cheka and enable it to keep in touch with the activities of foreigners and the extent of their intercourse with Russians.

Negotiations with Latvia dragged on for several months, the chief objects of discussion being the economic provisions of the treaty. Finally it was signed and the negotiations with Lithuania began. They were successfully concluded in a few weeks.

Meanwhile, other negotiations no less interesting than Ioffe's were going on. The Russian Government had openly espoused the cause of the Turkish

<hr>

2. John Maynard Keynes (1883-1946) was a highly influential British economist. Among many works, he wrote *The Economic Consequences of Peace* (1919), in which he criticized the harsh treatment of Germany in the settlement to World War I and predicted its economic collapse.

nationalists in Anatolia and the notorious Djemal Pasha, accompanied by Halel Pasha and the *effendi*,[3] arrived in Moscow to secure recognition of the Angora Government under Mustapha Kemal.[4]

I found Djemal a most charming person, frankly bourgeois and nationalistic in his ideas, and making no secret of his motives for seeking an alliance with Soviet Russia.

"Aren't you afraid of the spread of Bolshevik propaganda in Asia Minor if you sign a treaty with the Soviet Government?" I asked him.

"My dear lady," he said suavely, "if your house is on fire, do you ask the politics of the man who comes to help you put it out?"

His one aim, open and avowed, was to secure assistance against the British controlled government at Constantinople, and he did not care on what terms he got it. As for the danger of Bolshevist propaganda, he was counting on conservative Islam to take care of that. He was very careful to remove from my mind any idea that he was pro-German, claiming that the Turks were forced into the position of becoming allies of the Germans in the Great War; that after the war he and Enver and Talat[5] had wished to come to an understanding with England, but had been driven by British imperialism back into the arms of Germany.

The Persian peace delegation arrived shortly after, then the Chinese, with a special train loaded with rice and tea, which they sold quite openly at speculative prices in Moscow, no doubt paying their expenses for the entire trip. At this time an agreement was concluded between the Soviet Government and the Peking Government, under which the latter was to operate the Eastern Chinese railroad, wherein the former Imperial Russian Government had a large interest. Simultaneously, I believe, negotiations, less open in character, were going on with the Southern Chinese Government.[6]

Then there were the Bukharans, to whom I have already referred, and the Khivans,[7] who had about this time made a Soviet revolution to order. Later,

....

3. She is referring here to Ismail Enver (1881-1922), who was a leader of the Young Turk movement.
4. At the end of World War I, the Ottoman Empire collapsed, but the Turkish portion of the empire reorganized quickly into the state of Turkey under the leadership of Mustapha Kemal (Kemal Ataturk).
5. Mehmad Talat (1874-1921), also known as Talat Pasha, was a leader of the Young Turk movement who also took part in the Armenian genocide. He was assassinated in 1921.
6. After China's revolution in 1912 and overthrow of its monarchy, the country remained divided until the success of the Communist Revolution in 1949.
7. In February 1920, the Khorezm People's Soviet Republic succeeded the Khanate of Khiva, when Khan Sayid Abdullah abdicated. In October 1923, it was transformed into the Khorezm Socialist Soviet Republic, and in February 1925, it was divided between the Uzbek SSR, Turkmen SSR, and Karakalpak Autonomous Oblast.

when the Khan of Khiva came to Moscow, he was arrested and interned in the Andronovsky camp, just why I was never able to discover.

The delegate from Afghanistan was most picturesque, tall, slender, dark, with wonderful eyes, and he spoke English fairly well. One day I met him in the Savoy Hotel and he invited me to tea, whereupon he began what I presume was a typical Afghan courtship. This was the substance of our conversation:

"You long in Moscow?" he asked.

"Four months," I told him.

"You got husband at home?"

"No."

"You find a man here?"

"No."

"You young, and you look healthy. I got plenty wives in Afghanistan, but here it is very lonely. I don't want Russian woman — I always wanted English woman. We marry now, what you say? We stay married while I'm here or I take you back to Afghanistan. Fine country. You be first wife."

All this time, he was coming nearer and nearer with the most intense expression, which did not take my fancy by any means. I told him I'd have to think it over until the next day, then made my escape as soon as I could.

There were other delegates not as official, but just as important and more mysterious. For example, Dr. Mansur, an Indian nationalist of whom I have already spoken, who lived at the Savoy, lectured at the General Staff College in Moscow, and conducted courses in the Foreign Office school of Oriental languages. He was always busy receiving couriers and mysterious individuals who came from Berlin and Tashkent, where there was a Far Eastern Soviet propaganda center. Mansur was very intimate with Meyerhoeffer, who had stayed on in Russia after he was superceded by the official Austrian Mission. He was a Moslem convert and a strong supporter of Pan-Islamism and was also in receipt of constant communications from India, Asia Minor, Vienna and Berlin.

The Sinn Feiners[8] had their delegation and were often in conference with Soviet leaders. So also were the Korean nationalists whose leader, Pak, I knew very well. Mexico was represented by M.N. Roy,[9] an East Indian, with a handsome Mexican wife.

---

8. Sinn Fein is an Irish political party organized in 1905 to advocate for Irish independence.

9. Mandabendra Nath Roy (1887-1954) was a Bengali international revolutionary who was active in India and Mexico.

Besides the British Labor Delegation, there was an official Italian Labor delegation, and I saw something of several of the members, among them Dugoni, one of the Serratists who were exceedingly unpopular with Moscow. At that time were laid the foundations for the open breach which later took place in the Italian Socialist party. Lenin was pressing the delegation to support a revolution in Italy; the more moderate members represented to him the impossibility of attempting to inaugurate a Soviet regime in Italy without the assurance of the support of other countries. Italy, they said, had a supply of coal for three weeks, bread for a month, and raw materials for six weeks, and an attempt at revolution would only result in an economic blockade which would starve out Italy in a short time. In spite of these statements, the abortive attempt to seize control of the factories by the Italian working men was made in the summer of 1920 at the instigation of Moscow.

The Italians, like the British, lived at the Delovoy Dvor, formerly one of the best hotels in the city, which was reserved for Trades Union and Third International delegates. I was forbidden to go there, but I nevertheless was a frequent visitor and this did not help to make me popular with the authorities. The Italians brought all their own food, had macaroni and chianti every day. Like other foreign visitors who remain a short time, they had no idea of the privations and difficulties of the ordinary citizen in Moscow.

A German labor delegation was at the Savoy. The Germans were all working men, mostly Communists and they had come to draw up a convention with the Soviet Government for mass colonization in Russia. Negotiations between them and the All Russian Council of Trades Unions dragged on for a long time without results. The Germans wished to take over control of entire factories with their own personnel and to establish their own colonies. Russian living quarters did not suit them; they demanded the right to obtain building materials, construct their own homes, run their own cooperatives, and to bring a certain amount of money into the country with them. All these demands were not agreed to by the Soviet authorities. Meanwhile, they were quietly investigating conditions for themselves, and it was evident that, while thoroughly in sympathy with Communistic principles, their orderly German ideas, deeply rooted in tradition and strengthened by training, could not be adjusted to the life about them.

One of them said to me: "It's all very fine for everyone to be a productive worker, but I consider that my wife who runs my home and bears my children is just as much of a productive worker as if she worked in an office or factory. I don't want her to go out to work. I don't want to eat in a public dining room;

I want her to stay home and cook for me. It may be that I can buy just as good shirts at one of the government stores as she makes, but she's always made my shirts and I like the way she makes them. It may be all right to have your socks mended and your suspender buttons sewed on at a cooperative mending shop, but I like the way she does it. I'm not a religious man, but I want to have my children left free in matters of religion. I don't want them taught Atheism any more than I want them taught Catholicism or Lutheranism."

This was the attitude of most of the Germans and, owing to this as well as political and economic reasons, the German scheme for mass colonization was temporarily, at least, abandoned.

For a time Cachin[10] and Froissard, the French Communist delegates, stayed at my guest house, and while they were there it served as a rendezvous for all the French Communists in Moscow. Among them was Jacques Sadoul,[11] who had come up from Kharkov, where he was stationed as military adviser for the Ukrainian Government. I suppose there has been more speculation about the attitude of Sadoul towards the Soviet government than any of the other foreign Communists in Russia. He was attached to the French Military Mission in Russia during the Great War. At the time of the March Revolution, he declared himself in favor of the revolutionists and afterwards went over to the Bolsheviks. In his absence, he was tried and condemned to death by a military court martial in France, and of course, whatever his convictions, he has burned his bridges and can never return to his own country unless there is a revolution.

Sadoul is, in appearance, a most attractive person. He is short, rather thick set, blond, with a ruddy complexion, with clear blue eyes, rather the Norman type. In conversation he is very animated, and extremely genial. He struck me as being thoroughly happy, absolutely at ease in his strange surroundings. He was dressed, when I saw him, in a knickerbocker suit of English tweeds, with woolen golf stockings, and smart brown shoes that betokened a rather fastidious care of appearances. He was more interested in hearing from the Frenchmen all about the latest happenings in Paris, even down to what was playing at the theaters, than in talking politics. With regard to Russia, he expressed himself as convinced that Communism of the military stamp was the only force which could keep the country from lapsing into chaos.

---

10. Marcel Cachin (1869-1958) was one of the founders of the French Communist Party in 1920.

11. Jacques Sadoul (1881-1956) was a French Communist resident in Russia during World War I and the Russian Revolution. He returned to France in 1924 and was active in the French Communist Party, working as a correspondent for *Izvestia*. He was awarded the Order of the Red Banner in 1927.

His wife, who had arrived from Paris with his brother some weeks before, was a Parisienne to her fingertips, beautifully dressed and seemed decidedly out of place in her surroundings. She impressed me as being Communistic rather out of loyalty to her husband than from personal convictions and complained bitterly of the persecutions she had been subjected to in Paris on his account. Monsieur Sadoul, the brother, reminded me more of a floor walker from the Bon Marche than anything else. He was a timid, delicate looking little man, and was the only person I saw in Russia who wore a frock coat and stiff collar. Black bread and kasha disagreed with him; he was evidently bewildered and not a little frightened by the strange new forces with which he found himself in contact, and I think he heartily wished he was back on the Boulevard Raspail, talking about Socialism in a cafe.

Rene Marchand,[12] who is one of the ablest French publicists in Russia, gave me quite a different impression from that which I received from Sadoul. For some years before the Revolution he was correspondent for the *Paris Temps* in Petrograd; he also was mysteriously converted, publishing his declaration of faith in a rather remarkable pamphlet entitled "Why I rallied to the formula of the Social Revolution." He is a tall, dark, distinguished looking man, who says very little and appears at times to be suffering under a great nervous strain. He lives simply and very poorly with his wife and children, at the former Hotel Metropole, works very hard, and sees few visitors. Judging purely from superficial indications, I would be inclined to believe the gossip current in certain circles which has it that Marchand's conversion to Communism was due to pressure rather than to conviction.

Pascal,[13] the Frenchman who writes the "letters" that are sent out periodically by Soviet radio describing social, political and economic conditions in Russia, is a suave, exceedingly agreeable man. He was formerly a priest, more lately member of the French Military Mission to Petrograd, and is now a Communist. Strange to say, he has remained a staunch Catholic and goes to mass every Sunday.

The most energetic and able of the French Communists in Russia is Henri Guilbeaux.[14] He has rather an interesting history. During the war he was on the

---

12. Rene Marchand was a French journalist and publicist who was rumored to be a Cheka informant.
13. Pierre Pascal (1890-1983) was a part of the French Military mission in early Soviet Russia. In the early 1930s, he left the Communist Party because of Stalin's purges.
14. Henri Guilbeaux (1885-1938) was a French Communist who was a supporter of Leon Trotsky.

staff of a French newspaper, and took part in the Zimmerwaldian movement,[15] attending the congress. For this and for alleged treasonable correspondence with German Socialists, charges were preferred against him and he was compelled to leave France. He remained for some time in Switzerland and then drifted to Russia. He is an occasional correspondent of *L'Humanite, Le Populaire*, and other French Socialist papers. He is always chosen by the Soviet Government to show around distinguished French-speaking Socialist visitors. He is extremely cultivated, being an author of some distinction, very witty, and an able propagandist.

One of the most picturesque delegates to the International was the veteran German Revolutionary, Clara Zetkin.[16] She is a fat little German Hausfrau in appearance, and always wears a black silk dress, with a lace collar and a large cameo brooch. Her cheeks are as ruddy as winter apples and her gray hair is parted and drawn to a demure little knot at the back of her head. In spite of her seventy-six years, her speaking voice is wonderfully clear and she is just as full of revolutionary fire and spirit as if she were sixteen, instead of seventy-six.

I also saw something of Bilan and Stoklitsky,[17] American delegates to the International. Bilan was a quiet, unassuming man with a rather attractive personality. I was told that he was a Norwegian by birth. It seemed to me, judging from his conversation, that he was giving the Soviet authorities a rather exaggerated idea of the importance of the Communist movement in America. McLaine and Quelch,[18] two of the English Communists, were very alert, intelligent men. Most of the other Anglo-Saxon delegates whom I met were either naturalized Russian Jews, or immature youths, who seemed to regard Communism rather in the light of a great adventure. All the delegates made a sort of clubhouse of the headquarters of the Third International in

---

15. This refers to the Zimmerwald Conference held in Switzerland from September 5 through 8, 1915. It was an international conference of socialists which came out in opposition to World War I, and marked the beginning of the end of the coalition between revolutionary socialists (communists) and reformist socialists (social democrats) in the Second International.

16. Clara Zetkin (1857-1933) was a highly influential German socialist and fighter for women's rights. She went on to serve in the German Reichstag from 1920 until her death in 1933.

17. Two competing American Communist parties had been founded in 1919. The Communist Party of America sent two delegates to the Comintern conference, Alexander Stoklitsky and Louis Fraina. Stoklitsky was Translator-Secretary of the Russian Socialist Federation and a founding member of the Communist Party of America. The Communist Labor Party sent four delegates, including John Reed (journalist and author of *Ten Days That Shook The World*) and Alexander Bilan. Moscow forced the factions to unify into the Communist Party of the USA in 1921.

18. The delegates from Great Britain were William McLaine and Tom Quelch.

the Dyeneshny Pereulok, formerly the home of Count Mirbach,[19] the German Ambassador, who was assassinated in 1918. I was never allowed to set foot within its sacred precincts.

I did not meet Zinoviev, the chairman of the Congress, but I frequently heard him speak at meetings. He is a rugged, unprepossessing looking individual of a distinctly Jewish type, with an extremely forceful, dominating personality. It is this quality which has given him his present position. Zinoviev is not popular either among his colleagues or among the working classes. Several times during the summer at meetings in Petrograd, he was hooted down by factory workmen. Once he appeared at a meeting wearing one of the black leather coats that are much affected by the Red Army men and commissars. He spoke of the fact that it was

Lenin with Comintern delegates

necessary for the workers to make great sacrifices to assure the prosperity of the Soviet Republic. "Suppose the fellow in the leather jacket sets us the example," shouted a voice in the audience.

Among the foreign visitors at my guest house at this time was a Hungarian journalist named Holitscher.[20] He was a very delightful person; sympathetic, but not blind to the flaws in the Soviet Government; more of a literary man than a politician. Through him I met Dr. Varga, formerly Commissar of Education in the short-lived Hungarian Communist experiment. He was a dark, intense little man, one of those to whom Marxism is a cult, but apart from his fanaticism he was a man of broad general culture, quite different from Bela Kun,[21] whom I

19. Wilhelm Graf von Mirbach-Harff (1871-1918) was German ambassador to Soviet Russia in 1918.
20. Arthur Holitscher (1869-1941) was a Hungarian journalist and writer who wrote about his travels to many parts of the world, including the United States.
21. Bela Kun (1886-1938) was a Hungarian communist who led the Hungarian Soviet Republic in 1919.

saw very often. The latter impressed me as being a decidedly coarse, materialistic person, very much of an opportunist.

There were also several French correspondents and two Italians, Dodone of the *Cornere delta Sera*, and Panunzio[22] of the Socialist paper *Avanti*. Dodone, who was formerly an Italian officer, was under house arrest during his entire stay, which was limited to the prescribed two weeks for correspondents. Panunzio stayed longer and his visit terminated in a rather unpleasant experience. At the time of the Polish armistice negotiations at Minsk, he went with several other correspondents to attend the conference, intending, so he told me, to go directly from Minsk to Petrograd and leave the country.

About four weeks afterwards I was startled to see Panunzio appear in my room one morning, haggard, dirty, collarless and with a scraggly beard. He told me that he had been arrested in Minsk by the Cheka without a word of explanation, and brought back to Moscow, where he was imprisoned for three weeks in the Lubyanka 2, accused, much to his amazement, of espionage. He was not allowed to communicate with any of his Socialist friends, and would probably have been there indefinitely, except for the fact that his interpreter, to whom he had promised to write from Petrograd on a matter of business, grew suspicious and reported her fears to the members of the Italian Socialist Delegation then in Moscow, with the result that explanations were forthcoming and Panunzio was set at liberty. It seemed that, while he was in Minsk, the *Avanti* had published a dispatch with Moscow dateline in which were given statistics and information as to strength, equipment, distribution and morale of the Red Army. Although it was not signed and it was proved later to have been written by the Riga correspondent of the paper, Panunzio was suspected of being the author. It was thought that he had illegal means of sending correspondence out of Russia and he was detained on suspicion.

One day I went with Beach and Tanner,[23] two representatives of the English shop stewards, to meet two members of the Executive Committee of the Right Social Revolutionaries. These men were wanted by the Bolshevik authorities, so there was considerable mystery about it. We met by appointment in one of the squares in Moscow a Jewish gentleman, professedly a Menshevik, and formerly the correspondent of the United Telegraph Company in Petrograd. In view of what happened later and of several other circumstances, I am inclined

22. Sergio Panunzio (1886-1944) was an Italian socialist who later supported fascism.
23. Dick Beach was actually a delegate to the Congress from the Industrial Workers of the World; Jack Tanner was a delegate from Britain's Shop Steward's Movement.

to think he was playing quite another role, and was probably an agent of the Extraordinary Commission.

We accompanied him for several blocks, when he disappeared, after telling us to follow a young lady in a blue head kerchief who was strolling apparently unconcernedly up the street. Presently, she disappeared inside on an arched doorway. We did the same, following at a safe distance. Once inside of the hallway at the back of the court, she turned to us, and told us that she would take us to an apartment upstairs, where we would meet our men. I acted as interpreter for the Britishers during our half hour talk, after which they were obliged to leave and I stayed on for a cup of tea with the two Russians and our hostess, a teacher in the apartment which was used as a kindergarten. When I left, I found two soldiers armed with rifles in the hall. "Where did you come from?" they asked. I told them.

"Well, you must go back and stay," said one of them. "There is a raid of the Cheka on and no one will be allowed to leave the building."

Meanwhile, anyone was allowed to enter; perfectly innocent people calling on their friends were detained pending a room-to-room search. I went back to my friends, and found that the two Social Revolutionaries had disappeared as if by magic. The teacher, evidently very much alarmed, was still there, so we sat down and decided to make the best of it.

In a few minutes, two soldiers accompanied by a civil agent of the Cheka and the Chairman of the Housing Committee appeared and searched the apartment from end to end. Not a drawer was left unopened, not a paper escaped scrutiny, and they even went through the children's work and kindergarten material. Pictures were taken off the wall and examined, mattresses and pillows felt for concealed papers or documents; not a nook or cranny was left uninspected. Unfortunately some compromising papers were found in the teacher's desk and at the same moment her husband arrived most inopportunely. They were both arrested and taken away to the Cheka.

Meanwhile, I was told that I would be obliged to remain in the apartment until they had searched the whole building. Seeing that I was a foreigner, the chairman of the Housing Committee, a Lett who spoke German exceedingly well, tried to make matters as pleasant as possible for me. He asked his wife down, brought in the inevitable samovar, and invited me to have a cup of tea with bread and butter. It was then about ten o'clock and I had been there since six. After the search was completed, the Chekists retired, leaving a soldier on guard to see that no one left the apartment. He sat there motionless with his rifle between his knees, while my host and I talked in German. In a few minutes, I strolled over to the piano and began to pick out the melodies of a few Russian folk songs.

Up to this time he had been perfectly stolid and uninterested in the proceedings, then suddenly his whole expression changed.

"Fraulein," he said, in excellent German, "you speak German almost like a native. Have you lived in the Fatherland?"

I told him that I had spent much time in Germany. He hesitated. "Perhaps you could sing me a German song, just one," he begged.

"Yes, indeed," I answered, and sitting at the piano I sang one after another, a number of the homely German folk songs that are known to all the people, *Du, du liegst mir im Herzen, Ach, du lieber Augustin, Ich hatt' einen Kameraden,* and several others. He sat there spellbound and presently I noticed great tears, one after another, rolling down his lined cheeks. When I finished, for a few minutes he was unable to speak, then he said quite simply:

"Thank you, Fraulein, you have made me happier than I have been for six long years."

After that, little by little, the whole story came out. He was a German prisoner of war who had been captured during the Russian drive in East Prussia, in the summer of 1914. For five years he had been kept in prison camps or in the villages at compulsory labor, then he had given up hopes of ever getting back to the Fatherland again and had taken service with the Cheka, because, as he told me, he got better food and pay there than anywhere else. He had renounced his German citizenship just before the arrival of the German Repatriation Mission, his bridges were burned, he could never return to Germany, where he had a wife and three little children. Such instances among foreign nationals are not uncommon in Russia; they are part of the tragic aftermath of the Great War. I talked with my Latvian friends for several hours and it was two o'clock before the raid was over and I was allowed to go home.

CHAPTER XX
Al Fresco Adventures

*I*t was pretty hot in the dog days, and I was delighted when I received an invitation from some American friends, Mr. Hopwood,[1] formerly manager of the Kodak Company, and his two daughters, to spend a weekend in the country. We stayed in the house of an old peasant woman, a widow, whose son had been killed in the Great War, and who lived alone with her little grandchild. She belonged to the upper class of peasants, the Kulaks,[2] who have always owned their own land, and are still quite prosperous, representing the peasant bourgeoisie. In consequence they are much detested by the Communists, and they are rankly counter-revolutionary.

She had, until recently, made a very good living out of her cows and her small market garden, but the former had been requisitioned, only one being left her on account of the small boy who had to have milk. She was no longer able to work herself, she informed me, and owing to the tremendous decrease of manpower in the village, due to conscription and the number of peasants who had gone to the city as industrial workers, she had been unable to plant but a small part of her property. She gave us fresh eggs, a little milk, and some black bread. We supplied salt, sugar and real tea, much to her delight, for she had not tasted the last named for more than two years. She told us that the peasants in the village were bitterly discontented over the requisitions made by the government.

---

1. Samuel Hopwood was the stockkeeper for the Kodak Company in Moscow. In 1919, the Bolsheviks seized the Kodak facilities and refused to let Hopwood and his family leave Russia until later in 1920.
2. *Kulaks* were a wealthy group of peasants who owned land. In the late 1920s, Stalin began a campaign to "liquidate" the *kulaks*.

Each man had been compelled to furnish a certain number of *poods* of potatoes in proportion to the amount of acreage he had under cultivation. If he did not happen to have raised potatoes, he was obliged to exchange something he had raised with his neighbors for potatoes, and furnish the required amount. The hay crop was poor; even there in the country hay cost twelve thousand rubles a bale, and peasants who had had a poor harvest were compelled to buy hay for their horses and cattle. In many cases they were killing them, selling the meat on the open market rather than do this. She told me that all the peasants said there would soon be another revolution. As to where this revolution was coming from, how it was to be brought about, or what was to be their part in it, they had not the faintest idea. That seemed to me to be the weak point in all the opposition to the Soviet Government. Everybody was discontented, everybody expected the Soviet Government would be overthrown, but every man thought the other fellow was going to do it.

The sun was blazing hot and we were tired and dirty when we arrived at our destination on Saturday afternoon. We had walked at least ten *versts* from the station, and the village was situated near the Moskva River, which looked very cool and tempting.

"Let's go in bathing," said my companions.

"I'd like to," I answered, "but I have no bathing suit."

"That makes no difference," they answered. "Nobody wears a bathing suit in Russia. Come down to the river and see for yourself."

When I got there I saw the most startling sight I have ever witnessed. At this point the river made a sharp turn, throwing up a bank of fine white sand, which made an ideal beach. On the beach and in the water beyond were hundreds of naked people, men, women, boys and girls, all indiscriminately mingled. Some were standing knee-deep in the water chatting with their neighbors, others taking a sun bath, quite undisturbed; no one seemed in the least self-conscious or concerned.

"If it's the custom of the country, I suppose I can do it, too," I said, "but let's go a little further up the beach." So we withdrew to a slightly secluded spot, where we undressed, leaving our clothes on the bank in charge of the father of my two friends. They laughed at me because, as a vestige of Anglo-Saxon prudery, I kept on my hat until the last, but after the first agonized moment I quite forgot my embarrassment and never enjoyed a swim more in my life.

This utter absence of conventionality or self-consciousness was to me one of the most delightful things about the Russians. They act and dress exactly as they please on all occasions. In the streets in Moscow you see long-haired men, and short-haired women, girls without stockings, and on some occasions wearing men's clothes, while the men wear anything that suits their fancy. The regular summer costume of the un-Europeanized Russian is a pair of loose trousers, of linen or cloth tucked into high, soft boots, a linen or *pongee* blouse,[3] often beautifully embroidered in cross-stitch with bright colors, buttoning on the side with a high standing collar, worn outside the trousers. It is sometimes held in by a narrow leather belt, but more often by a bright-colored, knotted cotton cord with tassels.

Once, outside of the University of Moscow, I saw a distinguished professor talking to a friend. He had bare feet, wore long linen trousers, a Russian blouse, widely open at the throat, with flowing sleeves. A black opera cape was thrown back negligently over his shoulders. On his head he wore a small round skull cap embroidered in brilliant colors. He was perfectly unconscious of the fact that his attire was at all unusual. Of course, the scarcity of clothing has something to do with these eccentricities, but the Russians have always done as they pleased in respect to such matters.

We spent the night with our peasant friend, sleeping on her little wooden porch on huge feather beds, which she provided for us, and in the morning we paid a visit to an old Russian priest and to two children's summer colonies in the neighborhood.

The priest lived in a four-room wooden house like most of those in the village, with a large, glass-enclosed porch. He wore a faded brown cassock with the enormously long sleeves and corded girdle which is the traditional costume of the Svyaschennik.[4] His small, pig-like blue eyes squinted slightly when they looked at you; he had a monumental beard and a very red nose, which suggested that in the old days at least he had not been unacquainted with vodka and probably yet had a reserve tucked away somewhere. He owned a small piece of land on which he had a flourishing market garden, where he raised his own tobacco, a number of beehives and a fine lot of chickens.

His shock-headed children, eight in number, helped him work the garden, and altogether it struck me that he was probably living very much as he had before the Revolution. He sold us ten pounds of honey at an enormous price — 4000 rubles a pound — but, as he assured us, it was very fine honey. I found him densely ignorant, barely able to read and write. He knew nothing about

3. *Pongee* is a soft woven cloth exported from China.
4. *Svyaschennik* is a Russian term for priest or clergyman.

his parishioners, and they cared nothing for him, and contributed nothing towards his maintenance except the fees he exacted for burials, christenings and marriages. As a specimen of the old-fashioned country priest, he was very interesting and I could easily see how he and his kind would rouse prejudice against the church in the minds of the more enlightened classes among the population.

While we were walking from the village of Stroganov, where we had spent the night, to Troyki, several *versts* away, where we expected to visit a model children's colony, we had an experience which was particularly illuminating. It was Sunday, and along the road we met many groups of peasants, bearded, stalwart men loafing and smoking *makhorka*, rolled in newspaper, healthy looking peasant girls, mostly barefoot with bright colored handkerchiefs tied on their heads. As we passed, most of them stared at us in a distinctly unfriendly manner, and two or three times we were greeted with cries of "Yid." At first I was bewildered and my friend Mr. Hopwood explained.

"They think we're Jews," he said, "because we evidently come from the city, and are well-dressed. All the peasants hate the Jews."

The children's colony we had come to visit was a beautiful old house, which had formerly belonged to the Karzinkins, who were among the merchant princes of old Moscow.[5] It was run by the Commissariat of Public Health, under the direct supervision of Madame Semashko, wife of the Commissar. Madame Kamenev, wife of the Chairman of the Moscow Soviet, was also a member of the Board of Control. The house was situated in the midst of a fine park, with the remains of a beautiful flower garden, on a high bluff overlooking the river, and there was a large vegetable garden from which the colony drew most of its supplies. They had five cows and several horses.

The children's quarters were very clean and comfortable. The superintendent was a most intelligent Jewish woman, not by any means a Communist, but she was tremendously interested in the educational and cultural side of the work of the Soviet Government. The older girls were busily sewing on costumes for a little play that was to be given the following week. They all looked healthy and happy, and there seemed to be excellent discipline. Dinner was served at noon and consisted of a thick soup, followed by boiled beef tongue, with

---

5. The Karzinkin (also Korzinkin) dynasty of respected merchants traced back to Andrei Karzinkin (1755-1822), a former peasant who made his fortune in the tea trade and became a merchant of the first guild. The estate at Troitse-Lykovo was purchased by his son.

mashed potatoes, stewed fruit and white rolls. The older children had tea and the younger children each a big cup of milk.

In the grounds of the Karzinkin estate was the family mausoleum. It was a small white wooden building, rectangular in shape, the long sides being composed almost entirely of glass. Entrance was through a narrow passage, on one side of which was a kitchenette furnished with samovar and cooking utensils, on the other a small pantry, still stocked with fine porcelain. This passage opened into the main room, bright and sunny with growing plants on the sills of the large windows. It was carpeted with light brown velvet and contained luxurious armchairs, a big sofa and a table on which were still lying some Russian periodicals of three years past. At the further end of the room were eight graves, covered with growing ivy, each with a large stone cross at the head, on the arms of which were hung the Easter eggs which the Russians are in the habit of bringing to their dead at Easter.

It had been the custom of the Karzinkins to come frequently to the mausoleum, probably on all church holidays and on the name days of their dead. They spent the day sitting in the comfortable armchairs, chatting, reading and drinking tea. To my Western mind it seemed at first a rather gruesome idea, but in the final analysis there was really something beautiful about it. To these people the dead were no less real than the living; it was their way of bridging the gulf between the seen and the unseen world.

In the afternoon we paid a visit to another children's colony run by the municipality of Moscow. It was situated in one of the "Dacha" settlements where the small merchants of Moscow in the old days had cottage colonies where they spent the summer months. There were about sixty children living in five or six cottages, which of course had been taken from their former owners. They were clean and well run, but there was a marked difference in the physical condition of these children from those I had seen at the first colony. The explanation was simple — they were living on the regular ration assigned by the Commissary of Education, which runs the ordinary colonies. Their dinner was thin soup and kasha with black bread. For the sixty children, most of whom were below nine years of age, only twenty glasses of milk a day were provided. The other colony received the same allowance, but it was supplemented by the private contributions and resources of the wives of the commissars whose children were among its members.

I had another delightful midsummer outing at the "Neskuchny Sad,"[6] Sans Souci Park, a beautiful country seat on the Moskva, which was a gift of Catherine the Great to one of her favorites, Prince Orlov. The palace, a handsome building in the late eighteenth century style, was being transformed into a historical museum of Russian furniture under the supervision of a Russian nobleman, who had formerly collected such things as an amateur. The park surrounding the palace, though terribly neglected, is still a beautiful specimen of landscape architecture. There are charming vistas, apparently natural waterfalls, deep green pools with overhanging birches and a background of dark evergreens, small Doric temples in unexpected spots, their stone steps green with moss. The very decay of the grass-grown drives and winding paths makes them still lovelier. Here one Saturday afternoon I was a member of a picnic party with General Brusilov, his wife and daughter, General Polivanov, Minister of War under the Tsar and later under Kerensky, and a number of other Russians of the old regime. We walked until we were tired through the grounds, and then adjourned to the janitor's house, where we had tea on an upstairs veranda with a beautiful view of the river, beyond which was Moscow with its hundreds of gilded domes and cross-crowned minarets.

The janitor had been a soldier in one of General Brusilov's regiments. He still saluted when he addressed his former commander, calling him "My General," and his wife brought in the samovar with which we made our tea; and the cups were of rare old Russian porcelain of the eighteenth century. Each of us brought a contribution for our supper, which consisted of white bread and cream cheese, cold ham, butter, tea, honey, and small cakes. The conversation was mostly of the old days. General Brusilov indulged in reminiscences about his Galician campaign; Polivanov told incidents of official life in Petrograd. With such company, and in such surroundings, it was hard to believe that I was in Soviet Russia.

Finally our talk drifted to present day matters and I was interested to learn that Polivanov shared the ideas of Brusilov with regard to the Soviet Government. Like him, he believed that ill advised intervention had done more to strengthen the Bolsheviks than anything else. He believed that the Revolution would run an evolutionary course, that the Communists were, for the moment, the only party which could govern the country, preserve order, and keep the administrative machine functioning. Any radical change, he felt, must come

....
6. Neskuchny Sad (Enjoyable Garden) is a garden near Gorky Park in Moscow, along the river Moscow (Moskva).

from within rather than from without the country if it was to be permanent. The establishment of a new oligarchy, backed by foreign powers would, he was convinced, only plunge Russia into a new civil war, and the idea of foreign influence or intervention in any form was repugnant to his sturdy nationalism. Therefore he was one of the thousands of *Bezpartini* who were willing to work with the Soviet Government. Later, he accepted a post on the Commission sent to Riga to negotiate peace with Poland, and died there shortly after his arrival. There were wild rumors current in Moscow that he had been poisoned by Russian Counter-Revolutionaries who regarded him as a traitor, but I never heard anything to substantiate these reports.[7]

The parks and boulevards were always crowded during the long summer afternoons and evenings, for during June and July it is only dark for two or three hours and the people live in the streets nearly all night. In the parks there were numbers of open air concerts; on the boulevards were all sorts of amusements, fortune tellers, photographers who took your picture while you waited, jugglers, venders of *kvas* and lemonade and itinerant musicians. One of the last named was a most picturesque figure. He was an old man with a long white beard, and no matter how hot the weather he always wore a winter overcoat that reached to his heels. Every evening he played the flute in one of the open squares. When he had collected a large crowd, mostly children, he placed himself at the head of an impromptu procession and wound fantastically in and out among the paths, playing weird melodies like an antiquated Pied Piper. Just across from the Foreign Office under the walls of the Kitai Gorod (the Chinese city), was a small garden and there, in the long summer nights, another musician gave concerts for all who cared to hear. Sitting in the windowsill in the office of the Western section, waiting for war news and political bulletins, I passed some of the few restful moments of my stay in Moscow, transported to another world on wings of song, peaceful, immutable and serene. The performer was a little gray nightingale.

---

7. The historical record indicates that he died of typhus.

CHAPTER XXI
The Shadow of the Cheka

*D*uring the summer, the repatriation of prisoners of war which had been begun some months before by the arrival of the German Mission was given an impetus by the arrival of Czecho-Slovak and Austrian Missions and of Fridtjof Nansen,[1] the great Arctic explorer, who came to arrange for the repatriation of nationals whose countries had no official intercourse with Russia, on behalf of an International Committee working under the auspices of the Red Cross.

The German Mission, headed by a man named Hilger, was managed with true Teutonic efficiency. The Germans were the first in the field, and by the spring of 1920 they had succeeded in repatriating most of their nationals. On arriving in Moscow they regained possession of the former German consulate practically intact, also another building which was used as a home for destitute or invalid German soldiers. They purchased rations to feed their prisoners from Soviet stores at Soviet prices, and even got back the three original automobiles which had been in the possession of the German Mission before the assassination of Mirbach. Mr. Hilger, who was an extremely clever man and a born diplomatist, succeeded in establishing excellent relations with the Foreign Office and also with the German Soviet,[2] for every foreign country has its own Soviet in Moscow. By tactful management he was able to overcome the prejudice of the German Soviet against officers. Other Missions had great difficulties with their Soviets in this respect. In order to secure places in repatriation echelons,

----

1. Fridtjof Nansen (1861-1930) was a Norwegian scientist, explorer, and diplomat. He was awarded the Nobel Peace Prize in 1922.
2. This was an attempt in 1919-1920 to create a socialist state in postwar Germany. It is worth mentioning here that German assistance to the Bolsheviks was not insignificant in their rise to power.

prisoners of war must have their papers vised by the Soviet of the country to which they belong and this body invariably gives the preference to enlisted men, holding back officers as long as possible.

Mr. Hilger's activities were not entirely confined to repatriation, for he was also acting as the unofficial commercial agent of Germany and through him contracts were signed with the Soviet Government for the importation of large quantities of chemicals, drugs, medicines, surgical supplies, farm implements and tools.

The Czecho-Slovak Mission arrived in June and lived at my guest house. The chief was Mr. Skala, a former officer in the Czecho-Slovak Army in France; his wife, who acted as secretary to the Mission, was an American girl born in Chicago, of Czecho-Slovak parents, who had gone to Europe in 1915 as a member of the Serbian Unit of the American Red Cross. We became great friends, and she was of considerable assistance to me in carrying on the work I undertook later for the American prisoners.

The problem of the Czechs was a particularly difficult one. They were saddled with the work of repatriating about thirty-five thousand Czecho-Slovaks who had been captured in Siberia during the Kolchak retreat.[3] These men were scattered throughout Western Siberia, Southeastern Russia and Turkestan; some were in internment camps, others had been allowed to settle in the villages where they had gone to work; many had died or simply disappeared. It was a tremendous task to locate all these men, to secure transportation to Moscow, and finally to organize the echelons which left for Reval[4] twice a week.

The Russian organization through which the problem of repatriation was handled was the CentroEvak of which a Lett named Eiduk[5] was chairman. Every foreigner who has been resident in Russia, whether a civilian or prisoner of war, must receive his permit to leave the country through the CentroEvak and this permit must have the vise of the Foreign Office and of the Cheka.

....

3. At the outbreak of World War I, Czechs living in the Russian Empire petitioned Tsar Nicholas to be allowed to establish a national force to fight on the side of Russia and the Entente against Austria-Hungary, in order to secure an independent Czech state. When the Revolution abruptly ended Russia's involvement in the war, the Bolsheviks agreed to send the Czech Legions home by an easterly path. But when transportation and diplomatic issues during the Russian Civil War complicated the transfer, the Czechs seized much of the Trans-Siberian Railroad and sided with the Whites in the Civil War. Their evacuation was cited by the U.S. as one of the causes for its invasion of Murmansk in 1918. It was not until 1920 that the remaining Czechs (nearly 70,000) were evacuated home out of Vladivostok. An independent Czechoslovakia was born in 1918.

4. The Germanic name for Tallinn.

5. Alexander Eiduk (?-1938) was a poet, member of the Cheka, and the official representative to the American Relief Administration.

Foreign nationals arriving in Moscow from distant points in Russia are housed in enormous concentration points pending their departure, where they are supplied with rations and given a place to sleep.

I visited one of these concentration points near the Nikolai Station[6] with Madame Skala. It had formerly been an almshouse, and was packed from garret to cellar with a swarming mass of humanity of various nationalities: Letts, Estonians, Lithuanians, Poles, Italians, Greeks, Rumanians, Ukrainians and many others.

The Czecho-Slovaks were assigned special quarters where they were fairly comfortable, but the other nationalities were packed in helter-skelter, men, women, and children together with their filthy, nondescript baggage. I talked to a number of the Czechs, many of whom had heard nothing from their families for four or five years. In the hospital ward were numbers of men from Turkestan, desperately ill with malaria.

In one bed was an elderly man in a pitiable mental as well as physical condition. He was a Baron, but on his arrival in Moscow he had registered at the Czecho-Slovak Soviet under his Christian and family names without stating his former rank, thinking, very rightly, that as titles are not recognized at present in Czecho-Slovakia, it was not of the slightest importance. His family name was well known, however, and the zealous Czech Communists hunted him up in the *Almanach de Gotha*,[7] and accused him of some deep, counter-revolutionary design in thus concealing his rank. Only his extreme physical weakness and the energetic intervention of Mr. Skala saved him from being sent to prison.

At the Centro-Evak concentration point, the most picturesque inhabitants were the gypsies, large numbers of whom had been conscripted into the Austrian and Hungarian armies. They absolutely refused to live in the buildings, and had built themselves shelters of boards, scraps of old tin roofing, and blankets stretched on poles in the yard, where they bivouacked and did their own cooking. The Hungarians were in a particularly unfortunate situation. The counter-revolutionary government which followed the Hungarian Commune was intensely hated by the Soviet Government and there was nobody to represent their interests. The Austrians fared better and the repatriation of Austrian nationals was conducted in a fairly orderly manner.

I saw a great deal of Nansen during his visit to Moscow, as he stayed in our guest house at the Kharitonevsky. He was not allowed to bring his own secretary,

....

6. Moscow's Nikolayevsky Train Station, now called Leningradskaya.
7. The *Almanach de Gotha*, first published in 1763, was a directory of Europe's highest nobility and royalty.

as he was a Russian, and during his ten days' stay I acted as his secretary. The Russians, who have a tremendous respect for intellectual attainment, admired Nansen greatly as a scientist, but they gave him little encouragement on the diplomatic end of his mission, and I think he was rather disheartened by the result of his first visit. He was interested in providing transportation from Reval of the foreign nationals whom the Soviet Government was willing to permit to leave the country, but whose governments had not negotiated directly with Moscow on the subject. He had very uphill work to ascertain the approximate number of these people in Russia and the transportation facilities which would be given by the Russian Government. During his stay he purposely avoided making any investigations or meddling in any way in politics, but he used to spend hours every day sitting in my room, talking about Russia and also about the United States.

He speaks English beautifully and is very fond of America and Americans. His youngest daughter was at that time in New York, where she was studying singing. Nansen has changed very little since he was in the United States some years ago. In spite of his sixty-eight years, his tall form is as erect as ever, his blue eyes are clear, his complexion fresh and ruddy. He gives the impression of tremendous physical and mental vigor. His innate conservatism was profoundly shocked by many things he saw and heard in Russia, but the humanitarian rather than the political side of the situation appealed to him.

Fridtjof Nansen

He went nowhere in Moscow, and did nothing except have frequent conferences with Foreign Office officials.

The Danish Red Cross, as a neutral organization, confined its efforts entirely to the repatriation of civilians. Its chief, Dr. Martini, also acted as unofficial commercial agent for Danish interests.

The French Red Cross, which had no legal status, was in the charge of Mademoiselle Charpentier, who cared for all the French hostages and political prisoners, including a number of officers of the French Mission who had been interned since the October Revolution. She had retained the French Red Cross headquarters on the Chistoprudny Boulevard and the French home in the Milyutinsky Pereulok, securing her funds practically unaided from members of the French colony in Moscow, many of whom were allowed to remain at liberty, though without permission to leave the country, and from Russians, employing much the same methods as those used by Mr. North. She was often very short of funds, however, and resorted to many expedients, one of which got her into trouble. She asked a number of people to contribute the little gold and silver medallions with images of the Virgin or the Saints that are worn around their necks by Catholics, which she sold to obtain money to purchase food supplies. One day she was denounced as a speculator by a Polish woman to whom she had refused to give food, and was put in the Cheka, where she spent sixteen days, being finally released through the intervention of a liberal French journalist who happened to be in Moscow, and of the French Communists, who had not lost all their sympathy for their compatriots.

Mademoiselle Charpentier, after the departure of Mr. North, undertook to provide for British prisoners. When I first met her, she was also sending weekly food packages to Kalamatiano[8] and Royal R. Keeley,[9] the only Americans then known to be in prison in Russia, but this state of affairs did not last long.

The arrest of Mr. Keeley as he was leaving the country in May was followed by that of half a dozen others, among them Chabrow,[10] who had come to Russia as correspondent of the Federated Press; Thomas Hazelwood,[11] an American deserter from Vladivostok, who had worked his way across Siberia to Moscow; and Dr. Estes and Mr. Flick,[12] the former a journalist, the latter a motion picture operator who had come from Reval with permission of the Soviet Government; Dr. Lamare,[13] a man claiming American citizenship, who had lived for many years in Russia, and Albert Boni,[14] an American publisher, who was arrested

....

8. Xenophon D. Kalamatiano (1882-1923) was an American businessman and spy in Imperial and early Soviet Russia. He was captured and imprisoned by the Bolsheviks. He was released in 1921 as part of the arrangement that released other American prisoners like Harrison. He died in 1923.

9. Royal R. Keeley (1876-?) was an economic advisor to the new Bolshevik government in 1919. He observed and wrote about the economic conditions in Russia and found them to be troubling. He was arrested in May 1920 as he was trying to leave the country. He was released in August 1921.

10. Nathan Chabrow (aka Shaborn) was an American delegate to the Third International Congress. He was imprisoned by the Bolsheviks for counter-revolutionary activity.

11. Thomas Hazelwood was an alias for an American soldier named Russell R. Pattinger, who was part of the American Expeditionary Force.

12. Westen Burgess Estes was a doctor, dentist, member of the American Military Intelligence Division during World War I, and a friend of John Reed's. He was imprisoned in 1920 and released in August of 1921. John M. Flick was arrested with Estes in 1920 because of his association with Reed and Estes.

13. Dr. Lamare (also referred to as Dr. Lambie) was an American dentist who lived in Moscow for more than three decades.

14. Albert Boni was a correspondent for the *New York Sun* for three months in Russia in 1920.

after having attended the session of the Third International on the invitation of Karl Radek.

As I learned of the arrest of these people from time to time, I interviewed the Danish and Czecho-Slovak Red Cross officials with regard to the possibility of providing for them in some way, but they declined to take the matter up officially, as their agreements with the Soviet Government covered only their own nationals. Mademoiselle Charpentier was willing to undertake the work of supplying the Americans, but she had neither the time nor the funds, so I agreed to take them off her hands.

Then began one of the most interesting though one of the most dangerous and physically tiring of all my experiences in Russia. From the end of June until the 20th of October, when I was myself arrested, I had from six to eight Americans on the list of those to whom weekly food packages must be sent. They were in the Butyrki and Cheka prisons and the Andronovsky concentration camp. Through the kindness of the Czecho-Slovak Red Cross, I was able to send packages to the Butyrki and the Andronovsky, but those at the Cheka I always delivered myself. Tuesday was the day for the Butyrki, Friday was receiving day at the other prisons.

Every Monday and Thursday I went to the Sukharevka with several market baskets, and a big knapsack on my back, usually accompanied by Madame Skala, who prepared packages for the Czecho-Slovak prisoners. There we bought our supplies, hired an *izvozchik* to take us back to the Kharitonevsky, and devoted the afternoon to cooking and preparing the food packages. I tried to vary the contents from week to week, but the average package was as follows: three pounds of black bread, a sixth of a pound of tea or coffee, a quarter of a pound of sugar, half a pound of butter or bacon, a small amount of cooked meat or sausage, a few hard-boiled eggs or boiled potatoes, an earthenware bowl of baked beans, baked apples or boiled vegetables, cigarettes or tobacco, matches and once a month a cake of soap.

To secure funds was a rather difficult matter. I exchanged the American money I had brought with me at illegal rates through the speculators in Moscow's illicit stock market. The Soviet Government had fixed a legal rate for exchange of foreign currency, but it was so low that very few foreigners, even Socialists, chose to avail themselves of it. I was very much amused by the fact that several members of foreign Socialist delegations asked me to exchange their money for them at illegal rates. I also used money sent me by radio, by the Associated Press through the Soviet representatives in Copenhagen, and sold some of my personal belongings. I had an amusing time getting rid of a leather jacket and breeches. The sale of leather is controlled by the Soviet Government, as leather is among the prime needs of the Red Army, but I sold mine to a Chekist for a very good sum. I also received contributions from Americans and other foreigners temporarily in Moscow, and through the Czecho-Slovaks I had fifty pounds of sugar, twenty pounds of coffee, a dozen bars of chocolate and a dozen cans of condensed milk from the American Red Cross in Reval. I always obtained receipts from the prisoners for the articles received and occasionally requests for clothing or toilet articles which I bought on the Sukharevka.

On one occasion a prisoner asked for shoes, without stating the size. New shoes being utterly beyond my purse, I bought a pair of second hand shoes for twenty-six thousand rubles. To my horror they were returned to me the next day — they were too small. I had no money to purchase another pair, so there was nothing left for me to do, but to go on the Sukharevka myself, sell my shoes and buy a second pair with the money I received.

I went early in the morning and lined up in the shoe market, holding my goods in one hand, displayed to the public. Pretty soon a man came along and offered me fifteen thousand rubles. I told him that I would not sell for less than twenty-five thousand. Then another man offered me seventeen thousand. I held off for a higher price. Presently a small crowd began to gather, each man overbidding the other by a thousand rubles or so, until I was finally offered twenty-five thousand rubles which I accepted, when the first bidder offered me twenty-seven.

"I've already sold the shoes," I said.

"That doesn't make any difference," he returned, "I'm offering you more."

"That isn't the way we do business in America," I answered, whereupon he grabbed one of the shoes and I hit him over the head with the other.

At this juncture I saw a militiaman sauntering up in the distance, and decided it was high time for me to disappear. I snatched the shoe from my opponent, thrust both into the hands of the man who had offered me twenty-five thousand rubles, grabbed the money and vanished into the crowd. After that I found a very good pair of larger shoes for twenty-four thousand rubles, so I came out even on the transaction.

One day I received a message from Mademoiselle Charpentier stating that it was necessary for her to see me at once on an important matter. I went immediately to the headquarters of the French Red Cross, where I found her waiting for me with a tall, gaunt Yugoslav from the Koshchukovsky prison camp, in which were mainly Polish and Hungarian prisoners.

"This man has brought a note from a Polish prisoner of war who claims to be an American," she said. "He writes that he is ill, destitute and nearly starving. I can do nothing for him, as the French Government is now negotiating for the release of all prisoners, and as you know relations between France, Poland and Russia are such that aid from us to a Polish prisoner of war might cause a break in the negotiations."

I took the note — it was from "Corporal Frank R. Mosher," who stated that he had served during the war with the French Aviation Service, had later joined the A. E. F.,[15] had volunteered in the Kosciusko Squadron[16] of the Polish Army and had been taken prisoner near Kiev, where his plane was brought down by the Bolsheviks. He wrote that he was in very bad physical condition and asked for food and clothing from the French Red Cross.

I had never heard of "Corporal Mosher," but it was evident that he was an American, and that he had to be helped at all costs. It was impossible to do this openly. As the armistice with Poland had not even been signed, feeling against the Poles was running very high in Moscow, and I knew that the Foreign Office could not, even if it were willing to stretch a point, wink at aid to Polish prisoners, particularly as, according to all accounts, the Russian prisoners were anything but well treated in Poland. In fact, the previous year I had myself seen a most disgraceful Bolshevik prison camp at Bialystok, where decent conditions were assured the prisoners only after repeated and vigorous intervention on the part of the American Red Cross.

Something had to be done, however, as quickly and as secretly as possible. I went back to my room at the government guest house where I was staying, made up a food package from supplies I happened to have on hand, and took them back to my Yugoslav acquaintance at the French Red Cross. He had been a prisoner since the early days of the Great War, when he served in the Austrian Army, and, like all prisoners of this class, enjoyed a considerable amount of freedom and was allowed to go into Moscow several times a week without an escort. He had become acquainted with Mosher in the Koshchukovsky camp, where the latter had been transferred to from Kiev, and had agreed to smuggle out his letter to the French Red Cross.

....

15. The A.E.F. is the American Expeditionary Force which was the first American force sent to World War I, led by General John G. Pershing.
16. The Kosciusko Squadron was an airborne unit that fought in the Soviet-Polish War.

With the package I sent a message to Mosher asking him what he needed and I arranged to meet our go-between the next time he was permitted to leave the camp, at a safe place where I was sure I would not be observed. A few days later I received the list, which showed that Mosher was in need of practically everything: blanket, pillow, clothing, toilet articles, food. "And if you can," he wrote, "for God's sake send me a pipe and some tobacco." He also asked to know my name. I was afraid to write, but I sent back word that I was Mrs. Harrison, the correspondent of the Associated Press in Moscow.

Little by little I managed to buy all the necessary articles, including the pipe, in the Sukharevka. This itself attracted no attention, as I was in the habit of going there several times a week to purchase supplies for the other American prisoners, but I had to smuggle them in small quantities to our secret meeting place, making sure all the while that I was not being observed or followed. After I had sent in my name to Mosher, I was both horrified and delighted to receive a tiny note.

"My name is not Mosher," he wrote, "I gave it when I was captured because it happened to be on the underwear I was wearing, which I had received from the American Red Cross. I am Merriam C. Cooper[17] of Jacksonville, Florida, and I know you well. Don't you remember the last time we danced together at a ball at the Hotel Bristol in Warsaw?" He then explained that he had taken Mosher's name, with his rank of Corporal, first, because as Captain of the Kosciusko Squadron, his name was well known to the Bolsheviks and they had been particularly anxious to get him, and secondly because he knew that, in the event of an exchange of prisoners, enlisted men and non-commissioned officers invariably had the first chance.

I certainly did remember only too well, and I knew Captain Cooper's record in the French and American armies. Here was a most important prisoner masquerading under a false name, and I, the only person who could help him, was myself constantly watched and under suspicion. If he were found out, the consequences to both of us would be anything but pleasant.

It was necessary to take extra precautions, but I managed to send him weekly or semi-weekly packages, even money and books, without being caught in the act, and I secretly forwarded a note from him to his parents in Jacksonville,

....
17. Merian C. Cooper served as a pilot in the Kosciusko Squadron in the Polish-Soviet War. He was shot down and imprisoned. Harrison helped him while he was in prison during the summer of 1920; he escaped later that year. When Harrison was released, he was there to meet her. Later they would travel across Persia and make the documentary movie, *Grass*, in 1925. Later, in the 1930s, he was the director of *King Kong*.

adding a few lines to say that I was looking out for him, and asking them not to mention the fact that they had had news from him except to the members of their immediate family, as his identity was not known to the Soviet authorities.

Our clandestine intercourse kept up for over a month, after which, much to my relief, he was transferred to the Andronovsky prison camp. There, of course, it was perfectly natural that I should learn about "Mosher" from the other prisoners, who invariably reported the names of any additions to their number.

When I was arrested later, and cross-examined by the Cheka as to my relations with American and British prisoners, my chief dread was that they would ask inconvenient questions about "Mosher," but his name was never mentioned. I never heard anything more about him until I arrived in Riga and learned that he had escaped from prison in April, when he had reason to believe for the first time that his identity was suspected. When we met a few days later in Berlin, I heard his own story of his escape, and how he beat his way to the frontier with two fellow officers.[18]

Merian C. Cooper in his Polish Air Force uniform

In September when the French Red Cross left under an exchange agreement with the Russian Government, I undertook to provide temporarily for the British civilian prisoners, eight in number, and several elderly English ladies, who had formerly been governesses in Russian families, and to send bread to twenty-six British officers from Siberia, who were interned in the Andronovsky camp. Since June I had been sending weekly food packages to Mrs. Harding,[19] an English woman who came to Moscow as correspondent of the *New York World*, and was arrested immediately after her arrival.

I did all this work openly, although I had no permission whatever from the Soviet Government. In fact it would have been quite impossible for them to give me official permission, unless I had some authorization from my own government or from the American Red Cross, and this was out of the question, owing to the policy of the State Department to have no dealings direct or indirect with Moscow. The Foreign Office was officially blind to what I was doing, and I continued to send packages to the prisoners until my arrest.

....

18. She is referring to after she was released in late July 1921.
19. Mrs. Stan Harding was a British agent who thought Harrison turned her in to the Bolsheviks. She held a grudge against Harrison for decades. In the 1930s, she tried to block the publication of Harrison's autobiography (see Introduction).

Occasionally I learned of the arrest of other Americans, and in September I sent food and clothing to a Mrs. Schwarz,[20] who was confined with her husband in the Andronovsky camp. I had met the Schwarzes in the Foreign Office in July, just as they were apparently on the eve of leaving the country, and had imagined that they were long since back in America. I was told of their plight by Patrick Quinlan,[21] an Irish-American and labor leader who had also spent six weeks in prison.

In the early fall I met Washington Vanderlip, who was a guest at the Sofiskaya Naberzhnaya. He came with the outline of a scheme for the resumption of trade with Russia, claiming that the Republican administration, which he confidently believed would succeed the Democratic party, would be disposed to open commercial relations with Russia, recognize the Soviet Government, and to take concessions for the development of coal lands and the establishment of a naval coaling station in Sakhalin. His personal conductor was an Englishman named Humphreys, who had formerly worked in the Y. M. C. A. in Moscow, and was looked on as a member of the Foreign Office staff. Mr. Vanderlip was royally entertained during his stay in Russia and saw everything the Bolsheviks meant him to see. He also did a little private speculation on his own account. One of the transactions which happened to be known to me was the purchase of a number of paradise plumes and aigrettes, which he sold at a handsome profit in London.

During Mr. Vanderlip's stay, Clare Sheridan, the English sculptress, was also a guest at the same house, and she and Mr. Vanderlip were much in each other's company to the great delectation of the Soviet gossips. Mrs. Sheridan, who was invited by Kamenev during his stay in London to come to Russia and make the busts of Lenin, Trotsky, and other distinguished men, was at first regarded with some suspicion by the ever watchful Cheka, because she happened to be a relative of Winston Churchill. She was very discreet, however, resigned herself good naturedly to being personally conducted and apparently hugely enjoyed her stay in Moscow. I was at the opera with her one evening and we wisely confined our conversation to talk about art, theaters and such subjects.

....

20. Mrs. Schwartz and her husband were American delegates to the Third International and were in prison at the time of Harrison's arrest.

21. Patrick Quinlan was an Irish-American labor leader known as IWW leader William "Big Bill" Haywood's "little Irish lieutenant." He was accused of inciting the Paterson Silk Strike in 1913. He was briefly imprisoned in Russia in 1920. After he left Russia, he sent a letter to Lenin that covered many issues. In this letter he pleaded for Harrison's release and assured Lenin that she was not a spy (see Appendix).

I only saw Mr. Vanderlip for five minutes, after which we were interrupted by the entry of Humphreys, who announced that Mr. Vanderlip had to go to inspect some institution or other. The next day I was notified by the Cheka that I had no right to go to see Vanderlip or any other American in Moscow without its permission.

In the latter part of the summer, just before he left to attend the Eastern Conference of the Communist party at Baku, I met John Reed, leader of the American Communist party,[22] who had been released a short time previously from prison in Finland. He was looking very ill from the effect of the hardships he had undergone while in prison and he struck me as being rather dispirited; not that he believed any the less in Communism, but I think he saw some of the mistakes that were being made in Moscow and felt that he was powerless to prevent them. I frequently saw him at the Foreign Office in the evenings and we had long talks about Communism. He told me that he intended to return to America and face the charges then standing against him.[23] He impressed me as an intensely honest, rather fair-minded person, and I always felt that a certain spirit of bravado spurred on by what he regarded as unfair treatment in America pushed him rather farther than he intended to go in his radicalism. He was taken ill with typhoid fever immediately after his return from the Baku conference,[24] and died on October 19th.[25]

I also saw something of his wife, Louise Bryant, who arrived in the fall, looking very chic and pretty in her New York clothes. She was the only fashionable looking woman I had seen for such a long time that I was quite dazzled by her. In Moscow all the women were wearing the full skirts that were fashionable in 1917. I am sure that her chic tailor-made suit with its narrow skirt and straight lines afforded work for many home dressmakers. I liked Mrs. Reed very much, personally, and I felt sorry for her when her husband died, even risking a visit to the forbidden hotel of the Third International after his death in order to see if I could be of any assistance to her. The next day, when I was arrested, the

....

22. Actually, just one faction of the Communist Party at that time. Communists were expelled from the American Socialist Party in 1919, and they formed the Communist Labor Party (which Reed headed) and the Communist Party of America.

23. Reed had been indicted for sedition in 1919, soon after being acquitted on the same charges earlier that year, after a tough grilling before a U.S. Senate committee about Bolshevik propaganda in the U.S. He fled to Russia, hoping to gain Comintern support for his Communist faction.

24. Against his will, the Comintern had ordered him to attend the Congress of the Peoples of the East.

25. Reed actually died on October 17, his wife Louise Bryant at his side. He is the only American buried in the Kremlin Wall, at least fully. Apparently half of Big Bill Haywood's remains are in the Kremlin Wall; the other half are in Waldheim Cemetery in Chicago (Peter Cole, *Encyclopedia of U.S. Labor and Working-Class History*, vol. 1, p. 582. Routledge, 2007).

allegation that I had, under cover of sympathy, tried to get information from her about the Communist party was one of the accusations made against me. This was reasonable according to Bolshevist psychology, for it was exactly what a Communist would have done, under similar circumstances. In judging what are in themselves arbitrary, and often cruel acts of the Soviet authorities, many people fail to realize that the Communists are acting in accordance with the tenets of what is really not so much a political creed as a fanatical religion, based on an entirely new system of ethics.

Since I have been in America I have heard many rumors about the death of John Reed, all of them absolutely unfounded in my opinion. It has been said

that he was murdered, and a great deal of other nonsense. As a matter of fact, I believe that John Reed was not satisfied with the state of affairs in Russia. Like most foreign Communists, he was unwilling to accept the tactical dictation of Moscow. That he would have been arrested or in any way molested, however, I do not believe, much less murdered. He was in wretched health during his entire stay in Moscow, and he was not the only delegate to the Baku conference who came back with typhoid fever, which seems to have been epidemic there last autumn. Mrs. Reed told me that his treatment was not by any means what he would have received in

John Reed, 1913

New York. She did not approve of the methods of the Russian doctors; she did not believe that the Russian nurses knew their business, and she told me that his diet was not altogether what she would have wished for him, but she attributed all this to the universal shortage in Moscow, and I never had the impression that she felt the lack of up-to-date treatment was intentional. The only matter about which she took issue with the Soviet authorities was his burial in the Red Square in Moscow.

"John was a real American," she repeated over and over again. "I know he would have wanted to be buried on American soil."

Relief work for Russia was begun on a small scale during the summer by two foreign organizations, the English Society of Friends and the Joint Distribution Committee of America. The former was supervised by Mr. Arthur Watts, a young Englishman who lived at the Savoy, and consisted in furnishing food for children's dining rooms in Moscow and Petrograd. Up to the time of my arrest, nearly two hundred tons of food had been distributed in this manner. Mr. Watts' methods were much criticized by the more conservative foreigners. He was a Communist of the idealistic type and was quite content to receive and turn over in bulk the food supplies sent from England, leaving the distribution entirely to the Soviet authorities.

The Joint Distribution Committee, whose representatives, Judge Fischer and Harry Kagan of Chicago, and Max Pine of Brooklyn, signed a contract with the Soviet Government, operated through a local organization and got several trainloads of supplies through to the pogrom sufferers and the victims of the Polish offensive on the Berezina front and in the Ukraine.[26] They had no American representative in Russia and Mr. Watts was the only foreign relief worker who planned to remain in Moscow for the winter. I often appealed to him to help me care for the British, but got very little response from him.

At the end of September nearly all the foreigners had left Moscow, the weather was beginning to get very cold, the government guest houses were poorly heated, and the prospects for the winter were anything but cheerful. No new newspaper correspondents came in except a few representatives of the European Socialist Press. H. G. Wells was in Moscow for a few days but I was strictly forbidden to see him.[27] Owing to the scarcity of fuel, which was every day becoming more menacing, numbers of factories in Moscow were closed. Food was growing scarcer and at the same time it was announced that the government would shortly close all the markets and prohibit free trade. Nevertheless, life on the surface was going on very much as usual: the theaters opened with new programs, schools began on time, railroads were operating, though on a restricted schedule. Passenger trains were cut down, however, and it became increasingly difficult for private individuals to travel. To travel anywhere outside of a limited zone around any of the Russian cities it was necessary to have a special permit, stating the nature of your business, a release from the office where you happened to be working, besides the worker's book with which every citizen must be provided. After securing these documents,

26. Judge Harry Fischer, special attaché Harry Kagan, and labor leader Max Pine worked for the Joint Distribution Committee of American Funds for Jewish War Sufferers. This is the same committee to which Harrison refers.

27. Wells' account of his 1920 trip, which included an interview with Lenin, first ran as a series of articles in London's *Sunday Express*, and then were reprinted in book form, in *Russia in the Shadows*. An outspoken socialist, his review of Soviet Russia was quite negative. However, while in Russia during this visit, in 1920, Wells fell hopelessly in love with Countess Benckendorff, a.k.a. Moura Zakrevskaya, Màxim Gorky's secretary and mistress, and a Cheka plant.

you had to stand in line for hours at a stretch to obtain the tickets. There was an office of the Kazan Railway underneath the Hotel Metropole and it was no uncommon sight to see peasants sleeping all night on the pavement in order to be first in the line the next morning. As only a limited number of tickets were given out for each train, it was necessary to secure them a long time in advance.

The signing of the armistice with Poland produced little effect on the people. There was no rejoicing and no excitement, for there had been so many similar events in the past, which had always been followed by new wars and new mobilizations.

By this time I had begun to realize that not even the armistice with Poland would secure me permission to leave Russia. I was still looked on with suspicion, regarded as a person who knew entirely too much about the internal affairs of the country to be allowed to leave at such a critical juncture. A note from Mr. Colby,[28] then Secretary of State, to Chicherin, announcing continuance of the American Government's policy to refuse to have any intercourse with Russia until the formation of a government which would represent the will of the majority of the people, caused much ill feeling against Americans in general and this was heightened by the arrest of numbers of Communists in the United States, who, it was said, were held in Federal prisons under abominable conditions. This impression was fostered by the reports of the American political deportees and by the irritation which the Soviet Government felt at their presence, for they were mostly Anarchists and not persona grata in Russia any more than they were in the United States. It was evident to me that I and a number of other Americans would be retained as hostages and I was quite prepared to spend the winter in Moscow, hoping however, that I would escape arrest until some arrangement could be made for the care of my prisoners. Meanwhile I lived very quietly, going on with my work as inconspicuously as possible, seeing few people except the members of the Czechoslovak Mission and a few Russian friends, and waited to see what was coming next.

----

28. Bainbridge Colby (1869-1950) was Secretary of State from March 1920 to the end of the Wilson administration in March 1921. The reference is to a diplomatic note issued by Colby on August 9, 1920, which, in no uncertain terms, ruled out normal relations with the Bolshevik regime.

CHAPTER XXII
The Trap is Sprung

There is a current saying in Russia that every citizen "has sat, is sitting or will sit in prison." After eight months in Moscow, I had ample proof of the relative accuracy of this statement, so that when I was arrested on the night of the twentieth of October I was not taken unawares by any means. Indeed, for some time, as I have already stated, I had had reason to suspect that my turn was coming, and I often used to lie in bed at night listening to passing automobiles, wondering when one would stop at the door of the government guest house in the Mali Kharitonevsky Pereulok. A motor in a quiet street at night in Moscow nearly always means a "*zasada*," or raid, or an arrest, for none but official personages on official business use cars and the few commissars who work at night have no business to transact in the residential sections.

On this particular night, I had come home very late, about two o'clock as usual, from the Foreign Office, where everyone, including Chicherin, works all night, the news bulletin being given to press correspondents at twelve o'clock, and I was just preparing to go to bed when I heard a motor stop outside. In a few minutes there was a knock at my door. "It's all up," I thought, calmly, and without getting up from the sofa where I was sitting I called out in as cheerful a tone as I could muster, "Come in."

The door opened and a young, exceedingly well dressed, rather pretty woman came in, followed by two soldiers wearing the pointed caps of the Cheka and carrying the rifles which have almost entirely taken the place of revolvers even with the city militia. They were nice looking boys, not at all fierce or formidable, and they seemed rather reticent about stating their errand, so I thought I would help them out.

"I suppose you have come to arrest me," I remarked.

Without replying, the elder of the two boys handed me a small slip of paper. It was an order for my arrest, accompanied by a search warrant, written with a red pencil, and signed by Pyat, executive head of the "Secret Operative Section" of the Extraordinary Commission, which is the correct title in English for the Cheka.

At the same moment, the Commandant of the house arrived, rubbing his eyes, and looking very sleepy indeed. This was strictly in accord with the prescribed legal routine, which requires the presence of the Commandant or the chairman of the house committee whenever a search warrant is served.

The two men then began a thorough overhauling of everything in the room, and nothing escaped them. They were evidently experts at the job. All my personal belongings were gone over, my bags turned inside out and the space between the cover and the lining thoroughly examined. The bed was subjected to a rigid search, as was each piece of upholstered furniture, the carpet was turned up and the space behind the radiator received particular attention.

All my papers were collected down to the smallest scrap of writing—blank sheets were held to the light to detect possible invisible characters and my books were gone over page by page. As I had collected a number of books and pamphlets, made innumerable notes, kept copies of all my newspapers, articles and telegrams for eight months, there was much to be inspected. And then my money had to be counted. I had quite a lot of it, a million and a half rubles, for I was at that time supplying weekly food packages to eight Americans and a number of British prisoners and had to keep considerable cash on hand for my purchases in the market. The money was counted twice, I was asked to verify the amount, then money and papers were made into two packages to accompany me to the Cheka.

Meanwhile, I had been subjected to a personal search by the woman who had been sent for that purpose. She examined my pockets, felt in my corsets, my stockings and my hair, went over every inch of my fur-lined coat to see if it concealed any papers, but, much to my surprise, I was not compelled to undress, and I was treated most courteously throughout.

I asked permission to pack the necessary articles to take to prison with me, and this was immediately granted. Although warned that there was not room for much luggage in the automobile, I managed to take a bag containing toilet articles, a change of underwear, some chocolate and cigarettes, an army bedding roll with a pillow and a steamer rug and my big fur coat.

When the search was over I was asked to sign a document, witnessed by the Commandant, certifying that the search had been conducted in a proper manner, my room was closed, locked and sealed with a large red seal. I was then taken to the waiting motor, a fine English car, and driven through the silent moonlit streets to the prison of the secret section of the Cheka, which is in a building on the Lubyanka, in the heart of Moscow's business district, formerly the property of the "Rossiya" Life Insurance Company. From the outside it looks like anything but a prison. On the ground floor a row of unoccupied shops, divided by temporary unpainted wooden partitions, serve as offices for the Cheka. The car stopped outside one of these, and I was taken into a small, dingy room, with a railed space at one end, behind which were sitting two Chekists in front of a large deal table covered with documents and papers. Lined up along the railing were a number of other people who had evidently been arrested, all men except myself. I was the last in the line, and it was more than an hour before my turn came to fill out the questionnaire presented to me by the men behind the table. It was a most elaborate affair, evidently intended only for Russians, for among the questions to be answered were whether I had any relatives in the Red or White Armies. When this was over, my money was again counted, my valuables were all taken, including my wedding ring, and I was given a receipt for them, as well as for my typewriter and kodak.

This done, the commissars behind the table yawned, locked up their books and disappeared, and I was left alone with half a dozen soldiers. Then I was subjected to the only personal indignity I experienced during my ten months' imprisonment.

One of the soldiers, who was what we would call a fresh guy at home, proceeded to search me on his own account, accompanying the proceedings with a number of witticisms which, fortunately, I did not know enough Russian to understand, but which sent his companions into roars of laughter. They seemed to think it especially funny when I protested on the ground that I was an American.

"Much good being an American will do you here, citizenness," returned my tormentor scornfully.

Finally they had enough, and I was taken through a labyrinth of ground floor passages and up three flights of stairs to the office of the Commandant, where I surrendered my receipts, and was searched again, this time in a perfectly correct manner. The commandant, whom I afterwards got to know quite well from his daily visits, was the living image of "Kaiser Bill," and my Russian companions always called him "Vilgelm" behind his back.[1] Officially we addressed him as Citizen Commandant. He was a rigid disciplinarian, but absolutely just, and was always willing to listen to any reasonable complaints or requests.

By this time it was nearly six o'clock. I was desperately tired, and very thankful when I was taken to my room on the floor below. Here again the first impression was not that of a prison, though as a matter of fact the "Lubyanka 2" is the strictest prison in Moscow. Except for the armed sentinel at the door, the winding corridor into which I was taken might have been the hall of any second-class hotel anywhere in Europe. On both sides were numbered rooms. We stopped opposite number 39, the door was unlocked, the light turned on "for five minutes, so that you can undress if you want to," my guard informed me, the door was banged and locked, and I found myself in a small single room already occupied by three women.

Two were lying on the floor, and one on a bed of three boards laid across wooden horses and covered by a thin straw pallet. The only other articles of furniture were a deal table, and the "*parashka*," a large iron garbage can, which is unpleasant but indispensable considering the fact that prisoners are permitted to go to the toilet but twice a day.

On hearing the key turn in the lock, all three of my companions, who had evidently been "playing 'possum," sat bolt upright and began deluging me with questions as is always the custom in prison. Where was I from, why had I been arrested? I retaliated with a cross-fire in French and Russian, which resulted in the discovery that I was already acquainted with one of the prisoners, a pretty Jewish woman whom I had last seen at "The Bat," *Lyetushchaya Mysh*, one of Moscow's best known vaudeville theaters, with Mr. Michael Farbmann, the correspondent of the *Chicago Daily News*. The second was a young girl employed in the Foreign Office. Both had been arrested a few hours before I was and professed to be ignorant of the charges against them, though I suspected that my acquaintance was probably in for what is known as "international speculation," which means that she had had illegal business transactions with foreigners. The third woman, a young Russian girl, had been for six weeks in solitary confinement until our advent, which explained why she was the proud possessor of the bed. Hers was a most romantic story. She had fallen in love with a Hungarian prisoner of war,

---

1. The reference is to Germany's Kaiser Wilhelm (1859-1941), the late German emperor and first cousin by marriage to Tsar Nicholas II (the two sovereigns were also distant cousins by blood, sharing a great-great-grandfather in Tsar Paul I).

a near relative of Count Szechenyi,[2] who married Miss Gladys Vanderbilt[3] of New York some years ago, and was accused of being implicated in a plot for his escape, together with a number of Hungarian officers.

For more than a year, she had been taxing her slender resources to provide him with food and other comforts in prison, and I never told her that I had already heard that this same faithless Szechenyi was at the same time receiving food packets from a certain Princess Galitsin. She was what we would call in America a good sport. Though facing charges which might mean the death penalty if they were proved against her, she was always in the best of spirits, and made light of our hardships in the most delightful manner.

When our herring soup was served at noon, she assured me that it was fine for the digestion, and she told me that the six weeks in solitary confinement had been wonderfully soothing to her nerves. During all this time, she had had no books and no amusements, except conversation through a small hole in the wall near the steam pipe, with the man in the next room, a well known theosophist.

The morning passed without any incident except our matutinal[4] trip to the bathroom, where we all performed our ablutions together in a big tin trough with cold water. In the afternoon, I was taken to be photographed, full face, left and right profile, against a white screen on which my serial number was printed — as nearly as I can remember it was 3041.

That night, curled up in my bedding roll on the floor, for there had been so many arrests recently that there were not enough beds to go around, I slept well. Strange to say, I was not in the least nervous. After many weeks of suspense, the worst had happened, and my first feeling was one of relief, for it must be remembered that my status in Russia had always been illegal, I had been arrested once before, and I knew that I was subject to rearrest at any time.

The next day, shortly after dinner, a soldier appeared.

"Garrison," he demanded. "Here," I answered.

"*Na dopros*,"[5] he said, shortly. I was puzzled, for it was a new word to me. "That means," said my Russian friend, "that you are summoned to a hearing. You are lucky. Sometimes people wait for weeks before they are questioned by one of the judges."

2. Istvan Szechenyi (1791-1860) was a Hungarian politician.
3. Gladys Vanderbilt (1886-1965) was the daughter of American railroad owner Cornelius Vanderbilt.
4. Pre-dawn.
5. *Dopros* means an interrogation.

I followed my guard out into the hall, up and down a maze of stairways and passages, until I reached a familiar room, the office of Mogilevsky,[6] a member of the presidium of the Cheka, who had questioned me in the spring when I was detained for forty-eight hours on account of the fact that I had come to Russia from Poland, an enemy country, without the permission of the authorities.

Mogilevsky is a tall, slender, dark man, tremendously earnest and intensely fanatical in his Communistic beliefs, utterly unsparing of himself and others in his work, but he has his human side, as I discovered when I noticed a beautifully bound copy of Rabelais lying on his desk. I remarked about this and he told me that he had a weakness for old French literature.

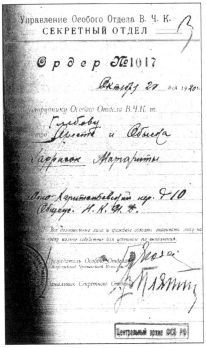

Harrison's Arrest Order of October 20, 1920, obtained from FSB archives

Our conversation in general, however, was not about literary subjects. I was put through a rigid cross-examination, lasting nearly three hours about my acquaintances in Moscow, my relations with foreigners, my relations with the prisoners to whom I had been sending food packages, and other matters, during which, while perfectly courteous, he made it quite plain to me that my position was exceedingly serious. In the midst of his questions a soldier brought in two glasses of tea with sugar, a box of cigarettes was at my elbow, and I sat in a big luxurious leather armchair. My answers were not altogether satisfactory, and the examination ended with my being returned to my companions in room 39, with the admonition to think things over and refresh my memory.

I had not been back more than a few minutes, however, when one of the prison guards appeared again.

....
6. Solomon Grigorevich Mogilevsky (1885-1925), an old Bolshevik who led the foreign department of the Cheka from 1921-1922, whence he was transferred to head up spy activity in the Caucasus and against Turkey. He died in an airplane crash.

"Pack your clothes," he ordered.

"Where am I going?" I asked.

"You'll see when you get there," he answered.

I started to put on my fur coat. "You won't need that," he said, and then I realized that I was probably to be transferred to solitary confinement, the thing I dreaded most, and I said good-bye to my newfound friends with a sinking heart, and followed my escort down the passage. It was just as I expected. I was shown into an empty room, the key turned in the lock and I was left alone.

CHAPTER XXIII
Odinochka[1]

The autumn days are very short in Moscow, and it was already beginning to grow dark, so I could see little except that I was in a small box-like room about nine feet square, with a large window, the panes of which were whitened, so that I could not see out. There was a plank bed, a small table and the *parashka*,[2] nothing more. It was very cold in the room, and for a while I walked up and down trying to keep warm and hoping that the light would soon be turned on. At that time I did not know enough about prison ways to realize that the guard had forgotten to turn on the light, and that I could knock and ask him to do so. Later I learned to knock and ask for all sorts of things, from a needle and thread to darn my stockings to a light for a cigarette. When we were short of matches we always knocked on the door, and when the eye of one of the prison guards appeared at the peephole, or *glazok*, which is covered on the outside by the swinging metal number plate, one of us would stick a cigarette through and get a light.

Ordinarily the peephole, though inconvenient if you happen to be doing anything against the rules, is not an unmixed evil, but in the "*odinochka*," as solitary confinement is called, it is nothing more or less at first than an instrument of torture. The guards are instructed to keep a close watch on prisoners in the *odinochka*, so at least every half-hour, day and night, the number plate is stealthily pushed aside and an eye appears in the peephole, gazes steadily for a minute, and disappears. For some time I was perpetually watching for the eye, but after a while I grew quite indifferent to it, and it did not even disturb

---

1. *Odinochka* means solitary confinement.
2. A *parashka* is a bucket used as a toilet.

my serenity when I was dressing, undressing, or engaged in any of the intimate mysteries of the toilet.

But to return to my first evening in the *odinochka*. In about an hour a boy appeared with a big copper kettle of the infusion of apple parings or dried carrots, which passes for tea in Russia these days, at the same time presenting me with a tin cup and a big wooden spoon, and turning on the light. While I ate the remaining portion of my day's ration of three-quarters of a pound of black bread, sipped my tea and nibbled a cake of chocolate, I looked around my new quarters.

The room was very dingy, but fairly clean. The walls were covered with a faded flowered paper that suggested the old rooming-house days, and scribbled all over, as high as a man's head, with inscriptions in various languages. Some were funny, some defiant, others despairing.

One man had written— "May 5, *dopros*" ... "May 7, *dopros*," and so on through a long series of dates until July 15, underneath which was written in Russian, "now I've told everything. This is the end." Another, a Frenchman evidently, wrote in a bold hand "*Rira bien qui rira le dernier.*" (He laughs best who laughs last.) A Dutchman wrote in his native language, "I lie here between life and death, but whatever happens I wish to testify to whoever may read this, that if I die, it will be as a loyal Communist." Underneath it a Belgian had written "*Vive la Belgique.*" An artist had sketched several soldier types, and a mathematician had covered many feet of wall space with problems in geometry.

There were also innumerable calendars, with each day checked off, and each ending abruptly. One, in English, running for three months, interested me very much, and I wondered if it could have been made by one of the four Americans whom I knew were in "Lubyanka 2," but I could find no trace of the identity of the man who had written it.

Finally this amusement palled, and I sat on the radiator to get warm, meanwhile taking stock of the situation. I had good cause to know that my position was very serious, but at the same time I figured it out that unless the United States actually went to war with Russia it was unlikely that I would be shot. Knowing the policy of our administration, I decided that it would probably be a waiting game on both sides, and that the only thing for me to do was to keep my nerve and my health as well, if possible, and wait to see what would happen. I had no reason either to complain of my arrest or to expect early liberation. It was simply the fortune of war.

When I judged it was about bedtime, for watches are not allowed prisoners, and mine had been taken with my other valuables, I lay down and tried to sleep, but sleep was impossible. My room was directly opposite the entrance door, where there was a constant stream of traffic. New prisoners arrived all night, others were being taken to or coming back from the *dopros*, and every time the door was opened there was a loud knock, followed by the challenge of the sentry, and a clanking sound as the chain which held it was unfastened. During slack times the other guards gathered round the sentry, exchanging jokes. Occasionally there were frantic knocks from prisoners who demanded in loud tones to be taken to the toilet; occasionally there was the sound of women's voices quarreling in another room, and I was continually haunted by the eye at the peephole. Finally I dozed off in sheer exhaustion. When I woke up it was light, and in a few minutes the door was opened and a woman's hand and arm appeared with a broom. From previous experience I knew that this was the signal for me to clean my room, so I jumped up, swept the floor, piled the refuse in a corner by the door, placed the broom beside it, and proceeded to carry out the rest of the day's routine I had planned for myself.

First I made my bed, which process consisted in conducting a hunt for the bed bugs who had invaded the sanctity of my bedding roll during the night; then I knocked and asked to be taken to the toilet, where I took a sponge bath in cold water. Soon came the day's bread ration, and a portion of sugar for two days, about two and a half teaspoons. I spread a clean piece of paper on the table and sat down to breakfast, after which I took a walk—five hundred times the length of the room and back. I repeated this every evening. At about eleven o'clock the Commandant appeared, took a quick appraising look around the room, and inquired if I had any request to make. I asked for paper, pencil and a few books. He told me that I must first have the permission of my *sledovatel*, the examining judge, but he did not explain that I might ask for permission; so I resigned myself to waiting until I was next called for cross-examination, as I thought I probably would be in a few days.

Dinner, consisting of a bowl of herring soup, followed by a bowl of *kasha*, the Russian national dish, a cereal made of various grains, most of which are new to Western palates, was served at noon. One sort, is I think, millet, another whole buckwheat. I had already learned to eat *kasha*, but I never could go the herring soup, though occasionally when I was very hungry I held my nose and ate one of the unpeeled potatoes that floated in it. Later the herring soup was varied, sometimes for some weeks at a stretch, by a thin meat broth, and on

Sundays, when we had no supper, it was thicker and sometimes contained a piece of meat. The soup and *kasha* were served in wooden bowls, some of them of the beautiful enamel work which is one of the most interesting of Russia's fascinating peasant industries. Supper was served at five, and consisted of soup only, followed by tea. This was my regular prison fare for eight months. Compared to that served in Soviet dining-rooms outside, it was a little better if anything, and knowing as I did, standards of life in Moscow, I realized that I was no worse off in this respect than thousands of other people. I can well imagine, however, that strangers who were arrested almost on their arrival in Moscow would regard it as starvation diet, and certainly no one could get fat on it.

In spite of all efforts to keep myself busy and amused the first day and the succeeding ones were terribly long. I resorted to all sorts of expedients to pass the time. In my bag I found some paper cigarette boxes and a cardboard toothpowder box. Out of these I made a pack of tiny cards, with a pencil I had managed to hide, through all the searches of my belongings. I was playing solitaire very peacefully when my enemy of the peephole looked in, saw me, unlocked the door and ordered me to give them up, for cards are not allowed in the Cheka. Then I played jackstraws with dead matches and a bent hairpin. Then I sang under my breath all the songs I had ever known, recited all the poems I remembered and gave myself oral examinations in languages and history.

I shall never forget a little incident which happened one day when I was feeling particularly blue, illustrating the kindliness of many of the prison guards, which I often experienced in the long months that followed. I had completely exhausted my supply of cigarettes and was wondering what on earth I would do without them when one of the guards appeared with the cigarettes which were part of the regular prison ration. The number given out varied with the supply — sometimes we received twenty-five a week, at other times, six a day and occasionally none at all for two weeks. On this occasion I asked him how many I was entitled to. "Sixteen," he replied. I suppose I must have looked disappointed, for after glancing at me sharply he counted out sixteen in a loud voice, laid down thirty-five on the table, and went away without another word.

Finally, when my first week was nearly up, the monotony and isolation had got on my nerves to such an extent that I decided I could not stand it much longer, and resolved on a bold stroke. I wrote to Mogilevsky and told him I had a very important communication to make.

In two hours I was called to his room. "Well, what is it you have to tell me?" he asked.

Solomon Mogilevsky

A 1919 demonstration in Lubyanka square. The Lubyanka building of the NKVD is the ornate building in the background, center.

"I want to tell you that it is very important for me to talk to somebody," I said. "You are the only person I can ask to talk to and I will be very glad to have you cross-examine me again. If you don't want to have any more conversations with me at frequent intervals please put me in a room with other people. I can't stand being alone any longer."

For a moment he just stared at me, then he did cross examine me again, and finally turned me over to his secretary, a studious young Jew with a passion for doing problems in geometry when he wasn't trying to solve personal equations. The end of it all was that I was informed that while I had failed to give a satisfactory account of myself, the charges against me would not be pushed at the moment, and that my request to be transferred to another room would be granted. After that I did not see Mogilevsky again for over two months. I was rather sorry on the whole, for although we disagreed on practically all subjects from Communism to herrings, of which he was evidently fond, for he often had a bowl of our prison soup for his dinner, his was a keen, alert mind and he was a very stimulating and resourceful enemy.

After my talk with his secretary I was transferred to the general room where I spent the next six months, with plenty of company, for we were rarely less than seven, and often as many as eleven or twelve for days at a time.

CHAPTER XXIV
Close Quarters

The room to which I was transferred was much larger than any I had seen before, but my first impression of it was that it was exactly the shape of the coffins that are used all over Europe. It was rectangular, about eighteen feet long, possibly seven feet wide at one end, and ten at the other. There were two windows, whitened of course, at either end. They were double, with an air space between, which we used for cold storage purposes, dropping food down on cords through a small pane at the top, which opened on a hinge. This little opening was our only means of obtaining fresh air, as the windows were hermetically sealed with putty. Through it, by standing on the sill, a glimpse of the courts into which the windows opened could be obtained, but not even a patch of sky was visible. During the six months I lived there I never saw the sun, moon or sky, except twice, once in December, and again in February, when we were taken out to one of the public baths with an armed escort, and I never left the room except for our morning and evening trips to the toilet, or when I was summoned to a *dopros*. It was well heated by steam, but the atmosphere was terrible owing to the utter inadequacy of the ventilation and the chronic aversion of most Russians to drafts.

When I entered, it was occupied by seven women, some sitting, some lying on their beds, which were spread with nondescript coverings, here a plaid shawl, there a silk quilt and a lace pillow, farther on another with only the straw pallet provided by the prison authorities. On a long table there was a miscellaneous assortment of cups and utensils. From under the beds protruded pieces of baggage of all descriptions, from peasant sacks and baskets to fitted dressing bags.

The women were just as conglomerate as their belongings. They all stared at me curiously, appraisingly, and, as I thought, in a rather unfriendly manner, but I afterwards learned to understand this apparent hostility and insatiable curiosity with regard to newcomers. Living as we did, in such crowded quarters, an addition to our number meant more physical discomfort; then she might be a spy. On the other hand, we were always hungry to hear the latest news from people who had just been arrested, and we welcomed anything that was a break in the monotonous prison routine. As a matter of fact, the Slavs are the kindliest, gentlest, most hospitable people in the world, wonderfully lovable and sweet-tempered. I was thrown almost entirely with them during my term of imprisonment, for I suspect that I was purposely isolated from persons from Western countries, and I never once had an unpleasant encounter with any of my fellow prisoners.

Besides Russians, I had Poles, Finns, Letts, Lithuanians, Estonians, Ukrainians and Jews as companions. They were drawn from every class of society, from great ladies to illiterate peasants; they represented every political party from monarchists to anarchists. There were some disagreements in our room of course, but on the whole we pulled together remarkably well and no backward male can ever tell me again that women are incapable of teamwork. In Russia there are no generalizations of this kind about women; there is no feminism, there are no "women's questions." Women are just people. Perhaps this is the result of the "broad" Slav nature, perhaps it is one of the good effects of the Revolution. But I have gone a long way from my story.

As I dumped my bags on the floor and looked around for a vacant bed, one of the inmates, a slender, aristocratic looking woman in a worn out tailor-made suit that had once been a Parisian creation, and wearing the shuffling straw slippers, known as *lapti*, which are given out to prisoners by the prison authorities, advanced to meet me with a smile, very much as if I had been a casual caller in a drawing-room.

"I see that you are a foreigner," she said in beautiful French. "This is very poor hospitality to offer you in Russia."

We both laughed, and then she helped me to unpack my belongings while we exchanged information. She was Mademoiselle Helena Sologub, a member of one of the oldest and most noted families in Russia. Their Moscow home, a beautiful old eighteenth century house on the Povarskaya, which is described by Tolstoy as the home of the hero Pyotr in his great novel *War and Peace*, is now used by the Commissariat of Education as a people's palace, where lectures and concerts of the "Prolet-Cult" are held. Up to the time of her arrest, Mademoiselle Sologub had been permitted to retain a room there. She had been accused of acquaintance with a White officer of whom she had never even heard, and had been kept in solitary confinement for two months. We became good friends and I was very sorry several weeks later when she was ordered to pack and leave. I did not know what had become of her until a long time afterward, when a prisoner arriving from the Butyrki, Moscow's largest prison, told me that she had been there for several months, finally being transferred to an internment camp.

My other fellow prisoners were three women clerks from the War Office, who had been arrested as witnesses in connection with an alleged counter-revolutionary plot in one of the departments, a Lettish Communist, who was arrested with her husband, suspected of being an "agent provocateur," the young wife of a naval officer, who was imprisoned in the adjoining room, and a sixteen year old girl from Archangel, who had been kept in the local Cheka, threatened with death, for six weeks, because she had repeated a remark she had heard to the effect that there would soon be a counter-revolution. I am glad to be able to say that Moscow had more sense than Archangel. After three weeks in prison she was questioned by a woman examiner and immediately offered her choice between being sent back to Archangel or remaining in Moscow and continuing her education. The fact that minors who are arrested are invariably questioned by women and treated with great kindness is a point in favor of the Cheka, though it is done with a view to ultimately making good Communists.

It is wonderful how naturally one drops into the routine of prison life. I was fortunate on arriving in finding a vacant bed at the narrow end of the room, next to the window. There was just enough space to move freely between me and the bed opposite, but I had light, the benefit of what little fresh air was to be had, and the windowsill to use as a bureau. Besides it was a wonderful strategic position, commanding a view of the whole room, and as the door was at the extreme end of one of the long sides, I escaped the eye at the peephole. Goings and comings affected me very little—I could sit up in my corner and survey the confusion with a delightful feeling of aloofness.

Occasionally, however, even my small measure of privacy was invaded. Eight beds covered the available wall space, nine or ten meant beds in the wide part of the room and the shifting of the table nearer the narrow end. Once, for several nights, a woman slept on the floor between my bed and my neighbor's opposite, and I had to literally walk over her to get out. There were then eleven of us, and there was absolutely no floor space left, so when another prisoner arrived at about two a.m., we cleared off our cups and dishes and put her on the table. When she had just gotten settled still another appeared, so we offered her our one chair, and she sat up for the rest of the night. These congested times were luckily not very frequent, and our average number was seven or eight.

Strange as it may seem, I was really very busy in prison, and while each day seemed interminable, the time on the whole passed very quickly. Realizing the importance of getting some exercise, I used to do Swedish gymnastics morning and night, to the constant wonder and amazement of my companions. One evening a woman who had just been arrested, after watching me go through my gyrations, asked me very seriously if that was the way we prayed to God in America.

Then there was the daily hunt for vermin. All the beds were infested with bed bugs and they had to be gone over several times a week. At first I did not realize the importance of special care of the hair, and consequently acquired what are known to the learned as *peticulosis* and to school children at home as "nits." It took me some time to get rid of them, and then only thanks to a good friend who gave me a fine tooth comb which was one of my chief treasures for the rest of my term of imprisonment. When we had prisoners from the South, we were pestered with fleas, the most elusive of all plaguey insects. I always inspected my underclothes twice a day, for we had many cooties,[1] especially when prisoners arrived from a distance, and cooties are not only disagreeable but dangerous in Russia, for they are the carriers of the dreaded typhus. Occasionally we had lazy fellow prisoners who refused to join in the daily hunt, but public opinion usually forced them to it in the end.

In spite of all our precautions, we had three cases of typhus during the winter. As soon as the diagnosis was clear, they were removed, and after each one we waited for two weeks to find out if we were infected. There were also several cases of syphilis in the acute state, one being that of a young girl who went suddenly insane in the middle of the night, and had to be taken off to the hospital. We had many cases of acute hysteria, and I was often kept busy for several hours applying cold compresses and administering valerian.[2]

We obtained all simple remedies from the prison dispensary. Medical service, while not adequate, was fairly satisfactory. There was a woman physician in charge of the prison, and she made periodical rounds of inspection, usually

1. Lice.
2. Valerian is an herb that was often used as a sedative.

once a week. There was a "*feldsher*," a third year medical student, who could be summoned at any time during the day or night, though occasionally he was not on hand when wanted; and there were cases in our room when acutely ill persons were obliged to wait for several hours without receiving medical attendance.

Prisoners requiring the services of a physician were supposed to register their names when the Commandant made his rounds, which was usually several times a week, and they received a visit from the "*feldsher*" some time within the next twenty-four hours. Simple remedies, such as soda, castor oil and aspirin, could always be obtained from the dispensary and prisoners were allowed to receive medicine from their friends outside. All drugs sent in this manner were subjected to analysis by the prison physician before being given to the inmates. Cases of acute illness were removed to the hospital as soon as possible, and the prison authorities were always on the watch for infectious diseases, which might cause an epidemic in the prison. But people suffering with chronic complaints received little attention and were not able to obtain the necessary care or diet. In the other prisons in Moscow, special rations are provided for such persons, but in the Cheka no arrangements existed for the *Bolnichny Stol*, the hospital table. Pregnant women and persons suffering from undernourishment received larger portions of the regular rations, that was all. During my eight months in the Cheka, five or six women who were expecting babies within a comparatively short time were kept on our floor for from two weeks to three months. The close quarters, bad air, and inadequate diet were particularly hard on them, and it seemed curiously inconsistent to me, in view of the Soviet Government's avowed principle of caring first of all for children.

The problem of keeping clean took much time. Occasionally I cajoled one of the guards into bringing me a kettle of hot water from the huge samovar machine in the court which supplied the prison, but usually there was no hot water to be had, so I used to save hot tea morning and evening in empty bottles that had been sent to the prisoners with milk. At night I took a tea bath in a small earthenware bowl that had been sent me by the Czecho-Slovak Red Cross, and in the morning I washed my underclothes in the same manner, one or two pieces a day. I made coarse lace with a crooked hairpin from linen threads drawn from an old bag, took Russian lessons from my companions and helped to mend the prison linen.

All the prisoners are allowed to wear their own clothes and no uniforms are provided, but those who are arrested without any baggage may obtain shirts and drawers, furnished once a week. At first men and women alike were provided with these garments, but after a while the privilege of wearing Russian B.V.D.'s was withdrawn from the ladies, owing to their proclivity for altering them to conform to the lines of feminine lingerie. The shirts we mended were sometimes *kazyonny*,[3] the regulation blouses, such as are furnished the Red Army. At other times we had shirts of all styles and materials, of finest linen, batiste and silk, sometimes with embroidered monograms. The makers' marks in the collar bands were from all parts of the world: Paris, London, Tokyo, New York, Budapest, Berlin. These garments had either been requisitioned from former bourgeois, or left behind by prisoners of all nationalities, who were either freed or met a grimmer fate. I often wove romances about the former owners as I patched and darned.

This work was purely voluntary. We liked it because it gave us needles and thread to mend our own clothes and the privilege of having scissors, which as a rule are strictly forbidden. I never realized before to how many uses one pair of scissors could be put. We employed them to cut our bread, open tin cans, trim our hair and fingernails, mend our shoes, and even to carve meat and sausage.

I believe, as a whole, the women prisoners under exactly the same conditions were relatively far more comfortable than the men. We took a great interest in keeping our room as clean as possible and we often managed to make our prison fare more palatable by simple expedients. For instance when the potatoes were badly cooked or frozen, as they usually were, we used to fish them out of our soup at dinner time, put them in one large bowl and mash them with a wooden spoon until they were reduced to a paste which we flavored with a little salt. Then we made them into croquettes and dropped them into our hot soup in the evening. Although we had a great many lice, I rarely saw a woman with underclothes as filthy as the prison underwear worn by the men. Of course it had all been boiled and laundered when we received it to mend, but the seams were coated with deposits of eggs from all sorts of vermin.

Besides, we were all very ingenious at inventing games and amusements. We had several packs of cards made of the mouthpieces of the Russian cigarettes, chessmen and checkers made of hardened bread and paper dominoes, all these being kept carefully hidden, for games are not allowed. One of our favorite pastimes was fortune-telling with cards, at which most Russian women are adept, and in which they believe implicitly. Once we had books, for two blissful weeks at New Years', but they were afterwards taken away from us. We often

....
3. *Kazyonny* means official in Russian.

sang Russian songs in the evening after the lights were out, in an undertone, of course, for we were not allowed to sing or to speak in tones that could be heard outside in the hall. Most of these songs were traditional melodies that had been sung in prisons in Russia and Siberia for many decades. I learned a great many of them at the time, writing down the words, but they were all taken away from me when I left the prison. Perhaps my favorite was "Baikal," a Siberian prison song that tells of the escape of a prisoner from the galleys in the mountains of Akatuy,[4] bordering on Lake Baikal; how he rigs up a boat from a herring tub, with a torn shirt for a sail and crosses the lake after running away from the penal settlements at Shilka and Nerchinsk. He calls on the Barguzin, the fair wind, to carry him across the lake. Good comrades had helped him to get away, the guards in the mountains shot at and missed him, the wild beasts have spared him, he has kept a sharp lookout while in the neighborhood of the towns, the peasants gave him bread, the young boys filled his pipe with *makhorka*; now he is covering the last stage of the flight to freedom—the trip in his frail craft across the "Holy Sea."[5]

Another song is called "*Slushay.*"[6] It begins:

Like the close of day, like the conscience of a tyrant,
The prison nights are dark,
Darker than the nights that come with the storm is the darkness of the dread prison.
Below the sentries march lazily, keeping an eye on the prison walls.
The poor convict at his window hears their challenge, "Slushay."

The song then described how the silence of the prison is deceptive. It is alive with the inarticulate murmurs of the prisoners who are thirsting for liberty.

Suddenly a noise is heard — a prisoner has broken his bars and jumped from the window. Something soft falls in a huddled mass at the sentry's feet; one prisoner is free.

Still another song which has long been a favorite and which I happen to remember as I translated it into English doggerel, runs as follows:

Dawn and noon and glowing sunset,
To my prison bring no light,

---

4. Akatuy mountain was a notorious *katorga* (forced labor) camp during the tsarist era, where criminals mined silver and lead. Later it became a camp for female political prisoners.
5. Baikal – often referred to as the "Sacred Sea."
6. *Slushay* (rhymes with "bye") means "listen" in Russian.

Watchful guards beneath my window,
Da ya ye, by day and night.

Little need you have to guard me,
Thick and strong my prison walls,
Iron bars twixt me and freedom
Da ya ye, deaf to all my piteous calls.

Chains! my clanking iron fetters,
You I cannot break or bend.
You will be my steel clad guardians
Da ya ye, till life shall end.

Then there were other songs which were very popular, the old revolutionary melodies, such as the *Varshavianka*, the *Red Flag*, and the funeral march of the Nihilists. The last named begins as follows:

Ye victims, who fell in the desperate fight
From love without measure for the people,
You sacrificed all that you could for their sakes
To bring them a life of happiness and freedom.

The last verse is:
When we accompany them to the grave
We say to our fallen comrades,
Farewell, brothers, you loyally trod
The shining road to freedom.

There were other present-day political songs which were very popular. One was *Yabloki*, which is sung all over Russia, the various political parties making up the verses to suit their fancy. *Yabloki*, I should explain, means "apples," and it is a slang word for describing what we should in America, term "boobs" or "simps." The chorus is:

O, little apple, whither away,
The Cheka will get you, some fine day—

One of the verses runs as follows:
I am in the Bochka[7] eating
Kasha from a bowl,
Trotsky and Lenin are boasting,
"We've swallowed Russia whole."
In the Bochka drinking tea,
Nothing more to fear,
My man is a Bolshevik,
And I'm a profiteer.

There was a satirical song which was much sung by the Social Revolutionaries. "He, he *Russky Narod*—Hey, hey, Russian people," which satirized the Cheka, the commissars and the Soviet system of government.

Besides there were many beautiful folk songs, of which I never tired, all with plaintive, haunting melodies, and the oldest of all the Russian national songs, the ballad of *Stenka Razin*, the first Russian revolutionary, who was executed in 1572, in the Red Square, which took its name from his execution.[8]

Still another popular amusement is one that is not considered good form in other countries, but which is perfectly correct in Russia at the present time. This was looking through the keyhole. If anything exciting was going on outside, we took turns. The young wife of the Naval officer next door always had the right of way when the occupants of that room were taken out to or returned from the toilet, and I had first call when General Klembovsky[9] went out for his daily walk. He was in solitary confinement for a long time in a room opposite ours, and I was interested in him because I had often met his wife, before my arrest, at the Cheka when she was bringing him *peredachas* or food packages, and I was bound on a similar errand for the American prisoners. Besides, he was chairman of the committee of Former Generals acting as an advisory commission to the General Staff of the Red Army during the war with Poland, of which my great friend, General Brusilov, was a member.

Speaking Russian, I was able to learn the meaning of many mysterious noises that went on in the Cheka, which have often struck terror to foreigners unfamiliar with the language, and to read the prison rules posted on the doors,

7. *Bochka* is slang for a low-class restaurant.
8. Stepan (Stenka) Razin (1630-1671) was a Cossack rebel from the Don River region who was executed for his rebellion. Harrison is incorrect on the dates of his life here.
9. Vladislav N. Klembovsky (1860-1921) was a Russian general during World War I.

which kept me from the innocent violation of regulations and the consequent penalty of the dark room or the cellar, called the *podval*.

During my entire stay in the Cheka no one from our room was ever sent to the *podval*, but two women were put in the dark room. One of these was a young Russian girl who had demanded to be allowed to go to the bathroom out of her regular turn. We happened to have a very disagreeable guard that day and he refused to let her go. Upon this she grew very indignant, which caused bad feeling; then a little later she demanded to be allowed to go to the corridor and get a glass of water. This was also refused and she told him what she thought of him. A few minutes later he appeared. "Na dopros," he said. She followed him out of the room and instead of being taken to the examining judge's office, she was taken to a small room on our floor, absolutely dark except for a little light that came in from the transom. It contained no furniture, not even a wooden bed. She was kept there for twenty-four hours without any place to sit or lie down on, but she received the regular prison fare. We prevailed on the guard to take her a blanket and a plate of food.

The guards sounded much gruffer than they really were, and very often apparent threats were only rough jokes or friendly admonitions. Nothing was to be gotten by threatening them, but they were almost always responsive to dignity and quiet good breeding. Many of them were actually in sympathy with us, and not a few were deserters who had been condemned to be shot and pardoned on condition that they should work in the Cheka.

Once we were all playing cards and, although we sat with our backs to the door, the guard, who was looking in through the peephole as usual, suspected something of the kind and burst into the room very suddenly. I seized the cards and crumpled them up in my fist.

"You're playing cards," he said severely.

"Never," said I. "We never play cards in this room."

"What have you got in your hand?" he demanded.

I partly opened my clenched fist. "Only a little waste paper," I said casually. "How's the weather this morning?" whereupon he burst out laughing and left the room.

The many stories afloat about the nightly shootings in the cellars of the Lubyanka are absolutely without foundation at the present time. Prisoners condemned to death are kept in solitary confinement for a time, then taken to be shot to a place which I was told is in the Baransky Pereulok, an out-of-the-way street. During my stay in the Lubyanka I only twice heard the automobile which is supposed to drown the noise of the shooting at night, and then only for twenty minutes or so. Once I heard a prisoner on our floor being taken out to be shot. He had completely lost his nerve, and struggled all the way down the hall with his captors, yelling piteously all the while — "Oh, God, I won't go, I won't go."

In general I believe that the number of political executions in Russia at the present time is very small in Moscow, all but the most flagrant conspirators and spies being condemned to internment camps or prisons.[10]

10. Harrison is correct only in relative terms, and only given her qualifier of "Moscow." First, much worse was yet to come. The first GULAG precursors were not built on the Solovetsky Islands until 1922, and it would be another 15 years before the purges reached their horrifying apogee. Second, while Alter Litvin ("The Cheka," in *Critical Companion to the Russian Revolution: 1914-1921*, Indiana 1997, p 318) estimates that the Cheka murdered "at least 10,000" in the years of the Red Terror (1918-1919), killings of an unprecedented scale were taking place in 1920 in the Kuban and the Don, where 300-500,000 were killed or deported in the wake of the Whites' defeat on the Civil War's southern front (*The Black Book of Communism*, Stephane Courtoie *et al*, Harvard 1999, p. 102).

CHAPTER XXV
Prison Holidays

*I*t would seem, naturally, that holidays would be harder to endure than other days in prison, but as a matter of fact this was only partially true. Sunday was, as I have already stated, no different from any other day except that we had a little thicker soup at noon, and no supper. The Soviet holidays, of which we had three important ones, the anniversary of the November and March Revolutions and the birthday of Karl Marx,[1] were the same as Sundays in so far as our rations were concerned, but the day before every prisoner received a *peredacha* from the Political Red Cross. On the seventh of November, the day of the Bolshevik Revolution, we each got half a pound of butter, a pound of sugar, a quarter of a pound of salt, a quarter of a pound of coffee and fifty cigarettes. The articles were distributed by the prison guards, who came in with big trays heaped with packages. When the coffee was being given out I asked our guard, "What kind of coffee are you giving us — Sovietsky?" Soviet coffee, I should explain, is a brew like nothing else in the world. At different times I was told that it consisted of roasted bread crumbs, powdered acorns, roasted barley and cow peas. Sometimes the better qualities were mixed with a little chicory, or flavored with something that resembled vanilla. Our warder evidently considered we were all counter-revolutionaries, for he answered with a wink—"No, Nikolayevsky." At New Year's, Christmas and Easter we received just about the same.

The last two holidays with their home memories were the hardest of all to face, and I shall never forget the two weeks just before Christmas. Some of us, including myself, were foreigners. We knew that there was no hope of our

....
1. May 5, 1818.

release before the great holiday, but there were several Russian women, detained as witnesses, or on relatively unimportant charges, who hoped up to the last minute. One of them was a woman with three small children. That she was in prison owing in large part to her own stupidity did not make her plight any the less pitiful. She had some time before her arrest received a letter by underground mail from her brother in Riga. He enclosed a sum of money, and wrote at length about his plans for the future, sending messages to several of his friends in Moscow as to how to get out of the country. At the close of the letter he instructed her to destroy it as soon as she had read it. Womanlike, however, she wanted to keep it, and hid it under the mattress on her bed. Shortly afterwards there was a raid in the apartment house where she lived, for hidden money and food supplies, and the letter was found quite by accident. She and her sister were immediately arrested and the three children were left alone in the apartment, dependent on the care of neighbors, with Christmas coming on.

The poor woman, who was really utterly ignorant of politics, was grilled and cross-examined repeatedly as to the acquaintances referred to in her brother's letter, and no doubt they were all arrested as well. She spent most of her time in prison weeping or laying out the cards to see whether she would be freed for Christmas. On Christmas Eve the first thing in the morning she reached for the pack under her pillow. The first card was *gromadny radost* — great joy. "I know I'm going to get home today," she declared triumphantly, but the morning and afternoon passed without a summons. Finally at about nine o'clock in the evening, when she had sobbed herself to sleep on her straw pallet, a guard appeared. "Dmitrova," he called. "*Sobiraytes s veschyami*" (pack your clothes). In less time than it takes to tell it, we had waked her up, packed her things, for she was too dazed to do anything but cross herself, and say "Thank God," and she was hustled off, sobbing but radiant.

All of us followed her in our thoughts to the little room we could picture to ourselves, with its small wood stove, its jumble of trunks, boxes, pots and pans, parlor, dining and bedroom furniture, its pile of wood in the corner, the sack of potatoes under the bed, where three small children were huddled together, tired out with waiting for Matushka[2] to come home. Perhaps she would still be able to get a Christmas tree at the last moment. We wondered, and meanwhile we finished trimming our own tree. It was an immense stroke of luck that we had a tree at all, and we owed it to the fact that three days before Christmas we had been taken out to the public baths with an armed convoy, and marched for

2. A endearing Russian diminutive for Mother.

some distance through the snow-covered streets. They were selling trees in the Trubnaya Square, through which we had to pass, and we managed to pick up a number of branches which had broken off and lay scattered on the snow. When we got back to our room we tied them together and stuck them in a bottle, which we covered with white paper that had been wrapped around a package received by one of the prisoners.

Then we set about making decorations. I had some silver paper in my bag that had been wrapped around a cake of soap. This we made into festoons of little silver balls, stringing them together on the thread we received to mend the prison linen. Another woman had a piece of red cardboard that had been part of a cigarette carton, and I had a red label from a can of condensed milk. We cut these pieces of paper into red stars, which we attached to the end of every twig. I complained of a toothache, and received some raw cotton and iodine to put on my tooth from the prison dispensary. We used this to powder the tree, giving the effect of snow. One of the women contributed a little gold chain she wore around her neck with an image of the *Mat Boga*, the Mother of God, and the Christmas tree was done. We thought it was very beautiful.

A clean white towel was spread on the table, and then we prepared our feast. It consisted of a tin of American canned beef which had been sent me by the Czecho-Slovak Red Cross, two salt herrings, a rice pudding that had been sent another of the prisoners, prison bread, butter and sugar sent us by the Political Red Cross and tea, an extra ration of which had been served to us at ten o'clock. We hid it under our blankets and pillows to keep it hot till midnight when we planned to have our supper. The guards had promised to give us light till one o'clock, which they invariably did on great holidays, and we spent the early part of the evening playing games. Promptly at twelve o'clock we all stood around the table. We were a strange cosmopolitan company.

First there was Pani Pavlovskaya, a Polish woman, who had been arrested some weeks before because she had had a telephone conversation with a strange man who wanted to rent one of her rooms. The Cheka had been listening in, as it does on two hundred and fifty telephones daily in Moscow, and it happened that the gentleman in question was suspected of being a counter-revolutionary. Pani Pavlovskaya had no babies to go back to, and her husband had deserted her and left the country in the first days of the Revolution. But she had a King Charles spaniel and a canary bird, and she was as much worried about them as if they had been a pair of small children.

Next was Elizaveta Eduardovna, a pretty young German girl married to a Russian. Her husband was in another prison. She had been arrested some weeks before, and up to that time had no knowledge of the charges against her. Then there was Anna Ivanovna, a Little Russian,[3] prostitute by instinct, spy by profession, with the temper of ten devils; the dramatic talent of a great artist. Anna Ivanovna's weakness was that she loved pretty things to wear and good things to eat and drink. She had sold herself for a pair of new shoes at the age of fifteen, had abandoned her baby for a man who promised her a green silk dress, and had betrayed a group of Estonian Communists for a bottle of champagne. I had won her heart by giving her a box of red nail salve with which she rouged her cheeks. She was generous to a fault, impulsively affectionate, and if she had lived at another time and in a different environment I am not sure that she would have been what the world calls an abandoned woman.

Next to Anna Ivanovna stood Maria Casimirovna, a Lithuanian peasant woman, one of the refugees who had been driven into Central Russia at the beginning of the German offensive, and thence to Kharkov, where she was arrested for having, like the good Catholic she was, carried a letter from a Polish priest to a compatriot who was accused of espionage. Maria could neither read nor write, but she spent hours every day poring over her missal, which she knew from cover to cover by heart, or telling her rosary. She seldom talked and never complained, but she just grew paler and thinner, day by day, until, when she was finally released some weeks later, she was almost too weak to walk.

Then came a Lettish Communist named Vera Ivanovna, a delicate young girl, still weakened from six months in the Central Prison at Riga. She had come to Moscow, had entered the service of the Cheka, and had been denounced as an agent provocateur. Although her position was very serious, for such charges against Communists, if not disproved to the entire satisfaction of the Cheka, are punishable with death, she was not afraid; but she was heartbroken to think that she had been misjudged by her own comrades.

The remaining members of our party were Olga Petrovna, a Russian woman, the sister of an old general who had been arrested for failure to declare the possession of a lot of family silver, which she was accused of secreting for counter-revolutionary funds, and myself.

Before beginning our supper, Pani Pavlovskaya, in accordance with the beautiful Polish custom, broke into seven pieces our substitute for the

----
3. "Little Russian" is an old term for someone from Ukraine, which during the Russian Empire was known as *Maloros*, or "Little Russia"

consecrated Christmas wafer, an American soda cracker, the last of a box I had in my possession when I was arrested, giving one to each of us with a kiss, and wishing us a happy Christmas. We in turn divided our bits with our particular friends, wishing them the same. Then we sat down to our simple Christmas repast. During supper each of us told where and how she had spent the preceding Christmas. I had spent mine in Warsaw with the Polish American girls known as the Gray Sisters, who were doing social service work under the auspices of the Young Women's Christian Association, and I had had my Christmas dinner at the American Legation with a crowd of fellow Americans.

After supper, one after another, we sang our own Christmas Carols, and the story of the Holy Night was retold in seven languages. I sang Phillips Brooks' hymn, *Oh, Little Town of Bethlehem*, not only because it was one of the loveliest carols I know, but because it was written by an American.

Finally Elizaveta Eduardovna, our German comrade, made a short speech which I don't think any of us who were there will ever forget. She said that although we were celebrating Christmas in prison, far away from all that had made previous Christmases dear to us, she did not believe that in the future we would look back on this Christmas as an altogether unhappy one. Prison had taught us one of the great Christmas messages — the message of good will towards men. Thrown together by fate under the worst possible conditions of mental anxiety and physical discomfort, we had learned to live together in peace and comradeship, to lay the foundation for a real international based on love and forbearance. She hoped from her heart that each of us would spend the next Christmas in our own homes, but she asked that wherever we were, we would stop for a minute on Christmas Eve and send a silent message of good cheer to every member of the present company.

No one spoke for a moment — then the silence was broken by Anna Ivanovna who burst into a fit of wild, uncontrollable sobbing. Vera Ivanovna flung herself on her bed face down, saying over and over again, "Oh, Mother, Mother." The rest began to undress, talking about trivial matters to carry on, and I busied myself in my corner with seven mysterious packages containing seven tiny pieces of chocolate, which I had saved for the occasion, for I had told all my companions about our American Christmas, and I wanted to illustrate it by playing Santa Claus. When they had gone to sleep I slipped one under each of the wooden headrests that were supposed to serve as pillows. After all, I thought, it is possible, if you only try hard enough, to have a real Christmas anywhere.

On New Year's Eve, according to the Russian custom, we all played fortune-telling games, very much as people do in America on Halloween. First we tried our luck with the cards, then, in order to find out who was to be our future husband, we drew slips from a pile on which were written a number of men's Christian names. I told of the American custom of walking backwards down the cellar stairs at midnight with a lighted candle in one hand and a mirror in the other. As we had none of the necessary paraphernalia, we rigged up a substitute apparatus. Our only chair was put on one of the beds. With many smothered giggles and suppressed screams, we mounted in turn on the chair, holding in one hand a lighted match, in the other our only mirror, the tiny one in the lid of my pocket powder box, and gingerly descended the three steps from the chair to the bed and thence to the floor. One of the girls solemnly averred that she saw the face of a dark man in the mirror.

Finally we played another rather gruesome game. On a number of tiny slips of paper were written the possibilities for the future that were facing us at the time—a meeting, a journey, an enemy, cross-examination, liberty, prison, death. These slips were placed on a table underneath a towel, and there were three drawings. I drew prison twice, and the last time a journey. This meant that I would not be released for some time, but that I would eventually get home. The death slip was drawn once by an eighteen-year old girl who was arrested as a witness and knew perfectly well that she was in no danger, so we could afford to make light of it.

Our Easter celebration was the most elaborate of all, for the Russians make more of Easter than of any other holiday. The spiritual significance of the Resurrection appeals strongly to the innate mysticism of the Russian temperament, and the more material side, largely manifested by an inordinate love for the fleshpots, finds expression in the great feasts that are spread in all Russian homes to celebrate the festival which marks the end of the long, cold winters, with their interminable nights. It happened at that time that all of my companions, except a Polish girl arrested for espionage, were Russians. One was a Communist and one a Jewess, and the rest Orthodox. There were nine of us in all. Most of them had families in Moscow and had received wonderful Easter *peredachas*. Our Easter table was really so beautiful that the guards themselves stared open-mouthed at it every time they opened the door. On Easter eve we fasted according to custom, and supper was served at midnight.

The table was covered with a beautiful drawn work linen cloth that had been sent us by a relative of one of the prisoners. In the center was a nosegay of flowering shrubs in a pottery bowl. It was surrounded by a ring of gaily colored Easter eggs and flanked by the traditional Easter dishes, *paskha*, a concoction of sweetened cream cheese, molded into a pyramid, on each side of which was a cross in high relief, ham, and the *kulich*, an enormous loaf of sweetened bread with raisins, prepared according to a special recipe. In addition we had vinagrette, pickled herrings, and small cakes, known in Russia as *pirozhki*.[4]

On the stroke of twelve we all stood round the table. Our *starosta* (the room chairman) turned to the woman on her right, and kissed her on both cheeks. "Christ is risen," she said simply. "Christ is risen, indeed," was the answer, and this was done by each woman in turn all around the table. Then, as we ate our supper, through the open window we could hear the bells of the Moscow churches in the distance. In all the churches there is a midnight service beginning with the reading of excerpts from the lives of the twelve apostles. After the first the bell tolls once, after the second twice, and so on until twelve is reached, when all the bells in Moscow together burst out into a mad carillon.

I know of nothing more beautiful than the Moscow church bells; there are literally thousands of them. Tradition imputes forty times forty churches to Moscow. As a matter of fact, the guidebooks state that there are four hundred and thirty-five, not counting the private chapels, and each has its chime of bells. Most of them are not constructed on the Western European plan. Instead of being rung by means of a pendulum they are struck by little hammers and the sound is unusual, but often mellow and very lovely.

Our lights were put out at one o'clock, but it was at least five in the morning before the last chimes died away. According to custom, our table remained spread for three days, and everybody who came into the room, including the guards and the man who gave out the prison linen, was invited to share our Easter feast.

---

4. *Paskha* is a rich Easter cheesecake made from eggs, *tvorog* (cottage cheese), butter, sugar and cream. *Kulich* is a traditional, delicate Russian Easter bread. *Pirozkhi* is plural of the word *pirogi*. They are small Russian pies with a variety of fillings.

CHAPTER XXVI
The Mills of the Gods

The physical isolation of prisoners in the "Lubyanka 2" is about as complete as possible, but nevertheless we were anything but isolated intellectually from the outside world, and from those confined in other prisons. Though we were without newspapers we were well informed of everything that was going on in Russia. We knew of all the new decrees, all the negotiations with foreign governments, local and general economic conditions, and our constantly changing population was an accurate reflection of the political situation.

During the first weeks of my imprisonment, the majority of the political prisoners were persons arrested in connection with an alleged counter-revolutionary plot in the war office. All the employees of one department, two hundred in number, had been arrested together with the department head. A number of naval officers and their wives were also arrested for the same reason. This was in the days when peace negotiations with the Poles were dragging on at Riga, and there was a good deal of disaffection in the army. Most of those arrested were held as witnesses. There seems to be no arrangement for subpoenaing witnesses in Russia. They are simply locked up until they have given the necessary testimony, or if the case is a very important one, until it is brought to trial, the principle being that it is better to isolate them.

After this excitement had died down, we had persons arrested for illegal intercourse with foreign missions. All governments which had signed diplomatic or commercial treaties with Russia sent delegations to Moscow, and naturally at first there was much intercourse between them and private citizens. Many persons who had friends or relatives abroad received letters or packages from them through foreign missions; then, the members of the missions were usually very well housed and entertained delightfully, and besides there was always the chance for the less scrupulous to send valuables out of the country or to do a little profitable private business.

The Soviet Government, however, regards all official delegations from bourgeois governments as espionage organizations, so the Central Executive Committee issued a decree forbidding Russian citizens any intercourse with foreign missions except through the intermediary of the Foreign Office. Few people were aware of this decree, though it was published in the newspapers, for papers are not on sale; the only way for the average citizen to get the news is to read the papers posted in the streets and public places, and most people have no time for this in the scramble for food and the ordinary necessities of life. Consequently, many unsuspecting persons were arrested. Among the cases of which I had personal knowledge from being thrown with the actual culprits were the following:

A well-known comic opera singer signed a contract to appear at a concert at the Estonian Mission. She was unable to fill the engagement owing to a cold, but nevertheless she was arrested and spent three weeks in our room. Although she was never in the slightest danger, she was very temperamental and took her arrest most tragically. After every *dopros* she would walk the floor for some time with a handkerchief around her head declaring that she had never believed that a woman could be made to suffer so; then she would lapse into violent hysterics and consume huge doses of valerian, after which she revived and entertained us all with clever impersonations of celebrated actors and accounts of her experiences and love affairs in Russia and other parts of Europe. She was convinced that imprisonment was making her hair gray, so she feigned a sore throat and got peroxide from the dispensary which she dabbed on her locks four or five times a day. Finally she was released through the efforts of her latest flame, a well-known Communist, who sent her wonderful *peredachas* nearly every day, though other prisoners were permitted to receive them only once a week, and we missed her very much when she left us.

A young Estonian woman married to a Frenchman who had become a Russian citizen, and who was expecting her first baby in three months, was arrested for having received a case of condensed milk from her sister in Reval and she spent a month in prison.

One night a very pretty Lettish girl, just married to a Russian, was brought into our room. For three weeks she was in complete ignorance as to why she had been arrested. At the first *dopros* it transpired that she was accused of espionage because she had had the members of the Lettish Mission to tea in her apartment. She was released after seven weeks. Still other cases were those of a young girl employed in the Foreign Office who had accepted a pair of shoes from a member of the Persian Mission, and the wife of the president of the Political Red Cross, who was arrested for having had a telephone conversation about the loan of an automobile to take food packages to the Butyrki, with one of the members of the Estonian Mission, and detained for forty-eight hours.

An old lady in destitute circumstances, a Czecho-Slovak by birth, who had taken Russian citizenship at the beginning of the Great War, but who was already registered for the resumption of her own nationality, was accused of espionage and kept in the Cheka for nearly two months because she had received food packages from the Czech Mission. Her alleged offense was rendered more grave by the fact that she was employed as a translator in the censorship department of the Moscow general post-office.

The Kronstadt rebellion[1] sent us its quota of witnesses from Petrograd, the defeat of Wrangel furnished us with several "White" prisoners; we had the aftermath of the war with Poland in a number of unfinished espionage cases, and of the peace with Latvia in the arrest of many Communists who had been deported from Latvia under the provisions of the treaty.

One of the Polish espionage cases was particularly interesting and I happened to hear the whole story. A party of five persons engaged in commercial espionage was arrested at Kiev in July, 1920. There were three men and two women. One of the men, becoming frightened, turned informer and was released, the rest being brought to Moscow. Both of the women were in my room in the autumn. One was condemned to an internment camp until the conclusion of peace with Poland, as was one of her male companions; another became converted to Communism and entered the service of the Polish section of the Cheka. The remaining member of the party, an intensely nervous man, was placed in solitary confinement because he had refused to give the required information, and hung himself in his cell.

The Lettish Communists were accused of being agents provocateurs in spite of the fact that most of them had spent several months in the Central Prison at Riga, where they were treated far worse than in Russia, many of them being beaten. I actually saw the scars on the arms, legs and breasts of several of them.

. . . .

1. The Kronstadt Rebellion was a rebellion of the Kronstadt military garrison on Kotlin Island near Petrograd in March, 1921. The rebellion was fueled by discontent over Bolshevik Civil War policies and sought to restore power to the soviets rather than political parties. After several attempts, the Red Army and Communist party members brutally subdued the uprising.

One told me that they would have starved to death in the Riga prison had it not been for the nourishing supper given them daily by the American Red Cross. It was very pathetic to see these women, all of whom had suffered much and most of whom I believe were sincere and devoted Communists, held in prison in the country where they had hoped to find an asylum. Among them was a trusted courier of the bureau of the Third International, and she was held for four months because she refused to give testimony against her sister, who was accused of espionage.

In the late winter, unsettled conditions in the Donsk Oblast[2] sent us several Cossack women prisoners, the most interesting among whom was a young girl recently married to the Commander of the Second Army. She accompanied him on army business to Moscow, where he was arrested on the charge of having encouraged peasant revolts by refusing to carry out what he thought were unreasonable requisitions among the Don peasants, and she was held as a witness. Believing in his absolute sincerity and devotion to the Soviet Government, she waived her right to refuse to testify as his wife, and was cross-examined several times, once from midnight until nearly four in the morning. She came back utterly exhausted and terrified for fear her testimony would be misinterpreted. I don't know if this was the case or not, but I heard late in the spring, long after she had left us, that she was in the Butyrki Hospital expecting the birth of a baby, and mercifully kept from the knowledge that her husband had been shot.

Our prison diet was about the same all winter. In the morning, anywhere from eight to ten-thirty, we received tea, made of apple parings and dried carrots, or Soviet coffee. I was never able to find out exactly what the latter was made of. We were usually allowed to take as much as we pleased. The tea was followed by our daily ration of from five and a half to eight and a half ounces of black bread, according to the supply on hand. Sometimes it was eatable, at others absolutely impossible and always without salt. The best was made of a combination of dark barley, oats and bran. Frequently it was adulterated with a substance that gave it the consistency of clay, the color of dirty putty. Every other day we received two and a half teaspoons of sugar, or, when there was no sugar, its equivalent in honey or bonbons. Our dinner, which was served at one o'clock, consisted usually of salt herring soup, chiefly eyes, tails and backbones, thickened with a little cereal or containing unpared, half boiled potatoes. In

----

2. Oblast is Russian for "province" or "region." The Donskoy Oblast is southeast of Moscow along the Don River. It has been the traditional home for Cossacks for many centuries.

the winter they were invariably frozen and almost black. Sometimes we had, instead, horse soup with salted cabbage. The cabbage was frequently almost uneatable, as most of the half rotten cabbages are salted to preserve them. Once in a while we had a treat — soup with salt pork or mutton, containing slices of salt cucumber. The second dish was *kasha* or boiled cabbage. The *kasha* was always edible and usually sufficient, but it required considerable patience to eat the variety made of whole wheat, for it was full of hulls. I used to pick them out and make a sort of *chevaux de frise* with which I decorated the edge of my bowl. For supper we had the same soup as that served at dinner, followed by tea.

Many of the prisoners received *peredachas*, or food packages, from their friends and relatives, and sometimes we lived high when we happened to have a number of rich bourgeois companions. Knowing as I did the prices of food on the open market, I used to wonder at the quantities of white bread, cake, cheese, sausage and other luxuries received by many of the prisoners. Of course in many cases it meant that the families of the prisoners were selling their last possessions, but in others it was evidence of the enormous amount of hidden wealth that still exists in Russia.

For the first three weeks I received no food packages, and then the first *peredachas* came from the Czecho-Slovak Red Cross. I shall never forget my joy when I heard my name called for the first time, and saw the signature of Mr. Skala, the head of the Czecho-Slovak Mission, on the list which accompanied the package. He and his wife had been good friends of mine, we had lived in the same house, and I felt that the small slip of paper was the one link which connected me with the outside world. The *peredachas* from the Czechs were often meager, but each week there was something, with the exception of intervals of several weeks at Christmas and Easter, and three weeks after my transfer to the Novinsky prison,[3] when they evidently lost sight of me. They also sent me shoes, needles and thread, soap, and other necessities. Besides, as time went on, I began to receive occasional *peredachas* from my Russian friends who were released from prison. Thanks to one of them, after six months I had sheets and a pillowcase, a wrapper and many other small comforts.

As the winter wore on, it became evident that my case was being held in abeyance to see what developments would take place in the international situation. I was seldom called to a *dopros*. Once, in January, I was informed by Mogilevsky that "Mr. Vanderlip, acting as the official representative of

---

3. Moscow's most famous women's prison was located on Novinsky pereulok, in the capital's Arbat region, from 1907 to the 1950s, when it was torn down.

President-elect Harding, had practically concluded negotiations for large mining concessions and the lease of a naval coaling station on the island of Sakhalin, and that in view of this fact all the American prisoners would probably be released in a few weeks." This was the last time I saw Mogilevsky until the day I left Russia, and there was no more talk of freedom until I was urged in the spring to write to the State Department, practically transmitting an unofficial proposal from the Soviet Government for my release, conditional upon the release of Communists then in prison in the United States, or the opening of negotiations for the resumption of trade relations with Russia. This I always refused to do.

While I was in prison I received three letters from relatives in the United States, and was allowed several times to write home. On arriving in this country I learned that none of these letters had been received.

I had several visits from employees of the Foreign Office who came to inquire after my health. One was from Santeri Nuorteva,[4] who was for some time chief of the English and American department of the Foreign Office. He was later arrested and the rumors as to the reasons for his arrest were various. One had it that he joined the noble army of speculators, another that he was the secret agent of a foreign government.

Following Mr. Nuorteva's visit, I had a rather amusing experience. When he asked me if I wanted anything, I told him, no, nothing particularly, except a bath, as I had not had one for four months. That night at half-past two a guard suddenly opened the door, turned on the light and demanded "Garrison!"

"Here," I answered sleepily, wondering vaguely at the same time whether I was to be taken out and shot, as prisoners condemned to execution are usually removed at night.

"To the bath," he announced solemnly.

I was taken upstairs to a very clean bathroom with plenty of hot water, supplied from the tank attached to a huge porcelain stove in the corner, a nice porcelain tub, clean towels and a piece of soap. Needless to say I took advantage of the opportunity, and in addition to bathing did a week's washing. This bathroom was ordinarily used for prisoners who were brought in from the provinces covered with vermin or afflicted with some infectious disease, which rendered them dangerous to their fellow prisoners. It was no time to be

---

4. Santeri Nuorteva (1881-1929) was a Finnish-Soviet journalist who emigrated to the United States in 1911. In 1920, he was expelled from the United States to Soviet Russia for his socialist views.

particular, however, and I never bothered as to whether or not there were any germs left in the tub.

In the early spring the government became particularly active against the members of other Socialist parties, and then began what was the most interesting part of my term in prison, for I had as companions a succession of party members. Our room became a real forum for the discussion of all questions of the day and even of the past. There were some old revolutionaries, among them a Maximalist who remembered the activities of the Nihilists and the assassination of Alexander II, and who had played an important role in the revolution of 1905. While opposed to Marxism on general principles, she had taken no part in activities against the Soviet Government, and indeed had helped to keep the underground Communist organization alive in the Crimea under Denikin and Wrangel. She was a clearheaded, unemotional person, and the circumstantial stories she told me of persecutions under the White *Kontrazvyetka*[5] were as bad as any I have ever read in the Northcliffe papers,[6] of the horrors of the Bolshevik regime. She had been engaged in educational work during the past year, and was arrested because, on coming to Moscow on a Kommandirovka, that is to say, official business, connected with her department, she had happened to share a room with a Social Revolutionary against whom there were conspiracy charges. Although old and in bad health, she was kept in the Cheka from the middle of February to the middle of March, then being transferred to the Novinsky prison from which she was released shortly before my arrival there in June.

Another, a Left Social Revolutionary, had also been one of the leading spirits of 1905, had spent much time in prison under Nikolai and was an old friend of Lenin. She escaped with him via Finland, and she described to me their journey to Helsingfors[7]—how they hid in closed summer dachas, bungalows near the Finnish coast, doing all their cooking at night so the smoke would not be seen; how they sneaked into Helsingfors by twos and threes, obtained false passports and were smuggled into steamers bound for England or Sweden. After that she spent many years in exile in Switzerland. When arrested, she claimed that she was not an active party worker; nevertheless following the obstructionist policy of the Left Social Revolutionaries, she refused to be photographed and was supremely indifferent to prison discipline, talking in a loud voice, though talking in undertones was a rigidly enforced rule of the prison, summoning

5. Counterintelligence.
6. Northcliffe papers refers to an English conglomerate that published many newspapers.
7. Helsinki, Finland.

the guards and demanding whatever she wanted. Failing to persuade her to be photographed, the guards resorted to stratagem. She was summoned to a fake *dopros*, but when she found out what was up she sat down on the stairs, refused to move, and dared her escort to violence. Then she demanded immediate release, or transfer to the Socialist section of the Butyrki prison, and announced that she would begin a hunger strike within twenty-four hours. Receiving no answer, she struck, and starved for five days, after which she was taken to the Butyrki.

The same thing happened in the case of another Left Social Revolutionary, a young, handsome and exceedingly brilliant woman from Kharkov. She had been condemned to a term of imprisonment in the Butyrki, but as her health broke down, she was transferred to a prison sanatorium from which she escaped, beating her way back to Kharkov without money, papers or documents. The authorities were on her trail, however, and she was arrested almost immediately and brought back to Moscow, absolutely without baggage and still wearing the clothes in which she had made her escape some two weeks before. Naturally she was very dirty and covered with vermin, but she refused to bathe, comb her hair or change her underclothes or eat any food until she was returned to the Butyrki prison.

"I am filthy," she said cheerfully. "I shall probably infest you all with vermin."

In spite of this fact, which was undoubtedly true, I found her a delightful companion, and I was sorry on my own account when she was transferred to the Butyrki three days later, though thankful for her sake.

At this time obstruction among the Social Revolutionaries in the Cheka became general, there was a feeling of tension in the air, mysterious noises were heard from various parts of the building, yells, howls, and the sound of breaking glass. One man, in solitary confinement in our corridor, who had been kept for six weeks without a *dopros*, spent a whole morning kicking on his door. For this he was confined in the cellar *podval* for several days. (The *podval* is used for the punishment of unruly prisoners. It is cold, damp, dark, infested with rats and vermin.) On being returned to his cell, he smashed the window and the transom and made kindling wood of his bed.

Another prisoner, on being summoned to a *dopros*, sent word that he had nothing to say to the *sledovatel*, and therefore did not care to go, but if the *sledovatel* had anything to say to him he would be glad to have him call.

Then the Anarchists, a number of whom were arrested at about that time, began to practice obstruction. Twelve of them went on a hunger strike simultaneously, one, a very pretty girl about eighteen years old, being in my room. I later met her in the Novinsky prison, from which she was released in July, as she had tuberculosis. The Anarchists caused still more excitement, armed guards were posted along the corridor and we had the feeling that a storm was going to break. The situation was finally relieved, however, by yielding to the demands of the obstructionists, and Left Social Revolutionaries and Anarchists were transferred to other and better prisons.

All movements of this kind were concerted and simultaneous. They were even supported by similar action in other prisons, thanks to the underground railway that exists among all political prisoners. The prisoners in my room were in constant communication with others in and out of prison. One means of communication known to the authorities, but which they were unable to control, and in some cases tolerated with a view of trapping the unwary, was by means of writing on the walls of the bathroom. The Socialists had their ciphers, which were unreadable, but others wrote messages that were sometimes interpreted with disastrous results. Then there was prison telegraphy by means of tapping on steam pipes or walls. There were numerous pipes running through our room and sometimes we heard three or four furtive telegraph messages going on at once.

Those of us who were not politically minded used to have very entertaining conversations with the men in the next room, in which, by the way, Captain Kilpatrick[8] of the American Red Cross was confined for several weeks, unfortunately before my arrival. This was the way it was done. There was a steam pipe that ran along the narrow end of our room close to the floor and passed into the next. We found that by lying flat on the floor and putting our lips to the pipe the sound could be carried to the next room. The person on the other side also lay on the floor, putting his ear against the pipe. Later the men dug a little hole around the pipe, and we passed through notes, all of course absolutely non-political in character because there might have been a spy in the room adjoining. One of the men, who was an artist, drew sketches of all of us as he imagined we would look, and we had a great deal of fun.

There was a girl in our room who developed a real romance by means of our clandestine correspondence. She had already had a novel and rather romantic

8. Captain Emmet Kilpatrick of the American Red Cross was captured and imprisoned by the Bolsheviks. A newspaper article in the *New York Times* in May 1921 mentioned that he had gone insane while in prison. An article in the *New York Times* in 1920 noted, though, that Kilpatrick had been killed in southern Russia. In the end, he was moved from prison to prison and spent long periods of time in isolation. He was released at the same time as Harrison.

escapade. She was a Russian, but had lived for some time in Tiflis,[9] the capital of Georgia, where she was a student at the University, and when Georgia went Red she decided she would like to get out of the country, so she contracted a Soviet marriage with a Turk, in order to leave with him for Constantinople. Of course it was only a *manage de convenance* and they were to part as soon as they got to Turkey, but at Batoum,[10] where they were to take the steamer, the Turk was arrested for espionage, accused of being an English agent, and brought to Moscow with his Russian bride, who was held as a witness against him.

Once I was summoned to our improvised telephone and to my surprise heard a familiar voice at the other end. It was that of the Commandant of the government guesthouse where I had lived so long, and whom I had last seen taking part in the search of my room. "Margarita Bernardovna," he whispered, "I want to tell you that all your baggage is sealed and quite safe." He also gave me news of my Czecho-Slovak friends and other people whom I had known at the Kharitonevsky. He was accused, it seemed of speculation, but he was shortly taken away and I don't know what became of him.

We always posted sentinels at the door while these clandestine conversations were going on, but several times we had narrow escapes. Once, one of the girls was lying on the floor talking through the pipe, when the guard, who had approached on tiptoe, opened the door very unexpectedly. I just had presence of mind enough to kick her as a warning not to get up and then I sat down unconcernedly on the bed under which she was lying and swung my feet. Finally we began to feel that we were suspected and we were still more uneasy when a Finnish girl who had been really imprudent, even going to the extent of throwing notes out of the window to compatriots who worked at the electric saw in the yard below, was detected, and taken off to solitary confinement. One night, March 24th, to be exact, at about eleven o'clock, guards came to our room and ordered us to pack immediately. We were sure that everything had been discovered and that we were bound for the *podval*. There was nothing to do but make the best of it, so we collected our belongings and prepared to spend our Easter underground. Our stuffy, overcrowded room suddenly looked very comfortable, and we filed out into the corridor, a disconsolate procession of nine women, laden with miscellaneous baggage of every description.

9. Tbilisi, Georgia.
10. Batumi, Batum or Batoum, Georgia is a Black Sea port city.

CHAPTER XXVII
An Attic Cell

$\mathcal{M}$uch to our surprise, however, we were taken upstairs, not down, and found ourselves on the top or garret floor, which had formerly been used for employees. Evidently the congestion had become so great that it had been necessary to transform this floor also into prison quarters.

The room into which we were shown contained about as much floor space as the one below, but it was shorter and wider. The walls, which had been newly painted, sloped at a sharp angle on three sides, making it seem smaller, and there was only one small dormer window, giving most insufficient light, and hermetically sealed. As usual I made for the bed nearest the window, but even there it was intolerably close, the air was damp, cold, permeated with the smell of fresh paint. The beds were new, and therefore absolutely clean, but we had mostly old pallets, which were anything but above suspicion.

We unpacked and went to bed, but no one was able to sleep. The atmosphere was absolutely stifling and as chill as a vault. To add to the other smells, our *parashka* was without a lid. We knocked repeatedly on the door during the night demanding air and a lid for the *parashka*. The former request was refused, and we were told that there were no lids for the *parashkas* on that floor, but that they were being made. I remained in that room until the beginning of June, but we never received a cover and we had to make a piece of old porous bagging answer the purpose.

By morning, we were all fairly gasping for breath, had turned various shades of white, green or yellow, according to our various complexions, and we were so weak we were hardly able to move. We demanded the Commandant; the *Nadziratel,* or officer on duty - who was one of the few brutal guards, a Lett by the way - refused to send for him. Finally we wrote a collective Zayavleniye[1] to Menzhinsky, the head of the Secret Section of the Cheka. It simply said:

"We are suffocating. If you don't believe it, come and see for yourself," and it was signed by all of us.

Now the writing of these petitions is one of the inalienable rights of prisoners that has never been questioned. Our warder was afraid to hold it back and sent for the Commandant. In two hours he arrived, and I think he was frightened himself at our appearance, for he ordered the window to be broken open immediately. After that it was never closed, but we were strictly forbidden to look out of it into the courtyard. Of course we did look when we were not observed, and it was an unfailing source of amusement to us, for it was opposite the registration office, where all prisoners who are discharged or sent to other prisons receive their papers, and the *predvaritelnaya*, or general detention room, where prisoners are frequently held pending commitment or cross-examination.

By standing on one of the beds, in the shadow, a little back from the window, we had a good view of all who passed through, and when our companions were taken out we always arranged for them to give us a sign to show whether they were to be set at liberty. Sometimes we were indiscreet and were reported on by someone opposite; then there were threats to close the window or we were told that if anyone appeared at it the sentry had orders to fire, which he actually did once or twice to frighten us.

During the weeks that followed, we endured other physical discomforts the chief of which were the frequent breakdowns of the plumbing, which necessitated repairs that kept us from going to the bathroom sometimes for eighteen hours at a stretch, and the breakdown of the apparatus for boiling water. When this happened, as it did several times, water had to be boiled on the prison stove, we were only allowed a cup of tea apiece morning and evening, though we usually cajoled the guards into giving us a little more, and there was no boiled drinking water in the cooler in the corridor to which we were usually allowed access. Once, during the very hot weather in May, this state of affairs continued for a week at a time.

Meanwhile, the political situation continued to be very interesting. Nearly all the prisoners were Socialists, Mensheviks, Right Social Revolutionaries and Jewish Bundists, belonging to the seceding faction of the Bund that did not

---

1. A petition or proposal.

unite with the Third International. We continued the political discussions begun downstairs, but there were no more hunger strikes and no more obstruction.

Having a majority of Socialists, we instituted a Commune, and as I was the oldest inhabitant in point of length of imprisonment and all the indications were that I was a permanent fixture, I was appointed Food Administrator. We pooled all our *peredachas*, and every day I had to plan menus for the three meals. Sometimes, when most of us were receiving food packages, we lived sumptuously; again, when there were many from other cities, with no connections in Moscow, there was hardly enough to go around. It must be remembered, however, that all the food we received from the outside was cold, and we had no means of heating it. After eight months of perpetual picnics I began to find this very trying.

In our new room we started several new amusements, one of which was Swedish gymnastics, the other Spiritualism. We never had a real medium, but we drew a circle on a large sheet of wrapping paper, marked letters and numbers around it, placed an overturned saucer on it, with an arrow indicator marked on one side, and then put our fingers on the saucer, very lightly, but in such a way as to form an unbroken circle of contact. Then we kept perfectly still. In a few minutes the "spirits" began to get busy spelling out remarkable messages to the credulous. I used to have great fun with this, imperceptibly guiding the saucer so that it would stop opposite the letters I wanted, and my companions never caught on. Once or twice, however, when I did absolutely nothing we made some experiments that had really interesting psychic results.

There was an old Lithuanian peasant woman in the room, who looked upon our proceedings with grave disapproval, regarding them as nothing less than necromancy. She always sat in the far end of the room and crossed herself when we began. One night she was sitting there as usual when she suddenly jumped up with a wild whoop and commenced switching under the bed with a handkerchief. "There he is; I see him!" "What is it, Christina?" we cried, thinking that it was probably a rat, for we were pestered with a plague of mice.

"The Devil," she answered promptly, and nothing could make her believe that she had not seen the Evil One in person lurking under our beds.

We had a number of peasants at different times during the winter, and they were all interesting types in their way, but the funniest was Anna Ivanovna "Kapusta." "Kapusta" in Russian means cabbage, and that was just what Anna Ivanovna most resembled with her face and figure exactly like a full-blown head of early cabbage. She was arrested by mistake for a person with a similar name who was supposed to have been implicated in the Kronstadt rebellion and she was released after ten days when the error was straightened out.

Her account of her arrest, during which she unconsciously implicated herself still further was one of the funniest I ever heard. "I'd just come home from work, sweating all over," she said, "when a fellow comes into my room and says I'm arrested."

"'Why?' I asks."

"'Haven't you had relations with sailors from Petrograd ?' says he."

"Sure," I answered, "the fellow I goes out with is a sailor."

"'Give up your papers and documents,'" he orders real sharp, so I hands him out my worker's certificate and my prayerbook which was all the documents I had. "'Where's your party card?' he asks."

"I knew I had to have a bread card, but I'd never heard of them things and I told him so. He wouldn't listen to nothing else, just brought me along and threw me into this room. Wait till I get out of this, I'm going back to the village."

Anna Ivanovna had had quite enough of being part of the class-conscious proletariat, and I am sure she kept her word.

I was asked by several of my friends to give a series of talks on foreign countries, to be held every evening after supper, so I brushed up my history, geography and economics, and told them all I knew about America, France, Germany, and the British Empire. They were insatiable in their desire for information. I drew geographic and economic maps of the various countries, showing their physical features, various zones of production, natural resources, explained the origin of the people, outlined their history down to the present day, sketched the Great War to its close, and the effect it has had on industrial, social and political conditions the world over. They also wanted to know all about literature, art, architecture and national customs.

In return they told me all about Russia, for they were exceedingly well up on all subjects pertaining to their own country. Our talks extended over nearly a month, and their interest never flagged. This to me was very remarkable. The Russians possess in a wonderful degree the faculty of forgetting their own personal problems and of complete absorption in purely abstract or impersonal questions. I don't believe that anywhere else in the world it would be possible to find a group of nine women, all in prison with no immediate prospect of release, isolated from their families, suffering great physical discomforts, and many of them facing serious charges, who would be interested in such matters.

This attitude on the part of most of the women with whom I was thrown and my blessed sense of humor were the two things that enabled me to carry on through ten long months of imprisonment. Under such conditions you have either got to go under or live for things of the mind and spirit. There is no middle course.

In studying the types with whom I was thrown I found that the old aristocrats, trained party workers and simple peasants were the people who stood imprisonment best. The weakest, the most spoiled and also the most treacherous and dishonorable, with few exceptions, were members of the former middle bourgeoisie. They lived best, complained the most and betrayed their companions the oftenest in prison. Sometimes they almost made me class conscious.

Occasionally the terror of some of these poor people who had been arrested without any warning had its comic side. Once an old lady was brought to our room, carrying as her sole piece of baggage an empty milk can.

"I was so flustered when I was arrested," she said, "that I grabbed the first thing in sight." This same old lady, although she was never in the slightest danger, being held merely as a witness, was obsessed with the idea that she was to be shot. One night her plank bed slipped off the trestle which supported it and fell to the floor, old lady and all, with an awful thud. She waked up shrieking:

"I'm shot, I'm shot."

It was a long time before we could convince her that she wasn't dead.

In the late spring, I was at last able to get some books after I had in vain appealed to my *sledovatel* all winter to let me have some reading matter. The Commandant of our prison was removed and a Lett appointed in his place. Several times I had occasion to ask small favors of him, which he always granted, and I noticed that his manner towards me was a shade more friendly than towards the other prisoners. I imagined that this was because I never had hysterics, never made a scandal, which is the Russian for making a scene, and never made unreasonable demands, but I was soon to know the real reason.

One day I asked him if he could let me have some books. He said nothing, but the following afternoon a guard came and called out "Garrison to the Commandant." People who had committed some breach of discipline were usually summoned before the Commandant for reprimand or punishment, and I wondered what I had done. When I arrived at his office he ordered his assistant to leave and shut the door. Then he said very kindly: "You asked for books. I have a few here that have been confiscated from the prisoners' baggage; you can look them over and take your choice."

I thanked him, went to the bookshelves in a corner picked out two, and then he said quite abruptly: "You are an American. America is a great country. Tell me all about it."

I sat down and talked to him for about twenty minutes. When I had finished he said quietly: "I have a brother in America. I've often wondered how he was living for the past seven years. I meant to go there myself, too, but I was caught by the conscription at the beginning of the Great War. Thank you very much."

So that was the secret of his kindness to me. He had once wanted, and perhaps still secretly longed to be an American himself. Before I left the office I had persuaded him to give me a pencil and paper, giving him in return my word of honor that I would not let them out of my hands. After that I was able to exchange my books every week or so. There were a number of interesting Russian novels, some good French classics and several German books to choose from. On his shelves I noticed also a number of missals in the old Slavonic that had evidently been taken from priests.

Periodically throughout my term of imprisonment in the Cheka we were annoyed by spies. I say annoyed merely because anyone who has been in prison for a certain length of time, or who has ever been in prison before, knows how to size up and detect a *nasyedka*.[2] She is sometimes very clever and plausible, and inexperienced persons often fall for her. Safe general rules are never to trust a person until you have been together for at least two weeks, or unless you know his or her antecedents and record, never to trust anyone who talks too openly at first against the government and to beware of people who are called frequently or at unusual times to a *dopros*. Even then, mistakes are sometimes made with disastrous results, and newcomers are often amazingly indiscreet before they can be warned.

Once a young girl employed in one of the Soviet offices was brought to our room in the middle of the night. Before anyone could stop her she burst out, "Oh, I'm so frightened I don't know what to do. My brother was arrested last year, tried for counter-revolutionary activities and condemned to ten years in prison. He escaped from the Butyrki three months ago, and has been hiding in Moscow ever since. The Bolsheviks think he has left the country, but he often comes in to see us. He is living" — here she named the street and house number. "I feel sure they have found out something, and they are going to cross-examine

---

2. Stool pigeon.

me about him." As it turned out there was no spy with us at the time, but if there had been, the brother would have been captured the next day.

When the girl was summoned to a cross-examination it turned out that she was accused of having received a present from a member of a foreign mission. She was thoroughly frightened and released on her promise to resist such blandishments from Oriental gentlemen in the future.

The *nasyedkas* were of two types: the agents who simply listened to the conversations that went on, and the provocateurs who tried to get the prisoners to implicate themselves and others by involving them in illicit intercourse with their comrades in other rooms or with persons at liberty. There was an interesting case of that sort in the early spring. A young Jewish woman, a member of the Social Revolutionary party, who had been in prison for several weeks, was suddenly told to pack her things, as she was to be freed within an hour. So saying, the guard left the room. This was rather unusual, as prisoners are generally not told their fate until they are taken to the Commandant's office, and if they are to be released they are not left alone for a minute while packing for fear that they may secrete notes from other prisoners. The girl, who had been arrested before was well aware of this fact, and her suspicions were immediately aroused. She refused all requests to take out notes from her fellow party members, as well as one from an apparently much persecuted Menshevik, who begged her to take a message to party headquarters, and seemed bitterly disappointed when she refused.

She was then taken downstairs and searched from head to foot by a woman with a minuteness and in a manner which ordinary decency prevents me from describing in detail. Nothing of course was found. After this she was released, but, happening to remember that she had left something in her, room, she went back to the Commandant's office to ask for it and was immediately rearrested and locked up on the same floor, although not in the same room she had previously occupied. It was perfectly evident what had happened. The Menshevik with whom she had been in prison was an agent provocateur, she had offered to send out a message herself and had tried to persuade the other Social Revolutionaries in the room that it was perfectly safe to do so, in order to obtain information that would lead to the arrest of persons then at liberty. The Cheka had never intended from the first to release the girl and if she had not happened to return to the office she would have later been rearrested in her own home.

At one time a woman was brought to our room in the middle of the morning, which was unusual as most people are arrested at night. She seemed like a rather stupid, unintelligent person, but kindly and good-natured. I had several friends who spoke some French and German and we often conversed in those languages. She always professed that she was sorry she could not join our discussions, as she was unable to speak either language. There was a young girl in our room, almost a child, who for no apparent reason, took a violent dislike to our new companion. One day the child, who was a fiery little thing, got into a violent dispute with her, and to get even dropped her slippers into the *parashka*. The woman protested, whereupon the little girl threatened to beat her. No one interfered, for she was not a popular person, and the woman was terrified. Turning to me, she shrieked in perfectly good French, "*Madame, Madame*, save me from this little wild cat! Oh, *mon Dieu*, the child will kill me!" It was rather amusing, but it did not cause us any uneasiness, because no one had trusted her from the beginning and it only confirmed our suspicions.

In spite of all my interests and activities, and the systematic efforts I made to keep in good physical shape, the long confinement without air or exercise began to tell terribly on my health and in the late winter I started to run a persistent temperature, a bad cold in December had left me with a bothersome cough, and I was very weak. I spoke several times to the physician about my condition, but she said that she could do nothing for me as she only had the power to send people to hospitals. I also wrote several times to my *sledovatel*, asking to be transferred to some place where I could have fresh air and sunshine, but received no answer. Finally one day when I was feeling particularly ill, one of the medical students who had frequently had occasion to visit our room asked me if he could do anything for me. I told him that no medicine would do me any good, and that all I needed was air and sun. He promised to ask the doctor to write a recommendation for my transfer to another prison. I heard nothing more for a week, and then one afternoon, quite unexpectedly, a guard appeared with the order, "Garrison, pack your clothes." I had given up hope of ever hearing my name called that way, but I staggered to my feet, got my belongings together, said goodbye to my friends, half walked, half fell down four flights of stairs with my heavy baggage. Then I was taken to the court through which I had seen so many of my companions pass, and to the registration office, where I received my transfer papers to the Novinsky and the receipts for my valuables, which however, were retained in the Cheka. Then I was assigned an armed escort, and to my amazement, taken, not back into the court to join an echelon of other prisoners, but out into the street.

CHAPTER XXVIII
Wherein a Jailbird Turns Jailer

$\mathcal{F}$or a moment I was dazed by the unexpectedness of what had happened. I had thought that I was to be taken to the Novinsky in the big Black Maria which was ordinarily used to transfer prisoners from one place to another, and which I had often surreptitiously looked at from my attic window as it was being loaded in the court below.

But here I was, thrown out into the Lubyanka Square, with my escort, a good-natured, stupid Russian boy about seventeen years old, with no idea as to where I was going or how I was to get there. I simply knew the name of the prison, that was all. The dazzling sunlight blinded my eyes, and I felt like a mole that has suddenly come up from months underground. The noise of passing trolley cars, carts and *drozhkis*[1] deafened me, and I was confused by the stream of passersby. Still thinking, quite naturally, that as I was ill, some means of transportation would be provided for me, I waited for my guard to call an *izvozchik*, one of the picturesque cabbies who were waiting nearby for fares, but he made no move, and stood quite dumbly with my bedding roll over his shoulder and his rifle in one hand.

"Well, aren't you going to requisition a *drozhki*?" I asked finally.

"I have no authority to do that," he answered. "We've got to walk."

"I can't walk," I protested. "I am much too weak. Go back and tell the Commandant that I must have a cab," but this he resolutely refused to do. He made no move to go on, but continued to gaze stolidly in front of him at the passing crowd. Seeing that there was nothing to be done, I resolved to try to

....

1. A horse drawn carriage used for public transportation.

foot it to the Novinsky, but as I was very weak and hampered with a bag and knapsack into the bargain, I had grave doubts as to whether I could make it.

"Let's walk, then," I said, "but we must go very slowly. Where is the Novinsky prison?"

"*Ne znayu* (I don't know)," was the unexpected answer.

Under the circumstances, there was nothing for me to do but put myself in prison again, so I walked up to a gentleman who was passing and asked him the way to the Novinsky. "I am a prisoner, and am being transferred from the Lubyanka," I explained, "but my guard hasn't the faintest idea as to how to get there."

Under ordinary circumstances in an ordinary country anyone would have been astonished to say the least, at such a question, but nobody is ever astonished at anything in present-day Russia. Without any comment, he explained the easiest route to get there, and then added very kindly, his voice betraying the sympathy he did not dare put into words — "But you can't walk there, it is very far, at least six *versts*, and you have a lot of baggage to carry." Then he lifted his hat and passed on, a bit hurriedly, for it isn't very safe to be seen talking to a prisoner in the street.

For a few minutes I stood undecided, not knowing what to do; then I had an inspiration. I had no money, and I could not pay an *izvozchik*, but I had two cans of American corned beef in my bag. Perhaps I could find one who would accept that as payment. I negotiated with three without result, explaining that I was a foreigner, ill and being transferred from the Cheka to the Novinsky prison, but that I was out of money and could only pay in American canned beef. I got out a can as a sample, it was examined, weighed and turned down, and I was about in despair of ever being able to get locked up again when I struck an old man with one leg who agreed to take me.

I was about to get into the *drozhki* when I saw an acquaintance, a woman with whom I had spent more than three weeks in the Lubyanka. She dashed up to me, kissed me on both cheeks, and exclaimed effusively how glad she was to see me out again; but when I explained that I was not free, but on my way to another prison, she cast one frightened look about her and scuttled away down a side street, hardly waiting to say good-bye. Then my guard and I, having piled the baggage in front of us, took our places on the back seat of the *drozhki*, he with his rifle between his knees, both of us smoking cigarettes and chatting very amicably.

When we arrived at the prison, I was very nearly all in, my head was spinning, my knees wobbled, and I felt that I had a high temperature. If I could only get somewhere so I could rest! The gloomy brick facade of the prison, which is a substantially built structure, dating from Imperial times, and has long been used as a criminal prison for women, did not look as forbidding as it would have under ordinary circumstances, and it was with a feeling of positive relief that I saw the face of the warder appear at the door in answer to my ring.

Inside, I at once realized that I had come to a very different sort of place. Instead of a "Chekist" in a tall cap, I found a pleasant-faced, gentle-voiced woman in the room for the reception of prisoners, who took my name, asked me a few necessary questions and turned me over to a woman attendant to be taken to the prison hospital for a medical examination. Afterwards she and I became great friends. She was a prisoner herself, the widow of a White officer, which constituted the sole reason for her being in prison, for she was one of the least politically-minded persons I have ever seen.

When I left the office and was taken out into the court on my way to the hospital, I felt as if I were in a sort of terrestrial paradise. The court was a large one, with grass and flowering shrubs, and brilliantly flooded with sunshine. Here and there were benches on which women were sitting, talking, knitting and sewing, a girl was strumming the balalaika, little children were making mud pies. In the center was a small white church, behind it a library. Around were the prison buildings, on one side of which were the one-story offices from which I had just come, on the other the hospital, also a one-story building with a row of large open windows, facing the Western sun.

At the back, a large, arched gate led to the street, and at the left of the quadrangle was the prison proper, with barred windows, it is true, but with growing plants and flowers in them, doors wide open, people coming and going. To the right was a workshop, and at the bottom of the yard, which sloped slightly, was a building which I afterwards found contained the schoolroom, kitchens, repair shops and a large recreation hall. Just as I was about to enter the door of the hospital, I heard a wild shriek of joy from the yard, followed by a glimpse of a familiar figure running towards me, and in a minute two arms were around my neck. One of my best friends, a Social Revolutionary with whom I had spent many weeks in the Cheka, had recognized me. Others followed suit, and soon I was the center of a perfect mob of former friends, being kissed violently and repeatedly on both cheeks to the accompaniment of exclamations of "Margarita Bernardovna," "*Slava Bogu*" (thank God), and overwhelmed with

A portion of Novinsky Prison in the 1920s.

questions as to the fate of other friends who had been left behind in the Cheka. We had all lived through much together, and we had never expected to see each other again. It was very wonderful.

I was swept off to the dispensary, rescued from the medical examination, and from quarantine, where I would ordinarily have spent two weeks. "Margarita Bernardovna is the cleanest woman I ever saw," explained one of my friends solemnly to the "*feldsheritsa*,"[2] the nurse who was examining all newcomers. "She washes all over twice a day, and she has no infectious disease."

Then I was carried off in triumph to a large, airy room, where at first I nearly fainted. Someone made hot tea for me, someone else helped me unpack and get to bed, where I lay, quite weak, but very happy and holding a sort of impromptu reception.

The next day, I began to take up the regular prison life, which, barring the food, that was worse than in the Cheka, was as pleasant and as nearly normal as life can be in any prison.

I occupied a room with eleven other prisoners, with two exceptions all "politicals." Our beds were composed of iron tubing covered with a canvas slip that was as comfortable as a good hammock. They were fastened to the wall with hinges and turned up against it in the daytime, leaving the floor space free. At the foot of each bed was a small chest on long legs, known in prison slang as a "dog," which served to hold our belongings and as a bench. There was a long table with two shelves underneath, where we stored all our provisions and utensils. All of the other rooms were similar, though some were larger, holding as many as twenty-four women, and on each floor were two large, clean

---

2. A female medical assistant.

bathrooms with modern plumbing and plenty of toilet facilities. In addition, there was a Russian bath in the office building where we could get hot water practically whenever we chose. Technically, each room was supposed to go to the bath once in ten days, but as a matter of fact those who cared to bathe every day could go there whenever they wanted to. They very seldom did, however. Russian ideas of bathing seem very peculiar to the Anglo-Saxon. Every morning they energetically splash themselves with cold water down to the waist, and once a week if they are very fastidious, once a fortnight if they are really particular, and once a month if they are just ordinary people, they go to the bath, where they spend hours, scrubbing themselves with a handful of vegetable fiber called "*mochalka*,"[3] pouring innumerable basins of scalding water over their bodies, steaming themselves till they are parboiled, and ending with a cold douche. They could never understand why I bathed every day and only took ten minutes to do it. The criminals were allowed out from eight until ten and from six until bedtime and the new arrivals, who were kept in quarantine for two weeks, took their exercise between two and four in the afternoon. The political prisoners, with the consent of their examining judges, were allowed to see their friends or relatives at intervals and *peredachas* were allowed every day. The criminals, subject to good behavior, were allowed to see their relatives on Sundays.

Every morning the rising bell rang at seven, followed immediately by the *proverka* (inspection), when the *nadziratelnitsa* (woman superintendent) counted us to see if anybody had vanished during the night. Then the doors were opened and we were practically allowed to come and go as we pleased. There was visiting between the rooms until nine in the evening, when the *proverka* was repeated and the doors were locked for the night. Some effort was made to separate the political prisoners, of whom there were relatively few, from the criminals. They were confined as nearly as possible in separate rooms. The former were allowed to exercise in the yard from ten to twelve in the morning and from four to six in the afternoon.

It was very amusing to see the way they evaded the authorities when permission was not forthcoming. The Novinsky was situated halfway down the slope of a steep hill, above it and overlooking the prison yard was a large church with a tall bell tower.[4] The relatives of prisoners to whom permission

---

3. A whisp of bast.

4. The prison was located near what is today Moscow's Novy Arbat, a wide avenue with large, book-shaped skyscrapers, about where the Moscow Dom Knigi (House of Books) is presently located and, ironically, just a street away from the American Embassy Complex. The nearby church was likely the Church of the Nine Martyrs.

had been denied for a *svidanye*[5] went up in the tower of the church and yelled to the prisoners in the yard. This started immediately after dinner on Sundays and continued till late in the afternoon. It began like this: Ivan Petrovich, whose sweetheart, Olga Nikolayevna, had perhaps punched her roommate in the head that week and therefore was not allowed to see him, would take his stand in the bell tower and shout her name until it attracted the attention of someone in the yard. Then the name was taken up and repeated by the prisoners until Olga Nikolayevna was found. She was pushed to the front of the crowd and then forming a megaphone with her hands she held long distance conversations with Ivan. Sometimes eight or ten of these conversations went on at the same time, with the result that the noise was simply deafening. Occasionally, when one of the women was prevented from hearing what was said to her by her too vociferous companions, a fight ensued, which usually ended in somebody getting hysterics and a number of hair-pullings. The authorities never interfered with these conversations unless the political prisoners took part in them. On several occasions, this took place and their unlucky friends in the bell tower were promptly arrested.

Church services were regularly held in the little church and as the Russian calendar is nearly entirely composed of Saints' days, there was mass morning and evening almost every day. It was always crowded and two women were appointed every day to clean the brasses and sacramental vessels. There were nearly always fresh flowers on the altar, contributed by the prisoners.

We could get all the books we wanted from the library behind the church and I found there all the Russian classics, many interesting bound volumes of the best magazines, plenty of good French books and a few English and German magazines and novels. The Socialists, who were in a class by themselves and had special privileges in certain respects, also had the newspapers every day; and as I had many friends among them, I shared all their interests and activities.

The Socialist room, which held twenty-four, was occupied by Right and Left Social Revolutionaries, Mensheviks and Anarchists. Among them were many old party workers as well as a number of girls from the student groups, all keen, intelligent, alive to all the questions of the day. I found them fully equal to, if not superior to the men of a corresponding stage of intellectual and political development. They were just as courageous, just as well trained as party workers, and shared equally with them in organization and the more dangerous conspiratorial work. We often had political debates in the evening,

....
5. A visit.

"disputes," the Russians called them, without any appreciation of the humorous significance of the word, and frequently brilliant papers were read on various aspects of the political and economic situation. At other times we had musical evenings, singing all the beautiful Russian prison songs and innumerable folk and student songs. Several of the girls played the balalaika very well and they accompanied the singers, also playing music for the folk dances that were often a feature of our impromptu performances. There was one pretty little Anarchist, only eighteen years old, who danced Cossack dances better than anyone I've ever seen off the stage. In a pair of blue bloomers, tucked into high boots, a red shirt and a black astrakhan cap, with her bobbed golden hair, she made a very picturesque boy, and her partner was a slender little slip of a dark girl who had been in prison for six months for complicity in an alleged Social Revolutionary plot, but had lost none of her high spirits.

Several times we had birthday parties, once in honor of the wife of Victor Chernov,[6] leader of the Right Social Revolutionaries, who escaped nearly a year before to Estonia. Olga Alexiyevna Chernova was first arrested more than a year ago, while her husband was still in Moscow, with her youngest daughter, who was but nine years old. After Chernov's escape to Estonia, she was arrested again and spent over six months in the Butyrki prison, where she was one of the editors of the prison newspaper gotten out by the Socialists. In the early spring, a riot took place among the Socialists in the Butyrki, planned as a demonstration to encourage their comrades still at liberty. After this, most of the men and many women were sent to provincial prisons, where they suffered untold hardships. Madame Chernova and several others were transferred to the Novinsky. Madame Peshkova, the wife of Gorky, was much interested in trying to obtain permission for her and her children to leave Russia, but up to the time of my departure the Soviet authorities were obstinate in their determination to hold her indefinitely as a hostage for her husband.

In spite of the fact that she had been in prison for nearly a year, Olga Alexiyevna had lost none of her interest in life. At her birthday party she read a very clever poem, "taking off" each of the party groups among the politicals. We had a delicious supper prepared by the two cooks appointed for the day, for the Socialists have a commune and pool all their *peredachas*. It was followed by games, speeches, and the presentation to Olga Alexiyevna of a number

6. Victor M. Chernov (1973-1952) was a co-founder of the Socialist Revolutionary Party in 1901. He was a member of the Provisional Government and elected Chairman of the Constituent Assembly in January 1918. After 1921, he left Russia for Czechoslovakia and eventually the United States.

of prison-made birthday gifts. One of these was a workbag woven from the vegetable fiber which was used for hand scrubs in our Russian baths. On it was most artistically applied a little *izba*, or peasant's cottage, made of twigs picked up in the prison yard, with a roof of birch bark. The landscape was completed by an artistic grouping of trees made from sprigs of arbor vitae which grew in the prison yard.

At our political meetings we discussed the new decrees, of which the most important were the "Prodnalog," or natural products tax, imposed on the peasants this year instead of the former system of requisitioning, the new wage scale and method of payment for factory workers, and the system of leasing factories to private capital, known as the "Arend" system. My Social Revolutionary friends believed that the government had by no means abandoned its plan of eventually establishing a Communist state in Russia, but they felt that the economic reforms being instituted would become permanent, as many of the Communists were gradually coming to realize that they could not proceed so far in advance of the rest of the world, that Russia could no longer maintain her position alone as the vanguard of the Revolutionary movement. She must give the rank and file time to catch up, as it were.

The fact that no general amnesty was declared, they pointed out, indicated that the Communist Oligarchy was determined to hold the political power in its hands, that it would be a long time before Russia would be able to institute anything approaching a popular form of government. They were profoundly discouraged as to the outlook for independent party activity for the future, and for the most part bitterly opposed to the political activities of the emigres and plotters of all parties outside of Russia, who, they said, had done far more harm than good by their abortive, ill planned conspiracies. They had great hopes from the then newly formed All-Russian Famine Relief Committee, but predicted just what has subsequently happened, that unless all foreign relief was conducted through its agency, the Soviet Government would find a pretext for putting it out of the way and arresting its most influential members.

The interests of all the politicals were looked after by the political *starosta*, or chairman, who is elected on the creation of a vacancy, and continues in office until she is released from prison. Ours was an extremely keen, energetic Menshevik. It was her business to distribute the *peredachas* sent by the Political Red Cross, and keep a list of those eligible for them, to give semi-legal advice to all the political prisoners, and to decide on matters of discipline and general policy.

The Political Red Cross, of which I have spoken several times in the preceding chapters, is one of the most remarkable organizations in Russia. Despite its name, it is absolutely unpolitical in character. Under the Czar it existed as an illegal organization for the purpose of giving assistance to all political prisoners. Under the Soviet Government it has only a semi-legal status, and receives no official support, being merely tolerated. Its members consist mainly of *Bezpartiny* non-partisans. Its funds are raised entirely by private subscription. In spite of many handicaps, it has for the last two years sent weekly food packages to all the political prisoners in Moscow, with the exception of those in the Cheka. There it is only permitted to send collective *peredachas* to be distributed to all prisoners alike, on Soviet or church holidays. In the other prisons, its representatives are allowed to visit the politicals periodically. In addition to providing food, the Red Cross supplies clothing and medicine and other necessaries to the prisoners. It also supplies counsel and legal advice to persons whose cases are about to come up for trial, furnishes funds and transportation to discharged prisoners who have been brought to Moscow from a distance and have no means of getting back to their homes, conducts a bureau of information, to supply information to the relatives of many persons who have been arrested and apparently disappeared, as to their whereabouts or their fate. The Political Red Cross also looks after all foreign nationals detained as prisoners, who are not being provided for by their own countrymen.

The Anarchists while in prison received regular *peredachas* from their comrades, who had organized what was known as the "Black Cross." It was to me a very curious and significant fact that they should have chosen this name for their organization. Acknowledging no code of laws, human or divine, they could find no better symbol for humanitarian work than the symbol of the Cross. On several occasions the Anarchists' *peredachas* were very wonderful, containing chocolate, coffee, jam, and other unheard-of luxuries. At the same time, an account was published in the papers of a mysterious robbery of one of the government stores. I was told by several persons who knew that the *peredachas* of the Anarchists came from this source.

Most of the Socialists were a very cheerful lot. Few of them were facing serious charges, nearly all being held in accordance with the general policy recently adopted by Lenin of keeping all the leaders of opposition parties under lock and key, but occasionally we were brought face to face with the real thing, as in the case of a friend of mine, who, with her husband, was accused of complicity in the Siberian peasant rebellion last February. They were taken to

Omsk for trial. Another was the tragic case of a young woman physician, a Left Social Revolutionary, who had been tried and condemned to death in Kharkov and was brought to Moscow for retrial in a dying condition from tuberculosis. A particularly pathetic feature of her story was that she had been living in safety in Switzerland at the beginning of the Revolution, and voluntarily came to Russia, aflame with Revolutionary ideals, eager to help in the regeneration of her country. There are many like her, real Revolutionaries at heart, who are sacrificed by the inexorable Juggernaut they have set in motion.

I did not stay long in the "*otdeleniye*," as the main section of the prison is called. My cough grew steadily worse, I had a constant temperature, and the prison physician decided that I should be removed to the hospital.

CHAPTER XXIX
Prison De Luxe

*I*n the hospital I slept in a real bed for the first time in more than eight months. It was a pretty decrepit bed, and had a straw pallet instead of a mattress, but it was a bed for all that. The hospital diet, too, was far better than that in the prison proper.

In the morning we received three-quarters of a pound of bread, two lumps of sugar or a small portion of honey, about half an ounce of butter, margarine or lard, three teaspoonfuls of Soviet coffee, occasionally a tablespoonful of salted caviar, and every other day a handful of dried apples. The usual herring soup was often replaced by a meat broth, the second dish at our noonday meal was rice or *mannaya kasha,*[1] a cereal similar to our cream of wheat, and we were given a good-sized portion of South American corned beef several times a week.

The doctor was a most intelligent and sympathetic woman and the nurses were kindness itself. The dispensary was woefully lacking in medicines and supplies, but it was remarkable how well the staff managed with next to nothing. For example, there were two hypodermic needles and one syringe. With this equipment, two hundred and forty-eight prisoners received the necessary cholera inoculations within three weeks, and I and a number of other prisoners were given daily injections of arsenic.[2] We had only one clinical thermometer, but the temperature of every patient was taken twice daily. Numbers of prisoners not hospital patients received dispensary treatment or hospital rations, and there was a good dental clinic once a week.

....
1. Semolina kasha.
2. At this time, compounds with arsenic were still being used as antibiotics and to treat syphilis.

After all I had been through, the Novinsky hospital, for all its deficiencies, was a haven of rest. There were only three of us in the cheerful little room I occupied: myself, a Polish lady who was accused of espionage, and our *nyanka*, or attendant, a ruddy-faced buxom peasant girl as innocent looking as a baby. She was up for the third time, the first offense being the receiving of stolen goods, the second hiding a deserter, and the last, for which she was serving only a three-year sentence, for being an accessory to the murder of her own sister by her brother-in-law, whom she afterwards married. He was her second husband, the first having been killed in the war. A large framed lithograph of the latter adorned the wall of our room. In one corner of it was stuck a photograph of the former. She was lazy and an incorrigible thief, but kindhearted, generous and impulsive. If we missed anything and remarked about it she would get down on her knees before the icon in the corner, weeping copiously and howling like a dervish, declaring that she had never taken as much as a kopek's worth from anyone. At the same time, if she had anything good to eat she always insisted that we should share it with her, and I couldn't help being fond of her in spite of everything. The attendants in the other two rooms of the hospital, one of which held twelve, the other six persons, were both professional thieves, one a railroad station pickpocket, the other a "Madame" who made a business of robbing her clients.

I was allowed absolute liberty in the hospital, with permission to spend the entire day in the yard if I chose, and I found talking to the criminals and studying their psychology a fascinating occupation.

One of the most interesting types was Kuzina, the queen of the Moscow Apaches, who had the record of having been arrested twenty-eight times, and of having served several terms in prison, though she was only twenty-three years old. She had twice escaped from prison. Her third attempt was an unsuccessful but almost extraordinary performance. Finding the Novinsky a difficult place to get out of, she simulated insanity, with perfect success, and was sent to a hospital for the criminal insane. It proved just as hard to escape from as the Novinsky, so she turned sane again, and demanded to be sent back there. Being refused, she resolved on what is known in prison as obstruction, but her method was unusual, to say the least, and certainly showed a great deal of physical courage and determination. She put a wad of newspaper on her chest, set fire to it and burned herself most horribly. "If you don't send me back, I'll do something worse next time," she said, and she was returned to the Novinsky.

She absolutely ruled the other criminals, they quailed before her and she was merciless in punishing those who violated the prison code of ethics. Once she led a mob against a woman who was suspected of being a *nasyedka* (spy), and they beat her until she was rescued almost unconscious by the prison guards. She would never steal from anyone in prison, but her example was followed by few of the others. Stealing was the universal rule. The prisoners stole from the prison kitchen, from the workshop, where they made clothes on government contracts, and received half a pound of bread extra a day in payment, and they also stole from each other. Thefts, if discovered, were punished by beatings, face scratchings and hair-pullings, but the thieves were never informed on, even by the attendants, for most of them stole too if they got the chance. Nothing was safe.

Once I took my bedding roll out into the yard to air, spread it on the grass, and sat down on a bench beside it to read. Two girls were lying in the grass near me, very innocently it seemed. I did not notice that they moved, but when I got up to go in the house I found that the canvas sheet that covered the pad had been torn off near the top and carried away. I afterwards saw slippers made of it being sold for a bread ration.

A flourishing trade was always going on inside the prison, not only in stolen articles, but in food brought in from the outside, and it was possible to buy almost everything for money, also smuggled in, or for bread. Twenty-five cigarettes cost one bread ration, ten fresh eggs cost three bread rations, and you could have your laundry done for two.

Other clandestine vices flourished too. Although cards were forbidden, there were plenty of decks, and gambling was universal. The women gambled away their bread rations, their *peredachas*, their clothing even. One woman I knew lost everything she had in one night, except her chemise, and the next morning she was compelled to get one of the prison dresses to wear. Unnatural forms of prostitution were also common.

I don't know whether it is the case with a similar class of criminals in other countries, but most of those I met seemed to take a personal pride in their achievements. There were few who pretended to be either innocent or repentant, though most of them were very religious and attended church assiduously.

The speculators formed a class all to themselves. Most of them were sordid and uninteresting, but there were a few picturesque characters, such as a brilliant woman engineer who had embezzled millions from the Supreme Economic Council, had been condemned to death, reprieved and finally sentenced to ten years in prison; and a young girl, who with several confederates had robbed the railroad administration of tons of supplies. She was such a capable executive, however, that she had charge of giving out all the supplies for the hospital.

The most attractive inmates, for they could scarcely be called prisoners, were the children. There were at least twenty of them; from babies in arms to sturdy little boys and girls four or five years old. Many of them had been born in prison, others had been brought there with their mothers, the Soviet Government permitting them to keep their babies with them, if desired, until they reach the school age. From the point of view of the morale of the mothers, it is an excellent thing, enabling them to lead something approaching a normal life, and the children do not fare badly by any means. They were given a special ration similar to our hospital ration, but with more fats; children up to two years of age received milk daily.

They were subjected to periodical medical inspection, and when ill were sent to a nearby children's clinic for treatment. Nearly all were rosy and healthy, and it was great fun to play with them in the yard. One, a small boy four years old, was a great chum of mine, and he always called me by the name by which I was known to the criminals—the "Afrikanka." Popular ideas as to geography and nationality are somewhat hazy in Russia. I was the only foreigner, and when I first arrived there were many speculations as to my nationality. One of the prisoners who had played in vaudeville with a troupe of negro minstrels announced that I had come from the same country. They were Africans, therefore I must be an African, too, in spite of the slight difference in complexion. The name stuck, notwithstanding all my explanations.

Amusements were not altogether lacking in our prison routine. There was a dramatic club, which gave performances of classic comedies nearly every Sunday. The government furnished the members a fixed monthly sum for the purpose of buying stage properties and make-ups. Occasionally we had a concert with outside artists from the best theaters, and there were often impromptu dances in the prison yard.

There were also two social service workers, who supervised the giving out of books from the library, distributed mail to prisoners and conducted several classes for illiterates. The political prisoners were barred from taking part in the official amusements and activities of the prisoners. I think the government was afraid they might contaminate the criminals.

The prison kitchen was one of the most popular places. From early morning till late evening it was filled with women of all descriptions, who were allowed to do their own cooking. I often went there to make tea or prepare some special dish for myself. Everybody stood around the stove, keeping an eagle eye on her own skillet or saucepan. If you turned your head for an instant you might find it had disappeared. Some of the dishes I saw cooked there were perfectly wonderful. One woman had twenty pounds of white flour sent to her and she made rolls, jam turnovers and tarts galore. Other women made delicious soups and ragouts and all the mothers prepared special food for their babies. It was well to keep a sharp lookout in the kitchen, for fights often occurred. Once I narrowly escaped being hit by a potful of hot soup that was thrown by one woman at another one just behind me. The privilege of using the kitchen was one that I greatly appreciated, for it was often possible to make very palatable dishes, even out of the regular prison rations.

Among the prisoners was a small group of women the reason for whose detention I could never understand. With the exception of one, Mademoiselle Sheremetyeva, a lady of distinguished family, who belonged to an affiliated organization, they were all members of the Salvation Army. They were very simple women, absolutely devoid of political ideas, but they were accused of having been the tools of counter-revolutionary organizations, just how had never been explained to them. The opposition of the Communists to the established church on the grounds that it has always been used as a means for the enslavement of the masses, is perfectly understandable from their point of view, but to anyone who knows the purely unpolitical and essentially proletarian character of the Salvation Army the world over, the arrest of its members on these grounds appears positively fantastic. The Salvation Armyites held a song service in one of the rooms in the "*otdeleniye*" nearly every evening, and it often made me very homesick to hear the familiar melodies, such as *Onward Christian Soldiers, Throw Out the Lifeline*, and many others sung in such a strange environment.

So far I have described the better side of our prison life, and the more fortunate of the prisoners, but there was a very dark side indeed. The Novinsky is used as a concentration point for prisoners in transit to internment camps, most of them what are known as Counter-Revolutionaries, and hundreds pass through every month on their way to distant points. It seems to be the policy of the Soviet Government to send those sentenced to internment as far away from their homes as possible, which inevitably brings about unnecessary hardships. Families are often separated in a manner recalling the German deportations from Lille during the Great War;[3] those interned are cut off from the possibility of receiving food supplies from their relatives still at liberty; delicate persons accustomed to the warm climate of Southern Russia are sent to the far North.

There were a number of women from the Crimea, arrested as the aftermath of Wrangel's collapse, who were being sent to Archangel. Several of them were old ladies over seventy.

One, who was the widow of a general, had been arrested because her name had been found on a list of subscribers to the food cooperatives which existed under the Wrangel regime. Prisoners from Kiev and the Ukraine were on their way to Yaroslavl. One day, a mother with seven children, the youngest a two-year-old boy, the oldest a girl of seventeen years, arrived from Rostov en route for Perm. The entire family was being deported because the mother had hidden her son, who had been with the White Armies. The boy was found in the house and shot, the father had escaped and his wife had no idea as to his whereabouts or his fate.

In justice to the Soviet Government, however, it must be stated that all cases are reviewed in Moscow before the prisoners are sent on to their destination, with the result that some are released and sent back to their homes.

We also had a number of prisoners who had been condemned to death in the provincial Chekas on absolutely insufficient evidence. These were mostly espionage cases from White Russia or the Ukraine, and they had been rescued from death in the nick of time by inspectors from the Central Office of the Extraordinary Commission, who periodically visit the provincial prisons. Two young girls who had been saved in this manner had been condemned to death without trial at Mogilev on the testimony of a single individual, that they had been friendly with members of the Polish Commission at Vitebsk, and had spent a month in a condemned cell from which prisoners were taken nightly to be shot. They told me that every night before going to bed they put on clean clothes so that they might die decently.

I was told by many of these prisoners that the food in most provincial prisons was utterly inadequate and prepared without the slightest regard for ordinary rules of hygiene. In many of the provincial prisons they got nothing but half a pound of bread a day and one bowl of soup. Men and women were kept in the same rooms, prisoners were often beaten by the guards. A Polish lady who came from Rostov told me that her husband had been shot two weeks after

---

3. In April, 1916, the German government issued a proclamation requiring people from occupied Lille, France to be relocated to the countryside to work the fields. This often meant the splitting of families.

the signing of the treaty with Poland. Some of the prisoners from the provinces had been held for six or eight months simply because their papers had been lost. Such conditions frequently exist in the "Gub Chekas," as the provincial Chekas are called. There, much depends on the character of the individual commissar or *sledovatel*. Some of them are utterly unfit for their jobs, others are very humane. I knew a Polish woman who told me that her life had been saved by her *sledovatel* at Vitebsk. The head of the local Cheka was anxious to clean up the congestion of the prison and ordered a number of persons shot, herself among them, but the *sledovatel* insisted that he had not sufficiently looked into her case, and managed to hold it over by a series of *dopros* until the arrival of the agents of the Extraordinary Commission from Moscow. The government is doing all in its power to control this sort of thing, but so far it has only been partially successful.

Among the transients were numbers of immigrants from White Russia and Poland who wished to resume their Russian citizenship, and had crossed the frontier without papers or credentials. Many of them were destitute and virtually starving. Some had relatives in distant parts of Russia, others had simply wandered east from the war-devastated regions in search of work and food. The majority of these were soon sent to their destinations or to parts of the country where living conditions are comparatively good, under the supervision of the Commissariat of Labor.

Altogether, life in the Novinsky was bearable and quite interesting. I had many good friends among the prisoners and on the prison staff, only one member of which, by the way, as far as I could discover, was a Communist. During my stay there I had two visits from my *sledovatel*, the head of the American bureau of the Cheka, the first shortly after my arrival when he came to inquire as to my health, and to see if I was in need of anything. Several times I asked for money to buy milk and eggs, and for the rest of my baggage, which had been sealed on my arrest, but this request was never granted. I had everything I needed, however, for my wants were cared for by my Russian friends, to whom I shall always owe an undying debt of gratitude.

CHAPTER XXX
Release Number 2961

By the middle of July we had begun to realize from accounts in the papers that the famine situation was so serious that the Soviet Government would be utterly unable to cope with it, and all my friends insisted that it would not be long before I was released from prison. "Russia must accept help from foreign governments," they said, "and the first condition for relief from America, will, of course, be the release of all prisoners." I had begun to have faint hopes, but I dared not acknowledge them even to myself. They had been stirred by the fact that Royal R. Keeley had been released from prison and I had, a week or so previously, received a small *peredacha* from him, with a message that he was well, stating that he would try to get permission to see me. This permission was not granted, nor was a note which he wrote delivered to me, but the fact that he had been released pointed to a more lenient attitude towards foreigners.

Then one day, July twenty-third, to be exact, the very day, though neither he nor I knew it at the time, of the receipt of the Hoover offer on behalf of the American Relief Administration, I had my first visit from anyone not a Soviet official, in more than nine months. It was from Senator Joseph I. France,[1] of Maryland, my own state, of whose presence in Moscow I was not even aware, until I met him face to face. Senator France, who had been in Moscow for some weeks, had made repeated efforts to see me, and had interceded with Chicherin and Lenin on my behalf, though, up to that time, without any prospect of

....
1. Senator Joseph I. France (1873-1939) was a Republican senator from Maryland from 1917 to 1923. He was the first U.S. Senator to visit Bolshevik Russia, in 1921. While there to study the economic situation, he intervened on behalf of American prisoners like Harrison to secure their release. He even met with Lenin concerning these prisoners.

success. He had done this at the risk of considerable unpleasantness to himself as one of the conditions upon which he obtained, through the influence of German friends in Berlin, permission to visit Moscow, was that he should not meddle with the question of the American prisoners.

Early in the afternoon I had a summons to go to the Commandant's office. There I found Kovalski, head of the American Bureau of the Cheka.

"I have brought you a visitor," he said; "I think you will be rather surprised to see who he is." At the same time he threw open the door of an inner room with a fine dramatic gesture, and I saw standing before me a tall man in a suit of real American clothes. It was curious that I should have noticed the clothes first, but I did, and then I recognized inside of them Senator France, with whose appearance I was familiar from his pictures in the newspapers, though I had never before had the pleasure of meeting him.

For a moment I was dazed — then came two curiously inconsequent thoughts, both of which I dismissed immediately. The first was, "Heavens, has the Senator run amuck and turned Bolshevik?" The next, "Perhaps, oh, perhaps, he has come to take me home."

Meanwhile, I heard myself in a far-away voice asking him quite composedly when he had arrived in Russia and where he was staying, casually as if we had met in the Senate Lobby at Washington. But Senator France went straight to the point, telling me in a few

Senator Joseph France

words that he had seen Lenin, Chicherin and Litvinov about my case, that they had until that morning given no encouragement, but that they now showed signs of relenting, and that if all went well, he might be able to take me home with him on the following Monday. Our talk was short, but I managed to get some news from him and to give him a number of messages for friends and relatives at home.

After his departure and until Monday afternoon I did a great deal of thinking, all of which as it turned out, I might have spared myself. At first I was inclined to refuse to leave, even if he should be able to secure permission to take me with him, because I felt that I wished to remain in Russia until all the other prisoners were released. Then my Russian friends told me that it was quixotic and unpractical to have such notions — that if I got out of Russia I could do much to get the other prisoners out, and that I would be insane to voluntarily stay behind, where I could do them no good whatever. I was still weighing the matter in my mind when Monday came and went, without any word from Senator France. "There you see, fate has decided it for me anyway," I said to my roommate, and I resolutely put the idea of freedom out of my mind, and returned to prison routine.

On Wednesday evening, July twenty-seventh, I was feeling rather ill, and was going to bed early, about ten o'clock, when Kovalski appeared alone and ordered me to pack my bags and accompany him to the Cheka, saying that my case would be brought up for trial in the morning, but not hinting at the probable outcome. The nurse in the hospital refused to let me go out at night as I had a temperature at the time, so Kovalski left, saying that he would return the next morning at nine o'clock. I was just about to turn in half an hour later when the door was abruptly thrown open, admitting two prison guards and a woman attendant, who searched me and my belongings without a word of explanation, examining everything including my pillow and mattress most minutely, and taking every scrap of written or printed matter in my possession, among which, much to my regret, were the lovely prison songs I had been collecting and writing down with such interest during long months in the Cheka.

"What does this mean?" I gasped, when I had recovered from my astonishment, for though an *obysk*, as the searches are called, are frequent in the Cheka, they are rare at the Novinsky, and I had done nothing to cause suspicion.

"It means that you will be deported tomorrow," said one of the soldiers, a genial looking chap, with a broad, kindly grin. At this the other, a severe looking personage in a black leather coat, annihilated him with a look, and I was unable to extract anything more from him.

For the rest of the night, sleep was impossible. I spent most of the time talking to my roommate, Pani Franziska, a dear elderly Polish lady.

The next morning I got up early and packed all my belongings, but the entire forenoon passed without a word from the Cheka. This did not surprise me, as I was by this time thoroughly accustomed to Russian dilatoriness. I spent the morning talking with my intimate friends. My best friend was a Jewish woman who had been kindness itself to me. We had first been together in the Cheka, and afterwards met at the Novinsky. When I arrived there I was utterly unable to eat the prison food, and it was thanks to her that I managed to get back my strength. She received *peredachas* twice a week from her family, and always shared everything with me, even going to the extent of writing home and ordering sent her the dishes she thought would tempt my appetite. She provided me with toilet articles, linen sheets, soap, a real knife and fork and a glass to drink out of instead of the tin cup I had used so long. She was one of the most delightful persons I have ever met, and we spent many hours together, talking of art, literature and many other subjects. She was tremendously interested in Russian art, particularly the old icons of which she had made an exhaustive study. In addition she was simple goodness and honor personified. In politics she was what is known as *Bezpartiny*, but she had been arrested and held in prison for four months as a witness. Her continued detention was owing to the fact that she refused to give testimony which she felt might be damaging to other people in whose activities she had had no share. Most of my other friends were Social Revolutionaries, but I had one who was an Anarchist and another who was a Menshevik.

I visited nearly all of the rooms in turn, saying good-bye to my friends among the criminals, who wished me luck, and suddenly I realized that a very close tie was about to be broken. Prison friendships are about the most real things in the world. People know each other as they are, without hypocrisy or concealment, and if they grow to care for each other under such conditions it is something that lasts.

For some time before the motor came to take me to the Cheka, which was not until early afternoon, we sat in my room, talking of past good times, making plans as to how I was to let them know if I was transferred to another prison, wondering as to when or where we would meet again, for we were quite sure that we would somehow. Then, when the attendant came to tell me that the motor had arrived, we all sat down, and for a minute there was silence, in accordance with the beautiful Russian custom of thus wishing godspeed to anyone who is about to set out on a long journey. Finally the stillness was broken by Pani Franziska, my Polish room mate, who made the sign of the cross on my forehead. "God bless you, my child," she said brokenly. It was hard for her to see me go, perhaps to freedom, for she had been in prison for fourteen months on a baseless charge of espionage, later disproved and she had been promised repatriation over two months before, but her papers had never been received by the Polish Repatriation Commission from the Cheka. At the last I was nearly smothered under an avalanche of hugs and kisses, and deafened with the chorus of cheery *Vsyo khorosho*, which meant literally "All's well," and *Do svidaniye*, the Russian for *Au revoir*, from half the inmates of the prison, who accompanied me to the door of the Commandant's office, and peeped through the bars of his window to wave their hands in a last greeting. In spite of my hopes as to what the future had in store for me, it was hard to say goodbye to my Russian friends, to whom I could from the bottom of my heart apply that much abused word — *Tovarischi* — comrades.

I found Kovalski waiting for me in the motor. He told me that if all went well he hoped to have good news for me later, but nothing more. On arriving at the Cheka I was taken to the *predvaritelnaya*, a detention room on the ground floor where prisoners awaiting commitment or cross-examination are often held for several days. It was a long, narrow room, filled with the wooden beds I have already described, but without the straw pallets given out to the regular prisoners, and it was packed with homogeneous mass of humanity, men and women of all classes and nationalities. People were lying two on a bed, and one enterprising individual had gone to sleep on a shelf high up on the wall. It was indescribably dirty, and there was only one window, which afforded utterly inadequate ventilation for so many people.

There, much to my surprise, I met two acquaintances. One was a woman whom I had known at the Novinsky. She was dying of tuberculosis, and literally fighting for every breath in the close atmosphere. In spite of her serious condition, she had been kept for three days, waiting for her *dopros*. The other was a Frenchman, whom I had met the previous summer, when he had come to Moscow from Novorossisk, where he had started an import and export business between that port and Marseilles. He had been arrested on his third trip to Moscow to sign a contract with the Supreme Economic Council for the importation of general merchandise. His principals in France were unaware of his predicament, he had been in prison five weeks, without *peredachas*, without the possibility of communicating with his friends in Novorossisk, and he was in wretched physical condition, but like a true Frenchman, he did not fail to apologize for his straggly beard and his collarless state. I also talked to a young Swiss boy, a Communist, who had no idea why he had been arrested, and a German Red Cross officer, who had been held in another prison for several months.

Finally, after what seemed to me an endless wait, my name was called, and I was taken by an armed guard to the American Bureau, where, instead of judges, I found Kovalski waiting for me with the papers that had been taken from me the night before. He asked me several questions about them, which I was able to answer satisfactorily, but he was evidently suspicious of some cross-stitch patterns I had drawn for my lace work. Finally he was convinced that they were not ciphers, and then he told me that my release had been decided on, at the same time handing me an insignificant looking bit of paper, very like a department store check, but which was a written order for the release of "Citizeness Garrison, Margarita Bernardovna, Number 2961." He told me that Senator France had delayed his departure in order to accompany me and that I was to leave with him for Riga that evening if an automobile could be procured to take me to the station.

In a few minutes, my former examiner, Mogilevsky, came in to say goodbye, telling me at the same time that all other Americans would be released within a few days, but that as Senator France had been interested in my case, and had shown himself most sympathetic to the Soviet Government, I would be permitted to leave with him in advance of the others.

"We have been enemies, it is true," he said, "but it was, as you realize, part of a big game. I hope that you feel that it was nothing personal and that some time, under happier auspices, you will come back to Russia."

I assured him that I felt the same way, which was quite true, and added that I sincerely hoped I would come back under different conditions. It was rather amusing, I reflected, how the same expression could be used with equal sincerity by two individuals with radically different points of view, but I merely smiled, shook hands and said goodbye. Kovalski told me that it would be impossible for them to deliver my baggage, money and valuables at such short notice, but that they would be sent to me at Riga. I told him that I wished the money sent to the Political Red Cross for the relief of Russian prisoners, and signed a transfer, which he promised to deliver to the office of the Red Cross. Then I was taken back to the general waiting room, where I spent an anxious hour or so, for it was growing perilously near train time. Finally a soldier came to take me to a waiting automobile, in which I was whirled to the station, at the rate of about sixty miles an hour, arriving just seven minutes before the departure of the train.

The platform was filled with a hustling, jostling crowd of homegoing Letts, busy porters carrying trunks and boxes, preoccupied couriers with dispatch cases, distinguished foreign visitors saying good-bye to commissars, Soviet officials, going abroad on various missions. I saw the tall figure of Senator France, which was easily distinguishable among them, and in a few seconds I was beside him. A few minutes later I was installed in a sleeping compartment, watching the receding station platform.

We had a comfortable, though uneventful trip to Riga, arriving on the morning of the second day. The only incident that disturbed the composure of the Senator and myself was at the border, where we were held for about six hours for no apparent reason. I had known of so many instances where persons, who had been permitted to leave Moscow were rearrested on the frontier that I did not quite believe in my good fortune until I was actually on Latvian soil.

My first act after greeting the friends who came to meet me at Riga was to indulge in the luxury of a tub bath for the first time in nearly a year, my second was to buy a Rigan outfit to replace the costume I had worn during my entire term of imprisonment, an exceedingly dirty suit of khaki cloth, a man's pongee shirt, a hat made in prison from the tail of the same shirt, and a pair of men's shoes sent me by the Czechoslovak Red Cross. Then I had a real dinner. I stayed in Riga for several days, after which the Senator and I left for Berlin, where I met many friends, among them Captain Cooper, who had come from Warsaw to meet me. Ever since his escape from Russia in April he had been working unceasingly for my release. The best news I had in Riga was the confirmation of what I had already heard from Mogilevsky: that owing to the Soviet Government's acceptance of the terms of Mr. Hoover's offer, all the American prisoners would probably be in Riga within a week or ten days. In Riga I also saw lists of the packages containing food, clothing and toilet articles, which had been sent me during my imprisonment, none of which had ever reached me.

In the few quiet moments I was able to snatch between calls, writing newspaper articles, and trips to the shops to replenish my scanty wardrobe, I looked back on the events of the past eighteen months, during which I had lived on black bread and kasha. From a material standpoint I had suffered, it was true, but I felt that I had gained immeasurably from another point of view. I knew the heart of Russia, and no one in these troublous times of transition can ever know it unless he lives with the Russian people both in and out of prison. I had gained a just perspective, and I felt that I understood all that is good and all that is bad, and all that is historically inevitable in the great upheaval which is, in spite of everything, modernizing Russia.

AFTERWORD

*T*hough this is an afterword, it is by no means an afterthought. It is rather a summary of the thoughts that have been running through my mind while I have been setting down what I saw and heard during eighteen months in Soviet Russia.

It seems to me that the world at large has overlooked an all-important fact in considering the Russian Revolution — its beginning, its present form and its development are following a logical historical, evolutionary process. The great powers of the world have done all that they possibly could to hinder this evolution by blockades, intervention and intrigue. They have never done the obvious thing as far as Russia's internal politics are concerned, which is to let them alone. By isolating Russia, they have brought about the very thing they were trying to prevent, a prolongation of the Communist dictatorship and postponement of the process of evolution.

No one can understand the situation in Russia without realizing what is actually the case, that two revolutions have taken place in that country. In the towns a small minority, less than ten percent in all of the population, have made a proletarian revolution, conducted by the class conscious workers with Karl Marx as their God, and Lenin as his prophet. The remaining ninety percent have made an agrarian revolution, they have done away with the feudal system and have gained possession of the land. The vast majority of them are illiterate, haunted by the traditions of serfdom, suffering from the shock of seven years of war, blockade, and internal disorder, with a capacity for endurance that is utterly incomprehensible to Western minds, utterly devoid of political opinions, patriotism, or a sense of racial unity. Ask the average Russian peasant what he is. He will answer — not that he is a Russian, not that he belongs to any political party, but simply that he is a person — *Ya chelovek*. He is inherently opposed to Communism, for as a matter of fact he knew something of a form of village Communism under the Tsar. It meant that the land belonged to the village, not to him, and it was parcelled out to him by the village Mir or Zemstvo Council.[1] Now he has his land, and he intends to keep it. Bolshevism is bad, because the Bolsheviks make requisitions; they shut up the cooperatives; he can no longer get tea, sugar, salt, boots and clothes, seeds and farm implements; but Tsarism was worse, because then he did not have the land. Of the two extremes, therefore, he prefers Bolshevism to Tsarism. Discontent with existing conditions will drive him to sporadic revolt, but as long as he is left alone and has a voice in his village Soviet, he does not care what kind of central government there is in Moscow. It is despotic, yes, but then he has always been accustomed to some form of despotism. If he cherishes any personal resentment against the government it is because he believes it is a government of and by the Jews. The dominant political factor in Russia today is fear of anarchy. Few of the peasant uprisings that have taken place in Russia or Siberia within the past few years have been the result of any concerted political movement, but rather of local conditions.

The more intelligent of the peasants are beginning to grope in a vague way towards the idea of a representative form of government. They realize dimly that they are the real proletariat of Russia, that they are represented in the proportion of one to one hundred and twenty-five thousand in the All Russian Council of Soviets, while the town proletariat is represented by one to twenty-five thousand. This, to them is radically wrong — some day it must all be changed. The Social Revolutionaries are preaching this doctrine, and winning converts through the Peasant Unions, but so far they have not been able to organize the vast masses of the peasant population, partly through the ban on free press, free speech, and the all powerful police organization of the Communists, partly owing to the apathy and inertia of the peasants themselves, and their lack of class solidarity.

Universal education, particularly the abolition of illiteracy in the Red Army, will eventually act as a boomerang against the Bolshevist Government by teaching the peasants to think for themselves, but this will be a long and a tedious process. Until it is completed there will be no possibility of establishing the government which I believe to be best suited to the needs of Russia – a democratic federation of sovereign states, held together by a national assembly,

---

1. One of the Great Reforms of the 1860s was the creation of rural *zemstvos* or land councils, where many local decisions were made.

elected by universal suffrage, on the principle of direct representation. This state will probably have many socialistic features, comprising the socialization of key industries and a widespread cooperative system. There will be a uniform system of free education and social maintenance, and there will be laws restraining the concentration of capital in the hands of a few individuals, but the rights of private property will be respected.

Meanwhile Russia will, for some time, necessarily be a prey to minority government. The question is, whether it is better to have the country ruled by a Communist or a Reactionary oligarchy. Of the two evils I believe the former is the lesser one. The Communists, numbering perhaps three quarters of a million in all, of whom probably ten percent are absolutely sincere and devoted Marxists, are in complete control of the governmental apparatus, and if they were swept away tomorrow there is no party which is prepared to take their place. They exercise iron discipline in a country where discipline is an unknown quantity. Backed by the best organized secret police and the best propaganda service in the world, they have suppressed all expression of free opinion, and legalized party opposition.

The leaders of the Communist party are mostly men who have lived a large part of their lives in Western Europe or America and have studied the organization of party machines in all countries. They have always known what they wanted and have had a program when other parties were in a chaotic condition. Their big men are undoubtedly idealists, working with altruistic aims for what they believe to be the good of humanity, but on the Jesuitic principle that the end justifies the means, and in accord with Marxian philosophy, which rejects all bourgeois ethics.

It must be remembered that these are men who all their lives have been hounded and persecuted, and they have, in many respects, distorted values. They are the exponents of the second stage of every revolution. First must come the work of preparation. The men and women who prepared the Revolution have long since been swept away and are living in exile or confined in Russian prisons. The men who occupy the center of the stage today are the iconoclasts, whose work is to destroy, the new broom that sweeps clean, the scalpels that have cut deep into the old order and removed the sound flesh in order to get at the source of the disease. The men who will come next will be the reconstructionists, and little by little, the iconoclasts will give place to them. Until this comes about by a process that is historically inevitable, there will be no government in Russia any better than the present one.

The universal corruption, the many acts of cruelty and the parasitic growth of the new bourgeoisie since the beginning of the Revolution are not all to be laid at the door of the Communist party. They are partly due to the inheritance of Tsarism, partly to the tendency of all undesirable elements to come to the surface in times of universal demoralization and revolution.

Russia is essentially an agrarian country; its future prosperity will be dependent on the goodwill and cooperation of the mass of peasants who form the agrarian population. In order to reconcile the two opposing elements of town and country and to put the nation on a sound social and economic basis, it will be necessary for the Revolution to go back many steps over the road it has travelled. That many of the Communist leaders recognize this fact is shown by the development of distinct Right and Left wings, within the party, by the tendency against centralization and bureaucratism and by the opportunist policy of Lenin, who in an effort to preserve the political balance of power is coquetting with the bourgeoisie and fighting the other socialist parties.

The dictatorship of the Communist party has been continuously strengthened during the past four years by the many attempts at intervention. I cannot too strongly emphasize the fact which I have tried to bring out in the preceding pages, that the men and women of varying political opinions, who have quietly carried on in Russia throughout the Revolution, are, for the great majority, of the opinion that the ultimate form of government in Russia must be worked out by a gradual process of evolution. They are the people who have kept the schools and universities going, furnished the bulk of officers for the Red Army and of physicians for the public health service, the agricultural experts who have helped to avert a still more ghastly famine, the factory experts who have kept alive what is left of Russia's industries, the engineers who are running the mines and the railroads. They have developed a new nationalism based on real patriotism, a quality which hitherto has never existed in Russia, and they are opposed to intervention in any form or to the forcible overthrow of the Soviet Government.

It has been said that aid to Russia through Soviet controlled institutions will have the effect of strengthening the Communist party by making the people believe they owe the improvement in conditions to the present regime. The effect in my opinion, will be just the opposite. Famine relief and contact with the outside world will strengthen the morale of the Russian people and give the few men who are capable of undertaking opposition party activities sound human material to work on. At the same time it will help to accelerate the changes which are taking place within the Communist organization itself and will force the Bolsheviks to undo with their own hands, much of what they have already done.

So much for the political factors which are making for evolutionary changes, and now for the economic factors which are for the present, the more important of the two.

Inheriting an unsound economic fabric, weakened by the Great War, the civil war and the blockade, hampered by embryonic industrial and trades union development and a backward agrarian population, the Communists have completed the ruin already begun, by the introduction of an economic system which, even if it is admitted that it is practicable, as the basis on which to run a prosperous government, presupposes a highly developed industrial organization and a large, class-conscious mass of industrial workers. Even under highly favorable conditions they could never have succeeded, in my opinion, in establishing a sound Communistic state in Russia, though their tremendous dynamic energy and their remarkable educational propaganda might have produced somewhat better results.

No private individual or corporations can hope to derive immediate profit from trade with Soviet Russia, but there is danger that if the great powers do not come to the aid of Russia, the present economic collapse will be followed by a collapse of the entire political and social system, with a tendency to revert to utter anarchy. The good features of the Soviet Government will be swept away with the bad and Russia will lapse into barbarism. Personally, I believe that state capitalism will be the next development in Russia. The new decrees, while permitting the development of private capital, still uphold the principle of state ownership; therefore, the only adequate protection for foreign interests doing business in Russia will be afforded by a *de facto* recognition by all the great powers, the appointment of general commercial agents with consular powers and the guaranteeing against loss of all interests undertaking trade with, or internal development in Russia, by means of national or international organizations under the official protection of a single government or an aggregation of governments.[2]

Frankly, I have no idea as to how this can be brought about, but it can and must be done if the world is ever to get out of the present tangle. The Russian Government has not the money to furnish large credits; no satisfactory

---

2. This is a reference to the New Economic Policy (NEP) that Lenin enacted in 1921 to help regenerate the Russian economy by easing War Communism and allowing limited free markets.

working basis has as yet been found for concessions; the supply of raw material for exchange is insignificant. Obviously the first thing to do is to devise some scheme for the reconstruction of Russia's transportation system, for without the railroads nothing can be done. Eventually it is impossible that some profitable way of doing business with a hundred and fifty million people living in a country which is probably richer in natural resources than any country in the world, and which needs everything from locomotives to shoe strings, cannot be found. The sooner this is done the sooner will the inevitable political readjustment between the agrarian and proletarian revolutions be made in Russia.

From an international standpoint, immediate foreign aid to Russia is even of greater importance. Such action by all the great powers will help to prevent a world economic crisis by opening new markets; it will assist in normalizing labor conditions and allaying the present industrial and social unrest, and it will do away with many of the delusions as to conditions in Russia, which have been fostered in the minds of the working class the world over by Communist propaganda to which Russian isolation has been a powerful ally. If the Bolsheviks succeed in building up their social, political and economic fabric, it will be, even with every outside assistance, a lengthy process, to be achieved only at the price of the sacrifice of many basic principles. Such a process of evolution is not likely to put strong arguments in the hands of the advocates of world revolution.

For the present, however, it is impossible to accord diplomatic recognition to a government which has, as its acknowledged object, the promotion of armed revolution in the countries with which it seeks to make diplomatic treaties. The promises of the Soviet Government in this respect are not worth the paper they are written on, as long as the Central Committee of the Third International guides the world revolution from Moscow.

There is a strong tendency among the radicals in all countries to break away from the dictation of Moscow. There were many quarrels and bickerings at this year's meeting of the Third International. The differences among the German and Italian Communists were thoroughly aired to the public, and there was a no less sturdy tendency towards independence in the matter of tactics among various other national groups, such as the Jewish Bundists, the Finnish Communists, the British, the French and Americans. These differences were still more marked in the congress of the Red Trades Union International, which was only just able to save its face and preserve a semblance of unity. All these indications point to a weakening of the power of Moscow in the international revolutionary movement. It is possible in the not too distant future that the

Russian Communists will be forced by radical opinion in other countries to give up their idea of a world propaganda directed from the Kremlin.

De facto recognition and trade with Russia will give an opportunity to prove the sincerity of the moderate Communists who claim that their world propaganda is largely a measure of self defense against the bourgeois governments who are bent on bringing about an internal economic, social and political collapse in Russia—that, given peace and a chance for peaceful development, they are willing to stop stirring up trouble in Asia, South America, Europe and the United States.

We may as well recognize the fact that the Germans will eventually dominate Russia commercially and perhaps economically. At present, in their desperate financial situation, German businessmen are willing to take chances and embark on enterprises which the large interests in other countries are unwilling to undertake. They have nothing to lose and everything to gain from the exploitation of Russia and they can afford to wait for returns.

But there is a political side to the situation. Things may not remain as they are in Germany. If the country swings more to the right, there will be a renascence of militarism, the desire for revenge on England, the old Berlin-to-Bagdad dream. I have told how I saw in Russia more than a year ago evidences that many Germans have not altogether abandoned it. There will be an attempt at political domination with a view to utilizing the vast manpower and natural resources of Russia to bring about the "Day," which many Germans regard as only postponed for a matter of ten years or so.

On the other hand, if Germany ever goes Red, the Germans will practice Communism with deadly efficiency. It will be quite a different matter from Communism in Russia and they will introduce their brand into that country.

The English think they have found an antidote to all this, and to the old bugbear of Russian ascendancy in Asia, which might threaten their colonial possessions and their political supremacy on that continent, in their policy of Balkanizing Russia. The trend of British statesmanship is to permanently weaken the former Russian Empire by dividing it into a number of relatively small independent states, which will be easier to exploit commercially and politically. That is the meaning of their support of various efforts at intervention, which has always been withdrawn at the critical moment. The British do not want any side to come out on top. The French are only looking for one thing in Russia – gold.

What then should be the policy of the United States? We distinctly want a strong and a united Russia. The United States is the only country that can look at the Russian question dispassionately at the present time. It has no political axe to grind in Europe, no need to exploit the natural resources of Russia, for its own are just as great. It needs new markets and new routes of trade, orders for its idle factories, cargoes for its great fleet of rusting ships.

The whole matter may be summed up as follows: We may not like the Soviet Government, but it is a real government. To refuse to help and continue to isolate Russia will have the effect of completing the economic ruin of the country, with the consequent reaction upon world economics, of strengthening the political dictatorship of the Communist party, pushing them still further in their tactical program of promoting world revolution, and perhaps of finally driving them in desperation to military aggression. The eventual outcome will be anarchy or possibly a reaction far more bloody and far more terrible than the Communist regime. The only way to bring about a government in Russia which will represent the will of the great mass of the people is to give them a chance to develop the moral force to express that will in action. This can only be done by giving them peace and food. It is up to the American people to give them that chance. Therefore I believe that our only sane policy from the political and the economic as well as from the humanitarian standpoint is cooperation to the fullest possible extent with the Soviet Government.

APPENDIX
The Russian Socialist Federal Soviet Republic

The sovereign governing authority is the All Russian Congress of Soviets, consisting of representatives of Town Soviets and of the provincial congresses of Soviets. The former are represented in the proportion of one per twenty-five thousand electors, the latter one per one hundred and twenty-five thousand inhabitants. The All Russian Congress meets twice a year and appoints a Central Executive Committee of up to two hundred members. The Central Executive Committee is a continuous body and appoints the Council of People's Commissaries, which is the principal governing authority.

The President of the All Russian Congress of Soviets is M. Kalinin. Nikolai Lenin (Ulyanov) is Chairman of the Central Executive Committee and Ex Officio of the Council of the People's Commissaries.

The People's Commissariats, sixteen in number, with the Commissars holding office in August of this year, are as follows:

COUNCIL OF PEOPLE'S COMMISSARS

Commissariat	People's Commissary	Assistant People's Commissars
1. War	L.D. Trotsky	Sklyansky
2. Internal Affairs	F.E. Dzerzhinsky	M.F. Vladimirsky
3. Justice	D.R. Kursky	Not known
4. Ways & Communications	F.E. Dzerzhinsky	V.M. Sverdlov/Borisov
5. Finance	N.M. Krestinsky	S.E. Chutskaev
6. Education	A.V. Lunacharsky	M.N. Pokrovsky
7. Posts and Telegraphs	A.M. Lyubovich (Acting)	Not known
8. Public Health	M.A. Semashko	Z.P. Soloviev

9. State Control (Workers' and Peasants' Control)	I.V. Stalin	A.V. Avanesov
10. Nationalities (Non-Russian Nationalities of Russia)	I.V. Stalin	N. Narimanov
11. Agricultural	A.P. Sereda	N.N. Osinsky
12. Labor and Social Welfare	V.V. Schmidt	A.N. Vinokurov
13. Foreign Affairs	G.V. Chicherin	L.M. Karakhan
14. Food	A.D. Tsyuryupa	N.P. Vryukhanov
15. Foreign Trade	L.B. Krasin	Yazikov/A.M. Lezhava
16. Supreme Council of People's Economy	Bogdanov G.I. Lomov	V.P. Milyutin

Both the members of the Central Executive Committee and the People's Commissars are elected for three months, but the People's Commissars can be recalled or superseded at any time by the Central Executive Committee.

The local Soviets, which constitute the basic units of the whole system and are at the same time the organs of local government, are grouped according to successive areas of administration.

1. Town Soviets of one per one thousand inhabitants elected by factories, wards, trades unions and parties.

2. Village Soviets of one per one hundred inhabitants, which combine to form district (Volost) and County (Uyezd) congresses of Soviets on a basis of one per one thousand inhabitants.

3. Provincial (Gubernia) or Regional (Oblast) Congresses of Soviets, elected by both town and country Soviets.

The Soviet Republic at present includes thirty-nine provinces, of which nineteen are classed as Autonomous Federated Republics with complete freedom in the matter of local self-government. The largest of these is the Ukrainian Republic, with Kharkov as its capital. Rakovsky is Chairman of the Central Executive Committee of the Ukrainian Republic. The next most important is the Tatar Republic, with Kazan as its capital.

Electoral rights in Russia are extended to all persons over eighteen who "earn a living by productive work or by work of social usefulness." No distinction is made between Russians and aliens; excluded are "employers, persons living on investments, traders, monks, clergy, members of the former Russian reigning house, officials and agents of the police forces of the old regime, lunatics, minors and criminals." Political parties, to participate in elections, must recognize the Soviet authority. At the present time, the only party except the Communist party which nominates candidates is the Menshevik party.

Economic: By the constitution of the Soviet Republic, private property in land is declared abolished, all land being the common property of the people. Up to the present time, however, nationalization of the land exists only in principle, the peasants retaining possession of the land distributed to them after the October Revolution. All forests, mines and waters of national importance as well as all livestock and fixtures, model estates and agricultural concerns, are declared national property. All factories, works, mines, railways and other means of production and transport are brought under the Commissariat of Factory Control and the Supreme Economic Council with a view to their complete transference to the Soviet Republic.

The Supreme Economic Council is the controlling authority in production and distribution. Its members are appointed in agreement with the All Russian Central Council of Trades Unions. Under it are Central Industrial Departments appointed by the Supreme Economic Council in agreement with the Central Committees of the corresponding trades unions. Local organizations reproduce the same scheme with District Economic Councils and District Economic Departments. The actual management of the factories was at first in the hands of Boards, but these have since, in most cases, been replaced by one-man management.

Recent decrees have licensed the leasing of factories to private individuals or cooperative organizations. The government exacts an initial license fee and a fixed tax on the gross receipts. The operators must conform to the regulations of the Code of Labor Laws.

The Commissariat of Labor, which is controlled by the Trades Unions, fixes wages and labor conditions under the general provisions of the Code of Labor Laws. The Code of Labor Laws makes work compulsory for all males between the ages of sixteen and fifty, all females between the ages of sixteen and forty, except for medical reasons. Those who are ill or unemployed are entitled to remuneration at their usual rate of wages during the time they are not working.

Education is compulsory to the age of sixteen or until the completion of what would in America be considered as high school education. University courses and special technical courses are open to all who desire to avail themselves of them. University students receive free lodgings, fixed food rations and a small monthly stipend.

Justice is administered in Russia by means of the People's Courts and Revolutionary Tribunals. Military tribunals and the presidium of the Extraordinary Commission have the power to judge cases of espionage, counter-revolution and desertion.

SOCIALIST PARTIES IN RUSSIA

The Bolsheviks who, since the dissolution of the Constituent Assembly in 1918 have adopted the name of the Communist party. The Communist party at present exercises complete and absolute dictatorship in Russia. The programs adopted at its congresses constitute the government programs, and it is the nerve of contact between the government and the Trades Unions, Soviets, and other organizations. Membership, involving as it does both burdens and powers,, is jealously guarded. Access is not made easy, discipline is severe and expulsion frequent. The present membership is stated to be seven hundred thousand. They believe in the dictatorship of a proletarian minority composed of class-conscious workers. They are Marxists.

The Mensheviks are also Marxists like the Communists, but they differ with them as to tactics, being in favor of more power for the Trades Unions, less centralization and more freedom of speech and action. They are a small group. At present they are virtually disfranchised and their leaders, Martov and Abramovitz, are in exile.

The Left Social Revolutionaries approach the Bolsheviks very closely in their belief that the dictatorship of the Proletariat must be imposed by force, but they would have the chief power vested in the Soviets and not in a Centralized government. They believe in the socialization of all industries. Their leaders were Kankov and Spiridonova. At present their status is illegal as is that of

The Right Social Revolutionaries. They interpret the word "Proletariat" in its broader sense to include all workers, particularly the peasants. They believe in an organization of Trades and Peasants' Unions for economic and industrial administration, and in the vesting of the governing authority in a national assembly, elected by universal suffrage. They favor socialization of essential industries, extensive development of the cooperative system and the licensing, under certain restraint, of private enterprise and capital. Their leader, V. Chernov, is in exile, their prominent members are all in prison. Numerically the Right Social Revolutionaries are the largest of the opposition Socialist parties.

Anarchists recognize no form of government, but they are divided into two factions, those who believe that Communism is a necessary stage in the development of Anarchism and those who believe in putting it in practice by force. They are especially numerous in the Ukraine and in the neighborhood of Saratov. Their status is also illegal.

The Poalei Zion and the Bund are both Jewish Social Democratic or Marxist parties. The former cooperate with the Bolsheviks, the latter are divided into two factions of which one is in thorough sympathy with the Soviet Government.

Non-Socialist parties are non-existent as such. A few groups of Cadets and Constitutional Democrats still exist, but they are numerically insignificant and politically inactive. There is no organized Monarchist party.

TRADES UNIONS

Trades Unions, though nominally independent, are part of the Soviet State. Membership, December, 1920: 5,222,000.

The structure of the Russian Unions is based on the factory as a unit. Each factory has its committee, and this is the local unit of the union. These factory or shop units are grouped into industrial Unions with the factory as the basis, no matter what a man's trade. Entrance fee, half day's pay, subscription two percent of the pay. Membership is virtually obligatory. The Unions are as follows:

1. Medical
2. Transport
3. Mines
4. Wood
5. Land
6. Art
7. Public feeding and housing
8. Leather
9. Metal Industries
10. Communal Services
11. Education
12. Postal Services
13. Printing
14. Paper
15. Food
16. Building
17. Sugar
18. Soviet Institutions
19. Tobacco
20. Textile
21. Chemical
22. Clothing
23. Finance Department

COOPERATIVES

The Russian Cooperatives, the organs of distribution, work under State Control. Each district has a Cooperative Society, "Soyuz," on which state or local authorities are represented. The franchise is identical with the political franchise.

All Cooperative Societies come under the Control of the Centrosoyuz, which in 1920 was composed of ten members appointed by the government and eight electoral members.

Shares of individual members of the old cooperatives have been repaid to them, the value being insignificant, however, owing to the depreciated currency. Credit Societies are under the Nationalized People's Bank.

Recent legislation has restored a measure of independence to the cooperatives by permitting them to deal with peasants on an exchange basis and to buy and sell goods at fixed prices.

New Documents from Russian and U.S. Archives

The following letter to Nikolai (sic) Lenin, from American labor activist Patrick Quinlan, himself recently released from a Soviet prison (see page 222), was found in Marguerite Harrison's Cheka file and is transcribed on the following pages.

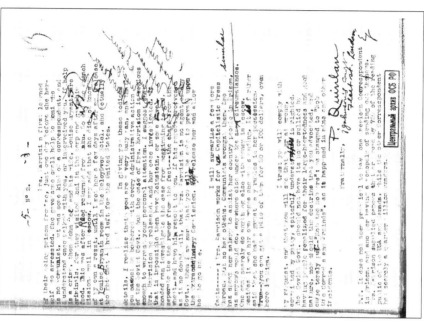

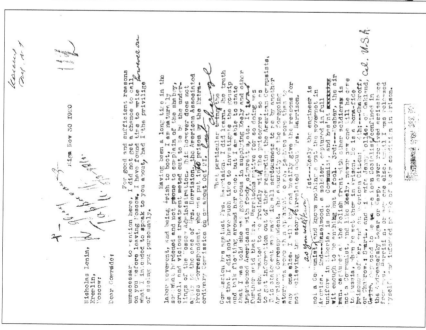

[Inscription: For the casefile of Harrison, M., 5/3-921g.]

Riga Nov 30 1920

Nicholas Lenin
Kremlin,
Moscow

Dear Comrade:

For good and sufficient reasons unnecessary to mention here, I did not get a chance to call on you before leaving Moscow. I have found time to write what I intended to speak to you about however, had I the privilige of seeing you personally.

Having ben a long time in the labor movement, and being Irish to boot, I am naturally somewhat hardened and not prone to complain of the shabby, cruel, and vicious treatment meted out to me by the underlings of the Moscow Administration. This however does not apply to the case of Mrs. Harrision, the American Associated Press Correspondent, who was put into prison by the Extraordinary Commission on or about Oct 21 last.

What particular charge the Commission has against Mrs. Harrision I did learn. The truth is that I did not have much time to investigate the gossip and talk floating around her case, but I am able to state that I was told she was generous in supplying Keely and other imprisoned Americans with food, cigarettes, etc. It was further said that Mrs. Harrisons motive for so doing was that she wanted to be friendly with the prisoners, so as to get information out of them regarding the American Communists. This statement was made in all seriousness to me by another American Correspondent. The absurdity of the foregoing story was more than apparent to me, perhaps more than to any one else. I will try and breifly give the reasons for not believing the story circulated about Mrs. Harrison.

1st --- Keely the engineer is not a Communist, as you well know, and knows nothing about the movemnet in America. 2nd --- Hazelwood, a soldier, captured in full uniform in Siberia, is not Communist, and has'nt wit enough to be anthing but a fool. 3rd;--- Mosher, the air man, captured at the Polish front with other soldiers, is not a Communist, and like Keely never saw one till he came to Russia, when he met them in prison. He is a bona-fide prisoner of War, and an American Citzen: 4th; --- Chabroff, or Chabrow: Swarts and 1 wife Jenny Hollie, of Oakland, Cal. USA. Supposed to be American Socialists confined in the Andreanefsky Lagar or Camp, never received assisstance from Mrs. Harrison, or any one else, until I was released myself, and informed people of their condition in prison.

Mrs. Harrison first learned of their being in prison from me, just one day before she herself was aresstted. She gave some small help to Boni who is no Communist, but was some kind of a corresspondent, and I understand once talked with you, or interveiwed you. If help is a crime, then John Reed and his wife, Louise Bryant, are criminals, for they visited Boni in the camp and gave him food. This was after Reed returned from Baku. So did the French Mission whil in Moscow. I may add that she did not know of my own arrest, until I met her a few days after my release at Louise Bryant's room in the DeloyDvor Hotel, she actually thought that I had left for the United States.

In giving you these tedious details, I realize that you are a very busy man, and that you cannot be bothered with every Administrative action of the Soviet Govt., but the case of Mrs. Harrision is serious enough to warrant your personal attention. I suggest that Mrs. Harrision be released and her case investigated. If that is impossible then have Reinstein, or some level headed man investigate the case from beginning to end, seperate the rumor from the fact --- the chaff from the wheat --- and have him report to you. If his report proves as it no doubt will, that Mrs Harrision is no agent of any Govt., then I am sure that you will be able to prevail upon the Extraordinary Commission to release her and allow her to go home.

I will summarize a few more facts-----: Mrs. Harrison works for the Capitolistic Press Bureau, but so has other. Communists amongst them. She has spend her salary to assisst her country people in prison as anyone would do, anywhere else under the similar circumstances. One can scarcly do anything else with money in Moscow. Besides it was her own wages she was spending. It is further said that she had a great many rubles in her possession. True—you can get a pile of them for 50 or 100 dollars, even here in Riga.

I trust you will comply with my request, and that you will see that a great wrong, committed by petty, spiteful understaffers is righted. The Soviet Govt. should not have its honor sullied by having people penalized for their large-heartedness and good nature, nor should the doctrine that you advocated, and once tersely put—"Rob the Robbers": be changed to "Rom the Comrades and Friends," as it happened in mine and other incidents.

Fraternally,
P. Quinlan
Johnson's Court
Fleet St. London

p.s. It does not seem practical to hav one American Corresspondent in prison, and another having a monopoly of sending out the news. Mrs. Harrison supplied papers that are read by 75% of the reading public of the USA and Canada, while the other Corresspondent has scarcly a quarter million readers.

[Stamped: Central Archive FSB RF]

[*An inscription showing through from reverse side of page two is illegible, but appears to be also sending the letter into Harrison's file.*]

A letter from Ludwig Martens (see page 28) to Governor Ritchie, conveying the contents of a letter from Chicherin, in which he clearly asserts that Harrison is a spy for military intelligence, which she was.

C O P Y

RUSSIAN SOCIALIST FEDERAL
    SOVIET REPUBLIC

Bureau of the Representative
in the United States of America.

    Room 304
110 West 40th Street,   January 7, 1921.
    New York, N.Y.

Hon. Albert C. Ritchie,
Executive Department,
Annapolis, Maryland.

Dear Governor Ritchie:

        I have received today from the Commissar for Foreign Affairs at Moscow the following detailed cablegram of reply to my recent inquiry regarding Mrs. Marguerite E. Harrison:

        "Martens
        "Representative of the Russian Socialist
        Federal Republic
        "New York

        "Marguerite Harrison professional spy employed by American Military Intelligence Department. Was illegally smuggled into Russia last spring by the Polist authorities on the request of the American representative in Warsaw. Gathered military information, forwarding it to Poles and Americans. Arrived in Moscow, her identity was established and she was arrested. Confronted with overwhelming evidence she confessed and offered her services to the Russian Extraordinary Commission, revealing American and British spies as evidence of loyalty. Worked for the Extraordinary Commission until October when she was rearrested as it became evident that, while she gave some valuable and correct information, she continued to sell herself to our enemies. She cannot be released. She is in good health and is treated much better than America would treat prisoner under similar circumstances. Nothing prevents her from writing to her relatives, and vice versa, except that the United States Government does not permit mail communication between America and Russia.

                                (Signed) Chicherin,
                                    "Commissar for Foreign Affairs"

        I believe that this cablegram contains all the information sought by the several relatives and friends of Mrs. Harrison who have recently applied to me on her behalf. I am forwarding a copy of this message also to Senator France who was among those who made inquiry. I will ask you to be so kind as to transmit this information to any other friends and relatives of Mrs. Harrison who may be entitled to know the facts. Especially, I would ask you to advise Mrs. Bernard M. Baker, the mother of Mrs. Harrison, at Santa Barbara, California, who recently telegraphed me regarding this matter but whose full address I do not know.

        This cablegram should be a complete assurance to Mrs. Harrison's relatives and friends, regarding her present health and her complete personal comfort and safety.

        I will ask you to treat this communication from the Commissar of Foreign Affairs as confidential, except for the private information of those personally interested in Mrs. Harrison. I do not intend to make any public use of this cablegram, unless I am compelled to do so by further misrepresentations in the press regarding the case of Mrs. Harrison.

        In response to a recent inquiry from Mr. J.S.Ames of Johns Hopkins University, regarding the possibilities of sending supplies to Mrs. Harrison, at this time, I referred Mr. Ames to Dr. D.H.Dubrowsky, the American Representative of the All-Russian Jewish Public Committee, with offices at room 302, 47 West 42nd Street. This Committee is now in a position to forward food and clothing parcels to Soviet Russia and I have the assurance of Dr. Dubrowsky that his facilities are at the service of Mrs. Harrison's Friends.

Martens - page 2.

I appreciate fully the natural anxiety of Mrs. Harrison's relatives, and I am glad to be able to give them this assurance of her complete personal well-being. You will understand, of course, that under the circumstances this is all I can do in the matter at this time.

Yours very truly,

(Signed)   L. Martens.

Representative of the Russian
Socialist Federal Soviet Republic.

Marguerite Harrison's application to work for Naval Intelligence.

NAVY DEPARTMENT
OFFICE OF NAVAL INTELLIGENCE

INFORMATION BLANK

Must be filled out fully and carefully. Unless presented personally, it must be accompanied by photograph taken within two years

Name (initials only not sufficient)   Date

Marguerite Elton Harrison.   September 15, 1918.
Address   Telephone number

1206 North Charles Street, Baltimore, Md.   Mount Vernon 6530.
Age   Height   Weight   Place of birth

39   5 ft, 6 in.   125 lbs   Baltimore, Maryland.
Native born or naturalized   Date and place naturalized

native.
Legal residence   (Town)   (State)   (Country)

1205 N. Charles St.   Baltimore.   Maryland.   U.S.A.
Married or single   Full name of husband or wife

widow.   Thomas Bullitt Harrison.
Complete list of every place you have resided during the past six months (specify from date to date)

Have lived in Baltimore only.

Name of grade school   From   To   Did you graduate?

St. Timothy's School.   1889   1896   yes.
Name of high school   From   To   Did you graduate?

"   "   "   "   yes.
Other education or training

Passed entrance examinations to Bryn Mawr and Radcliffe colleges, Taking a special course at the latter institution.

Foreign countries, cities, towns, or localities with which familiar

The British Isles., France, Holland, Germany, Italy, Austria, Switzerland, Am
Foreign languages with which familiar, and extent of familiarity

familiar with all parts of Switzerland, Northern Italy, Rome, Naples, Tyrol.

I have absolute command of French and German, am very fluent and have a

good accent in Italian and speak a little Spanish. Without any trouble I

could pass as a French woman, and after a little practice, as German-Swiss
Where was your husband or wife born?   (Town)   (State)   (Country)

3. Mosher Street.   Baltimore   Maryland   U.S.A.
If not native born, when did he or she come to the United States

Full name of father   Address

Bernard Nadal Baker.   Santa Barbara, California.
Full name of mother

Elizabeth Elton Livezey.   deceased.
Where was your father born?   (Town)   (State)   (Country)

Where was your mother born?   Baltimore   Maryland   U.S.A.
                                        (Town)   (State)   (Country)

"   "   "

What is your father's nationality? (See note below)

American.

NOTE.—The answer to this question has no necessary connection with your father's citizenship. Answer as to your father's parents—whether they were English, Scotch, Irish, French, German, Spanish, Italian, Austrian, or what.

What is your mother's nationality? (See note above)

American

Is your father living?   Is your mother living?

yes.   no.

If not native born, has your father become naturalized?

When did he come to the United States to live?   (Year, month, day)

If not native born, when did your mother come to the United States to live?   (Year, month, day)

If you were not native born, when did you come to the United States to live?   (Year, month, day)

Have you any physical defects?   Minimum salary expected

no

Do you use stimulants?   Tobacco?   Drugs?

no   no   no

General history (a brief and general statement in chronological order of entire life to date, including names of secret societies or clubs)

I was born on October 23,1878,was educated at St.Timothy's private school at Catonsville near Baltimore.In 1901 I married Thomas Bullitt Harrison,a stock broker in Baltimore,and we had one son,born in 1902.My husband died in June 1915.In December 1914 I started an interior decorator's shop,leaving it in June 1916 to accept a position as member of the State Board of Motion Picture Censors,which I now hold.In addition I have been for two years a staff reporter on the Baltimore Morning Sun,covering news assignments,police court work,feature stories,and also acting as musical and dramatic critic.I have been in Europe fourteen times,and have spent much time in Switzerland,Italy,France and England.I speak French and German almost without accent.I have been much on steamers,and am familiar in a general way with ships of the merchant marine.I also worked for a week in the ship yard of the Bethlehem Steel Corporation in Baltimore,writing an account of my experiences in shipbuilding work.I was the only woman employe in the yard.

(DO NOT WRITE IN SPACE BELOW)

Index

A

Abramovich, Raphael 147
Abrikosova, Anna I. 144
Administration, American Relief 17
agriculture 179
Akhmatova, Anna 165
Aksyonov, Ivan Alexandrovich 165
Alexandra, Empress 7
Allen, Clifford 182
All-Russian Central Executive Committee 85
All-Russian Council of Trades Unions 85-6, 88, 131, 153
alphabet reform 77
Alsberg, Henry 151
American Communist Party 223
American Jewish Joint Distribution Committee 164
American Red Cross 16–17, 265
Ames, Joseph S. 9, 17
Anarchists 14–15, 147–156
Andronnikov Monastery 121
Antonov-Ovseenko, Vladimir A. 183
Armistice 59
Associated Press 70
August 1920 Affair of the Tactical Center 113
Avanti 178, 202
Azerbaijan 124

B

Baker, Bernard 8
Bakunin, Mikhail A. 167
Balabanova, Angelica 13-14, 84, 90-93
Baltimore Sun 9, 10, 17, 18, 25, 28
Barkatullah, Maulana 123
Barry, Griffin 73
Beach, Dick 202
Bedny, Demyan 165

Berezina 29
Berger, Henning 171
Berkman, Alexander 14-15, 65, 148-150
Bilan, Alexander 200
Bim-Bom 174
Biryukov, Pavel 32, 116
Blake, Arthur M. 21
Blavatskaya, Helena 112
Bobrov, Yevgeny 165
Bolshoi Opera 170
Bonch-Bruevich, Vladimir D. 32
Boni, Albert 216
Brailsford, Henry Noel 127
Brusilov, Alexei A. 22, 109-113, 142, 171, 210, 247
Brusilov, Madame 142
    trial of 112
Bryant, Louise 223
Buchanan, Sir George 110
Budyonny, Semyon M. 189
Bund, Jewish 154
Butyrka Prison 113
Buxton, Charles 178
Byednota 76

C

cabbies 127
Cachin, Marcel 198
Cadet Party 110, 311
Cavelier, Rene-Robert 45
Ceci, Lord Robert 85
censorship 71, 133
Chabrow, Nathan 216
Chaliapin, Fyodor I. 170–171
Cheka 3, 10, 10–11, 14-19, 27, 57, 74, 79-84, 99, 113-119, 122-130, 133, 144-145, 149-151, 159-161, 166-169, 172, 174, 194, 199, 201-

204, 212-213, 216-217, 221-228, 229, 232, 237, 241, 243, 246-249, 252-253, 259, 263, 264, 268, 272-278, 283, 291-296
Chekhov, Anton 171
Chernov, Victor M. 281
Chertkov, Vladmir C. 115
Chicago Daily News 61
Chicherin, Georgy 11, 12, 59, 63-68, 70-74, 85, 124, 226, 227, 292, 293, 308
children's issues 208
Children's Theater 175
Chita 19
Churchill, Winston 222
church rites 103
Clayton, John 73
Colby, Bainbridge 226
Comintern 13, 68, 82, 84, 184, 186, 193–320, 200-201, 223
Commissariat of Labor 309
Commissariat of Nationalities 55
Commissariat of Public Health 77, 133
Communistic Work 76
Communist Labor Party of America 200
Communist Party of America 200
Communist Party of the USA 200
consumer issues 106, 108, 162
Cooper, Merian C. 16, 20, 220
Cornere delta Sera 202
corruption 96, 105, 159, 217
Cossacks 86, 87, 145, 155, 260
Curzon, George N. 67
Czapski, Andrew O. 67
Czech Legion 213

D
death and dying 103
Decembrist Revolt 45
de La Salle, Sieur 45
Denikin, Anton I. 60, 83
divorce 98
Dom Soyuzov 89
Drizdo, Solomon A. 88
Dukes, Paul 122
Duma 110
Dzerzhinsky, Felix 10, 27, 128, 190, 307

E
Economic Life 76
education 35, 133, 136, 309
Eiduk, Alexander 213
Emerson, Gertrude 21
Enver, Ismail 195

Estes, Westen Burgess 216

F
family issues 91, 98
famine 180
Farbman, Michael 61
Far Eastern Republic 19
Feinberg, Joe 71
First International 45
Fischer, Judge Harry 225
Flick, John M. 216
Florinsky, Dmitry 122
Foreign Office 28, 57-64, 67, 70-78, 82, 105, 112, 117, 118-125, 132, 151, 157, 163, 165, 166, 169, 178, 192-196, 211-215, 219-223, 227, 230, 258-259, 262
foreign policy 12–13
Fraina, Louis 200
France, Joseph I. 18, 292
French Red Cross 16–17
Frick, Henry Clay 149
funeral of high party official 65

G
Geltser, Yekaterina 169
Georgia 124
Germanova, Maria 175
Gibson, Hugh S. 67
Gippius, Zinaida N. 172
Goldman, Emma 5, 6, 13-15, 22, 65, 148-150
Goldoni, Carlo O. 172
Goldschmidt, Alphons 123
Gorky, Maxim 98, 171
Grass 20
Guilbeaux, Henri 199
Gumilyov, Nikolai 165

H
Haden-Guest, Leslie 183
Harding, Mrs. Stan 18, 221
Harding, Warren 17, 72
Harrison, Marguerite
    anti-semitism 22
    arrest 16
    begins journalism work 9
    care for prisoners 216
    death 21
    death of first husband 9
    death of second husband 21
    espionage 9, 18
    feminism 21

first arrest 117
gains correspondent status 67
Grass 20
marriage 8
provocation of 125
Red Bear or Yellow Dragon 20
release from prison 292–298
second arrest 227
second marriage 21
There's Always Tomorrow 21
Unfinished Tales from a Russian Prison 20
writing *Marooned in Moscow* 18
Harrison, Thomas 8
Harrison, Tommy 8–9
Hazelwood, Thomas 216
Herzen, Alexander 168
Herzog, Rudolph 178
Holitscher, Arthur 201
Hoover, Herbert 17
Hopwood, Samuel 205
hygeine 133

I

Icon of the Iberian Virgin 141
Industrial Workers of the World 88, 202
Ioffe, Adolf A. 63, 193
Izvestia 76

J

Jakopo 30
Johnston, Vera 112
Joint Distribution Committee of American
    Funds for Jewish War Sufferers 225
Judaism 82, 151–153, 182

K

Kagan, Harry 225
Kaiser Wilhelm 230
Kalamantiano, Xenophon 15, 216
Kalinin, Mikhail I. 87
Kamenev, Lev Borisovich 66, 81, 188, 208, 222
Kamenev, Sergei S. 188, 222
Kammerny Theater 172
Kapp Putsch 126
Karakhan, Lev Mikhailovich 72
Karlin, Anna 29, 31-33, 36, 118-122
Karzinkin dynasty 208
Keeley, Royal R. 15, 216, 292
Kerensky, Alexander 7, 99, 111
Kerzhentsev, Platon 75
Keynes, John Maynard 194

Kharitonevsky Guest House 60, 63, 64, 78, 118,
    123, 166, 169, 192, 214, 217, 266
Khorezm People's Soviet Republic 195
Kilpatrick, Emmet 265
Klembovsky, Vladislav N. 111, 247
Knipper-Chekhova, Olga 175
Knox, Alfred W.F. 75
Kodak Company 205
Kolchak, Alexander 75, 83
Kollontai, Alexandra 13-14, 90-93, 97-98
Koonen, Alisa 172
Kosciusko Squadron 16–17
Koussevitzky, Sergei A. 166
Krasin, Leonid B. 12, 22, 68, 87, 178, 308
Krasnoschokov, A.M. 125
Kremlin 82, 91
Kronstadt 131, 259
Krupki 42
Krupskaya, Nadezhda 32, 94, 97-98
Krylov, Ivan 135
Kryzhyanovsky 131
Kulaks 205
Kun, Bela 201
Kursky, Dmitry I. 130

L

labor issues 107, 132
Lamare, Dr. 216
Landsbury, George 72-73
Latvian peace negotiations 194
Le Journal 178
Lenin, Vladimir 10, 13, 15–16, 17, 22, 32, 45, 52,
    66, 68, 80-87, 94, 98, 113, 128, 147-148, 168,
    174, 184, 186, 197, 201, 222, 225, 247, 263,
    283, 292-293, 299, 302-303, 307, 313-314
Litovtseva, Nina 175
Litvinov, Maxim 28
Litvinov-O'Grady Agreement 120
London Daily Herald 151, 178
London Daily News 178
Lososvky, Alexander 88
Lubyanka 19, 74-76, 119, 128, 144, 202, 229-
    230, 235, 238, 248, 257, 275-276
Lunacharsky, Anatoly 32, 128, 133, 134, 307

M

Magrini, Signor 178
Mamontov, Konstantin 189
Manchester Guardian 75
Marchand, Rene 199
Marchlewski, Julian 190
marriage 98

Marsillac, M. 178
Martens Bureau 28
Martov, Yuli O. 147
Marx, Karl 73
Marxstadt 181
Maximalists 133
Mayakovsky, Vladimir V. 165
McCullagh, Francis 75, 82, 138
    arrest of 118
McLaine, William 200
medical facilities 43, 54, 135
Mensheviks 310
Metropole Hotel 71, 72, 118, 119, 199, 226
Meyerhold, Vsevolod 165
Military Intelligence Division 9
Mirbach-Harff, Wilhelm Graf von 201
Mogilevsky, Solomon G. 19, 232
Morozov, Ivan 169
Morozov, Savva 169
Moscow Anarchists' Club 65
Moscow Art Theater 171
Moscow Ballet School 108
Mosher, Frank R. 16, 219

N

Nansen, Fridtjof 212
Napoleon 6, 29, 34, 56
New Economic Policy 303
news distribution 77
New York Evening Post 28
Nezhdanova, Antonia N. 169
Nicholas II 7, 37, 110, 120, 124, 128, 230
Nihilism 66
Nikitskaya Circus 174
Nikitskaya Theater 172
Niles, Blair 21
No Man's Land 33
North, Reverend Frank 120
Novinsky Prison 261, 275
Novodevichy Cemetery 104
Novodevichy Convent 142
Nuorteva, Santeri 262

O

Obshchestvo Zdravookhraneniya Yevreyev 30
Old Believers 145, 181

P

Pale of Settlement 54
Panunzio, Sergio 202
Pascal, Pierre 199

Pate, Maurice 72
Paterson Silk Strike 88
Pattinger, Russell R. 216
Peter the Great 158
Petliura, Symon V. 84
Petrovsky, Gregory I. 189
Pilsudski, Josef 117
Poale Zion 154
Podbelsky, Vadim 65
Poland
    peace treaty with 63
    war with 190
political trials 112
Polivanov, Alexei A. 111
Portable Theater 171
Pravda 76
Proletcult 134
public meetings 81

Q

Quelch, Tom 200
Quinlan, Patrick 222, 313

R

Radek, Karl 12, 22, 68-69, 70, 75, 217
Ransome, Arthur 72
Rasputin, Grigory 7
Razin, Stepan 247
Red Army 189
Red Bear or Yellow Dragon 20
Reed, John 5, 6, 22, 66, 200, 216, 223-224, 314
religion 139–146
Ritchie, Albert 9, 18
Rodzianko, Mikhail V. 113
Rosta 68, 74, 75, 76, 77, 82, 118, 167
Roy, Mandabendra Nath 196
Russell, Bertrand 178
Russian American Steamship Company 47
Russian Famine Relief Committee 113
Rykov, Alexei I. 131

S

Sadoul, Jacques 198
Samara 180
Saratov 97, 145, 177, 180-182, 311
Savoy Hotel 63, 196
Schmidt, Vasily V. 132
Schwarz, Mrs. 222
Scriabin, Alexander 166
Second World Congress of the Comintern 186
Sedova, Natalia I. 94

Selby, Gertrude Mathews 21
Semashko, Nikolai A. 133
Sereda, Semen P. 132
Shaw, George Bernard 184
Sheridan, Clare 5, 72, 222
Shop Steward's Movement 202
Siemens Electric Company 12–13
Singer Sewing Machine Company 60
Sinn Fein 196
Snowden, Ethell 183
Socialist Revolutionaries 153, 310
Society of Woman Geographers 21
Sologub, Helena 240
Sparticist Revolt 69
Stalin, Joseph 55
Stanislavsky, Constantine 171
Steklov, Yuri M. 63
Stoklitsky, Alexander 200
Stolypin, Peter 45
Stroganov Institute 136
Sukharevka 157–164, 217
Supreme Economic Council 309
Sverdlov, Yakov M. 178
Szechenyi, Istvan 231
Szeptitzki, Stanislav 31

T
Tairov, Alexander 172
Talat, Mehmad 195
Tanner, Jack 202
Ten Days That Shook The World 200
The Bat 174
There's Always Tomorrow 21
Third International 184, 186, 197–204
Tikhon, Patriarch 22, 138, 139, 140
Tolstoy, Alexandra Lvovna 114
Tolstoy, Leo 115
Treaty of Brest-Litovsk 10–11
Trifon, Metropolitan 143
Trotsky, Leon 12, 13, 22, 45, 57, 60, 63, 80-87, 94, 145, 147, 153, 174, 183, 187-189, 199, 222, 247, 307
Tsarskoe Selo 77
Tukhachevsky, Mikhail N. 189
Turkestanov, Boris P. 143

U
Underwood & Underwood 28
Unfinished Tales from a Russian Prison 20
United Telegraph Company 202

V
Vanderbilt, Gladys 231
Vanderlip, Washington B. 72, 222, 261
Virgin of Smolensk icon 143
Vitebsk 38, 55
Volga region 179

W
Walker, Herschel 72
Wallhead, Richard Collingham 184
Warsaw 29
Wells, H. G. 225
Williams, Robert 183
Wilson, Woodrow 11–12, 17
women's issues 13–14, 91
World War I 7
Wrangel, Peter N. 73, 191

Y
Yevreysky komitet pomoshchy zhertvam voiny 30
Y.M.C.A. 52
Young Turks 195
Yudenich, Nikolai N. 60, 83
Yusupov, Felix F. 169

Z
Zetkin, Clara 200
Zimmerwald Conference 200
Zinoviev, Grigory 22, 82, 153, 201

Acknowledgements

$\mathcal{A}$ relative recently asked me how I came across Marguerite Harrison. Much to my embarrassment, I could not remember. Like many people, I read broadly on many subjects, including Russian-American relations, and somehow she just kept popping up. Even though most of my published work has been on the nineteenth century, she just kept intriguing me as I worked on other topics. I also thought of many different ways to produce a work on her. However, she is a difficult figure to research. She wrote a lot about her own life and adventures in books and articles, but there has been very little scholarly attention paid to her. She seems to be one of those people who is mentioned in passing, but without much in depth discussion. So, in the end, as I read and reread her book, I decided the best way to present Harrison's time in Russia was to present her own words, now ninety years later, to the reading public.

In undertaking a project like this, there are many debts of gratitude. First, I would like to thank Paul Richardson of Russian Life Books, for recognizing that this was a worthwhile project. I appreciate his interest and attention to detail. In Russia, I want to thank Alex Soloviev, Yuri Zaretsky, and, especially, Nikolai Matronov for their help. In the United States, I want to thank Norman Saul, Matt Miller, Lee Farrow, Lubyov Ginzburg, and Robert H. Davis for their comments on a conference paper I gave on Harrison and for their support of Russian-American studies. At College of DuPage Library, I would like to thank Marianne Berger and Prema Ramnath. I would like to thank Steven Usitalo for all of the conversations on all things Russian and otherwise over the past many years. They are a great source of stimulation and support. My family has been, as always, a great source of support. My parents continue to demonstrate a limitless support for the work that I do. I appreciate that very much. My children, Meredith and Matthew, went on a great adventure to Russia a few years ago. Perhaps one day one of them will write of their adventures. In the end, though, there is only one person to whom I could dedicate this book. My wife, Michele, is an extraordinary woman in her own right. She has endured two Russian adventures that did not involve a prison sentence, but I know they were taxing, especially when her interests lie elsewhere. For those reasons and many more, this book is dedicated to her.

William Benton Whisenhunt
Sycamore, Illinois
January, 2011

About the Author

Marguerite Harrison was born in the late 1870s to a prominent Baltimore family. Her early life was somewhat uneventful, but when her husband died in 1915, that all changed. Through her work as a journalist for the *Baltimore Sun* during World War I, she began to work simultaneously as a journalist and spy, first in post-war Germany and then in post-revolutionary Russia. After her first imprisonment in Russia (which is the central fixture of this book), she returned to Russia (only to be imprisoned again), traveled across Asia, trekked the Middle East, wrote illuminating accounts of her adventures, co-founded the Society of Woman Geographers, helped produce perhaps the world's first film documentary (*Grass*), and authored an autobiography of her first sixty years.

About the Editor

William Benton Whisenhunt is Professor of History at College of DuPage. He is the co-author (with Marina Swoboda) of *A Russian Paints America: The Travels of Pavel P. Svin'in, 1811-1813* (McGill-Queen's University Press, 2008), the co-editor (with Steven A. Usitalo) of *Russian and Soviet History: From the Time of Troubles to the Collapse of the Soviet Union* (Rowman and Littlefield, 2008), and author of *In Search of Legality: Mikhail M. Speranskii and the Codification of Russian Law, 1826-1833* (East European Monographs, 2001). He received his Ph.D. in Russian history from the University of Illinois at Chicago and was a J. William Fulbright Senior Scholar at Ryazan' State University in Ryazan', Russia in 2006.

14474356R00174

Made in the USA
Lexington, KY
03 April 2012